Christian Fundamentalism in America

ALSO BY DAVID S. NEW

*Holy War: The Rise of Militant Christian,
Jewish and Islamic Fundamentalism* (McFarland, 2002)

Christian Fundamentalism in America

A Cultural History

David S. New

McFarland & Company, Inc., Publishers
Jefferson, North Carolina, and London

277.3082
New

LIBRARY OF CONGRESS CATALOGUING-IN-PUBLICATION DATA

New, David S.
    Christian fundamentalism in America : a cultural history /
David S. New.
        p.   cm.
    Includes bibliographical references and index.

    ISBN 978-0-7864-7058-7
    softcover : acid free paper ∞

    1. United States—Church history.   2. Christian
conservatism — United States.   3. Conservatism — Religious
aspects—Christianity.   I. Title.
    BR515.N465 2012
    277.3'082—dc23   2012012932

BRITISH LIBRARY CATALOGUING DATA ARE AVAILABLE

Front cover image © 2012 Shutterstock

Manufactured in the United States of America

McFarland & Company, Inc., Publishers
    Box 611, Jefferson, North Carolina 28640
    www.mcfarlandpub.com

Table of Contents

Preface

Not since the Civil War have Americans been so divided regarding the direction, the goals, and the ethos of their nation. There is talk of two distinct cultures— the "Reds" and the "Blues." A great divide threatens the fabric of American society. At issue is the American identity — what it means to be an American.

There is in America today "a war of ideology, it's a war of ideas, it's a war about our way of life,"[1] involving "basic commitments and beliefs that provide a source of identity, purpose, and togetherness for the people who live by them."[2] Words and phrases like "truth," "justice," "the public good," "right and wrong" are bandied about, larded with the deepest hopes and fears, marinated in the highest and noblest principles and ideals.

Competing systems of ultimate moral value —"the commitment to different and opposing bases of moral authority and the world views that derive from them"[3]— are at stake. It comes down to religion — the final authority for making moral and lifestyle judgments, for deciding what is right and what is wrong, what is acceptable or unacceptable, how we should live.

The broader cultural division into "Reds" and "Blues" reflects a religious division into conservatives and liberals. E. Brooks Holifield remarks upon this polarization of American Christianity: Protestants have been busy "'rearranging' themselves along ideological lines: Differences about ethics, politics, and theology ... loom larger than historic denominational commitments ... [there is] evidence of 'culture wars' among the laity and a 'two-party system' among the clergy."[4] Holifield finds Protestants more theologically divided than ever before along conservative/liberal lines. Conservatives of any one denomination have more in common with conservatives of other denominations than with liberals of their own denomination. The same holds for liberals.

Surveys indicate that with regard to religion the United States is almost evenly split down the middle: 43 percent identifying themselves as "liberals" (19 percent as "very liberal"); 41 percent as "conservatives" (18 percent as "very conservative"). Only 16 percent are unwilling to identify with either group.[5]

1

This religious dichotomy is particularly significant for the United States, a preeminently religious nation. It is a division which goes right to the core, the bedrock of American nationhood — the concept of "one nation under God." Beginning with its first colonists, America was conceived to be a religious entity. Americans have high aspirations, high ideals, for their nation, *as a nation*. That is how the United States differs from other nations. Observing that "religious radicalism in the United States" is "truly as American as apple pie,"[6] Kevin Phillips states, "No other contemporary Western nation shares this religious intensity and its concomitant proclamation that Americans are God's chosen people and nation."[7]

Religion has always been front and center in the American ethos. Traveling in the United States early in the nineteenth century, French statesman and author of *Democracy in America* Alexis de Tocqueville remarked on the religiosity of the American citizenry. Nothing has changed in our time. University Professor of Sociology and Theology at Boston University Peter L. Berger writes, "By any measure, the United States is the most religious country among the Western democracies."[8] Surveys support this statement: only half the percentage of western Europeans consider religion "very important" in their lives, compared with Americans; the United States gets a 67 on a "religion index," compared with 21 for Denmark and the 30s for Britain, France, West Germany, the Netherlands, and Norway.[9] American scholar Harold Bloom remarks, "No other Western nation ... matches our obsession with religion."[10]

Robert C. Fuller notes, "The United States is arguably the most religious nation on earth."[11] Public opinion polls back this up: ninety percent of Americans believe in some Higher Power;[12] as for other religious beliefs: the devil, 65 percent; hell, 73 percent; heaven, 90 percent; miracles, 79 percent; angels, 72 percent.[13] Sixty-two percent of Americans attend a place of worship.[14] One in four Americans are affiliated with a conservative Protestant church (fundamentalist, evangelical, Pentecostal), another one in six with a mainline Protestant church.[15] William G. McLoughlin observes, "America today has proportionately more church members, more church wealth, and more church activity than any other nation in the world."[16] By contrast, in Western Europe secularization is the norm; less than ten percent of the population regularly attend church.[17] British commentators have described church attendance in their nation as in "catastrophic decline."[18] Kevin Phillips finds "the intensity of religion in the United States"[19] in sharp contrast "to the secular and often agnostic Christianity dominant in Europe, Canada, and Australia."[20]

It follows that politics in America would have a stronger religious flavor than in other nations. As pollster George Gallup observes, "Religious affiliation remains one of the most accurate and least-appreciated political indicators available."[21] Susan Page writes, "The religion gap is the leading edge of the 'culture war' that has polarized American politics."[22] Liberal versus conservative is a universal political phenomenon (in Canadian politics, for example, there is a Liberal Party and a Conservative Party), but this division in other nations lacks the religious animus found in the United States.

In recent times much of that animus has resulted from a resurgence of conservative Christianity, especially in its more extreme manifestation — Christian fundamentalism. The so-called Christian Right[23] has brought division among the American citizenry to the surface. Religious conservatives speak of a "war being fought for the soul of contemporary America."[24] Conservative Tim LaHaye remarks: "We are in a cultural war in this country, and there are two worldviews ... 180 degrees in opposition."[25] For those of the Christian Right, and for many conservative Christians, "under God" means exactly what it says: the United States should be a nation governed by the principles of Christian belief and morality.

In 1989 a book with the title *Fall from Grace: The Failed Crusade of the Christian Right* was published. Its author said that "the Christian Right crusade of the 1980s" was "defeated and exhausted."[26] Nothing could be further from the truth. The Christian Right is stronger today than it was in the 1980s. In his book *American Theocracy* Kevin Phillips elaborates on "religion's new political prowess"[27] in America. He notes that "religiosity, biblical fundamentalism, and theology" are "increasingly vital keys to U. S. electoral behavior."[28] He says that during the administration of George W. Bush the Republican party became "the first religious party in U. S. history."[29] The White House implemented "domestic and international political agendas that seem to be driven by religious motivations and biblical worldviews."[30] Many among the American clergy are alarmed at these developments. Ordained Baptist minister Bill Moyers warns, "For the first time in our history, ideology and theology hold a monopoly of power in Washington."[31]

Because of its religious foundation, this cultural and political divide continued into the Obama administration, and is likely to continue into the future. Christian liberals and conservatives feed off one another. Each seems to drive the other to more extreme positions. In this way each has contributed over the decades, over the centuries, to the development of the other.

In his book *Culture Wars: The Struggle to Define America*, James Davison Hunter writes, "...most discussions of the tensions in American society fail to consider the historical context. The truth of it is that the contemporary culture war evolved out of century-old religious tensions."[32] It is impossible to make sense of the cultural and political rift in America today without an understanding of its religious basis. This means going back to the beginning of American history, to the time of the first colonists. The Puritans of the Massachusetts Bay colony set the tone for what David W. Wills calls "the nation's collective religious destiny."[33] Wills talks about "the enduring legacy of the Puritan tradition in America"[34]: their idea that the new settlement should become a "holy commonwealth," a "city upon a hill," a "new Jerusalem."

Puritan beliefs became part of the DNA of American religion, of the American national ethos. These beliefs evolved over the generations, shaped by the pressures of a liberal environment — so the story of Christian fundamentalism is also the story of American Christian liberalism; they grow side by side, each in a sense the complement, the counterpart, of the other.

Because the Puritan seeds of Christian fundamentalism grew in the isolated soil of a new continent, Christian fundamentalism is a distinctly American innovation within the evolution of broader Christianity. Christian fundamentalism is *American*. In no other nation is Christian fundamentalism as dominant as in America.

To trace the history of the evolution of American religious conservativism[35] and its complement — religious liberalism, is to trace a dimension of the American spirit, to delineate a major strand of its specific national DNA.

The history of America, *as a religious nation*, a nation "under God," begins in 1620 when a tiny vessel arrived at a new continent filled with brave souls seeking freedom and religious liberty. Their story has charmed the hearts of Americans for generations: Plymouth Rock, the first Thanksgiving — adventure, heroism, humble folk defying the odds and succeeding. These settlers bore a significance beyond their number. They provided a vision, a symbol, for the many thousands, then millions, who would follow. Since that time religion has always been a significant force in America.

The success of these pioneers encouraged a group of Puritans to form the Massachusetts Bay Company and set sail for the new world with a sense of divine mission: "We shall be as a city upon a hill, the eyes of all people are upon us." They would be "a new Jerusalem," God's people, God's nation. Theirs was an eschatological community which believed not only that a glorious millennium was imminent, but that by its own actions it could precipitate its coming. The locus— America. An ember had been lighted that would never go out, even to this day.

But with the passing of a century this sense of mission and expectation was in decline. Prosperous times and new thinking competed for the attention of the populace. It was the age of the Enlightenment. Enter Jonathan Edwards, a strict Puritan who is able to integrate the new scientific thinking with religious tradition. Edwards and England's preaching sensation George Whitefield usher in the "Great Awakening," an explosive religious revival which renews, and diffuses throughout the colonies, the belief that the millennium is about to unfold in the midst of America, God's chosen people.

The Great Awakening brings the American colonies together as never before; it is America's first mass movement, its first experience as a nation. The expectation of an American millennium spreads among the populace. Belief in the millennium provides a framework for political and economic events, a perspective. This animating ideal of the future propels American colonists to make a decisive break from tradition, pushing a large mass of the population toward revolution. After the Revolution millennialism provides the new American nation with cosmic purpose: its "Manifest Destiny" is part of God's plan. This new nationalistic spirit, bolstered by and permeated with a vibrant religiosity, has remained a peculiarly American form of nationalism to this day.

Beginning early in the nineteenth century and lasting for several decades, a period of revivals known as the Second Great Awakening melded personal and national aspirations within a millennial context. Charles Grandison Finney believed that vigorous lay evangelistic preaching could save enough souls to inaugurate the thousand years' reign of Christ on earth.

By contrast, William Miller insisted that such human efforts to bring on the millennium were futile. In Miller's end-time scenario, known as *premillennialism*, Christ would have to return to vanquish the forces of evil and decay, *before* the millennium. Based on their interpretation of various passages of the Bible, the Millerites calculated the specific date for Jesus's arrival — October 22, 1844. Millerites donned white "ascension robes" and climbed the highest hills and perched on rooftops to await the Second Coming of their Lord. October 22, 1844, would go down in history as "the Great Disappointment." Nevertheless, the Millerite end-time scenario would become an integral part of one form of Christian hope in America from this point on.

Millerism nourished an explicit polarization of American Protestantism which remains to this day, forcing the center of American religious orthodoxy to move left or right. A new liberalized evangelicalism, following Finney's lead, resulted: God worked through human beings and their churches to progressively bring on the millennium.

With the best of his ability, and within the confines of traditional American Puritanism, Jonathan Edwards had come to terms with the forces of the Enlightenment. But the Enlightenment spawned critical thinking which moved beyond anything Edwards could have conceived, or would have been willing to accept. The Bible came under attack. To counter this menace, Princeton Theological Seminary was founded, determined to be a bastion of American Calvinism, a defender of the faith, of the Bible. Up to that point Protestantism had no fully integrated theology of biblical authority. The

Princeton theologians instituted two innovative concepts which have become part of contemporary conservative Protestant belief: that God dictated every word of Scripture, and that the Bible is free from error, even regarding the most recent discoveries of science.

Meanwhile, in Europe figures like Rousseau, Kant, Schleiermacher, Feuerbach, Harnack, and Strauss were advancing liberal thinking along other lines, later to be developed in the United States by Parker, Emerson, Bushnell, Rauschenbusch, and others. Liberals insisted that Jesus's "divinity" was an accretion of the early church; Jesus had never proclaimed himself divine. More important than Jesus himself was his teaching: the gospel of love and the infinite worth of the human soul. To understand the Bible literally was to deviate from the intention of its authors. Jesus meant not that he would return in physical form, but that he would be present spiritually after his death, working in and through the church to gradually bring about God's millennial Kingdom.

Then there arose in Ireland a figure whose theology would invigorate the conservative Calvinist forces in American Protestantism and guarantee them a sure place in the future. John Nelson Darby maintained that only divine intervention (the Second Coming of Christ) could bring on the millennium, not human action. The "true church" had nothing to fear regarding the eschaton; during "the Rapture" Jesus would gather it up before the violence of the end-time. In America almost a century later "pre-tribulational" pre-millennialism would become a crucial part of the fundamentalist end-time scenario.

Darby introduced a new method of interpreting the Bible which, he maintained, eliminates apparent contradictions in Scripture, allowing it to be read literally. Darby brought his dispensationalist hermeneutic and his eschatology to the United States where they quickly caught on with conservatives. During the latter decades of the nineteenth century Princeton-oriented Calvinists joined dispensationalists in a common cause against liberalism. The apocalyptic aspect of the First World War supported the pre-millennilists' view of history as regressive rather than progressive, thereby vastly increasing their numbers.

After the war this new, distinctively American, religious movement was christened "fundamentalism." Opposing the secular materialism and religious indifference of the 1920s, fundamentalists like Billy Sunday reminded America of its Puritan beginnings, its God-given destiny as the hope of the world.

Then in 1925 the "Monkey Trial" dampened, even extinguished, liberal and denominational fears of fundamentalism until the societal changes of the late 1960s and early 1970s caused many to return to a more conservative form of Protestantism and set the stage for a public resurgence of conservative

Christianity. Conservative Christians have fashioned a subculture which fully mirrors and duplicates the wider suburban American culture, but with the important label "Christian" affixed.

Their beliefs make conservative Americans vulnerable to charismatic rogue preachers, false prophets who make cunning use of the Bible, resulting in tragic minor apocalypses. Social scientists maintain that an accurate, truthful portrayal of these religious groups is essential for understanding contemporary religious life in the United States; they are but a variant of what is found in fundamentalist churches.

The biblical book of Revelation is the key source for conservative Christians—fifty-nine percent of Americans believe that its prophecies will come true.[36] Falsely interpreted, the book of Revelation is an explosive fuse, the breeding ground of dangerous religious eccentricity. It has led to fatalism, causing people to retreat from this world and abandon the fight for human progress and betterment. Too often has Revelation been used to sanctify our natural human tendencies of revenge and aggression, to bless our demonization of enemies, leading to excesses, atrocities, and violence, on both the individual and national scales.

In the end, we return to the concept of the American millennium, the city upon a hill—a belief, a hope for the future, from the time of the first colonists.

1

"As a City Upon a Hill"

"Land ho!" came the cry from aloft. There was an eager rush to the gunwales to catch a glimpse. Dozens of eyes squinted, peering hopefully into the distance.

It took some time—for most passengers lacked the trained eye of the sailor or his vantage point aloft — but at last one of those who history would recognize as the "Pilgrim Fathers" confirmed the sailor's sighting. Upon which, the sea-weary voyagers fell to their knees and thanked God for bringing them safely to the New World. The journey from England in the staunch little ship *Mayflower* had taken sixty-five days.

Sixty-five days in which all aboard had wondered if the cold stormy waters of the Atlantic would be their grave. Crossing the ocean was still an adventure in 1620. And the Pilgrims had already lost one ship. The *Speedwell* had sprung a leak shortly after departing Southampton in August and had to put back to Dartmouth for repairs. After a brief interval the two vessels once again set sail, but this, too, was a false start. The *Speedwell* was still giving trouble; it would have to be left behind. Only the *Mayflower* would voyage into the unknown.

On September 16, overcrowded and underprovisioned, the tiny vessel sailed out of Plymouth harbor and into the history books. It was the beginning of a story which would charm and gladden the hearts of Americans for centuries to come: brave souls seeking freedom and religious liberty, living without ostentation in stark unknown surroundings. The Mayflower Compact. Plymouth Rock. The first Thanksgiving. It was a classic narrative with all the ingredients. Adventure. Heroism. Humble folk defying the odds, and succeeding.

This small band of settlers would bear a significance beyond their number. They would provide a vision, a symbol, for the many thousands, then millions, who would eventually form an independent nation "under God." A nation whose currency would bear the words "in God we trust." "A nation with the soul of a church," British author G. K. Chesterton would write roughly three hundred years in the future.[1] A nation whose citizens would regard church attendance as of much greater importance than would the populace of the nation from whence came the Pilgrims.[2] Religion has always been a significant force in America. And it all started at Plymouth Rock.

But the Pilgrims had not set out with noble dreams of great accomplishment. They did not see themselves as crusaders. They were not out to change the world. Devoid of any particular self-consciousness or self-importance, they were humble folk, with humble goals. There was only one gentleman among their number. They were of lower middle class backgrounds—farmers, artisans, small shopkeepers. They hadn't come to make money, to grow rich in a new land. Nor did they have pretensions of an intellectual bent. For the first fifty years in America they lacked even a public school, and sent not a single individual off for a university education. They had left their homeland behind and braved the winds and seas of the Atlantic and come to this virgin land for one purpose — to worship God as they pleased.

In addition to its crew of forty-eight, the *Mayflower* had set sail with one hundred and one passengers. Not all of the passengers would meet our definition of "Pilgrim," in the sense of being religiously motivated. Thirty-one were children, of whom seven were waifs and idlers, unrelated to the adults aboard. Fourteen of the adults were servants and hired artisans. Only slightly more than half of the total—fifty-six—were adult Pilgrims in the full sense of the word.

Only one passenger died during the voyage, and two were born. This record of good health was remarkable. Disease was rampant on board ship in those times. Sir Francis Drake lost 600 from a crew of 2300 on his famous voyage around the world a mere forty years earlier. The *Mayflower* had been for several years a carrier for the wine trade. Such vessels had a reputation among sailors as "sweet"— believed to be conducive to good health. As for the Pilgrims ... no doubt they attributed the preservation of their numbers to the watchful care of their heavenly Father.

Their story began in Nottinghamshire, in the obscure village of Scrooby, a stopover on the great northern post-road. There a small group of men, mostly untutored farmers and farm hands, formed themselves into an independent church.

Ever since the reign of Henry VIII England had been in a state of religious chaos and persecution. For almost a century one could never be sure that one's particular brand of Christianity, even if for the present time in vogue, would remain so. For this was the age of the Protestant Reformation on the European continent, a time of great religious and political upheaval. Separated from the continental mainland by a watery barrier, England had its own form of Reformation.

When James I ascended the throne in 1603 there was hope that the new king might be tolerant of other forms of Christianity than strict Church of England. Such hope was soon dashed, and many set out to found separatist or independent churches. The group at Scrooby was one of these.

The nucleus of this group consisted of three individuals. John Robinson, a graduate of Cambridge, had been a Church of England clergyman. William Brewster, a cultured man having spent some time at Cambridge, was the most influential layperson in the new congregation. William Bradford, only sixteen when the group had begun meeting in Brewster's home several years earlier, quickly became a leading figure. He was a literate man of sound judgment, a student of several languages including Dutch, French, Latin, Greek, and Hebrew. He would eventually become governor of the young settlement at Plymouth and write its history.

Although there is no evidence that either the civil or ecclesiastical authorities had any desire to interfere with this small separatist congregation, its future could never be guaranteed and life was never completely comfortable for those outside the established church. So in 1607 a decision was made to leave England for Holland, where a neighboring congregation had already found a home. At the start of the trip the group was stopped by customs officers and some of its members held in custody. But they were soon released and charges dropped, despite an obvious breach of civil law (taking money and goods out of the country without government permit). There was no indication of religious persecution.

By the following year they had established themselves in the university town of Leyden. As others of like mind crossed the channel and joined, the congregation grew to number almost two hundred. But making a living in their new homeland was never easy and the separatists feared losing their identity as English citizens if they remained too long in this foreign environment. The idea of planting a settlement in the New World was attractive. Guyana — ironically the site of Jonestown where another group of religious separatists would meet a violent end three and a half centuries later — was first proposed because the living would be easy. But that idea was voted down for fear of tropical disease and the Spaniards. The big problem was money. The Leyden group had none. So in 1617 they contacted the Virginia Company in London.

England had been slow to make inroads into the New World despite an early start. Even before Columbus made his celebrated voyages the Italian, Giovanni Caboto (John Cabot) had requisitioned the sovereigns of Spain and Portugal. Having met with failure there, he moved to England where King Henry VII proved amenable. But a papal bull had divided land in the south between Spain and Portugal, the two nations which had explored these regions. Cabot would have to sail north, Henry decreed.

He did, and in 1497 brought back news about regions which would later become part of Canada. Stirred by these reports, Henry furnished a second expedition along the coast which went possibly as far south as Chesapeake Bay. But that was it. Other than fishing expeditions, the English showed little interest in the New World for more than half a century, despite having prior claim to the northern regions based on Cabot's exploration.

Under Queen Elizabeth several exploration expeditions were sent out and some failed attempts at settlement made, but it wasn't until the Spanish fleet — the "invincible armada" — was defeated in 1588 that England gained that mastery of the seas which would allow the fruition of imperial dreams.

Suddenly English merchants and capitalists were eager to turn the New World to profit. As the saying goes, It takes money to make money. So money was eagerly invested. But soon the balance sheets were found wanting. Money out, but none coming in. A small settlement was made at the mouth of the James River in a tract granted along the Virginia coast, but by time the separatists from Leyden were contacting the Virginia Company it had lost over 200,000 pounds.

Fortunately the separatists had an influential contact within the Company. It took time and much negotiation to secure a settlement patent and sufficient financing, but finally, on July 22, 1620, after many annoying delays thirty-five of the Leyden congregation under William Brewster sailed out from Delft Haven on the *Speedwell*, leaving behind their beloved pastor John Robinson and the majority of his flock. Others joined the Leyden contingent in Southampton, along with a second ship, the *Mayflower*.

The initial feeling of joy and triumph on first sighting land in America after a long voyage quickly dissipated as those on the *Mayflower* took full measure of the reality of their situation.

The original plan had been to arrive in late summer, but delays made this impossible. Now it was November, a bleak gray unwelcoming month, with winter fast on its heels. As William Bradford wrote in his history, "For summer being done, all things stand upon them with a weatherbeaten face, and the whole country, full of woods and thickets, represented a wild and savage hue. If they looked behind them, there was the mighty ocean which they had passed and was now as a main bar and gulf to separate them from all the civil parts of the world."[3] There was no going back. The Pilgrims could only move forward. Bradford's words conveyed the Pilgrim's predicament in plain forthright language: "They had now no friends to welcome them nor inns to entertain or refresh their weatherbeaten bodies; no houses or much less towns to repair to, to seek for succor."[4]

The original intention had been to settle far to the south near the Hudson River. Instead they found themselves off the barren craggy windswept shore of Cape Cod, no place for settlement. But dangerous shoals prevented their going south, and the cantankerous crew refused to weigh anchor until the Pilgrims found a site for settlement.

Clearly, settlement would have to be outside of the area designated in the Virginia Company's land grant, on land which had been granted to another company. The Pilgrims found themselves operating outside the law, with a patent which was invalid in these regions. But what choice did they have? The ship's master and company told them to hurry up and find a safe harbor nearby: take the shallop and explore, or we shall put you and your possessions ashore and leave without you.

Only after three expeditions in the shallop did the Pilgrims find a satisfactory site with a harbor fit for shipping. Here there was a small clearing — an abandoned Patuxet (native) village. Those in the shallop went ashore. December 21. Plymouth Rock. Bradford was unenthusiastic: "It was the best they could find, and the season, and their present necessity, made them glad to accept it."[5]

Five days later the *Mayflower* arrived and the Pilgrims finally set their feet upon land. Fortunately the weather was unseasonably mild. They quickly set about erecting a common building. But this was soon abandoned for individual dwellings. This was done in haste for the natives had been heard yelling in the thick forests and a few of these aboriginals spotted skulking about.

Fear of the natives was exaggerated. A few years earlier tens of thousands had succumbed to a plague probably introduced by French traders. Historians estimate that the native population had decreased by ninety percent.[6]

Food soon became an urgent issue. The supply aboard ship was rapidly being depleted and the ship's master reminded the Pilgrims that sufficient quantity had to be preserved for the crew's voyage back to England. Jamestown was too far away to be of help. But this was of no immediate concern, as the Pilgrims expected to live off the land. Most were farmers and could grow whatever was needed — albeit this would have to await warmer weather. For the time being, the local waters were known to be teaming with fish and the forests would surely be filled with wild animals.

But the newcomers had little success fishing and hunting. During the first month ashore they managed to catch only a single cod; their first fish was a live herring that happened to wash up on the rocks. As one historian humorously phrased it, "The Pilgrims seemed likely to go down in history not as Founding Fathers but as the world's worst fishermen."[7] For some time their major source of nourishment was shellfish dug out of the beach and groundnuts found in the woods.

By the time their skills at living off the land improved, it was too late. Their constitutions weakened by a long sea voyage and exposure and hunger, the Pilgrims succumbed to disease and illness, resulting in death. Often two or three died in a single day. Soon so many were bedridden that only a half-dozen were available at any one time to fetch wood, tend the fires, prepare food, and attend to all the other mundane tasks of living, as well as care for the sick and bury the dead. By the end of March forty-four — almost half of the small company — had died. It served them well that they had come to this new land not for material gain but to embody a spiritual ideal. A high sense of religious purpose gave them strength to endure whatever hardships they had to face.

Ironically it was the indigenous peoples who proved the greatest help. Late in March one from their number walked boldly into the settlement and asked — in English!—for a drink of beer. Short of beer, the settlers generously regaled him with food and drink from their meager supplies, hoping to establish good relations. He was an Algonquin from Maine where he had picked up some English from the fishermen who frequented that coast. He spent the night with the settlers and left with gifts, promising to return.

A week later he did, this time with a friend, a Patuxet named Squanto, a survivor from the group which had cleared the forest where the settlement stood. Squanto taught the Pilgrims how to fish and hunt, and how to plant corn, squash, and beans. As well, he proved a valuable channel to the other indigenous peoples in the region. Soon his services as a guide, interpreter, and intermediary bore fruit. A leader of the Pokanoket made a pact with the settlers hoping by so doing to ensure their help against the rival Narragansetts to the west.

Despite a trying first winter, not a single Pilgrim returned to England when the *Mayflower* sailed for the homeland in April. William Bradford was made governor in place of the former governor who had died of illness, and summer and autumn saw the little settlement prospering. Twenty acres of corn were harvested, and a single gaming expedition provided enough fowl for everyone for a week. Trade in beaver pelts had begun with the natives, and in November a ship from England replentished supplies. To celebrate their new-found good fortune the Pilgrims invited the local chief and ninety natives to a feast. Rejoicing in the spirit of peace and friendship, the natives supplied five deer for what became the first Thanksgiving.

But their trials were not over. The summer of 1622 brought crop failure. Drought withered the corn, and the settlers had to resort once again to a diet of fish, clams, and nuts.

As the years passed the Pilgrims learned how best to live in their new environment. William Bradford, elected governor for thirty one-year terms, was a tower of strength. Happy to live as a caring community, without theological dispute, quietly worshiping their God, the settlement at Plymouth never developed into a trading center and grew in population only slowly. But their steadfast perseverance demonstrated to those of similar religious convictions back in England that a colony of settlers could survive the harsh conditions of the New World and live in peace as a church of their own founding. Moreover, an idiosyncratically Christian foundation had begun for what in the centuries to come would become *the* preeminent Christian nation.

Back in England news of the success at Plymouth encouraged the thinking of the religiously like-minded Puritans.

The Puritans have long been the object of crude caricature: "neurotic individuals who condemned liquor and sex, dressed in drab clothes, and minded their neighbors' business."[8] As Allen Carden writes at the beginning of his book *Puritan Christianity in America*, "Use the word 'Puritan' or 'Puritanical' today and many modern minds are flooded with images of dour, austere, repressive, colorless people who perceived life as something to be endured rather than enjoyed."[9]

Yet historian Perry Miller notes that, contrary to popular caricature, "the Puritans enjoyed a vigorous and productive sexuality, ... they drank staggering quantities of rum," and indulged in "petty animosities, village gossip, and displays of sheer spite."[10] As historian Sydney E. Ahlstrom observes, "Puritanism at its core ... was something more than an austere exodus from the fleshpots of Egypt or a resurgence of experimental piety."[11] It would be their religious beliefs, rather than their morality, which the Puritans would pass on to the generations that followed in America. Here would be their legacy.

The term "Puritan" was originally a derisive name[12] for those who wished to "purify" the Church of England. Unlike the Pilgrims, who separated themselves from the English Church because they thought it beyond reform, the Puritans wanted to reform it from within. By the beginning of the seventeenth century Puritanism had become a strong and established movement in England.

Puritanism in England was an expression of a distinctive religious movement found on the European continental mainland known as the Reformed tradition, a major strand of thinking coming out of the Protestant Reformation and closely associated with Calvinism.

Reformed theology placed special emphasis on the power, transcendence, and unknowableness of God. The Reformed God was the God of the Old Testament — fierce, slow to forgive, angry, threatening. Their outlook dominated by what Ahlstrom calls "this austere Hebraic legacy," the Puritans saw life as one titanic struggle "to cajole the Almighty."[13]

But nothing could be done about the afterlife. God had predestined some individuals to eternal salvation, others to eternal damnation. It didn't matter what you did in this earthly existence; no number of good acts, no sterling moral character, could earn you eternal life if God had already damned you. The biblical book of Revelation told of "the book of life." If your name was not written there, you would be cast into the lake of everlasting fire.

Reformed theology insisted that God's law, as found in the Old Testament, be the basis for reforming the Church of England. Rites, offices, ceremonies, celebrations not found in the Bible — that included Christmas — were to be prohibited. The Reformed tradition, in distinction from other streams of the Protestant Reformation, sought to enliven the "Old Testament world view" and "to make God's revealed Law and the historical example of Israel an explicit basis for ordering the affairs of men in this world."[14] Those of the Reformed tradition observed the sabbath "with almost Judaic austerity and legalistic rigor."[15] So much did they love the old covenant, the Law, the Reformed often named their children with names from the Old Testament.

The Puritans wanted to reform the Church of England in a specifically Reformed manner. They first had grounds for optimism when Queen Elizabeth appointed Edmund Grindal Archbishop of Canterbury in 1575. He encouraged the preaching function of the clergy and removed overt papists from office. More importantly, he allowed the Geneva Bible to be printed in England. Puritanism was a "movement of the Book" and the Bible its "fountainhead,"[16] and the Geneva Bible was *the* Bible of the Puritans, for it was packed with marginal notes of strongly Calvinistic persuasion.

When a year later Elizabeth suspended Grindal, Puritan hopes were put on hold. In 1603 the queen died and was succeeded by James 1. James came from Scotland and was steeped in Calvinist doctrine. Surely the golden age of Puritanism was about to unfold. With great optimism Puritans presented the new king with the Millenary Petition in which they requested religious reform. Once again their hopes were dashed, for James was no devout Calvinist and showed little interest in religious reform.

Things turned decidedly worse when his son Charles became king in 1625. Charles married Princess Henrietta Maria of France, a fervent Catholic, and favored William Laud, a bishop of decidedly popish inclinations. Laud persecuted Puritan ministers — either they conformed to his views or risked losing their license to preach. Moreover, under Charles the Church of England adopted several Catholic practices. Then, in 1629, Charles dissolved Parliament — at the time packed with Puritans and a major hope for religious reform — and decided to rule England on his own. Parliament would not meet again for eleven years.

Leaving England for the European continent was not a practical Puritan option, for there Protestantism was in dire straits. That very year in France a Huguenot rebellion against the Catholic king was suppressed by Cardinal Richelieu, and the emperor of the Holy Roman Empire proclaimed the Edict of Restitution which stated that all church properties secularized since 1552 must be restored to the Catholic Church. The Roman Catholic Counter-Reformation was in full swing, and on German soil—the home of Protestantism—Protestant and Catholic forces waged all out battle in the Thirty Years' War. It seemed that everything which had been accomplished in the direction of church reform since Luther's declarations in 1517 was being undone.

There remained one clear answer to the Puritan dilemma: follow the lead of the Pilgrims and migrate to the New World. So in that dire year 1629 a group of Puritans formed the Massachusetts Bay Company, secured a charter from the king, and elected John Winthrop future governor.

Early in the next year a fleet of well-provisioned ships gathered at Southampton. It was to be England's largest colonial migration. The soon-to-be colonists were more affluent, better educated, and of a higher social class than those who had come over in the *Mayflower*. Instead of starting out in debt for their venture, these people had already paid their way. On March 29, 1630, four ships carrying a total of 400 passengers set sail, with Governor Winthrop on the *Arbella*.

On June 12 the *Arbella* disembarked at Salem, where a small advance colony had been established. Soon the center of the colony was moved to what became the town of Boston, the site of a fine harbor at the mouth of the Charles River. By the end of the year sixteen more ships would arrive, boosting the total population of the new colony to over one thousand persons. Over the next decade "New England" would prosper, its population rising to over twenty thousand.

As had been the case with the Puritans of "old" England, the Bible took center stage in the life of the new colony. Morning and afternoon services on the sabbath focused on the sermon, and the sermon focused on Scripture, usually on a single verse. Each and every word would be milked for its practical value, often with the original Greek and Hebrew consulted to provide every possible shade of meaning.

Sermons were long—six hours of services on Sunday and an additional lecture once a week similar to Sunday's sermon. Increase Mather, a leading New England pastor, wrote, "Men are most sleepy at sermon time. Before the sermon began they were not drowsy, and after the sermon is ended they are not so; but just at that season when they are called to attend the word of God, they are apt to drowse and sleep."[17] The reverend pastor need not have been surprised, for such had been happening since the time of the apostle Paul, as is related in the biblical book of Acts: "And there sat in the window a certain young man ... and as Paul was long preaching, he sunk down with sleep and fell down from the third loft" (20:9). The good Puritan reverend observed, "This is as Satan would have it."[18]

Sermons were not entertaining homilies. Every statement of a sermon was to be supported by Scripture. It didn't matter how godly a man the preacher might be, his personal opinions counted for nothing. As had been the case in England, the Old Testament was given prominent place, for regarding Holy Writ, there was "no part unprofitable."[19] In a sample of 500 sermons preached in five Massachusetts communities during the seventeenth century, 42 percent were based on the Old Testament.[20] The stern forbidding God of ancient Israel was very much alive in New England.

The Bible was not the focus of attention only during religious services. It furnished "a perfect rule of faith and holiness, according to which all doctrines are to be tried, and all controversies decided."[21] The Bible was truly a book for all seasons, applicable to all facets of life. It was not only *a* source of authority, it was the *only* source of authority for all matters of faith and practice. The celebrated Boston pastor John Cotton published a children's catechism in 1646 with the revealing title *Milk for Babes Drawn out of the Breasts of Both Testaments*. It answered sixty-two questions with 66 citations from the Old Testament and 106 from the New. In two brief tracts on the church, each of about a dozen pages, he cited the Bible a total of over five hundred times.[22]

The Puritans emphasized the private daily reading of Scripture. Read, study, meditate. All were encouraged "to examine our selves, and bring our services to the test and touchstone of the Word of God."[23] The true Puritan would properly be *obsessed* with justifying *every* action and thought and feeling with words from the Bible — that was the ideal, anyway. It was common practice for an individual to keep a journal which recorded how closely his or her daily life tallied with the standards found in Holy Writ. Even children spent considerable time reading the Bible and tracing their spiritual development.

Wrote Joshua Moodey late in the seventeenth century, The Bible is "the Christians' Apothecaries Shop ... reproof, correction, doctrine, instruction, etc. all these are there to be had."[24] Scripture was to be the Puritan's constant friend: a comfort in times of adversity and loss, an advisor and guide in times of trial and uncertainty. In a contemporary manual on Bible study John White noted three distinct sequential psychological stages the Bible reader could expect to experience: "First, the wounding and terrifying. Secondly, the converting and renewing. Thirdly, the comforting and reviving of the heart."[25]

This arduous soul-searching existence was a part of a covenant the colonists had made before disembarking in the New World. On the good ship *Arbella* Governor Winthrop had already declared that "we shall be as a city upon a hill, the eyes of all people are upon us"[26]— words that indicate a distinct sense of mission.

What did Winthrop mean by the words "city upon a hill"? A hint can be found in Cotton Mather's ecclesiastical history of New England, *Magnalia Christi Americana*, published in 1702. Here he describes John Winthrop as "our New English Nehemiah" in connection with "our American Jerusalem."[27] Mather did not have to explain to his Bible-reading public who Nehemiah was—that he had led the ancient Israelites from their captivity in Babylon and rebuilt Jerusalem, that city upon a hill.

"A city upon a hill" is Jerusalem. But not the historical Jerusalem. Mather writes: "Our glorious Lord will have a Holy City in America; a city, the street whereof will be pure gold."[28] This was the "new Jerusalem" mentioned in the biblical book of Revelation, which would descend from heaven at the end-time, whose street "was pure gold."

The Puritans were apocalypticists; they believed in the Second Coming of Jesus Christ and the attendant end of this earthly world. They based these beliefs on an interpretation of various passages in the Bible, particularly the book of Revelation, also known as the Apocalypse — hence, the term "apocalyptic."

Apocalypticism was at the very core of Puritanism. The very bedrock of Puritan belief was apocalyptic; it was the driving force behind all that the Puritans believed, said, thought, and did.

Allen Carden writes, "The American Puritans' eschatological [end-time] expectation is a significant aspect of their theology, oftentimes overlooked by historians."[29] J. F. Maclear notes that historians do not give "adequate weight to the Puritan scheme of apocalyptic history and its impact on early New England thought and institutions."[30] Maclear insists that "millennial ideas" are "central to Puritan faith and indispensable to its proper historical interpretation."[31]

It was all a matter of timing. As Paul Boyer has stated, "That the colonizing venture began at a time of intense apocalyptic awareness in England meant that it, like everything else in these years, took on an aura of eschatological meaning."[32] Reiner Smolinski has remarked on "the proliferation of eschatological theories in the early decades of the seventeenth century" and points to "millennialism" as a "defining feature in the sermon literature of the time."[33]

Although, as Stephen J. Stein notes, there was a decided "Americanization of the apocalyptic tradition"[34] as the Puritans grew accustomed to life in the New World, the origins, once again, lie in the mother country, England.

England was so awash in apocalyptic expectation in the seventeenth century that it would have been unimaginable for the Puritans not to have partaken of this spirit. The Stuart kings realized the subversive power apocalyptic thinking had had throughout history, which was part of the reason they opposed the Puritans. Ben Jonson, a poet and playwright known for his satiric realism, became a favorite at the court of James I. The king must have enjoyed Jonson's *Bartholomew Fair* which ridiculed apocalypticism, finding the ubiquitous Antichrist in everyday objects.

John Milton considered his time one of great eschatological significance. His celebrated *Paradise Lost* is a commentary on the book of Revelation.[35] Cambridge University was a hotbed of Puritan apocalypticism. In his *Clavis Apocalyptica* Cambridge scholar Joseph Mede wove biblical passages from here and there which dealt with, or in any way hinted at, apocalyptic into a single end-time narrative. This work proved so popular among Puritans that a Puritan-dominated Parliament ordered it reprinted. Mede's collected works circulated widely in England and later in America. Even Isaac Newton, famous for his leading role in the scientific revolution, was an ardent apocalypticist. Voltaire said that Newton wrote a commentary on Revelation to show that he was human, to compensate for his obvious superiority in other areas of endeavor. Newton's successor as professor of mathematics at Cambridge, William Whiston, wrote several books on eschatology. With whispers of the end-time everywhere, Quaker leader George Fox quipped that every thunderstorm produced expectations of the End.

Awash in eschatological expectation, Puritans in England found a spiritual nudge in Robert Cushman's *A Sermon Preached at Plymouth in New England*, published in London in 1622. It suggested that God was about to pour end-time wrath upon the homeland for its sinfulness. It was time "for such as have wings to fly into this wilderness."[36] As well, Cushman published a tract titled *Reasons and Considerations Touching the Lawfulness of Removing out of England into the Wild Parts of America* which was included in a narrative describing the Pilgrims' first months in the New World.

This idea of a God-given shelter in the wilderness as a sanctuary from the apocalyptic wrath to come was taken up by John Winthrop. One year before the Puritans departed England for America Winthrop wrote his wife that "the increasing of our sins gives us so great cause to look for some heavy scourge and judgment to be coming upon us"; if they remained in England they must soon "drink of the bitter cup of tribulation."[37] Winthrop searched Scripture and found overwhelming evidence that God intended the Puritans to go into the wilderness of the New World where they would be protected from his wrath. In a comprehensive study on the topic Avihu Zakai concludes that Winthrop's "eschatological zeal ... was responsible more than anything else for his existential decision to lead the Puritan exodus out of the sins of the Old World and its corrupted history."[38] "These eschatological expectations and apocalyptic visions ... were in time to become the predominant reasons and justifications for the Puritan migration to New England."[39] The old

England was soon to be subject to God's eschatological wrath. It was time to plant a new England.

Historian Ahlstrom notes, Puritanism in America presented a "drastic break with the old order in Europe." Here it developed "in unexpected and unprecedented ways," so that by the time the colonies declared their independence "they had become the most thoroughly Protestant, Reformed, and Puritan commonwealths in the world. Indeed, Puritanism provided the moral and religious background of fully 75 percent of the people who declared their independence in 1776."[40] Ahlstrom writes, "All over the world New England is known as the place where Puritanism achieved its fullest, least inhibited flowering."[41]

Once they arrived in the New World the Puritans began to develop a full apocalyptic theology. A leading figure in this was the minister of Boston's First Church, John Cotton. As J. F. Maclear comments, "Emigrants to the Bay brought with them an eschatological excitement which was probably more intense than that of the Puritan mainstream and flowered under John Cotton's influential preaching."[42] Cotton gave several series of lectures on, and wrote a commentary on, the book of Revelation. He believed that the very act of eschatological preaching would cause Satan to be bound. Cotton said the colonists had a grave responsibility: they were to establish a purified church, for their very activity in this regard would help bring about the coming reign of the Lord with his saints. Thereby the colonists were active participants in the coming eschaton. The millennium was waiting in the wings; it was up to the colonists to perform their role.

2

The Great Awakening

A strong beginning had been made. The Pilgrims had led the way by example. Following their lead the Puritan colonies around Massachusetts Bay had set up an eschatological community that believed not only that a glorious millennium was imminent, but that its own actions it could precipitate its coming. An ember had been lighted that would never go out, even to this day.

In *The Puritan Origins of the American Self* Sacvan Bercovitch proposes "to trace the sources of our obsessive concern with the meaning of America."[1] He concludes, "The New England Puritans gave America the status of visible sainthood. The subsequent impact of their concept cannot be overestimated ... it contributes significantly to ... the American Way ... American identity ... American dream, manifest destiny, redeemer nation...."[2] Philip F. Gura concurs: "The New England mind has indeed contributed something basic to that nebulous thing called the 'meaning' of America."[3]

A sense of apocalyptic mission was certainly evident in New England. Many wrote and preached on apocalyptic themes. In 1653 Edward Johnson published the first history of New England, in which he declared the colony "the place where the Lord will create a new heaven and a new earth"[4]—a clear reference to the apocalyptic event mentioned in Revelation 21:1. One pastor wrote an account of the apocalypse in verse form. "For a century it was read in every household in New England.... Commentators sometimes suppose that Michael Wigglesworth's *The Day of Doom* drove Puritan children crazy, but it did nothing of the sort: they loved it."[5]

At mid-century Richard Mather urged his flock to "be patient for a while, for a very little while, for it [would] not be long afore the storm be over, and then [they would] have glorious days ... and Jerusalem ... come down from heaven."[6] All seemed certain that the millennium was about to dawn. The timetable could be moved forward by the godly living of the good people of New England.

Hope remained strong as the century drew to a close. In 1698 Cotton Mather wrote, "Such principles as we have at last produced in the American deserts ... [ensure] a great revolution ... e're long."[7] In 1730, in celebration of the centennial of the arrival of the *Arbella*, Thomas Prince addressed his fellow colonists. His hopes for an American millennium remained steadfast: "Let us cry earnestly for the spirit of grace to be poured forth on us.... There never was any people on earth so parallel in their general history to that of the ancient Israelites as this of New England."[8]

But with the passage of time had come many changes. The British colonies which would become the United States were divided into three economic and cultural regions: the large plantations of the South, the commercial and industrial Middle colonies, and the small subsistence farms of New England. The total population had risen to 840,000; that of Massachusetts to 150,000.[9] The tight controls on public morality which had enlivened the original Massachusetts Bay colony could hardly be expected to prevail with such an expanding populace.

The wider world beckoned. With increasing commerce and literacy, New England, and particularly Boston, remained in close ties with the mother country and the European continent. Every major town in New England had its own weekly newspaper, so events and ideas in distant places were soon discussed in local taverns and coffee houses. Where once the clergy had had a virtual stranglehold on the domain of the intellect, a new secular intelligensia was coming into being.

It was an exciting time for new ideas, for this was the Age of Reason, the Age of Science, the Enlightenment. Newtonian physics had demonstrated that the force which made the apple fall to the ground held the moon in its course around the earth and the planets in theirs about the sun. It seemed that the whole universe was subject to mathematical regularity. Nature was one vast mechanism, governed by exact immutable mathematical laws which human reason could discover and measure.

If the universe functioned as one vast orderly regular machine, where was the place for miracles? No one wanted to deny the existence of God. He was the Creator of the machine. But once he had set everything in motion and fixed its laws surely his work was finished. In this mechanistic universe there was no space for God to intervene in human affairs. He was no longer the Redeemer who reached down to save wayward souls.

This "natural religion," this "rational religion," was known as Deism. Deism did away with the scandal of the particularity and exclusivity of traditional organized religions, the scandal that God would reveal himself to a specific religious and ethnic community. The hard-core Deist regarded much of traditional Christianity as superstitious and intolerant. As this new rational religion was deemed accessible to all men and women by virtue of their faculties of reason, it found itself up against revealed religion, against the authority and teaching of the established church.

Many amongst the Christian clergy outrightly rejected such blasphemy. But some thought strident opposition might prove inimical to the continued existence of the church. Would it not be prudent to adapt Christian thinking to meet this new challenge?

Back in England Archbishop John Tillotson sought to demonstrate the reasonableness of Christianity. His printed sermons found a ready audience among many of Boston's esteemed clergy; they applauded his tolerance and spirit of moderation. But those of a stricter Calvinist bent found Tillotson's thinking dangerous, a menace to the traditional Puritanism which was the foundation of life in New England. The archbishop had come out against predestination, a hidebound Calvinist tenet: "I am as certain that this doctrine cannot be of God as I am sure that God is good and just, because this [doctrine] grates upon the notion that mankind have of goodness and justice."[10] Predestination, in other words, did not stand the test of human reason. Tillotson's good and more humane God would take into consideration the weakness of the sinner and the seriousness of the sin, rather than simply condemning all sins and sinners alike to an equally severe and eternal punishment. All of this had its effect, so that in the New England of 1730 Puritanism was no longer the vital force it had once been. The clergy and the church were no longer the dominant factor in people's lives. Prosperous times and new thinking competed for the attention of the populace. New Englanders were choosing the pleasures and profits of this world over their "errand into the wilderness." The countinghouse was becoming more popular than the meetinghouse.

Graduates of Harvard College and Yale College no longer went almost exclusively into the pastorate. The demands of an expanding population and opportunities for secular advancement meant that New England's brightest young men were increasingly not entering the clergy. As a result the clergy was debased; too many were of mediocre intellect and moral suasion, not up to the challenge of leadership, not up to confronting the issues of secularism. It was safer to hide behind stylized sermons of biblical exegesis no matter how dull and irrelevant to the issues of the time.

With a less than inspiring clergy, it is not surprising that attendance at church was becoming a formal weekly observance, accompanied by apathy and indifference. In too many churches the pews were filled with nominal Christians who paid mere lip service to the tenets of Puritanism. They attended according to the standards of polite and refined society, not out of passionate religious intensity. The atmosphere was one of relaxed, secure, and contented religiosity. As one contemporary minister commented, the richly dressed congregations of the time "had nothing further in view than to smoke and eat together, to tell a pleasant story, and to talk of the common and ordinary affairs of life."[11]

Some men of the cloth were profoundly disturbed by this growing laxity. The champions of strict orthodoxy considered any accommodation of Enlightenment philosophy to be supping with the devil. One began a new pastorate by informing his parishioners that he had no intention of compromising with the new thinking, of providing them with "a nice and philosophical account of the nature, influences and motions of the stars." Another clergyman was renowned as "fiery hot, his principles rigid to the highest degree, and his charity as cold as death in regard of all but those who thought as he did."[12] But, as historian Perry Miller quipped, he was unfortunately "the most indolent man in Boston."

In order to prevent a decisive rift in the religious fabric of New England there was needed an individual who could defend the faith of the fathers in terms of the new thinking, without compromising the essentials of Puritan doctrine. In the small hamlet of East Windsor in the hinterlands of Massachusetts was born on October 5, 1703, just such an individual, the only son in a family of ten daughters.

Jonathan Edwards came to Boston as the son of a pastor, but more importantly the grandson of the illustrious Solomon Stoddard, the "pope" of the Connecticut River valley who had built an ecclesiastical empire free from the domination of the Boston clergy. Calvinism was in Edwards's blood. Not only were his father and grandfather clergymen, his family line was chock full of illustrious church names: Mathers, Hookers. His people had come over with the founding fathers and married into Governor Winthrop's family.

Jonathan Edwards was a religious man, a Calvinist among Calvinists. He made that abundantly clear as a young man still in his twenties at his first significant public appearance before the most distinguished of Boston's clerical leadership. The collected Harvard graduates saw in Edwards's invitation to give the celebrated Thursday Lecture (an institution since earliest colonial days) an opportunity to test the mettle of a graduate of the newly-founded Yale College. Would he remain steadfast in the principles of his grandfather's absolutist Calvinism, or would he bend it to the winds of the time, would he grant concession to the stirrings of the Enlightenment?

Edward's lecture proved a clear and stark and resounding confirmation of the strictest Calvinism. No whiff of the human role in salvation here: "God is under no obligation to any man: he is sovereign, and hath mercy on whom he will have mercy."[13] God could damn the most moral and devout of his creatures to eternal punishment. His will reigned supreme. Edwards could not be sure that even he himself might not be thrown into the pits of hell when his earthly days were over.

Unlike his Puritan predecessors, Edwards looked not just inward to his soul but outward with an Enlightenment gaze upon the natural world, where he saw God: "...looking up on the sky and clouds, there came into my mind so sweet a sense of the glorious majesty and grace of God.... God's excellency, his wisdom, his purity and love, seemed to appear in everything; in the sun, moon, and stars; ... in the grass, flowers, trees; ... and all nature."[14] Because of this Edwards very early became "involved in the creative process of conforming his inherited Puritanism to a larger manner of apprehending the world."[15]

Throughout his life Edwards communed with his God in nature. Abstemious of diet, austere and disciplined in all facets of his life, he found solace in long walks in the woods every day after dinner. Here he would note down any thoughts that came to him on slips of paper. If he was on horseback he pinned these slips onto his coat. Sometimes he would arrive home covered in slips of paper, like a tree with its leaves, whereupon his devoted wife would lovingly unpin him of his burden. In the evening he reworked his thoughts and added them to a growing list of "Miscellanies." He had begun gathering such notes while still in his teens. Over his lifetime he accumulated nine volumes of material, all carefully indexed, some of which consisted of elaborate treatises. Edwards was ever the conscientious student, meticulous in his thinking. Summer mornings he rose at four, winters at five; he spent thirteen hours a day in his study.

At the age of fourteen Edwards had discovered John Locke's *An Essay Concerning Human Understanding*, a seminal Enlightenment work. Edwards absorbed the ideas in Locke's *Essay* with more pleasure "than the most greedy miser finds when gathering up handfuls of silver and gold from some newly discovered treasure."[16] It is unlikely that more than a handful of individuals in America had read the *Essay* by this time — it was published in 1690. Edwards recognized that here was a work central to a whole new way of thinking which would soon render contemporary college curricula obsolete. Here was the gateway to the new century.

Edwards was fortunate to be attending the new college of Yale, for a benefactor from London had just donated his collection of eight hundred books covering every branch of the "new learning." Although these books were not part of the curriculum, the young scholar eagerly consumed their contents: cosmology, optics, atoms, philosophy, literature. At Yale Edwards was aware of the rumors "of a new philosophy that of late was all in vogue and of such names as Descartes, Boyle, Locke, and Newton, but they were cautioned against thinking of them because the new philosophy, it was said, would soon bring in a new divinity and corrupt the pure religion of the country."[17] The prudent Edwards decided not to "look as if I was much read, or was conversant with books, or with the learned world."[18] Instead, Edwards kept all these things to himself. As historian Miller remarks, "Edwards would not compartmentalize his thinking ... there could be no warfare between religion and science, or between ethics and nature. He was incapable of accepting Christianity and physics on separate premises."[19] It was immediately clear to this thoughtful young man that theology was dead if it could not be integrated with the new learning.

A practical laboratory for doing just that was about to unfold. At the age of twenty-three Edwards joined his grandfather in the pastorate at Northampton. Two years after Edwards's ordination, almost to the day, his grandfather died and he assumed full pastoral duties. Then, late in December of 1734, something extraordinary happened — several sudden and violent conversions among the parishioners of Edwards's church. One conversion followed another in rapid succession. As winter turned into spring the numbers of converted increased. By April of 1735 the conversion rate had risen to "at least, of four persons in a day, or near thirty in a week ... for five or six weeks together."[20] Soon virtually every citizen of the small town was among the communicants. Edwards estimated conservatively that the total number was "more than 300 souls ... (how many more I don't guess)."[21] "There are very few houses in the whole town into which salvation has not lately come, in one or more instances."[22]

Revivals — often referred to as "stirs" or "harvests" or "seasons"[23] — had occurred, on occasion, before in New England churches. Edwards's own grandfather had experienced five — an unusually high number — during his long and illustrious career. But none of these earlier revivals had been on the scale of that in Edwards's church. And it wasn't just the numbers. The town seemed almost transformed: "...people had soon done with their old quarrels, backbitings, and intermeddling with other men's matters. The tavern was soon left empty.... [It was] the minister's house that was thronged far more than ever the tavern had been wont to be."[24]

What happened as the congregation gathered for church service on Sundays must have been gratifying to the young minister: everyone was "eager to drink in the words of the minister as they came from his mouth ... some weeping with sorrow and distress, others with joy and love."[25] Edwards's style of preaching was anything but flamboyant. He did not wave his arms about or raise his voice. He read from carefully prepared notes in a quiet voice without gesture, his eyes fixed on the bell rope. A few phrases from one of his sermons shows why he found it unnecessary to wave his arms about or raise his voice. His words furnished a very clear and vivid depiction of the eternal punishment awaiting those who are not saved: "...you never, never shall be delivered ... endured these torments millions of ages ... your dolorous groans and lamentations, without any rest day or night, or one minute's ease ... your bodies ... will remain to roast through an eternity yet...."[26]

In August of 1733 Edwards had delivered a sermon which so enthralled his congregation that they persuaded him to publish it. He did. Early the next year *A Divine and Supernatural Light, Immediately Imparted to the Soul by the Spirit of God, Shown To Be Both a Scriptural and Rational Doctrine* came hot off the press, containing in miniature what would be the essence of Edwards's thought. The use of "scriptural and rational" is typical of Edwards. As Sydney Ahlstrom writes, "He infused the spirit of the Age of Reason into the faith of his fathers with a transforming sublimity equaled by no Reformed thinker of the century."[27] The "rational" part was based principally on his reading of Locke.

Edwards believed that evangelical preaching was the vehicle whereby the saint (the predestined saved soul) perceived the "supernatural light" imparted by the Spirit of God. He learned from Locke that a person acquires knowledge only from "experience." The mind, the soul, is a passive thing upon which impinge sensations. This was consistent with the Puritan belief that God's grace was simply received; one could not earn salvation by one's own efforts.

The preacher must furnish the impressions, the sensations, which result in religious conviction and passion: "Sounds and letters are external things that are the objects of the external senses."[28] To do this it was necessary carefully to choose the right words: "To extricate all questions from least confusion or ambiguity of words, so that the ideas shall be left naked."[29]

It might seem from this that the preacher, by using the right words, *causes* salvation in his congregation. Edwards makes clear that is not so. Everything, every idea, is dependent for its existence during every moment of its existence upon God. Edwards was not about to credit himself with the revival of 1734 to 1735 in Northampton. Instead, he called it "this work of God," "this remarkable pouring out of the Spirit of God," "this shower of divine blessing."[30]

But then things went sour. In May of 1735 Edwards's uncle by marriage, a man who suffered from insomnia and depression, despairing about his spiritual state, committed suicide. To Edwards this was the work of Satan, who was raging at the success of the revival. Thereafter the revival died out, as quickly as it had come. Edwards, no doubt devastatingly disappointed, observed that it "began to be very sensible that the Spirit of God was gradually withdrawing from us."[31]

It is ironic that just as the revival in Northampton was beginning to lose momentum, word of its amazing success began to spread. The pastor in a nearby town wrote to Benjamin Colman, a leading Boston clergyman, describing the Northampton revival. Colman arranged to have excerpts of this letter published in the *New England Weekly Journal*. Colman requested more details from Edwards. Edwards responded with an eight-page summary of the revival which Colman forwarded to two British Nonconformist leaders,

John Guyse and Isaac Watts. These two men decided an expanded version needed to be published. They considered the Northampton revival a "so strange and surprising work of God that we have not heard anything like it since the Reformation."[32] By late 1737 Edwards's 132-page account of the revival, *A Faithful Narrative*,[33] appeared in London bookstalls. Previous local revivals had gone unnoticed by a wider audience. Edwards's book assured that the Northampton revival would have broad significance.

In their preface to *A Faithful Narrative* the editors called for prayers encouraging the fulfillment of biblical prophecies "concerning the large extent of this salvation in the latter days of the world."[34] Was the millennium about to unfold? Events on the horizon would lead anyone steeped in biblical prophecy to wax hopeful.

At the same time that Edwards's *A Faithful Narrative* was being enthusiastically read by Britishers, Americans were reading about a young twenty-three-year-old preacher, not yet ordained, who was stirring the masses on the other side of the Atlantic. Newspapers were proliferating, made less expensive because of the extensive advertising they carried. Exciting news sold more papers; increased circulation brought in more advertising. Business and the propagation of new ideas went hand in hand. In Virginia, certainly no hotbed of religion, the *Virginia Gazette* reprinted a London newspaper's account of George Whitefield's first sermon in that city.

Whitefield was stirring up religious controversy in England. He had criticized the clergy of the Church of England, and was talking about something he was calling "the New Birth." He was denied access to the pulpit, forced to preach in the parks and open fields where his preaching was attracting ever increasing crowds. Then in 1739 the *Virginia Gazette* announced news of an event sure to excite anyone following the New England revivals— George Whitefield would be coming to America for a preaching tour throughout the colonies.

We know little of Whitefield's early life save what he offered in his self-promoting autobiography. Despite his claim, "If I trace myself from my cradle to my manhood, I can see nothing in me but a fitness to be damned,"[35] it is abundantly clear that Whitefield had never been anything but a good boy and a religious boy, raised in a family active and prominent in the Anglican church.

At Oxford University he joined the "Holy Club," a small group of evangelicals scorned and ridiculed by other students. There Whitefield fell under the spell of John Wesley who set him upon a strict reading diet: the devotional works of the continental Pietists, the Puritan classics, and the Bible. Especially the Bible. He "began to read the Holy Scriptures upon [my] knees, laying aside all other books, and praying over ... every line and word."[36]

Whitefield wore nothing but the plainest of clothing and fasted until he became ill. After months of such sacrifice he concluded that good works would not earn salvation. He adopted the Calvinist doctrine of predestination and parted from John Wesley who believed that salvation is available to all who accept it.

Whitefield's theology of "New Birth" was the forerunner of today's "born again." With regard to salvation, Whitefield claimed there was too much value placed on "letter-learning" and "head knowledge"—the intellectual affirmation of prescribed doctrine. He insisted that religious knowledge was accessible through the heart, not the intellect. Salvation was a new birth, the "union of the soul with God," "the indwelling of Christ," "an experimental knowledge of Jesus Christ."[37] Unlike traditional Puritan doctrine which said that salvation was a process which moved through successive stages over a period of several months, the New Birth was experienced in an instant. He cited testimonials of persons who could state the specific time and date when they had experienced the New Birth.

By the spring of 1739 Whitefield's fame was widespread. Newspapers advertised his preaching as a second Reformation. A recent convert, William Seward, was instrumental in promoting Whitefield's endeavors. Seward had been treasurer of the South Sea Company during the notorious South Sea Bubble and knew the power of hype. He applied new merchandising techniques: front-page newspaper ads in journals like the *Daily Advertiser*, which appeared to be news articles. Seward fabricated exaggerated reports on the size of the crowds at Whitefield's sermons: May 1, twenty thousand at Kennington Common, thirty thousand at Moorfields; May 7, fifty thousand at Kennington Common, twenty thousand at Moorfields; May 14, sixty thousand at Kennington Common, fifty thousand at Moorfields.[38]

Word that Whitefield would be coming to the colonies later that year generated excited expectation. Then the day arrived. On the cold evening of November 8 Whitefield mounted the steps of the courthouse in Philadelphia to begin his sermon. Benjamin Franklin's *Pennsylvania Gazette* estimated the crowd at six thousand, a huge crowd for a city of twelve thousand, too large for any of the city's churches. It was a well orchestrated event, the result of careful planning and meticulous organization. An innovative promotional machine had supplied American newspapers with regular reports on Whitefield's exploits in England over the previous six months. When the big day arrived riders circulated throughout the city drumming up interest and tacking up ads. As for the sermon itself ... it too was well rehearsed, having been given numerous times with slight variation—not extemporaneous, as it appeared.

New Birth was the key. Whitefield was to Puritanism what Henry Ford was to the automobile. His New Birth was the Model T of American Protestantism; it made Puritanism immediately accessible to everyone. Entering the Kingdom of Heaven was no longer a slow thoughtful soul-searching process; it happened in an instant and needed no complex theology. People lapped it up.

The crowds were real, not just some figment of journalistic imagination. Benjamin Franklin was at first suspicious of the large numbers reported by the press. But after first-hand observation he considered twenty-five thousand a reasonable estimate. Even an outspoken critic of the new revivalism, the Anglican priest Timothy Cutler, had to admit that Whitefield's claim of twenty thousand was accurate.

Part of this amazing success was due to what Frank Lambert calls "the commercialization of religion," of which Whitefield was the "pioneer."[39] Almost a century later the famous evangelist Charles Grandison Finney would acknowledge Whitefield's legacy in his handbook for the promotion of revivals, *Lectures on Revivals of Religion*. Whitefield established a model which would be repeated right up to the present by such celebrated evangelists as Dwight L. Moody, Billy Sunday, and Billy Graham. The secret was preparation: organization, advance notice, widespread use of the media, coordination with the local clergy, the use of "advance teams" which engaged in a pervasive publicity campaign.

Yet none of this would have succeeded without a receptive audience. Whitefield had little success in America outside the northeast where Puritanism had taken hold and laid the groundwork. Here he was preaching to people who wanted resolution to the religious tensions within Puritanism, people who wanted to be saved, to have their religious anxieties calmed. Whitefield's New Birth answered all of this religious unease within the framework of Puritan Calvinism. Whitefield, like Jonathan Edwards, was staunchly Calvinist. Hence, he succeeded in America where John Wesley, who was immensely successful in England, did not.

In physical appearance Whitefield was anything but prepossessing. He was so cross-eyed he gained the name "Doctor Squinitum." He was bald, but fortunately powdered wigs were in style at the time. Even one of his greatest admirers had to admit Whitefield was "corpulent." But none of this mattered when he was performing before an audience. As a boy he had been fascinated by the stage. He noted in his autobiography, "During the time of my being at school, I was very fond of reading plays, and have kept from school for days together to prepare myself for acting in them."[40] His flair for acting won him drama competitions. As a preacher he made use of his dramatic talents. Some of his greatest admirers were renowned actors of the time. None other than David Garrick once proclaimed that he would give a hundred guineas to be able to pronounce "O!" with Whitefield's depth of feeling. Like most actors, Whitefield fed off his audience — the bigger the better.

Whitefield possessed that intangible — charisma. One woman, who spoke not a word of English, told her Lutheran pastor that she had never been so moved as upon hearing one of Whitefield's sermons. An Enlightenment man, Benjamin Franklin had turned away from religion, yet even he felt attracted to Whitefield. At first finding the phenomenon of Whitefield good for his printing business, Franklin eventually came to like the man himself. Virtually polar opposites in religious outlook, the two men became friends. Franklin never ceased to be amazed that an individual of Whitefield's religious fervor could so easily sway him: "I happened ... to attend one of his sermons, in the course of which I perceived he intended to finish with a collection, and I silently resolved he should get nothing from me. I had in my pocket a handful of copper money, three or four silver dollars, and five pistoles in gold. As he proceeded I began to soften, and concluded to give the coppers. Another stroke of his oratory made me ashamed of that, and determined me to give the silver; he finished so admirably, that I emptied my pocket wholly into the collector's dish, gold and all."[41]

It was all in the magic of Whitefield's oratory. As Edwards's wife Sarah remarked, "He is a born orator. You have already heard of his deep-toned, yet clear and melodious voice. It is wonderful to see what a spell he casts over an audience by proclaiming the simplest truths of the Bible. I have seen upwards of a thousand people hang on his words with breathless silence, broken only by an occasional half-suppressed sob."[42] Like Coleridge's ancient mariner, Whitefield held people in a spell with his "glittering eye," and his audience listened "like a three years' child." Franklin witnessed the "extraordinary influence of his oratory": "His eloquence had a wonderful power over the hearts and purses of his hearers."[43] "...[E]very accent, every emphasis, every modulation of voice, was so perfectly well turned and well placed, that without being interested in the subject, one could not help being pleased with the discourse."[44] The pleasure felt by the listener, Franklin declared, was "of much the same kind with that received from a excellent piece of music."[45]

Where Whitefield dared to go others were sure to follow. Soon over a hundred clergymen were traveling about the country preaching for conversions, although few drew the widespread attention of a Whitefield.

This sudden burst of revivalist preaching would come to be known as the Great Awakening.[46] Perry Miller writes, "Jonathan Edwards had already put a match to the fuse, and Whitefield blew it into flame."[47] Historian of religion Sydney Ahlstrom called the Great Awakening "an apocalyptic outburst" which "rejuvenated the politically potent elements of the Puritan ideology" and "most important for the future of American Protestantism" made of "revivalism ... an institution."[48] Stephen J. Stein asserts that the Great Awakening was a "formative religious event" helping to shape the people's "self-conception and their understanding of history."[49] Historian Alan Heimert writes, "The watershed in American history marked by the 1740's can be understood best in terms of the degree to which, after the Great Awakening, the American populace was filled with the notion of an impending millennium."[50]

3

Bonfire of the Vanities

There was nothing out of the ordinary about the clergyman Jonathan Barber. Then one day he fixed upon a single verse from a tiny and obscure book of the Old Testament and became obsessed with what he took to be its special revelation in the words "an appointed time ... it will surely come, it will not tarry."[1] Could this be a reference to the end-time? He stayed up that night, wrought with religious agony. Flipping through the Bible at random, hoping to find answers, he came upon a passage that confirmed his wildest imaginings: "Yea, the set time is come."[2] Then he fell into a trance, to awaken just in time for his Sunday service.

He stumbled through the service that morning then, convinced the Holy Spirit was about to use him for its special work just prior to the coming Day of Judgment, he left his parish, and without money or change of clothing set out on foot to see his good friend and former classmate at Yale, the clergyman James Davenport. Davenport let him preach to his own congregation, whereupon Barber excitedly related his recent spiritual experience. Barber returned to his own church and ranted throughout his next service, saying whatever came into his mind. He again left his own parish, this time to go from village to village preaching to any group or individual who would listen. He had laid aside all study and meditation, he said, for the Holy Spirit was speaking through him, telling him what to say from one moment to the next. Then one day the Holy Spirit, it seemed, abandoned him many miles from his home. He loitered about for several months until the Holy Spirit told him to seek out George Whitefield. Barber immediately embarked ship and sailed to meet the great evangelist. Whitefield was impressed with Barber and asked him to join him on his journeys. After that little was heard about Jonathan Barber.

Such could not be said about his close friend James Davenport. Davenport, infused with Barber's spiritual enthusiasm, ranted at his own congregation for a full twenty-four hours and then collapsed. When he recovered he demanded religious confession of each of his parishioners. A letter written by an alarmed observer relates an episode in which Davenport predicted the exact day a woman, both mentally ill and dumb, would be delivered from her afflictions upon his fasting and praying over her: "On the very day [predicted] the woman died, without having spoken a word, or discovering any signs of being in her right mind."[3] Davenport insisted that his prediction had been fulfilled — the woman *had* been delivered ... to heaven.

Just as Barber before him, Davenport left his own church to preach wherever he felt directed. He would flip through the Bible and point at a passage at random, then interpret it as divine directive. Directed to a specific church where he was to convert exactly twenty persons, he walked over fifty miles, in places through deep snow, then strode boldly into that church and pronounced the elderly minister a blind guide leading his flock to perdition. Exactly twenty members of the congregation did respond and leave the church, thereafter conducting their own services.

For four years Davenport marched into churches uninvited and asked the pastor to give a testimonial of his conversion experience. If he refused Davenport declared him unfit to lead his congregation, even if the pastor had led his own revival. Then Davenport encouraged any laypersons who had "seen the light" to become itinerant preachers.

Like Whitefield, Davenport preached in the open air. His services, if they could be called that, were devoid of all form. As was remarked at the time, Davenport "had no text nor Bible visable, no doctrine ... nor anything else that was regular."[4] Davenport would walk among the people screaming exhortations, ranting incoherently, waving his arms. Sometimes as many as ten persons would accompany him in these acts, all screaming and carrying on at the same time — virtual chaos. This would go on for hours, far into the night. Contemporary descriptions tell it best: "Then he [Davenport] came out of the pulpit, and stripped off his upper garments, and got into the seats, and leapt up and down some time, and clapped his hands, and cried out ... and then betook himself to stamping and screaming most dreadfully."[5] An excerpt from the *Boston Evening Post* exclaimed, "His sermons are dull and heavy ... a violent straining of his lungs, and the most extravagant writhing of his body, which at the same time that it creates laughter and indignation in the most, occasions great meltings, screaming, crying, swooning and fits in some others.... Were you to see him in his most violent agitations, you would be apt to think that he was a madman just broke from his chains."[6] Another description from the same newspaper: "His gestures in preaching are theatrical, his voice tumultuous, his whole speech and behaviour discovering the freaks of madness, and wilds of enthusiasm."[7]

Gilbert Tennent lacked the flamboyance and wild chaos associated with Davenport, yet was just as vehement in his denunciation of his fellow clergymen. He castigated the majority of the clergy as unconverted "subtle selfish hypocrites ... [of] little worth, for all the bustle they make about them."[8] Tennent called his fellow pastors "swarms of locusts, the crowds of Pharisees, that have as covetously as cruelly, crept into the ministry in this adulterous generation."[9] Hence, he maintained, "it is both lawful and expedient to go from them to hear godly persons."[10]

Whitefield had been welcomed by most of the pastorate, even in conservative Boston, at first, because his preaching had an enlivening effect on New England religion. Many pastors preached the New Birth to their own congregations. Yet some among the clergy reacted negatively. "People wallowed in snow, night and day, for the benefit of his [Whitefield's] beastly brayings,"[11] fumed Timothy Cutler, Anglican priest at Christ Church in Boston. It wasn't long before rabble rousing figures like Barber, Tennent, and Davenport brought others among the clergy to Cutler's side. Rogue preachers, it seemed, were sprouting everywhere like noxious weeds. The early mood of acceptance began to abate. The anti-clerical diatribe of such rogue preachers obviously did not sit well with the majority of the clergy. Even those who at first were enthusiastic began to wonder if the revival movement was going too far.

Where at first the clergy had enjoyed any increase in church membership resulting from the revival movement, now just as many were losing members to wild cannons like Davenport. Ministers were criticized by their parishioners either for not going far enough or for going too far in their response to revivalism. And why, it began to be asked, was the pastorate even necessary, considering that the New Birth made all equal before God? Why not do away with clerical education and ordination, when any converted layperson could preach the gospel? Lay resentment was bubbling to the surface, causing the clergy to fear for the maintenance of its status.

When in 1741 Whitefield's *Journal* was published, some passages in this work were considered incendiary: "I think the ministers preaching almost universally by note, is a mark that they have, in a great measure, lost the old spirit of preaching.... It is a symptom of the decay of religion, when reading sermons becomes fashionable where extempore preaching did once almost universally prevail."[12] Whitefield had nothing good to say for the universities and the education they provided the future pastorate: "Their light has become darkness ... complained of by the most godly ministers."[13] Whitefield remarked that faculties and pastorate alike "do not experimentally know Christ."[14]

Things had gone too far. In 1742 the Connecticut Assembly passed An Act for Regulating Abuses and Correcting Disorders in Ecclesiastical Affairs. Stiff penalties were to be administered for uninvited preaching; all pastors would have to be licensed by local ministerial associations. A month later Davenport was arrested and tried before the Connecticut Assembly, no matter that Whitefield had said, "I never knew one keep so close a walk with God as Mr. Davenport."[15] Davenport was declared insane and unceremoniously escorted to the Connecticut border. Reaction to revivalism had begun in earnest.

A major figure in the reaction was Charles Chauncy, pastor at the venerable First Church, Boston. Chauncy was a man who favored direct statement over poetic embellishment. As a contemporary remarked, Chauncy "wished that someone would translate *Paradise Lost* into prose, that he might understand it."[16] Chauncy liked a rational and ordered existence, and lived his life accordingly. A close friend described his daily routine: "At twelve o'clock he took one pinch of snuff, and only one in twenty-four hours. At one o'clock he dined on one dish of plain wholesome food, and after dinner took one glass of wine, and one pipe of tobacco, and only one in twenty-four hours."[17] To a man of such regular habits the raw emotion displayed in the revival movement went against the grain of his being. Perry Miller writes, for Chauncy "emotion is something to be measured out in judicious quantities upon suitable occasions, and at other times stored in the refrigerator."[18]

Psychologically predisposed to calm rationality, Chauncy, while remaining a bulwark of Puritanism, favored the temperament of the Enlightenment. The Enlightenment condemned enthusiasm — the type of emotional response evident in revivalism. The problem with enthusiasm was that the subject believed himself in direct communication with God; he became a moral absolute unto himself, rather than submitting to Christian tradition and theology. As Locke had warned in his *Essay*, "immediate revelation" is nothing but "the conceits of a warmed or overweening brain."[19] The person experiencing such imaginings could become dangerous to society. Chauncy came to see revivalism as a menace.

He had good reason. What was to distinguish the inner voice of God from the inner voice of Satan? Look what happened to James Davenport. After being expelled from Connecticut he continued in his ways. Early in 1743 suffering from fever and occasionally delirious, he preached a sermon which "published the messages which he said he received from the Spirit in dreams."[20] Wigs, jewels, fine clothing, and books by worldly divines— anything that caused the soul to turn away from the Spirit and toward the idols of this world, were to be cast into the fire. Soon a great fire was set ablaze, around which crazed citizens danced and howled into the night. It was Savanarola's bonfire of the vanities revisited.

Then something snapped within Davenport's soul. It was reported in the *Boston Weekly Post-Boy* that someone from the crowd around the fire approached Davenport and told him "he thought the Devil was in him; Mr. Davenport said he thought so too, and added that he was under the influence of an evil spirit and that God had left him."[21] The same Boston newspaper reported the words of Davenport's closest traveling companion: "That although he had for three years past believed (and why not known) himself to be a child of God, he now thought he was a child of the devil and a Judas, and thought he should be hanged between heaven and earth and have his bowels gush out."[22] Davenport wrote to his old friend Jonathan Barber: "Take no part of the glory to yourself. Neither lean on your own understanding. Oh! Be not wise above that which is written nor leave the sacred unerring Oracle of Truth."[23] A year later he published a document titled *The Confession and Retractions of James Davenport*, then wrote his friend Barber that he was enjoying an inner peace he had never experienced before, that only now did he believe that God had finally entered his soul, that everything before had been the work of the devil.

The example of Davenport gave Charles Chauncy the necessary ammunition to wage war against the revivalists. He could reasonably claim that the spiritual enthusiast mistakes his passions for divine communication, that "he is under no other influence than that of an overheated imagination," a victim of a "bad temperament of the blood and spirits ... a disease, a sort of madness."[24]

Chauncy's chief opponent was none other than Jonathan Edwards. Next to Whitefield, Edwards was the most significant figure of the Great Awakening. Edwards was a formidable foe. His *Faithful Narrative* had gone through three editions and twenty printings. It was eventually translated into several languages and became a manual for revivalists, maintaining this status for over a century. It made Edwards a famous international figure, an expert on conversion and revival psychology. Edwards published several other works on revivalism, but two were particularly significant: *Some Thoughts Concerning the Present Revival of Religion in New England* (1742), and *A Treatise Concerning Religious Affections* (1746). The latter made Edwards's reputation for all time. It was used as a textbook in theological seminaries well into the nineteenth century and is still held in high regard. Sydney Ahlstrom remarks that such work made Edwards "one of the most important interpreters of religious experience and experiential religion in post-Reformation history."[25]

Chauncy was not of Edwards's intellectual caliber: "Chauncy was not an eloquent man.... When he once prayed God not to make him an orator, a friend replied that his prayer was long since granted."[26] Nor had he first-hand experience with revivalism: Edwards had corresponded with Whitefield, and Whitefield accepted an invitation to preach at his church in Northampton.

As both Calvinist Puritan and son of the Enlightenment, Edwards found himself in a balancing act between the Chauncys and the Davenports of his time. He believed in the new "religion of the heart" against its rationalist opponents. Yet Edwards believed, with Locke, that religious affections must be tested against some measure of objectivity. In all cases mere intellectual knowledge alone is insufficient; there must be some "sense of the heart."

Edwards did insist, however, that one can only be saved through the work of the Holy Spirit. He issued a warning to Chauncy and others: Those who in any way criticized or hindered the work of revivals "would do well thoroughly to consider whether this be not indeed the work of God."[27] Instead, Edwards maintained, "it behooves us to encourage and promote this work," for it would be "dangerous ... to forbear to do so."[28] And why might it be dangerous? Because America was to be the site of the coming millennium. "There is no such thing as being neuters," proclaimed Edwards, "there is a necessity of being either for or against the King that then gloriously appears."[29]

Certainly, as a Puritan, Chauncy was not against promoting the coming Kingdom. This was not the basis for his antipathy toward revivalism. Rather, he was against the display of "enthusiasm" that characterized the Great Awakening. Chauncy discerned in those public displays of emotion a rebellious spirit stirring to life among the great mass of ordinary people. In the larger cities there was developing a population of single men — newcomers from the countryside and overseas— which could mobilize at any time into an angry and rebellious mob. These people lacked a stake in the community and often suffered a frustrating and impoverished existence. A Boston clergyman spoke on behalf of his colleagues concerning his fear of those "murmuring against the government and the rich people among us...."[30]

This urban mob was a ready audience for revivalist preachers. Newspapers reported that most of those who came to hear Davenport, for example, were from the lower orders of society. Writes Robert Brockway, "This was all quite alarming to the Establishment ... some kind of popular movement which threatened their prestige and status."[31] Many among the lower classes seemed to take pleasure in Davenport's disparagement of the clergy, which they identified with the wealthy gentry. As Chauncy commented concerning revivalism, "It has made strong attempts to destroy all property, to make all things common...."[32]

Since most of the clergy came from the educated upper echelon of society they had good grounds to fear social unrest. Moreover, as Alan Heimert remarks, "...it seldom escaped notice that the 'most substantial and sensible people' inclined to the churches of rational religion."[33] Historian Ruth H. Bloch notes that, by contrast, the vast majority of revivalists came from the middle and lower classes: "The Great Awakening powerfully reaffirmed the radical and democratic elements of Reformation Protestantism."[34]

4

The American Millennium

Historian Robert Brockway makes a crucial point: "Evangelicalism was a populist religion. It was also apocalyptic."[1] Ruth Bloch concurs: "The Great Awakening ... raised and diffused intense millennial expectations."[2] Indeed, the Great Awakening was *essentially* millennialist. Historian Alan Heimert writes, "The Awakening had brought history to a critical juncture, a discernible confluence which disposed the Calvinist mind to 'look for the beginnings' of the millennium 'from year to year.'"[3]

But the Great Awakening was only an intensification of normal Puritan ethos—after all, that is what "revival" means. As Heimert observes, "The heart and soul of Calvinism was ... an implicit faith that God intended to establish his earthly Kingdom."[4] Millennialism was firmly ensconced in the Confession of Faith adhered to by all New England churches (the Savoy Declaration of 1658). Because millennialism was an implicit part of the Puritan tradition, phrases like "the Kingdom" carried apocalyptic significance. There was no need for explicit reference to millennialism.

This dual aspect of revivalism — its populist appeal and its apocalyptic spirit — presented a dilemma for many of the clergy. Although revivalism could be seen as a sign that New England was about to experience the millennium, its popular appeal raised fear of revolution against the privileged. This was not surprising. First, there was precedent. In the English civil wars and on the European continent millennialism had proven to be "a mighty engine of revolution" which "gave direction and meaning to rebellion."[5] Second, if the examples of history were not enough, cause for concern lay close at hand in the example of James Davenport. The General Court noted that he claimed "some extraordinary discovery and assurance of the very near approach of the end of the world ... that in a very short time all these things will be involved in devouring flames."[6] Expectations of an imminent fiery End could easily lead to lawlessness and civil disorder among the urban mob, especially when some revivalist pastors were preaching against the luxury of the well-to-do.

Nevertheless, large numbers of the clergy put aside their fears and trusted that divine Providence would somehow clear the way peacefully to the coming millennium. They put their whole-hearted support behind the revivalist movement, assured that the eschaton was thereby about to be fulfilled. The son of Boston minister Thomas Prince founded the periodical *The Christian History* "for the advancement of the Redeemer's Kingdom and glory."[7] For several years this magazine traced every step of the revivalist movement, linking accounts of local revivals into a larger narrative, furnishing widespread assurance that the Kingdom was making significant advances, always placing an "apocalyptic construction"[8] upon events. All over New England ministers were hoping that the events of the Great Awakening were a prelude to the end-time millennium. Typical was the comment of Peter Thacher, pastor at Middleborough, Massachusetts: "If it be the dawn of the glorious Gospel-Day, I trust the whole earth shall soon be filled with the knowledge of the Saviour."[9] John Moorehead of Boston was certain that the apocalypse was unfolding: "Let the guardian angels carry the news to heaven of the numerous converts: the Millennium is begun, Christ dwells with men on earth."[10]

An assembly of almost seventy pastors from all around New England gathered to sign a document titled *The Testimony and Advice of an Assembly of Pastors* in support of the revivals. This document remarked on the "plentiful effusion" of God's Spirit in the revivals and the resulting "enlargement of the Kingdom of Christ." It asserted that all of this had raised "the hopes of such as are waiting for the Kingdom of God, and the coming on of the glory of the Latter Days," and furnished "an earnest of the glorious things promised to the church in the Latter Days." Finally this document said that the revivalist movement must be defended against those who "despise these out-pourings of the Spirit."[11] Its chief defender was, of course, Jonathan Edwards. Edwards saw the Great Awakening as *the* apocalyptic event.

From his youth Edwards had been an ardent apocalypticist. Indeed, Perry Miller proclaimed Edwards "the greatest artist of the apocalypse."[12] At age eighteen he took up a pastorate in New York where he lived with the Smith family. He writes: "Sometimes Mr. Smith and I walked there [along the bank of the Hudson] to converse on the things of God; and our conversation used to turn much on the advancement of Christ's Kingdom in the world, and the glorious things that God would accomplish for his church in the latter days."[13]

Young Edwards kept a close eye on world events to see if any would portend the imminence of the end-time: "If I heard the least hint of anything that happened in any part of the world that appeared, in some respect or other, to have a favourable aspect on the interests of Christ's Kingdom, my soul eagerly catched at it, and it would much animate and refresh me. I used to be eager to read public news-letters, mainly for that end."[14]

As a young man, and all through his life, Edwards was an inveterate note maker. He compiled notebooks on all different topics, recording his own meditations and observations on the Bible, on Christian doctrine, on the natural world — anything that grabbed his interest at the moment. He eventually filled nine volumes of "Miscellanies" containing 1360 entries, some of which were elaborate treatises, along with three volumes of notes on the Bible.[15] All of these notes he meticulously indexed.

Edwards reserved separate sections in the "Miscellanies" under the headings "Antichrist," "Apocalypse," and "Millennium." Before he was twenty he began a separate notebook devoted to the book of Revelation. In these "Notes on the Apocalypse" he made a detailed study of every chapter of that biblical book, and noted every advance of Protestant Christianity throughout the world against Roman Catholicism (headed by the pope, the traditional Antichrist of Puritanism) and Roman Catholic nations: a Jesuit house struck by lightening, its library burned; a slow-down in Spanish commerce. The mature man continued to watch world events from an apocalyptic perspective. When soldiers from New England forced surrender at the vaunted French fortress at Louisbourg in 1745, he wondered if this indicated the pouring of the sixth vial of the Apocalypse. "I had great longings for the advancement of Christ's Kingdom in the world, and my secret prayer used to be, in great part, taken up in praying for it."[16]

None of this was inconsistent with Edwards's adoption of Enlightenment precepts. He read Isaac Newton's scientific work, but Newton's interests did not stop at the edge of the natural universe. Newton, who discovered the elements of differential calculus and the laws of gravity, devoted the last thirty-five years of his life to studying the fulfillment of biblical prophecy. He spent more years trying to determine the exact date for the pouring of the seventh vial (mentioned in Revelation) than he spent determining the orbits of the planets. Recent examination of Newton's private papers, which he kept secret during his lifetime, reveals that his calculated year for the dawn of the end-time was 2060. Edwards cited some of Newton's published speculations on this subject in his *A History of the Work of Redemption*. Most scientists of the Enlightenment in trying to capture nature in mathematical formulae were seeking to come closer to God; for them "the books of Daniel and of the Revelation were as much data as were Halley's tabulations of his comet."[17] In this regard John Maynard Keynes said that Newton believed "certain mystic clues which God had laid about the world ... were to be found partly in the evidence of the heavens and in the constitution of elements ... but also partly in ... the original cryptic revelation in Babylonia. He regarded the universe as a cryptogram set by the Almighty."[18]

It was, then, both as a child of the Enlightenment and in true Calvinist Puritan tradition that Jonathan Edwards "cast the revivals in an eschatological framework,"[19] in apocalyptic perspective, and "offered the fullest discussion of the Awakening's eschatological meaning."[20] Stephen Stein notes that "confidence about the ultimate outcome of history marks Edwards' eschatology from beginning to end."[21]

In his book *Some Thoughts* Edwards made his most optimistic eschatological pronouncements: "It is not unlikely that this work of God's Spirit [revivalism], that is so extraordinary and wonderful, is the dawning, or at least a prelude, of that glorious work of God, so often foretold in Scripture.... And there are many things that make it probable that this work will begin in America."[22]

Alan Heimert remarks, "Perhaps Edwards' most impressive achievement was to purge Calvinist millenarianism of all those seventeenth-century elements which were symptoms of cosmic despair."[23] In *An Humble Attempt ... Promises and Prophecies Concerning the Last Time*[24] Edwards argued against an interpretation of Revelation which held that there would be bad times before the millennium began. With such a negative interpretation, Edwards reasoned, people would focus on the "dismal time that shall precede" the millennium rather than look forward to the millennium itself. Such a negative interpretation would cause "a great damp to their hope, courage and activity."[25] Could anyone seriously expect, he asked, "that after all the increase of light that has been made in the world since the Reformation, there shall be a return of more dark time.... Satan's kingdom of darkness be more firmly established ... is this conceivable...?"[26]

A surge in millennialist spirit was not the only result of the Great Awakening. Overall church membership increased by an estimated twenty to fifty thousand.[27] But more important than the numbers was the new spirituality manifested in revivalism. There was a revival of many of Puritanism's emphases: praying, preaching, daily Bible reading, public testimonies of religious experience. Immediate individual religious experience took precedence over theology. There was a movement toward the heart and the spirit, and away from the intellect.

Where those who adopted the revivalist spirit were unable to make the desired changes in their own church they withdrew to form a new church. They ordained their own clergy from among their number, persons who felt called to preach and who had been "tested" by the congregation. Formal education was not a prerequisite. By mid-century New England had spawned nearly one hundred such "Separate" churches, many of which later joined the Baptists. Meanwhile the Anglican church benefited; it gained members who had defected from other denominations because they were repelled by evangelicalism. Not only did the Great Awakening cause a fracturing of American Christendom into new denominations, formerly monolithic denominations subdivided. The Anglican church developed an evangelical wing to accommodate its membership and prevent loss of numbers. Such a multiplicity of churches existed by 1760 that Gilbert Tennent complained that these "numerous and scandalous divisions" of the Christian church were a "torment to herself, a grief to her friends, and the scorn of her enemies."[28]

A new divisive spirit was afoot among the populace, the beginning of the religious dichotomy prevalent today. As Perry Miller phrased it, "New England in the eighteenth century was a laboratory for America, and it divided itself in two, into 'new lights' and 'old lights.' The split was the measure of this community's encounter with the parting of the ways in modern culture."[29] Jonathan Edwards was well aware of the developing two cultures, like children calling each other nasty names: "Such distinguishing names of reproach do, as it were, divide us into two armies, separated and drawn up in battle array, ready to fight one with another; which greatly hinders the work of God."[30] A warning from a wise and perceptive man, needed but unheeded today. Historian Frank Lambert says the Great Awakening was "a sustained, intensive struggle over meaning that may be termed an early American cultural war."[31]

Alan Heimert insists that the split ran much deeper than between clerical factions; there was a "fundamental cleavage within the colonial populace,"[32] a dichotomy between "evangelicals" and "rationalists" (or "liberals"). While there may have been debate over fine points of doctrine and polity *within* each of these two major divisions, fellowship among evangelicals transcended geographical and denominational boundaries. An evangelical in Massachusetts had more in common with an evangelical in Georgia, than he had with a liberal in his home town. The intercolonialism of Whitefield, Tennent, and Edwards had set the tone. As Ahlstrom observes, "Based on a wide and durable consensus, evangelicalism would become a powerful force in the future development of American culture."[33] From this point forward the two "religious philosophies" would engage in "a vital competition for the intellectual allegiance of the American people."[34]

While the Great Awakening left colonials with a dichotomy of religious philosophy, it united people throughout the colonies as never before, providing a unifying self-consciousness: "The Great Awakening also played its part in breaking down sectional and parochial feelings in the colonies and encouraging a new sense of American unity."[35] It was America's first mass movement, America's first experience as a nation. As Alan Heimert remarks, "The evangelical impulse ... was the avatar and instrument of a fervent American nationalism."[36]

This nationalism would eventuate in the American Revolution. As well as a feeling of oneness among the colonies, the Great Awakening contributed other factors which greased the wheels of independence. The Great Awakening fostered a new anti-authoritarianism among persons of all levels of society, and among the lower levels a democratization. The individual assumed a new consciousness, and demanded to be heard. The establishment had been successfully challenged. A precedent had been set. People were open to new ideas, ready to criticize and debate, ready to protest. The crowds which had gathered to hear Whitefield and other evangelicals easily morphed into the crowds which gathered in Boston in the early 1770s to hear speeches praising liberty.

Undergirding this new self-consciousness of the colonies as a unity vis-à-vis the outside world was the spirit of millennialism. As Ruth Bloch observes, "The Great Awakening ... raised and diffused intense millennial expectations"[37] and "carried the millennialism of American Puritanism throughout the colonies."[38] "Above all," writes Sydney Ahlstrom, "it [the Great Awakening] awakened millennial hopes that a covenanted nation ... could become an instrument of Providence in realizing the Kingdom."[39] Jonathan Edwards had renewed the original Puritan vision of the city upon a hill and the idea that America would be the seat of the coming millennium; the Great Awakening spread these ideas throughout the American colonies. This "master organizing principle" of "a special people with a messianic destiny," this "vision of a redeemer nation and a covenant people was dazzling, and none ... could escape its glare."[40] There was a "national sense of intensified religious and moral resolution.... Millennial hopes were kindled."[41]

The Anglo-French conflicts of the 1740s and 1750s offered the first occasion for celebration of such nationalist millennialism. As Nathan Hatch remarks, "Vivid perceptions of an external foe confirmed their sense of identity as God's elect people living in the end times and linked their lives to the cosmic war between good and evil."[42] It began with the defeat of the most redoubtable military stronghold in North America by a small force of untrained New Englanders lacking both heavy artillery and British naval support in July 1745 — the siege of Louisbourg which Jonathan Edwards hailed as having apocalyptic significance. As conflict with France widened, sectarian differences were momentarily held in abeyance. Liberal and evangelical clergy found common ground in the face of an external enemy described in language lifted directly from the seventeenth chapter of Revelation: "the offspring of that scarlet whore, that mother of harlots, who is justly the abomination of the earth."[43] Former critics of the Great Awakening now openly expressed millennialist hopes. Even Charles Chauncy joined in, as religious differences were muted in a general flowering of millennial expectation.[44] As Ruth Bloch observed, "More Americans thought about the Last Days in the late 1750s than ever before."[45]

This rising spirit of millennialism gained momentum in Revolutionary years as apocalyptic nomenclature shifted from French Roman Catholic shoulders to British backs. After England had ceded special Catholic religious powers to the defeated enemy in the Quebec Act of 1774, Harvard president Samuel Langdon suggested that "all the late measures respecting the colonies have originated from popish schemes of men who ... look on Popery as a religion."[46] Timothy Dwight, grandson of Jonathan Edwards, in a valedictory address to the students of Yale College in 1776, spoke of "the last thousand years of the reign of time,"[47] "the summit of American glory"[48] that was soon to be: "You now see the foundations of that glory laid."[49] Although Dwight had always abhorred the idea of war he urged his young students to participate in the oncoming conflict, and he himself served as a chaplain in the Revolutionary Army. A vocal patriot, he continued to preach the American millennium throughout the war.

Much of what Jonathan Edwards said and wrote could be taken as inflaming insurrection: "There are many passages in Scripture which do seem to intend that as well the civil as the ecclesiastical polities of the nations shall be overthrown and a theocracy ensue."[50] Those with sovereign powers should never be allowed to rule "contrary to true liberty"; instead, "the absolute and despotic power of the kings of the earth shall be taken away, and liberty shall reign throughout the earth."[51] "The days are coming, so often spoken of, when the saints shall reign on earth and all dominion and authority shall be given into their hands."[52]

These sentiments expressed by Edwards were commonplace in Puritan thought. Did this widespread spirit of millennialism, help bring on the Revolution? Historian Jerald Brauer believes that it did: "Religion was indeed one of the primary forces which impelled colonial American people towards revolution and sustained them in their actions."[53] He elaborates: "Revivalism provided one of the most powerful forces that ... offered a set of symbols and beliefs which were both a source of criticism and a vision of new possibilities."[54]

Belief in the millennium provided a framework in which to view everyday political and economic events, a perspective. Such a belief helps to shape, structure, formulate, articulate, what might otherwise be simply unfocused emotion. It legitimates, rationalizes, mobilizes. Historian Ruth Bloch understands this when she writes, "An animating ideal of the future was necessary to propel American colonists to make their decisive break from tradition.... In America in the 1770's most of this ideological leverage was provided by the millennial tradition within American Protestantism."[55] Bloch does not deny the contribution of Enlightenment principles, the intellect that fashioned the Constitution, but such sober cerebral ideology was hardly sufficient, she argues, to excite emotions, to push a large mass of the population over the edge toward a large-scale social and political transformation. Millennialism helped Americans understand "the ultimate meaning of the revolutionary crisis and the birth of the American nation.... The conviction that history was drawing to its glorious conclusion, when the world would be transformed into a paradise for the righteous, predisposed large numbers of American Protestants to throw themselves behind the revolutionary cause with a fervency that is otherwise hard to explain."[56]

But wasn't the Revolution about "liberty"? It was. The word "liberty" originally had a religious meaning. It meant religious salvation, liberty from the bonds of Satan. It also meant liberty from religious oppression, the kind the Puritans escaped by coming to America on the *Arbella*. For Jonathan Edwards civil and religious liberty were one. As early as 1724 he was describing the millennium as a time of civil and religious liberty. In sermons he spoke of the historic progress of Christianity toward "a state of liberty from persecution" and the "advancement of the church into that state of the glorious prevalence of truth, liberty, peace, and joy, that we so often read of in the prophetical parts of Scripture."[57] The millennium, he wrote, would be a time of "glorious liberty," of "liberty and glory."[58]

Nathan Hatch observes that "liberty always had a religious as well as a civil dimension."[59] This is evidenced in the words of Ebenezer Baldwin in 1775: The colonies will become "the foundation of a great and mighty empire ... to be founded on such principles of liberty and freedom, both civil and religious, as never before took place in the world; which shall be the principal seat of that glorious Kingdom, which Christ shall erect upon the earth in the latter days."[60] The religious connotation of the word "liberty" was to remain a specifically American way of thinking. When Alexis de Tocqueville visited the United States several generations later he commented, "The Americans combine the notions of Christianity and of liberty so intimately in their minds that it is impossible to make them conceive the one without the other."[61]

During the Revolution religious and secular thinking merged in the concepts of liberty and the millennium. Millennial thinking was prevalent during that era. As Bloch has noted, "Eschatological imagery from the beginning intermixed with constitutional arguments, contributing a cosmic dimension to patriot political understanding."[62] Millennial beliefs concerning the destiny of the revolutionary nation formed a seamless fabric with the political ideology of the patriots.

The revolutionary potential of millennialism, which during the Great Awakening had so frightened Charles Chauncy and others of the ruling class, was now turned outward against the mother country. As events intensified, millennial thinking extended beyond the Revolution against Great Britain. Revolutionary rhetoric began to encompass the whole world. The efforts of the colonies were on behalf of "all mankind." In New York pastor Abraham Keteltas preached that liberty "is God's own cause," that in the coming millennium America's revolutionary principles would have universal application and transform the world from "a vale of tears into a paradise of God."[63]

Millennial sentiments continued to be expressed as the War of Independence neared its conclusion. Victory at Yorktown in 1781 moved the sober and secular John Adams to indulge in millennial expectation: "The great designs of Providence must be accomplished.... Light spreads ... may it shine more and more until the perfect day."[64]

And then it was over. The colonies that had begun with a vision of a "city upon a hill" had become an independent nation. At war's end Connecticut minister David Tappan considered contemporary events "a principal link — a chain which is gradually drawing after it the most glorious consequences to mankind.... Hastening on the accomplishment of the Scripture prophecies relative to the millennial state."[65] A year after the conclusion of the conflict the Baptist Warren Association of Rhode Island was sure that this new independent nation would "advance the cause of Christ in the world" on its way "towards bringing the glory of the latter day."[66]

In a book titled *The Millennium* published shortly after the conclusion of the War of Independence and the founding of the new nation, David Austin wrote, "It seems no unnatural conclusion from ancient prophecy ... that in order to usher in ... the latter day glory two great revolutions are to take place; the first outward and political, the second inward and spiritual."[67] As historian Ahlstrom remarks, millennialism had become "a prominent and distinctive feature of American thought on the nature, purpose, and destiny of the nation.... This old Puritan conception of the Redeemer Nation ... was on men's minds on the first Fourth of July, and ... would become an enduring feature of American patriotic oratory."[68] A new nation. Glorious times, surely, lay ahead.

5

Democratic Evangelism

In 1781 on the occasion of Cornwallis's surrender at Yorktown, Timothy Dwight, grandson of Jonathan Edwards, chaplain during the War of Independence, preached a sermon at Northampton, the scene of his grandfather's revival. The American Revolution, he said, would mark a watershed in human history. The recent victory anticipated the coming millennium, expected to begin around the year 2000. The new nation would, indeed, be a city upon a hill, an example for the rest of the world.

Then, on the morning of May 9, 1798, Reverend Jedidiah Morse shocked his congregation at New North Church in Boston with the news that foreign agents were at work in America plotting to subvert God's new nation. He claimed to possess documents which proved that these agents were part of the same secret organization of anarchists which had planned the French Revolution.

Word of this conspiracy spread like wildfire. Within weeks a professor of divinity at Harvard, David Tappan, warned his senior class concerning this menacing plot. At Yale Timothy Dwight, now president of the college, in a Fourth-of-July address said that these saboteurs and infidels were part of the unfolding end-time. It was all in the book of Revelation, he insisted: the frogs were coming out of the mouth of the beast, and Satan's forces were gathering for the final struggle between good and evil. Fourth of July addresses in Connecticut and Massachusetts abounded with similar fears.[1] By autumn, despite a lack of hard evidence to back suspicions, pulpit and press were ablaze with millennialist fears of an international Masonic conspiracy plotting to destroy the religion and political order of the West.

All of this commotion stemmed from a obscure work by a Scottish theologian and professor of natural philosophy, John Robison — *Proofs of a Conspiracy against All the Religions and Governments of Europe*. Robison believed that for the past half-century secret orders of Masons had been promulgating heretical ideas "under the specious pretext of enlightening the world by the torch of philosophy.... Until, at last, an association has been formed for the express purpose of rooting out all the religious establishments and overturning all the existing governments of Europe."[2] This association was none other than the Bavarian Illuminati, in reality a minor group founded by Adam Weishaupt in 1776 and soon suppressed by the Bavarian monarch. But Robison claimed its members were leading lights in the French Revolution and that the association was still secretly active all over the world.

American millennialists put their own spin on this: the Illuminati were servants of Satan. Timothy Dwight feared that Americans might become "disciples of Voltaire" and "concubines of the Illuminati."[3] David Austin wrote that France was embarking on a "counterfeit millennium," "the millennium of Hell! ...The attempt of Satan to mount the millennial saddle...."[4]

The solution was simple. America must hold itself aloof from everything European. Had not Europe always been a seedbed of apostasy, a sinkhole of heresy? The minister of Hartford's First Church, Nathan Strong, could clearly see the danger of American flirtation with European ideology. America must stand alone, withdraw from contact with the evil manifest in Europe: "Come out of her, my people, that ye be not partakers of her sins, and that ye receive not her plagues." A year later, in 1799, the entire Congregational clergy of Massachusetts in concert gave expression to almost those precise words: "Come out of the infidel antichristian world, my people...."[5]

America must stand alone, God's people in an evil world.[6] America must harken back to the days of its founding Fathers, to the ideology of its first colonists—that America would be the site of the end-time millennium. As historian Ruth Bloch remarks, "Millennialism provided a major intellectual framework through which Americans understood the general course of history and defined their national purpose ... and became an essential ingredient of the national culture ... millennialism in its various forms had by 1800 become deeply imbedded in the thought and the character of the American people."[7] This "originally Puritan idea" would "become an integral part of the nineteenth-century creed of American manifest destiny."[8]

Ordinary folk empowered by the Great Awakening and the Revolution, believed that the average man and woman, with the aid of the Bible, could experience the New Birth without the need of an educated clergy. The laity turned to the Bible to test previously unexamined, and largely secular and political, assumptions about the millennium. Detailed exegeses of passages of biblical prophecy, often written by obscure unknown and probably self-educated laypersons fed an appetite for the exposition of biblical prophecy among the reading public which became ravenous by the mid-1790s. The number of eschatological publications between 1793 and 1796 averaged between five and ten times more per year than during the period from 1765 to 1792.[9]

The concept of the millennium was maleable. Liberal Protestants, often "tied closely in friendship to such secular thinkers as Jefferson, Franklin, and Paine" who "formed a kind of international network of Enlightened Protestants,"[10] had fostered a somewhat secularized concept of the millennium. According to this concept, closely allied with the Enlightenment theory of a progressive history of humankind, the millennium prophesied in the Bible would arrive at the end of a gradual, if not necessarily steady, improvement in the lives of human beings. Was not the successfully completed War of Independence and the resulting new nation the most obvious example of this unfolding? Biblical millennialist Benjamin Rush in a 1786 lecture to the American Philosophical Society remarked that science would some day be able to rid the world of "baneful vices" and change human moral character into the "likeness of God himself."[11] Princeton's Samuel Stanhope Smith proclaimed that there might be "no need of any other millennium than the general progress of science and civilization."[12]

When Thomas Jefferson became president in 1801 many Americans feared for the future of the nation. Jefferson had made no secret of the fact that he was a Deist, openly avowing his doubts concerning orthodox Christian beliefs. He had spent half a decade in infidel France absorbing the latest thinking of the "philosophes." The colleges were filled with students eager to adopt such new thinking. Among the students at Maine's Bowdoin College there was only one who professed Christian beliefs. The College of William and Mary was a "hot-bed of French politics and religion,"[13] according to a Virginia bishop, and these new ideas were sprouting even at Presbyterian Princeton.

At Yale "intemperance, profanity, gambling, and licentiousness were common," and most of the class "were infidels, and called each other Voltaire, Rousseau, D'Alembert, etc."[14] Yale's president, Timothy Dwight, decided something needed to be done, and right away. He challenged his students with stimulating topics such as "Is the Bible the word of God?" He set upon a preaching cycle which converted one third of the college's students, many deciding to enter the ministry. This was the beginning of what came to be known as the Second Great Awakening, a period of expanding religious enthusiasm over the next several decades.[15]

Following Dwight's example this new spirit spread to other colleges. Middlebury College, for example, had a succession of revivals spanning a decade. As students of these colleges joined the clergy and went out to pastorates the rate of local revivals increased. The laity once again caught fire; as one clergyman said of the time, It was an occasion for renewed "prayer for, and expectation of, the fulfillment of the promises respecting the later day Glory."[16]

This new spirit of revival blended personal and national aspirations within a millennial context. Historian Ruth Doan notes that it was during the Second Great Awakening that a new culture of evangelical Protestantism centered on the New Birth, the authority of the Bible, and "an anticipation of the coming millennium" provided a growing number of Americans with "an understanding of history" which "tied together identity, community, and nation."[17] This new nationalistic spirit, bolstered by and permeated with a vibrant religiosity, has remained a peculiarly American form of nationalism to this day.

During the Second Great Awakening evangelicalism and republican ideology became "mutually reinforcing, with evangelicalism providing a basis for the survival of the republic while also symbolizing the underlying moral meaning of being American.... The millennial hope lent urgency and promise to the American as well as the evangelical mission...."[18] By the 1820s orthodox American Protestantism "included a general Christian millennialism."[19] As historian Whitney R. Cross remarks, "Optimism took the form of belief in an early millennium. Just as the American political system would lead the world to equality and justice, so would American revivals inaugurate the thousand years' reign of Christ on earth before the Second Coming and the end of the world."[20]

New England had been the center of American religious orthodoxy beginning with its first colonists. But in this era of renewed revivalist spirit and a shift of religious influence from clergy to laity, it was about to pass the torch to the new New England — upstate New York.

Movement westward began with the new status of nationhood. By 1810 almost all of upstate New York had been settled, mostly by immigrants from New England. The population of Jefferson and St. Lawrence counties was almost homogeneously from Vermont. Oneida was a new Connecticut. Groups of families from the same area of New England had migrated en masse to their new abode in the west, later to be joined by others from the same geographic origin. It was as if parts of New England, along with its culture, had been transplanted lock-stock-and-barrel hundreds of miles west in the fertile valleys of upstate New York.

Then in 1825 in an act to symbolize the opening of the newly completed Erie Canal New York's Governor De Witt Clinton poured a keg of Lake Erie water into the waters of the Atlantic Ocean lapping against the shores of New York City. Now Great Lakes' commodities could travel east to the port of New York City and eastern manufactured goods could travel west as far as Buffalo. In celebration cannons were fired in sequence every five miles along the entire length of the canal. It was hoped that the reverberating boom of these cannons would echo in an economic boom the canal was expected to bring to the newly settled west.

Indeed, boom days followed in those regions directly served by the canal as its construction inched westward. Towns sprouted up along this westward path, and the boom economy encouraged even more immigration to New York State south and east of Lake Ontario. Commerce for the state increased tenfold between 1791 and 1831, and the population quadrupled between 1790 and 1820. The population of Ontario County alone doubled in the decade between 1810 and 1820.[21] During the 1820s the population grew more rapidly in western New York than in any other part of the United States: Albany gained 96 percent, Utica 183, Syracuse 282, Buffalo 314, Rochester 512.[22]

Just as New Englanders transplanted their communities and culture in their new homeland, so they also transplanted their religious fervor. As early as 1784 Connecticut churches began sending missionaries to the new New England. The winter of 1799–1800 saw a "Great Revival" in that newly settled area. The spirit of revivalism in western New York did not die thereafter, but continued to grow in a cyclical crescendo throughout the early decades of the nineteenth century. In 1824, well before revivalism reached its peak, almost one half of all Presbyterian clergymen in America resided in New York State, with more than half of this number serving in the area surrounding the Erie Canal.[23] The hunger for religious literature in western New York was voracious. In 1822 the American Tract Society of New York published three-quarters of all the tracts printed in the nation. The residents of New York State were purchasing more than double the number of Bibles bought in New England, and they donated more funds in support of the American Bible Society than Massachusetts and Connecticut combined.[24]

The area of New York State south and just east of Lake Ontario was so awash in religious fervor that historians have designated it the "Burned-over District." As Michael Barkun has noted, millennialism was a core ingredient in the religious legacy inherited from New England. The inhabitants of the Burned-over District "brought with them religious patterns in which millennial themes and emotional excitation were already present. They had grown accustomed to view the world as an arena in which God's plan unfolded in history."[25]

Into this environment came a figure who would gain renown as the greatest "religious leader in America since Edwards,"[26] an individual who "was a catalyst and often a prime mover in achieving the enormous shift that occurred in Protestant church practices and theology...."[27]

Charles Grandison Finney was "an enormously successful practitioner, almost the inventor, of the modern high-pressure revivalism which, as it spread, would have important consequences for the religious ethos of the nation as a whole."[28] New "measures" Finney made standard practice would become the means for greatly increasing church growth through massive numbers of conversions. Celebrated evangelists of future generations—

Dwight L. Moody, Billy Sunday, Billy Graham — would follow in his footsteps.

In 1794 Sylvester and Rebecca Finney, along with their brood of children, including two-year-old Charles, moved out from Litchfield County, Connecticut, and emigrated, as did many others at that time, into the frontier of western New York, into Oneida County, then later into Jefferson County. Charles Finney grew into a sturdy young man with a dynamic willful personality. Although he was engaged for a short while as a school teacher, he failed to put down roots and was twenty-six before he settled upon what looked to be a promising career — law. As was the custom in those times he spent three years studying under a practicing attorney.

Finney was intrigued by how often the legal texts he was studying referred to the Bible, particularly the Mosaic code. Finney purchased a Bible and began to read it. He noticed a correlation between the legal authorities and the Bible regarding the assumption of a free human will. Without free will there could be no reward and no punishment for human acts. This seed would remain lodged in the young man's cranium, only to sprout at a later date.

The young law clerk began to attend church, and discussed religion with the pastor. In 1821 there occurred a local revival, and after some soul searching Finney converted. Shortly thereafter he decided the law was not for him; he would become a minister. His pastor wrote to three seminaries recommending the young man, but Finney was rejected by all three. So his pastor undertook to educate the young man himself. Finney was licensed to preach by the local presbytery and, after a stint replacing his now ailing pastor, received a commission as missionary to the northern regions of the county. Finney was thirty-one.

But Finney soon discovered, much to his chagrin, that by 1824 the region was already "a burnt district." Looking back on that time later in life, Finney wrote in his memoirs, "There had been, a few years previously a wild excitement passing through that region, which they called a revival of religion, but which turned out to be spurious ... and resulted in a reaction so extensive and profound, as to leave the impression on many minds that religion was a mere delusion ... they felt justified in opposing anything looking toward the promoting of a revival."[29] The young missionary had before him an uphill battle.

To avoid negative reactions among the populace Finney resolved to keep emotionalism within strict bounds. Yet he must make his audience feel the power of the Holy Spirit. He determined to preach from the heart, responding to the pulse of his audience and the guidance of the Holy Ghost. He would use no notes, but preach "on the spur of the moment, without any previous preparation."[30] The time spent on preparing and writing a sermon might better be used in preaching, in actual delivery.

Finney recalled his first experience in church listening to a well-loved older pastor preach. Finney observed that he "read his sermons in a manner that left no impression whatever on my mind. He had a monotonous, humdrum way of reading what he had probably written many years before.... It seemed to be always a matter of curiosity to know what he was aiming at."[31] Not only were the elderly preacher's sermons dry, they bore no practical application to people's lives. A preacher could not be dull if he expected to arouse his audience to the point of conversion. "We must have exciting, powerful preaching, or the devil will have the people."[32] Yet "splendid exhibitions of rhetoric"[33] did nothing to move a congregation. So Finney spoke in simple cogent sentences, using the colloquial dialect, repeating, repeating, to drive home his point. He used techniques effective in the courtroom: he spoke clearly, modulating the tone, pitch, and volume of his voice, moving in an instant from shouting to a barely audible whisper. He made good use of the hands and body language.

Finney illustrated his sermons with anecdotes taken from the lives of his audience — housewives, farmers, millers. He spoke directly, using the word "you," rather than the third person of traditional sermons. Finney wasn't there to entertain, but to save souls with a good dose of hell-fire, portraying hell with all its horrors.

And those eyes ... hypnotic, piercing the core of one's soul, afire with the power of the Holy Spirit — none could avoid Finney's accusing unrelenting stare. A fellow preacher remarked, "those great staring eyes of his (never was a man whose soul looked out through his face as his did)."[34] When a heckler held up some silver dollars and shouted, "These are my gods," Finney fixed him with a withering gaze and the man converted.

Soon Finney's reputation as an effective evangelist was made. His mission to the hamlets and countryside garnered the attention of pastors further afield who invited him to lead revivals at their churches. In Rome five hundred conversions resulted from a population of about four thousand.[35]

News of Finney's success in Rome spread ten miles east to the bustling town of Utica, a commercial, financial, and shipping center located on the Erie Canal. In 1826 Finney converted one out of ten in the town and three thousand in the surrounding county.[36] At Utica he had the cooperation of Methodist, Congregationalist, Baptist, and Presbyterian churches and clergy.

Finney gradually adapted his style of preaching to suit a more refined and educated audience. He needed to; the Burned-over District was remarkable for the relatively high percentage of educated persons compared to other regions.[37] Nearly every boy and girl learned at least the three R's, the Bible usually serving as a reader. Historian Whitney Cross writes, "...very few native-born adults remained illiterate."[38] Persons who could read the Bible, and had read it since childhood, provided a population ready and eager for Finney's evangelism. Advanced education provided a leven of clerical and lay intellectual leadership: "In the year 1829 more New Yorkers went to college than the number from Pennsylvania and New Jersey together."[39]

Finney preached with great success not only to common folk but to the highly educated. College professors appreciated how Finney mixed emotion with logic. A contemporary journalist furnishes this description: "The discourse was a chain of logic, brightened by the felicity of illustration and enforced by urgent appeals from a voice of great compass and melody."[40]

Finney never stopped learning and improving. At Utica he resided for several months with Samuel C. Aikin, pastor of the First Presbyterian Church of Utica, a prominent church filled with literate refined parishioners. Aikin had graduated college and seminary and was well versed in theology. Finney and Aikin became close friends. Finney readily accepted Aikin's criticisms and eagerly followed his advice. Aikin introduced Finney to the works of Jonathan Edwards, which Finney delighted in, second only to the Bible. He often quoted Edwards in his sermons.

Yet Finney's youthful zeal did not give way to polished urbanity. His arrow was directed at the heart, the soul of his audience. He believed the human soul could respond. Here he differed from the Calvinist doctrine of predestination, of election, and the Calvinist doctrine that sin is inherited from Adam's fall, that all are so mired in sin as to be incapable of moral choice.

If Calvinism is right about this, why preach to elicit conversions? Finney believed we have the free will, the power, to obey God or not. We are not sinners from birth, powerless to do otherwise. We choose to sin. Conversion is a choice: "Gospel salvation seemed to me to be an offer of something to be accepted ... and that all that was necessary on my part, was to get my own consent to give up my sins, and accept Christ."[41] Here is where the concept of legal moral responsibility, which Finney had learned as a law clerk, came to fruition.

This conviction that our broken relationship with God could be healed by simply turning in repentance to Christ Finney derived from a close study of the Bible: "I have sometimes thought that I would only have two articles in a creed: first, that the Bible is the only rule of faith; and second, that every other creed under heaven is an abomination in the sight of God."[42] Finney called Calvinist doctrine a "wonderful theological fiction."[43]

Finney developed his ideas in an 1835 publication, *Lectures on Revivals in Religion*. Here he boldly asserted that revivals are not miracles, not completely the work of the Holy Spirit. Using as his text the thirteenth chapter of the biblical book of Matthew, Finney writes, "In the Bible, the Work of God is compared to grain, and preaching is compared to sowing the seed...."[44] This idea that the preaching of evangelists could bring about a revival was clearly contrary to what Edwards and many others had said.

From 1830 to 1831 Finney led a prolonged revival centering on Rochester concerning which historian Cross remarks, "No more impressive revival has occurred in American history."[45]

Rochester had been founded less than two decades earlier as the town of Rochesterville. Through the town flowed the Genesee River, providing what an atlas of the time described as "cascades of exceeding beauty." The river furnished local industry with an abundant source of power, enough to supply twenty-one flour mills, eleven sawmills, and several other factories and manufacturing interests.[46] When the Erie Canal connected Rochester to New York City in 1823, Rochester became an instant boom town. In the fertile Genesee Valley trees were felled, crops plowed under, as all available acreage was made available for the planting of wheat, wheat to be milled in Rochester. Where once half the profit was lost in transportation, now Rochester's flour could travel down the canal to New York and thence to world markets for a fraction of former costs. Before the canal's construction Rochester's mills produced 26,000 barrels of flour a year. By 1828 this figure had risen to 200,000, and by 1840 to 500,000.[47]

Flour production was up, but church membership was down. Churches were feuding and bickering, yet Finney was able to draw the churches together in a spirit of cooperation to support an evangelistic campaign. Thousands of members were added to the various denominations of Rochester and the surrounding areas. Indeed, the Rochester revival spread nationwide. By 1835 the proportion of Protestant church members to the national population had almost doubled.[48] Revivals were sprouting up everywhere —1,323 in New York State alone.[49]

This national manifestation reflected Finney's emphasis on the ability of the individual to choose his or her salvation, an idea that well matched the mood of individualism current during the years of Jacksonian democracy. Finney fed anti-intellectual and anti-clerical attitudes: "A minister may be very learned and not wise ... a minister may be very wise, though he is not learned.... When young men come out from the seminaries ... [they come] with such a load of theological trumpery ... irrelevant matters which are not necessary to be attended to ... and so they get cold in religion."[50] The minister who is best fit for the job is one who saves souls: "Success in saving souls is evidence that a man understands the gospel ... he has common sense."[51] Finney considered it "all a farce to suppose that a literary ministry can convert the world."[52] "Nothing is more calculated to make a sinner feel that religion is some mysterious thing that he cannot understand, than this mouthing, formal, lofty style of speaking, so generally employed in the pulpit."[53]

No longer need the laity depend on the clergy to save souls. Finney insisted that every Christian had a responsibility in this regard; every Christian must become an evangelist. And why? To bring on the millennium. As historian Ruth Doan writes, "...the millennial dawning did not have to await a sudden, supernatural intervention, but could rather grow gradually and progressively through the accumulating numbers of the saved."[54] Finney elaborated upon this theme in 1832 in an anniversary address, challenging all Christians to do their part to bring on the millennium mentioned in the twentieth chapter of Revelation. America would play a crucial role in the divine plan.

Doan notes that "millennialism ... was pervasive in America by the 1830s."[55] Keith Hardman speaks of "the millennial thrust of the times"[56] and historian Whitney Cross writes, "Orthodox Protestantism had long been developing a strong millennial tone ... the increasing number and magnitude of revivals heightened interest in the Second Coming, while they themselves fed on this same nourishing concern.... The phenomenal awakening of 1831 convinced multitudes the day must be quite near."[57] Finney was optimistic. In 1835 he wrote, "If the church will do all her duty the millennium may come in this country in three years."[58] Historian Cross notes, "By 1837 it had become habitual for Christians to interpret 'everything that deeply engages public attention' as a symbol of 'Messiah's kingdom' ... the more enthusiastic segments of orthodoxy in 1841 were 'laying out our plans upon this basis: *the millennium is at hand.*'"[59]

6

The Great Disappointment

In 1843 Finney attended a few Bible classes presented in Boston by a rather portly farmer-turned-Baptist-preacher who was promulgating the idea that Christian efforts to bring on the millennium were futile, that Christ would have to return first, to vanquish the forces of evil and decay. It was a view diametrically opposed to Finney's, so he invited the gentleman to his room and "tried to convince him that he was in error.... But it was vain to reason with him and his followers.... Believing ... that the advent of Christ was at hand, it was no wonder that they were too wild with excitement to be reasoned with to any purpose."[1] These two men represented the seeds of the two religious cultures which dominate Protestant America today.

This compact figure of a man standing before Finney would, as James Tabor and Eugene Gallagher remark, indirectly launch "what is arguably the largest indigenous religious movement in the history of the United States."[2] The "Adventist family" of churches which eventually grew out of the movement which followed his lead today comprises eighty-four groups and sects.[3] It was a movement which thrust premillennialism — the idea of an imminent Second Coming to be followed by Christ's millennial reign on this earth — front and center. Intimately connected with this was insistence upon a specifically literal interpretation of biblical prophecy. Ironically, all of this was on the back of the widespread revivalism fostered by Finney.

William Miller was a household name in his own time; his followers were known as Millerites. But his start in life was humble. When William was only a few years old his father, a veteran of the Revolutionary War, moved the family from Massachusetts to Low Hampton, New York. Young Miller's early days were steeped in religion. The family home was used for community religious services, and the boy's maternal grandfather and paternal uncle were both Baptist preachers. His pious mother took it upon herself to be responsible for the boy's personal salvation. She taught him to read using the Bible, then the hymnal and prayer book. Strict Calvinist doctrine worked on the boy's imagination. The depravity of human nature. The propensity to sin. The Last Judgment. And lurking over all of this, a black cloud — the fear of damnation.

One had to be forever watchful. "I was often concerned about the welfare of my soul, particularly in relation to its future destiny,"[4] Miller would later write concerning his youth. And so, at the tender age of ten, young Miller promised God he would be "a good boy."

Miller married in his early twenties and moved a few miles across the border into Vermont. Here there was a public library, and soon he became friends with Matthew Lyon, who owned an extensive library. Miller read Voltaire, Hume, Paine, Ethan Allen. Lyon was an agnostic who moved in a social circle of politicians and other influential individuals. It wasn't long before Miller himself became a figure of importance, winning election for sheriff.

Like his new friends Miller became a Deist, remaining so for twelve years. His god had created the world, but then retreated and was unavailable for human communication. The beliefs of his religious upbringing he now regarded as superstition. Religion was a "system of craft rather than truth."[5] As for the Bible, which had been thumped to death in his childhood home, it was not the revealed Word, but simply a human work of history and moral instruction. The idea that God would inspire a book that could not be understood, then punish human beings for not understanding, Miller found offensive to rational thought. He seemed determined to exact vengeance on his family for their religious indoctrination. In their presence Miller mocked the pulpit style of his preacher relatives, mimicking their "ludicrous gravity," their "words, tones of voice, gestures, fervency."[6]

Beneath all of this was a growing hatred of humanity, of life. At its foundation was a deep and abiding pessimism and cynicism. Miller's study of human history, beginning with the Bible — a "history of blood, tyranny, and oppression"[7] — had been terribly disillusioning: "I could discern no bright spot in the history of the past. Those conquerors of the world, and heroes of history, were apparently but demons in human form.... I began to feel very distrustful of all men."[8] Despite the fact that he was surrounded by friendly individuals, that his home was "a place of common resort," and that he and his wife had become a "central unit" in local society, Miller informed his children "that your father has vainly sought the friendship of men, and never could he discover any friendship only where there was a dependence." By his own description, Miller was "morose and ill natured."[9]

Miller was commissioned during the War of 1812 against the British. When he witnessed an American force defeat a British force three times its size Miller could only explain this surprising victory by crediting a higher power: "It seemed to me that the Supreme Being must have watched over the interests of this country in an especial manner, and delivered us from the hands of our enemies."[10]

Miller was everywhere surrounded by death. When spotted fever killed 6000 persons locally Miller himself became ill, and narrowly escaped becoming a statistic. He lost his grandfather and a close friend. Then Miller fell from the back of a wagon, hit his head, and remained unconscious so long he was believed dead. This got him thinking, to the point he became almost obsessed with death. His earthly existence might be terminated at any moment, and Deism offered no hope of a future existence. In a letter home his wife he wrote: "What a short time and, like Spencer, I shall be no more. It is a solemn thought.... No! rather let me cling to that hope which warrants a never ending existence; a future spring where troubles shall cease ... where never ending spring shall flourish, and love, pure as the driven snow, rests in every breast."[11]

Once his military stint was over and he was back in the community of his childhood, Low Hampton, Miller was plagued with darkness: "It appeared to me that there was nothing good on earth.... I began to think man was no more than a brute, and the idea of hereafter was a dream; annihilation was a cold and chilling thought.... The heavens were as brass over my head, and the earth as iron under my feet. Eternity! What was it? And death, why was it?"[12] Hounded by thoughts of death followed by oblivion, Miller took the first tentative steps toward returning to the religious traditions of his childhood. He began to attend church once a week.

Local revivals filled Miller's soul with unbearable emotional tension. Doubts battled fear, shame, and guilt. Miller thought of his mother and his father; he thought of his own children. Too long had his family encouraged, almost begged him to return to the faith. At last he succumbed. Forget Deism. "Suddenly the character of a Saviour was vividly impressed upon my mind. It seemed that there might be a Being so good and compassionate as to himself atone for our transgressions, and thereby save us from suffering the penalty of sin. I immediately felt how lovely such Being must be; and imagined that I could cast myself into the arms of, and trust in the mercy of, such a One."[13]

At last he could say good-bye to conflicting thoughts, tormenting contradictions. Within a year he became an "ornament and pillar in the church."[14] Miller began to argue his new position vociferously with his Deist friends. In an attempt to convince all naysayers, he hoped to completely convince himself.

Miller's heart was filled with hope, but his rational mind demanded more. To clear away any niggling doubts empirical verification of God's existence was necessary. "To believe in [the] Saviour without evidence would be visionary in the extreme."[15] So in 1816, at the age of thirty-four, Miller embarked upon an enterprise which would occupy him for several years, and change his life. And in turn, the lives of thousands of others.

To buttress his newfound faith, to prove that God does exist, he would prove that the Bible was completely consistent in all that it said. Since, he reasoned, such a consistent document of diverse revelation could only come from God, then God must exist. So he must prove to himself that the Bible's contradictions were only apparent.

Miller devised a set of "rules," fourteen in all. Among these: "Scripture must be its own expositor.... If I depend on a teacher to expound it to me, and he should guess at its meaning, or desire to have it so on account of his sectarian creed ... then his guessing, desire, creed or wisdom is my rule, not the Bible."[16] Miller insisted that any person could discover the truths hidden in the Bible should he or she simply search and study with sufficient diligence. "The Bible is a system of revealed truths, so clearly and simply given that the way-faring man, though a fool, need not err therein."[17] "The most important rule of all is, that you must have *faith*."[18] This democratization of the Bible would become a touchstone forever after in American Protestantism.

One of Miller's rules stated, "All Scripture is necessary..."[19] Both testaments, not simply the New, must be taken into account. For any text in the Bible to be understood a corresponding text must be found in both testaments: "Be sure you get one in the Old and one in the New Testament."[20]

Miller vowed, "Give me time, and I will harmonize all those apparent contradictions [in the Bible] to my own satisfaction."[21] It took him two years of intense study. As a result of all this hard work Miller came up with an astounding discovery: "I found, in going through with the Bible, the end of all things was clearly and emphatically predicted, both as to time and manner."[22]

The biblical books of Daniel and Revelation had long posed a challenging puzzle. Miller attacked the enigmatic passages in Daniel and Revelation with a special passion, determined to decode their obscure symbolism. After much study he concluded, "The World and all the wicked will be burnt up."[23] Just before this fiery destruction Christ would return and the dead saints ("saint" was Miller's designation for believers) would rise and, along with the living saints, would be "caught up to meet the Lord in the air."[24] Miller, of course, assumed he was one of these. So he was not afraid of the imminent destruction of the world; rather, he looked forward to the "delightful prospect" of the "joys of the redeemed."[25]

After the destruction Christ would descend and reign over the saints for one thousand years in "a new earth." After this millennium God would judge the wicked, sending their souls to everlasting agony in the lake of fire.

Miller's conception of the end-time, in which Christ returned *before* the millennium (premillennialism), clearly differed from the prevailing scenario in which Christ returned *after* the millennium (postmillennialism). In Miller's scenario Christ would initiate the end-time; human action could do nothing to influence the onset of events.

Miller's detailed study of the Bible provided more than just the end-time scenario. Based on several passages of Scripture he calculated *when* the world would come to an end — the year 1843. Wanting confirmation for this date, he developed twelve additional proofs over the next several years.

Historians are uncertain whether Miller can be credited with an original calculus to arrive at 1843. Biblical exegetes were notorious for grinding out various timetables for the end-time. One compilation of these listed nineteen British and American timetables published between 1768 and 1831, all of which predicted 1843 as the final year for this earthly planet.[26] It is possible that Miller came upon one of these earlier timetables. But none of the other exegetes attained anything like Miller's fame. Their timetables never became more than mere curios for antiquarians. It took the seriousness and intensity of a Miller to take his results out of the study and into the public arena.

But this did not happen quickly. At first Miller did nothing, fearing public ridicule. He kept coming up with personal objections, and for several years dueled with these imaginary problems. During that time, however, Miller was haunted with a fear for his own soul. He must quickly get to the largest possible number of people before the end came, because if he did not "their blood might be required at my hand."[27] God would surely punish Miller if he did not do all in his power to spread the saving message. The specter of his own damnation haunted Miller and eventually drove this falsely shy and retiring man out from the warmth and security of his own hearth into the madding crowd.

Then in 1826 Miller had a dream which convinced him that God would bless and support a mission to warn the world of the coming end-time. Miller interpreted this as a divine call. He believed himself to be the angel of Revelation 14:6–7, who warns the world of the upcoming divine judgment. This self-conception gave him the courage to finally broach the subject with family and friends, local residents and clergy. But the results were disappointing: "To my astonishment, I found very few who listened with any interest. Occasionally, one would see the force of the evidence; but the great majority passed it by as an idle tale."[28]

Fortunately for Miller, America was in the throes of the Second Great Awakening, an ongoing binge of religious revival. As David Rowe remarks, "The religious exercises accompanying revivals frequently convinced enthusiastic converts that God was pouring grace on the world to prepare it to receive the Millennium."[29] These revivals plowed the ground for Miller and prepared his way. There were ready crowds, eager to listen. In some other time Miller might have stood out as a lone eccentric; now he successfully rode the coattails of revivals. The revival became his vehicle to public exposure.

His opportunity for a first formal public presentation came amidst a local revival, when millennial hopes were high. As supervisor of Hampton Township, a recognized local figure, Miller was invited to expound upon his ideas in nearby Dresden. He was soon to turn fifty. It had been thirteen years since he had first concocted his end-time calculus.

News spread concerning Miller's Dresden lecture, and he received a few more invitations to speak. Then in 1832 Miller published a series of eight articles on the Second Coming in a Baptist newspaper, the *Vermont Telegraph*. So great was the response to these articles, the *Telegraph* reprinted them in pamphlet form. Suddenly laity and clergy alike wanted to hear Miller in person. As word spread he received more and more invitations to speak. In November 1833 the heavens seemed willing to help. A shower of meteors, one or two a minute, reminded those watching the sky of the passage in Revelation which prophesied that the stars of heaven would fall to the earth in the Last Days.

Miller was a colorless individual entirely lacking in personal magnetism. His appeal lay not in his person but in his message. His message caught on because it was rooted in the Bible, and his audience was favorably predisposed to Scripture. Miller cashed in on a biblical pietism which was the legacy of Puritanism. In Miller's words, the Bible "is a revelation of God to man ... you must prove all things by Bible, you must talk Bible, you must exhort Bible, you must pray Bible and love Bible, and do all in your power to make others love Bible, too."[30] With careful matching of contemporary events to biblical word, Miller was able to convince large numbers of people.

Nature seemed to cooperate in supplying signs that The End was fast approaching. Listening to Miller, people recalled the total solar eclipse of 1808 which had brought people to their knees in supplication, to their bellies in convulsions. The year 1827 had offered a brilliant auroral display in the heavens. There was the recent meteor shower. Even the weather provided signs of the end-time. The year 1816, "eighteen hundred and froze to death," "the year without a summer,"[31] was still etched in public memory. The spring and summer of that year featured some of the lowest recorded temperatures throughout western Europe and the northeastern American continent. Snow in parts of New England in June, followed by frosts in July and August, meant that some areas had snow and ice for twelve consecutive months. A cholera epidemic in 1832 which followed the sequence of towns up the Erie Canal bringing death to one out of every two stricken made one mindful of "the seven last plagues" of the fifteenth chapter of Revelation.

On the economic front the Panic of 1837, followed two years later with a second economic contraction and a full-fledged depression which lasted until 1844, raised fear that The End might indeed be near.

As the times got progressively more chaotic people became increasingly sympathetic to Miller's message. Miller said that the Bible predicted worse times as the millennium drew nigh, and that human efforts were futile. His words were ringing true.

Miller proved virtually indefatigable in preaching the cause, even to the point of ill health. Looking back later he provided these figures: from October 1, 1839, to April 15, 1841, 627 lectures, 4560 miles covered, 5000 conversions;[32] over a twelve-year period, 4500 lectures to at least 500,000 people.[33] But he was not the firebrand one might expect of the leader of such a successful grassroots religious movement. Indeed, as time passed he became not much more than its figurehead, its front man.

Beginning in 1839 the *Christian Palladium* published articles about the growing Millerite movement. The *Palladium* was the official journal in New York State for the Christian Connection, a loose confederation of independent churches formed during the Second Great Awakening. As such, it gave Millerism a respectable and wide publicity, and drew in many from the Christian Connection who became influential lecturers and supporters of the movement.

Joshua Vaughan Himes frequently contributed articles to the *Palladium*. Next to Miller he became the most important figure in spreading the Millerite message. Indeed, without Himes's support and hard work and dominant influence, Miller might have remained little more than an obscure individual predicting the end of the world. Miller would later remark that Himes did more than any other ten persons to spread the Millerite message.

Born in 1805, Himes was considerably younger than Miller, and considerably more energetic. He himself averaged one speaking engagement a day during the early 1840s, promoting the cause. He kept Miller going, when by Miller's own confession he was tiring: "I find that, as I grow old, I grow more peevish, and cannot bear so much contradiction. Therefore I am called uncharitable and severe."[34]

Himes's parents had intended him to attend Brown University and become an Episcopal priest, but his father's business failed and the young man apprenticed to a cabinet maker. As there was no Episcopal church in the town where he was apprenticing, Himes joined a Christian Connection church. These churches focused on the Bible as the only rule of faith. A few years later Himes was ordained and quickly established himself as a builder of churches. Invited to be pastor of a Christian Connection church in Boston which was on its last legs, he soon filled the pews.

Himes supported many radical social movements. This bothered the more conservative members of his church and he was asked to step down. Unfazed, he gathered like-minded members of his church to found a new Christian Connection church in Boston, the Chardon Street Chapel, which became a meeting place for reform groups. A contemporary observed, "Himes was by nature a reformer of men and things. He always wished evils done away with and the present condition of mankind improved.... Whatever work he undertook he entered into with a whole heart."[35] A man of such energy and enthusiasm, Himes was disappointed by the slow progress of reform, the internal bickering within the reform movement, and the reluctance of society to change.

Then in the fall of 1839 Himes met Miller at a Christian Connection conference. Miller's presentation so impressed Himes that he invited Miller to give a series of lectures that December. Himes found Miller's message revolutionary: "I could not believe or preach as I had done. Light on this subject was blazing on my conscience day and night."[36] Himes was hooked. His tremendous energy and enthusiasm would thenceforth be thrown behind Miller.

Within a few months Himes founded the first Millerite newspaper, *Signs of the Times*, devoted to the Second Coming. As editor and publisher, Himes solicited articles both for and against Miller's position; he insisted on open discussion. The paper was an immediate success—in less than a year 50,000 copies would be distributed—and drew numerous invitations for Miller to speak. Up to this point Miller had labored in the proverbial vineyard for almost a decade with only modest results. Himes was convinced that the whole world should hear Miller's message and quickly assumed a managerial role in the new movement.

One of his first acts was to call together those persons who had responded to Miller's message, irrespective of denomination, for the purpose of planning, organization, and discussion. The General Conference of Believers in the Second Coming of Christ at the Door met at the Chardon Street Chapel in October 1840. Here the network of contacts and influence widened. Similar organizational conferences followed.

Himes's involvement with reform groups gave him skills in organization and publicity and provided him with numerous influential contacts. Himes choreographed Miller's lecture itinerary so that his message would reach as many people as possible. Himes virtually created Millerism. He orchestrated it, he infused it with energy. Himes took Millerism to the big cities, he founded publications, he recruited leaders. He organized campaigns. He mobilized backers. He raised funds. He introduced contacts to contacts, forming influential networks of the like-minded. He micro-managed every facet of the burgeoning movement. Millerism hit critical mass and exploded.

Today's evangelists would envy Himes's promotional skills. One of his most successful public relations gimmicks was a gigantic tent, fifty-five feet high at the center and three hundred feet in circumference, which could seat up to four thousand people — reported to be the largest ever in America. Word that "the Great Tent" would arrive in a town was ballyhooed a few days in advance, ensuring overflow crowds. A traveling circus atmosphere prevailed; people who came simply to see the spectacle of the Tent got caught up in the excitement and listened to the Millerite message. A market had been created. It grew and grew at an explosive rate, becoming virtually insatiable. At some locations as many as 10,000 attended tent meetings. Small hamlets off the beaten trail desperately petitioned the Millerite organization: Come and enjoy our hospitality. Use our splendid convention facilities. Oh, and be sure to bring the Tent.

Himes was particularly adept in his use of the media of the time. Recently founded mass circulation newspapers were eager to build subscriptions and attract readers with exciting news and ideas, so Himes provided articles on the movement and thus gained free publicity.

Late in 1842 Himes launched a second newspaper, *The Midnight Cry*, in New York City, where it could take advantage of that city's dominance as a center of commerce, transportation, communication, and the distribution of information. Himes saw that one copy of *Signs of the Times* and *The Midnight Cry* went to every clergyman in New York State. During its first five months 600,000 copies of *The Midnight Cry* were distributed.[37] Book rooms were established in Buffalo and Syracuse. Promotional literature was distributed where it would have greatest impact — at transportation terminals, on railroad cars, and on canal boats. Charts depicting Miller's message in pictorial form were posted on the walls of railway stations and in railway cars. Mailings were sealed with stickers on which was printed Scripture concerning the Second Coming. By May of 1844 Hines announced that five million copies of Millerite literature had been distributed.[38]

All of this publicity brought its rewards. Himes estimated that there were 300 to 400 clergy who spread the word of the Second Coming.[39] Miller himself estimated that there were 50,000 seriously committed Millerites. Historians suggest that the number of adherents may have reached one million.[40] Considering that the movement was concentrated in New York State and that the population of the state was less than two and a half million at the time,[41] the upper figure would make of Millerism a religious epidemic.

Certainly the movement was widespread, covering New York State and New England. It supported journals in Philadelphia, Cincinnati, and Cleveland. Traveling preachers went into Michigan, Illinois, and Wisconsin, and considerable interest was aroused in Washington, D. C. It attracted persons from all sectors of the population and all economic levels, although somewhat favoring the upper part of the spectrum. Millerism caught on in rural communities better than it did in the larger cities, if only because the latter offered more competing interests and attractions. Millerism has been touted as "America's most significant millenarian expression."[42] Its influence would be felt for generations to come.

Millerism spread by means of literature, preaching, and lectures. Amongst the clergy, Christian Connection and Baptist preachers furnished the greatest numbers of supporters. Preachers spread the word from their own pulpits, and other local pulpits. Some among the clergy abandoned their pastorates to become itinerant preachers. In addition to ordained clergy a vast number of lay preachers and lay lecturers spread the word — by one estimate, five hundred.[43] It was quite common for a layperson, inspired by what he read in the Millerite literature or heard from a traveling lecturer, to turn amateur lecturer, spreading the word either locally or further afield.

Miller expected Christ to return sometime "on or before 1843."[44] As the year of reckoning approached excitement grew to a fever pitch. There were escalating demands that ambiguity concerning the date be resolved. Right from the beginning Miller had been loath to fix upon a specific date for the Second Coming. Yet specific dates were constantly appearing in Millerite publications, much to his annoyance. He continually published denials that he had ever "fixed on any month, day or hour."[45]

Then, as if on cue, a spectacular comet appeared on February 28, 1843. The most brilliant comet of the century, it blazed across the skies of both northern and southern hemispheres until April 1, visible even in broad daylight. The End, indeed, must be nigh. As one contributor to *Signs of the Times* wrote, "I could not but think of 'the signs of the Son of Man in Heaven.'"[46] Those who had doubted before, perhaps even scoffed, began to think that perhaps Miller was right, after all. Better to err on the side of safety.

Suddenly the signs of the approaching end-time — most, specters of the imagination — were everywhere. A cross on the face of the moon. Lights and haloes around Jupiter and Venus. Ordinary events took on a significance out of all proportion. Every fire, earthquake, bankruptcy, and act of immorality was a nugget hungrily seized upon by the Millerite press. Concerning the Millerite tendency to burden contemporary events with special religious significance, one skeptic wrote: "It is amusing to see how the most ordinary events are cited by the advocates of this new theory [Millerism], as proofs that 'the day of the Lord is at hand. ' The fire at Hamburgh ... the falling of the chandelier in the U. S. House of Representatives ...— these, and many other equally *remarkable* occurrences, are set forth as solemn warnings."[47]

Miller must have wanted to run and hide. He had never laid store in contemporary events. He had steadfastly maintained that the Bible is the only source of truth. It should be consulted, not the heavens. Natural events are "immaterial." For faith must rest "on the word of God, and such things are not needed to confirm it."[48]

The year 1843 passed without The End. Strangely, the Millerites held fast to their belief that The End was imminent. Their belief, if anything, grew stronger. Miller was feeling the pressure, and came up with a new timeframe. The prophets, he now realized, would have calculated time according to the Jewish lunar calendar, which meant that the year 1843 would not really end until March 21, 1844. This adjustment provided Millerites great relief.

But March 21 came and went. Christ did not come. Himes had never been strict about the exact timing of Christ's coming. Back in 1842 he had registered a note of caution: "As far as prophecy, in connection with history, presents evidence that may point to any particular time, it is our duty to consider it faithfully, but we have no right to be dogmatical respecting it; and we should consider how fallible we are, and how liable we are to be deceived."[49] When March 1844 passed into history Himes made no effort to obfuscate: "We freely say to all men that we expected our Savior before the present time."[50] Miller openly admitted he had been wrong about the date: "I confess my error, and acknowledge my disappointment; yet I still believe that the day of the Lord is near, even at the door; and I exhort you, my brethren, to be watchful, and not let that day come upon you unawares."[51] Himes concurred, "It is not safe, therefore, for us to defer in our minds the event for an hour, but to live in constant expectation, and readiness to meet our Judge."[52] Himes did not advocate waiting in idleness. Because The End was still to come, and until it did, the message must be broadcast through literature and lectures until all had heard. "We must work with more zeal, decision, and perseverance, than ever."[53]

Surprisingly, the largest camp meeting in Millerite history occurred just after the passing of the March deadline. As one said, "My faith has never been stronger in the glorious personal coming of our dear Redeemer than at present."[54] This renewed commitment had much to do with a desire to close ranks against strong popular ridicule. The "faint, the fearful, the half-resolved" were castigated. While some urged that Millerites must show understanding toward their weaker brethren, others took a hard stand: "God holds the fan in his hand, and will blow out all the chaff, before gathering all of the wheat into his garner."[55] The passing of predicted deadlines had been a test of faith. Those who failed, God would surely punish. God wanted only the most faithful.

But it was increasingly difficult to continue. A woman who lived through this trying time described the psychological turmoil experienced by the Millerites: Can you imagine, she writes, what it would be like to know "that at any moment ... there would come that fearful upheaval of the earth, that fiery rending apart of the heavens ... the shrieking of the damned, God himself would descend with a great shout to burn up the world, the sea and the dry land?... Waking in the night [was] a painful experience, and a thunder-storm a fearful ordeal, while every sunset brought the inner voice, 'The morning may never come.'"[56]

If a definite date could be set this stress would be reduced. Back in February Samuel S. Snow, an agnostic converted to Miller's ideas, had published a prediction that Christ would not come in March, but sometime in the summer. Although summer passed without Christ's appearance, Snow was undaunted. He fixed upon a new date. Basically he defended Miller's calculations ... provided that the Karaite calendar replace the standard Jewish calendar for determining the date for Yom Kippur, the Day of Atonement. What could be more appropriate, Snow reasoned, for Christ's coming — a day that would mark the final atonement of all sin — than the Jewish Day of Atonement? Snow's prediction was published in *The Midnight Cry*. Its logic so convinced leading Millerites that in no time they were preaching this new date.

Miller and Himes, disappointed over the failure of previous dates, were reluctant to accept this new date. Yet as October 22 approached, the mounting excitement proved too much. Finally, on October 6, they gave in and accepted the new revised date. For Miller, now suffering from illness, this new date must have seemed a desperate hope. His words in the October 15 issue of *The Midnight Cry* showed signs of the rancor he felt toward critics of the movement: "I am strong in the opinion that the next will be the last Lord's day sinners will ever have in probation; and within ten or fifteen days from thence, they will see Him whom they have hated and despised."[57]

As the big day drew close Millerites abandoned their traditional modes of living. Farmers left their fields uncultivated. Houses were not cleaned. Shops were closed up with signs in the windows proclaiming the coming of the Lord. At least one person stopped eating. Many Millerites engaged in unconventional, even bizarre behavior.[58] As historian Jonathan M. Butler remarks, "Flaunting their alienation from the old order, many threw themselves into an excitedly extravagant no-rules state."[59] Some wandered about in the nude. Others crawled through the streets on all fours, to be as little children for the Kingdom. There was "holy" kissing and "promiscuous" footwashing. There was self-starvation and sexual license. Joshua Himes was appalled at such "fleshly and selfish passions."[60] One Millerite reported that his group had given themselves up to "a tempest of real fanaticism."[61] Another group "withdrew entirely ... night and day, and all night long, neglecting almost wholly their temporal affairs, and in some instances leaving their little children to take care of themselves."[62]

Other Millerites saw things differently. With only days of earthly existence remaining, why not turn a moral leaf? Neighbors settled longstanding disputes. People made peace with former enemies. With little time left in human existence, one could afford to be pleasant. Because it would be unwise to meet the Lord with unconfessed sins, numerous crimes were confessed. One woman admitted to committing murder several years previously in far-off England. While it was doubtful she would ever be caught and punished (at least not by earthly authorities) she insisted that she return to England and be tried. A man sent $120 to an insurance company with a note saying he had unlawfully taken the money and wished to be forgiven. Another sent five dollars to the United States Treasury to reconcile himself with the government for unpaid taxes.

With the end of the world imminent, material wealth would soon be of no value. Loans were repaid in full. Business operators became scrupulous and honest. A merchant returned two cents a yard to a woman who had formerly bought cloth from him; with the Lord about to appear in the clouds he thought it best to be "moderate and fair"[63] in his dealings. Some shopkeepers gave merchandise away. Some Millerites sold their possessions and gave the proceeds to the needy.

In those last hours it was not just the Millerites who watched the skies. Events which would cause little concern under normal circumstances took on cosmic significance. When a fierce gale buffeted the city of Rochester and blew down the liberty pole many skeptics believed Miller might be right. In Ithaca a fire which lighted the night awakened one man to the fear that this might be the fire that was to consume the world, and for a moment he believed. Some who had hitherto mocked and doubted the Millerites' warnings cast themselves on Jesus's mercy during those last hours. Why take a chance? What if, after all, the Millerites were right? It was a time of soul-searching.

Then came the fateful day. October 22, 1844. According to eyewitnesses across New York State, the Millerites had donned white "ascension robes" and climbed the highest hills or perched on rooftops to await the Second Coming of their Lord and the end of the world.[64] So great was the demand for ascension robes, there was a temporary boom in the textile industry, despite generally depressed economic times. As Millerite fanaticism increased in the days approaching October 22, morality flew out the window. Thievery, murder, lasciviousness.... Millerites were inebriated with Last Days excitement. What were morals in such a state of psychological agitation?

October 22, 1844, was a time for prayer and waiting. Millerites gathered in their churches and tabernacles and meetinghouses to enjoy a deep sense of community. However, things were not everywhere peaceful. In Williamsburg, New York, a mob attacked the Millerite meetinghouse until the mayor intervened. When ruffians threatened violence in Lewiston a Millerite reported that "the magistracy of that town have more sympathy with the lawless mob than their innocent objects, upon which they wished to wreak unprovoked vengeance."[65] In Seneca Falls Millerites were able to force a violent mob armed with clubs and knives to retreat. A Methodist preacher "justified" the actions of the mob, saying that "the Millerites ought to be taken up; if other means fail, forcibly."[66] In Cincinnati 1,500 gathered in their tabernacle to the sound of a threatening mob outside. In New York City Millerite meeting places were closed by police order.

The scoffers and persecutors, even the death threats, assured the Millerites that The End was indeed imminent. Did the Bible not say this would happen in the Last Days? Surely this was just one more sign.

Many Millerites, fearing public violence, took a lower profile and remained within the safety and privacy of their own homes, or gathered quietly with others in their homes. In the hours which remained every tick of the clock meant that years of sacrifice and persecution would soon meet with reward and vindication. Centuries of Christian hope and expectation were now focused on a few short hours. The work God had begun in the garden of Eden was about to reach its culmination. How exciting to be alive at this moment!

Some Millerites expected the sun to darken at high noon. But twelve o'clock passed and it was just as bright as the hour before. Twelve o'clock, one o'clock, two o'clock, three o'clock.... Day passed into evening, and evening into night. The excitement was increasing. Jesus would soon appear. Come, Lord Jesus, come. How feverish those minutes approaching midnight! Christ would come at any moment.

And then the clock struck midnight. Eyes strained in the dark, ears sharpened to hear the slightest sound. All was attentiveness. But it remained dark and silent. How dark, how silent.

The vigil continued. October 22 was officially over. At least in the local time zone. But the day was not really over until the sun came up.

And then the sun did come up. A faint glow in the east filled hearts with despair and utter disappointment. What the Millerites experienced, what they failed to experience, on October 22, 1844, would go down in history as "the Great Disappointment."

One Millerite attempted to express what could hardly be expressed: "Our fondest hopes and expectations were blasted.... If this had proved a failure, what was the rest of my Christian experience worth? Has the Bible proved a failure? Is there no God, no heaven, no golden home city, no paradise? Is all this but a cunningly devised fable? Is there no reality to our fondest hopes and expectation of these things?"[67]

Many simply could not believe the evidence of their senses. Surely Christ would come. Perhaps there was some minor error in calculation. Perhaps the Lord would come in the clouds in a few more hours. The hours passed. In a few more days? The days passed. Some Millerites continued to wait, praying fervently, thus postponing the possibility of total despair. They watched and waited, disbelief held in suspension, for days, weeks.

To forestall almost certain public reprisal, Nathaniel Whiting, a leading Millerite, advised Miller on October 24 that "all who participated in this mistake [immediately make] public acknowledgement of their error.... Any shuffling on this point will authorize the community to say that we are not only credulous but absolutely dishonest."[68] This advice was not acted upon, and public response was in many places immediate and nasty. In Ithaca, Dansville, Scottsville, and Rochester mobs damaged and burned Millerite meeting places. The Millerites were reviled in the public press, from the pulpits of orthodox belief, and in the streets. One Millerite complained that there were "falsehoods, and ... all manner of evil about us ... we have become a proverb and byword in the land."[69]

Such public antagonism and the resultant feelings of embarrassment and disgrace, not to mention the overwhelming emotional disappointment, led many to abandon their erstwhile beliefs. Many had been swept up in the public excitement of the times; they had succumbed to a temporary lukewarm belief mostly out of fear that perhaps Miller and his followers were right. When October 23 dawned they stealthily slid out from the glare of their scorning neighbors, quietly returning to their former lifestyles. To cover their tracks many turned against their former brethren in the faith and, as Miller bitterly remarked, "were now mixed with the rabble, and mocking, scoffing, and threatening in a most blasphemous manner."[70] Everywhere the number of professed Millerites declined precipitously. In Oswego, for example, only fifteen out of one hundred remained true to the faith after a span of less than a year. New converts were nonexistent.

On November 5 Himes publicly stated that all reasonable dates had passed. He confessed that "the authorities on which we based our calculations cannot be depended upon for definite time."[71] Yet Himes continued to believe that Christ's advent was imminent. So, too, Miller, although he had abandoned the idea of fixed dates: "I am not yet cast down or discouraged.... I do believe in God's Word; and although surrounded with enemies and scoffers, yet my mind is perfectly calm, and my hope in the coming of Christ is as strong as ever."[72]

Along with Himes and Miller and other leading lights of Millerism, there remained a core of Millerites with a deep and abiding conviction. While the Great Disappointment had been devastating for many Millerites, it only incited others to a more fervent, if more desperate, faith. Indeed, surrounded by scoffers, those who remained steadfast considered themselves, even more than before, God's chosen few. Public mockery only served to reinforce the Millerites' feeling of martyrdom: We "rejoice that we are counted worthy to suffer for his sake."[73] As for those who scoffed, the Millerites relished the thought of the coming "day of vengeance"[74] when they would get their due.

In the interim Himes was concerned about those who had given up all their material possessions and might starve during the coming winter. He had never advised against abandoning one's secular lifestyle, and had always maintained that one should fulfill one's social obligations until the day the Lord comes. But now the time had come for those Millerites who had the material means to support their fellows in need, so that they would not have to resort to charity from those who were critical of the movement. Himes recommended that committees be set up in every city and town to receive and distribute contributions. "I doubt not that all will do their duty."[75]

Some Millerites tenaciously held to the idea that there had been some minor miscalculation of the exact date of Christ's return. There was no shortage of those willing to rectify the arithmetic. The first recalculation resulted in a date in November of 1844. That time passed and several different dates were set for the following spring. The spring of 1845 passed and new dates were set for 1846, 1847, and 1848.

But such a stratagem has its limitation. The vast majority of remaining Millerites realized the time had come for some hard thinking, something beyond the mere setting of new dates. What was to be made of the fact that Christ had not returned?

Some believed Christ *had* returned as predicted on October 22, 1844. But not in the flesh on this earth. Instead, he had returned in the spirit and separated the saints from the damned. The door had been shut for further salvation, for any who might henceforth seek mercy. Those who had not turned to Christ before October 22 were damned for eternity — a fitting end for scoffers and unbelievers. Despite the efforts of Himes and others to get Miller to publicly renounce the closed-door theory it is clear that Miller firmly believed that Christ had chosen the elect. As early as 1836 he had written, "After the door is shut, he that is filthy will remain so. There will be no use ... to warn people of their danger."[76]

Some Millerites believed the millennium had begun. As historian Cross writes: "God's chosen people had entered the millennium which followed judgment day and instead of inhabiting heaven, as they had anticipated, had been allowed to enjoy heavenly privileges on earth.... The present millennium led many of the most zealously sincere Millerites into remarkable extravagances...."[77] Certain that they were irrevocably saved, these Millerites saw no bounds to their behavior. They could not "sin"; they were the elect, the saints, God's chosen few. Moderate Millerites were aghast at such debauched behavior, but in their journals mentioned such acts euphemistically: conduct "not becoming a civil man";[78] one who kept "a very bad house";[79] "revolting and indecent ceremonies";[80] worship "in a nude state."[81]

Moderate Millerites continued to believe that the Lord would return. To bring some order consequent to the Great Disappointment and to combat the trend to radicalism, leaders of the moderate group gathered in Albany in April 1845. Here a committee was struck to examine candidates for a new clergy. With the institution of a church polity came a gradual, if subtle and implicit, slide toward postmillennial belief in the efficacy of human agency. Himes, in the beginning an orthodox postmillennialist, seemed to be returning to his former belief: "I am still of the opinion that we have more work to do, and that 'this Gospel of the Kingdom' shall be preached in all the world, and *then* shall the End come."[82] As a like-minded colleague commented, "The best way to hasten Christ's return is to labor with all our might in plucking sinners out of the fire; for when he has accomplished the number of his elect, he will descend in glory and power."[83]

Amongst this vast reservoir would come the seeds of the Seventh-Day Adventist Church, the largest group to trace its origins to William Miller.

In 1845, when it had finally become clear that Miller's prediction was mistaken, the Low Hampton Baptist church disfellowshipped William Miller. Many churches struck Millerites from their membership lists, even though the *Baptist Register* took a tolerant attitude: any Millerite who would candidly confess error was invited to "receive the welcome embrace of your brethren."[84] Miller was not about to make such a confession.

Separated from his former church community, suffering from physical illness, often haunted by regrets (his mother never accepted his apocalyptic scenario), Miller withdrew from the public spotlight in 1846. After that time only Himes took any interest in the man who had fathered the cause which bore his name. Himes continued to write regularly, providing news on the progress of the movement. At sixty-seven, his loyal friend Himes at his side, Miller was released from the material world he despised and detested.

Most of the important Millerite leaders had no part in the formation of the several adventist churches that derived in some way from the Millerite movement of the 1840s. Joshua Himes, however, did serve two of these churches— the Evangelical Adventists and the Advent Christians— before reverting to his roots, the Episcopal Church. As an older man he was ordained an Episcopal priest and went west to South Dakota where as a missionary he built up the body of Christ's church both in souls and with his bare hands in the physical construction of churches. When he died at ninety he was buried in a hillside in Sioux Falls, as he had requested; he wanted "to be on the top of a hill when Gabriel blows his trumpet."[85]

The Millerite movement fractured into a great many apocalyptic sects—twenty-five, by one count taken in 1855.[86] But the most significant legacy of Millerism lies not in the churches that evolved from it but in its influence on the future shape of American millennialism.

Millerism began an explicit polarization of American religion which remains with us to this day. Whatever might have been subtle or undefined regarding religious tendencies heretofore, was now cast into bright and unforgiving light. Millerism drove a sharp wedge into the American religious soul, creating a divisiveness which has yet to heal.

Millerism fostered an anti-church attitude which many conservative Christians maintain today. It was a Millerite manifesto in 1843: "If you are a Christian, come out of Babylon [the traditional religious denominations]. If you intend to be found a Christian when Christ appears, come out of Babylon, and come out now."[87]

Miller was against the institutionalized church and its clergy: "The World and Clergy vs. Miller."[88] He never grew tired of fulminating against the educated clergy, "the learned, the eloquent, the popular."[89] He fostered a spirit of anti-intellectualism which became a defining characteristic of many premillennialists far into the future. He railed against clergy who take "some novel idea from some of their 'standard writers' as they call their Reverend Masters" and add to it "a host of classical phrases, spotted over with a little Hebrew, Greek, and Latin, all obtained with a few months' study of old pagan philosophers, obscure writers, and classical blockheads."[90] Many Millerites were quick to adopt Miller's attitude. One wrote that the seminary is no more than the "workshop of the Devil, and the hotbed of all kinds of delusions.... It is there [Satan] keeps his library, or tool-chest, and there he manufactures his magicians."[91]

With their concept of an earthly conflagration, the Millerites flew in the face of the prevailing thrust of American religious tradition which asserts that the United States has a special place in God's plan as the center for spiritual and moral progress toward the Kingdom of God on this earth. If the whole world was to be burned to nothing, how could America be the site of the coming millennium? As Ruth Doan writes, the Millerites "had little room for a special destiny for America. The divine power was about to break through the heavens and set the whole world ablaze. Not the United States, but the believers in the advent near were brands to be plucked from the burning."[92]

In their belief of an imminent end-time the Millerites had forsaken this earthly future. As one contemporary of Miller observed: "Multitudes, who were formerly engaged in the various moral enterprises of the age, have lost all interest in works of practical righteousness and think and talk of nothing else but the burning up of the world."[93] Historian Whitney Cross pronounces Millerism essentially "the product of a pessimistic mood."[94] He finds it rooted in "deep pessimism" and "despair," a "compensatory dream," an "escape mechanism."[95]

That approximately one third of the local population of a major section of the American nation was seduced by Miller's ideas suggests that Millerism spoke to a deep need. This need did not disappear with the Great Disappointment. Miller had evoked the desire to escape from the chaotic changes and tensions of modern life, and he had given that desire a vision, an image, a hope. Christ's imminent Second Coming, the end-time conflagration, and a millennium which followed Christ's return would be integral parts of one form of Christian hope in America from this point on.

Stephen J. Stein notes that the word "eschatology" was not in use until the 1840s.[96] Miller and the Millerites can be credited for bringing eschatology front and center. Yet the reaction to Millerism was just as important in the evolution of American religious culture. Millerism forced the center of American religious orthodoxy to examine its assumptions and more clearly articulate its beliefs. In so doing, a new orthodoxy was formulated — a liberalized evangelicalism: God worked through human beings and their churches to progressively bring on the millennium. The new Protestant orthodoxy sided with Finney, against Miller. The die had been cast.

From this point forward for some time to come premillennialism would bear the Millerite cross.[97] As historian Ernest R. Sandeen comments, "In retrospect the Millerite movement appears to have virtually destroyed premillennialism in America for a generation."[98]

7

Threat from Abroad

Ernest Sandeen writes, "America in the early nineteenth century was drunk on the millennium ... men spoke the language of the Apocalypse...."[1] Until the Great Disappointment. "It took a long time for Americans to forget William Miller."[2] "The failure of his predictions disillusioned most of his followers and marked the whole millenarian cause ... with the stigma of fanaticism and quackery."[3]

But millennialism, a feature of specifically American Protestantism, did not die out. It could not. It was the essence of the American religious ethos, a cornerstone of the young nation, etched into the soul of its people. Because Miller had become "a theological leper" those who continued to boldly and publicly voice millenarian doctrine felt compelled "to take a stand against 'Millerism' as virtually the first sentence in every speech and the first paragraph in every treatise."[4] These stalwarts renounced any association with the Millerite movement, lest they be branded "as a band of fanatics ready to don ascension robes."[5] They insisted that the Second Coming was a doctrine held by the earliest Christians, not something dreamed up by the late William Miller.

Dedicated millennialists lost no time in seizing the field. Just four years after the Millerite fiasco, in 1848, David Nevins Lord founded the *Theological and Literary Journal*. Its purpose was to introduce some order into the interpretation of biblical prophecy, which Lord described as "wrenched by a thousand experimenters on the wheel of conjecture"[6]— no doubt with Miller firmly in mind.

But the Millerite disaster would prove insignificant to the continuation of American millennialism when compared to a threat which had been brewing in continental Europe for some time.

The seeds of this threat had been planted several centuries earlier. America was not the only "new world" at the time the *Arbella* set sail with its band of prospective colonists. Explorers were rapidly charting hitherto unknown regions of the world, lands inhabited by peoples unlike any in Christian Europe. Astronomers were discovering new worlds in the blackness of space.

The realization was fast dawning that our cherished globe might not be the center of this expanding universe of knowledge. Humankind's understanding of the universe and its place within it was about to be profoundly shaken.

Yet the natural world was proving to be governed by laws which fit nicely into the straitjacket of humanly devised mathematics. New philosophies were developed to encompass a newly altered way of perceiving. Whereas up to this point the primary authority in all things had rested with the church, scientific discovery had emboldened the human spirit with a new confidence in its own abilities—reason, the human mind. The *Arbella* had barely touched the shore of America when in 1637 the French mathematician and philosopher René Descartes penned the words "Cogito, ergo sum" ("I think, therefore I am"). Beginning with this only absolutely certain piece of knowledge—that I exist—Descartes proceeded to "prove" the existence of the world, of other people, of God. Indeed, to develop a whole system of philosophy.

Things had been turned upside down. God was relegated to the end of a progression of human thought, no longer its source. Whatever truths were out there to be discovered, human reason would ferret out. Observation and reason became the standards for discerning truth. No longer would it suffice to believe something based on tradition, because someone said it was true. Henceforth everything must pass the tests of reason and observation.

Humanity replaced God as the focus of concern. As the poet phrased it, "Presume not God to scan; the proper study of Mankind is Man"[7]—words published just months before Jonathan Edwards heralded the Great Awakening. In Europe it was another type of awakening. The Age of Reason. The Enlightenment.

With the best of his ability, and within the confines of traditional American Puritanism, Jonathan Edwards came to terms with the forces of the Enlightenment. But the Enlightenment spawned thinking which moved beyond anything Edwards could have conceived. Or would have been willing to accept.

Historians had long recorded the narrative of human affairs. But in the philosophy of Georg Wilhelm Friedrich Hegel history took on new meaning, new significance. In Hegel's philosophy of history everything was historicized. All of reality was subsumed within the Absolute Spirit, the "Geist," which was constantly becoming realized. Thanks to Hegel, history became a byword of the new thinking. This turn toward history would challenge the authority of religious tradition, the credibility of Christian beliefs.

Between 1810 and 1812 Georg Bartold Niebuhr published a seminal two-volume history of Rome. G. P. Gooch called Niebuhr "the first commanding figure in modern historiography, the scholar who raised history from a subordinate place to the dignity of an independent science, ... in whom the greatest historians of the succeeding generations found their model or inspiration."[8] Niebuhr's history of Rome was the first example of a new type of history—critical history—which took its lead from the critical thinking developed in the physical sciences. Niebuhr developed precise methods for searching out and assessing historical evidence. An attitude of skepticism was to prevail. Venerable traditions and vaunted authorities from the past must be carefully vetted. Niebuhr proved that traditions preserved by Livy and other ancient historians concerning the seven kings of Rome, accepted as fact, without question, for fifty generations, were mostly myth.

With Niebuhr, secular history and the historians who had written it came under suspicion. Ancient authorities and traditions were suspect. But what about religious history? Was not the Bible the prime source of religious history? Just because the Bible was part of the canon of sacred literature did not exempt it from historical inquiry. Why not treat Scripture in the same manner as other historical documents?

Ferdinand Christian Baur did just that. The first in a long line of influential and controversial biblical scholars known as the Tübingen School, Baur was fascinated by the example of Niebuhr's *History of Rome*, and determined to follow his lead. Nothing—neither cherished religious beliefs nor the fear of churchly authority—would get in the way of his search for truth. Hard at work in his study by four in the morning, Baur put out a tremendous volume of writing: his published works exceeded sixteen thousand pages—equal to one four-hundred-page book per year for forty years.[9]

Traditionally the history of church doctrine, of Christian theology, was assumed to begin *after* the era described in the New Testament. Baur insisted this was wrong; the New Testament *itself* was part of Christian history. Within the New Testament Baur found several varying perceptions of the persona of Jesus Christ, several differing incipient theologies. Early Christianity was not a monolithic whole. Here lay the roots of future theological conflict.

Baur believed that the earliest documents among the New Testament books were the epistles of Paul. Paul's letters gave Baur a window onto the beliefs of the earliest Christian communities. In his study of the books of Galatians and Corinthians Baur detected two rival factions among the early Christians—one led by Paul and distinctly Gentile, another led by Peter which maintained Jewish religious practices. Each of these parties had its own perception of the person and role of Jesus. Fitting these divergent theologies into the Procrustean bed of Hegelian dialectic, Baur claimed that the Petrine and Pauline parties were later reconciled in the Catholic church.

Baur maintained that not all the books attributed to Paul were written by him, and he observed a distinct difference between the fourth gospel and the other three.

After Baur each book of the New Testament would be studied in the historical context of its origin.

Biblical criticism had its seeds centuries before Baur. Thomas Hobbes had maintained that the whole of the Old Testament had been written after the Babylonian Captivity, at the time of Ezra and Nehemiah in the sixth century B.C., not many centuries earlier as tradition held. In his *Leviathan* of 1651 Hobbes cited many passages in the biblical text to prove his claim. For example, he said that Moses could not have written Deuteronomy because the final verses tell of his death.

The first truly systematic work of "biblical science" (as he termed it) was Baruch Spinoza's *Tractatus Theologico-Politicus*, published anonymously in 1670 for fear of ecclesiastical reprisal. (Spinoza's fears were not unfounded; in 1674 the Reformed Church of Holland banned both Hobbes's *Leviathan* and Spinoza's *Tractatus* and forbade either to be printed or distributed.) Spinoza tried to determine the author and date of each Old Testament book. He concluded that Ezra, not Moses, was the author of the Pentateuch (the first five books of the Old Testament). Moses had written a law book (Nehemiah 8:1—"they spoke unto Ezra the scribe to bring the book of the law of Moses") which Ezra incorporated into the Pentateuch. Spinoza said that Ezra also wrote Joshua, Judges, 1 and 2 Samuel, and 1 and 2 Kings. Later editors revised Ezra's work and added material from other sources, resulting in repetitions and contradictions.

Clearly the church needed to get into the act. In 1678 Richard Simon, a Roman Catholic theologian, published *Histoire critique du vieux testament* in which he attempted to prove that the text of the Old Testament was corrupt and, therefore, the Roman Catholic church, contra the Reformation, remained a greater authority than the Bible. Like Spinoza, Simon said that Moses had not written all of the Pentateuch; in addition he suggested that the books of the Old Testament had gradually been compiled in scribal schools, passing through many revisions before reaching their final form.

The first to openly proclaim the right of Protestant university scholars to engage in critical studies of the Old Testament free from tradition and ecclesiastical authority was Johann Gottfried Eichhorn, a German professor of philosophy and oriental languages. Eichhorn insisted that the Old Testament should be treated as any other book, not as some sacred holy-of-holies which had fallen from heaven. Following the anonymous work of Jean Astruc (1753), he explained the twinned narratives of Genesis as the result of the splicing together of two earlier pieces of literature. This and many other proposals he published in *Einleitung ins Alte Testament* in three volumes (1780–1783), immediately translated into English as *Introduction to the Old Testament*.

J. S. Semler, Professor of Theology at Halle, later to be regarded as the father of modern biblical criticism, said it was time to abandon belief in the "supernatural understanding" of the Bible. In his *Treatise on the Free Investigation of the Canon* he insisted that Scripture *contained* the Word of God, but was not identical to it. Semler maintained that the New Testament gave evidence of several varieties of Christian life and teaching.

Then in 1835 David Friedrich Strauss, a professor of New Testament at Tübingen and a former student of Baur, published his two-volume *Das Leben Jesu*. Translated into English by the novelist George Eliot as *The Life of Jesus* (1846), this book caused a widespread storm of protest like nothing before it. There was an attempt to have the book suppressed.

Strauss was no skeptic; he was not out to destroy the Christian faith. Indeed, he saw himself as a mediator, aiming to mollify the unpalatable conclusions of the rationalists. As historian Stephen Neill remarks, "There is no reason to doubt that, from his own point of view, he [Strauss] was a sincere believer, and was convinced that only through an interpretation of the Gospels such as he had given was it possible to save the Christian faith for the nineteenth century."[10]

Why had Strauss caused such a furor? He had concluded that it was impossible to write an historically accurate life of Jesus. This was because in the gospels of the New Testament the *facts* of Jesus's life were seamlessly mixed, and adulterated, with the *beliefs* of his apostles. Strauss maintained that to take the gospel accounts literally, as factual history, was to mistake the purpose of the writers. Strauss insisted that the gospels had great religious value, despite not being historically reliable.

In 1815, subsidized by Harvard College, Edward Everett boarded ship in Boston Harbor eager to cross the waters and begin biblical studies at Göttingen under the renowned biblical scholar Eichhorn. At that eminent German university he devoted himself to his studies, sleeping a mere six hours a day. Within two years he became the first American to earn a doctorate from a German university.

When he returned to the United States Everett taught at Harvard College, but left after only five years to pursue a political career. He made no effort to promote biblical criticism along the lines of German scholarship. He feared that he might undermine his own faith and the faith of his students if he pursued such studies further.

Harvard College then provided George Bancroft with a scholarship for three years of study at Göttingen. Bancroft resolved that his studies would not endanger his religious faith. His resolve held, and he attained the doctorate at Göttingen, then went on to study at Berlin under Hegel.

When Bancroft returned to the United States as tutor at Harvard, he took pleasure thrusting his German education up his colleagues' noses. His overweening pride and affected manners and Germanized conversation grated against one professor in particular, who insisted he conform to American standards of social intercourse. Within a year Bancroft left Harvard. Like Everett before him, he had no desire to propagate German biblical criticism. His impressions of German biblical scholarship influenced American opinion thereafter: "I never heard anything like moral or religious feeling manifested in their theological lectures. They neither begin with God nor go on with him.... The Bible is treated with very little respect, and the narratives are laughed at as an old wife's tale, fit to be believed in the nursery."[11] Historian Jerry Wayne Brown asserts that "Bancroft's emotional protestations against German scholarship served to establish a fear of German theology in America."[12] Historian Henry A. Pochman concurs: "...for fifty years to come, the accusations launched by him against German scholars and theologians are identical with those so widely repeated in the American press afterwards."[13]

While Everett and Bancroft had done nothing to promote German biblical criticism in America, a young student at Harvard Divinity School was diligently pursuing biblical studies along lines similar to those of the German critics. In one two-month period Theodore Parker read sixty-five books in five different languages, making detailed notes. He read widely — rabbinic literature, the church fathers, early versions of the Bible in the original languages. He was so proficient in Hebrew he was asked to teach it to Harvard undergraduates. Parker was finding the Bible to be a random collection of books of dubious authorship filled with varying doctrines.

Along with two classmates, Parker was asked to substitute for the editor of *The Scriptural Interpreter* (founded by a clergyman to promote religious education) while he was abroad. Eager to spread the news of German biblical criticism, Parker translated portions of Eichhorn and other German critics for the *Interpreter*. At times he and his fellow editors wondered if perhaps in their youthful enthusiasm they were overstepping the boundary of discretion. In their last number as editors they wrote: "We have found our greatest difficulty to consist in deciding how far we might properly oppose popular opinions."[14]

As a young pastor, Parker read Strauss's *Das Leben Jesu* — possibly the first in the United States to do so — with great excitement. He discussed with the Dexter Lecturer at Harvard the possibility of preparing an English translation of Strauss, but the project did not materialize. So in 1840 Parker presented the first American review of Strauss's work, in *Christian Examiner*, a major religious periodical.

Parker adopted the spirit of Strauss's approach to the Bible, while not following him in its finer detail. He remarked that the Bible contradicted itself, and was full of inconsistency and historical error. Not only were the first three gospels as much fiction as fact, the author of the fourth gospel "invents actions and doctrines to suit his aim, and ascribes them to Jesus with no authority."[15]

While critical, Parker did not find the Bible completely wanting: "Whatever is consistent with Reason, Conscience, and the Religious faculty, is consistent with the Christianity of Jesus."[16] The Bible can help clarify, and to verify, the religious truths God has implanted upon our soul, and to reveal "to us the truths we ourselves might ... discover at a more advanced state of progress."[17]

Parker wrote in his journal that he had to restrain his comments in *The Examiner*: "I could not say all I would say ... for this is not allowable, but the most the readers of that paper will bear."[18] Nevertheless, the Boston Association of Ministers was so shocked by Parker's unorthodox thinking it asked him to resign. He refused. He still had much to accomplish.

Parker believed it was time to introduce German critical scholarship into America: "Germany [is] the only land where theology ... [is] studied as a science, and developed with scientific freedom."[19] So he translated and published Martin Leberecht de Wett's *Critical and Historical Introduction to the Old Testament* at his own expense. Near the beginning of this work it is asserted that "the Bible is to be considered as an historical phenomenon, in a series with other such phenomena, and entirely subject to the laws of historical inquiry."[20] It is not to be "examined from a religious point of view ... a blind and indiscriminating belief."[21] Parker published several updated editions of de Wette's *Introduction*, but after more than a decade he was forced to concede failure: "It has never received any reasonable notice in America, for it favors the truth, and not the prejudice of any sect. It has never had a friendly word said for it in any American journal."[22]

Although Parker championed Strauss's work, it too did not have the compelling reception in the United States which Parker might have wished. Stephen G. Bulfinch's review, published five years after Parker's, criticized Strauss as carrying his methods to too great a length. Yes, there might be inconsistencies in the gospels, but these only served to underline the authenticity of the four witness's accounts. Even if the gospels were complete fiction, "Our feelings would tempt us to forgive the Evangelists who have so beautifully deceived, rather than the critics who so coldly disenchant us."[23] One year later George E. Ellis published a review of Strauss, admonishing the German scholar's destructive spirit and skepticism; Strauss's book was nothing more than a "mass of ... worthless speculations."[24]

However, Hancock Professor of Hebrew and Dexter Professor of Sacred Literature George R. Noyes thought it unwise to dismiss the German scholars.

In an 1847 address to the alumni of Harvard Divinity School he rued the lack of critical American biblical scholarship: "We do need an answer to a work so learned and plausible as Strauss's.... [It is not] desirable that the most elaborate exposition of the life of the Founder of Christianity should be the production of one who denies the divinity of his mission."[25]

Yet such was not forthcoming. As for the American public and the majority of its clergy, it was almost as if the attack upon the Bible by German critical scholars and Americans like Parker had never occurred. Historian Sydney Ahlstrom writes, "In countless congregations in the mainstream of American evangelical Protestantism, urban as well as rural, the older anti-intellectual patterns of revivalism held sway."[26] It would be decades before even a few persons became aware of the "new" thing called "higher criticism"— principally due to W. Robertson Smith's articles in the 1875 and 1880 editions of the *Encyclopedia Britannica*.

If such "modern" religious ideas were to be grappled with at all on the North American continent, it was in the Protestant seminaries. There, as Ahlstrom observes, "the challenges ... were primarily intellectual."[27] But this had its limits. American seminaries were not intended to be *freely* intellectual. In 1815 it was proposed that Harvard Divinity School have a separate building, for fear its students might "imbibe more of the spirit of the University than of the spirit of their profession" and come to understand the ministry "as an occasion of intellectual exercise and display rather than as a means of doing good to all classes in the community."[28]

On a summer day, August 12, 1812, Samuel Miller uttered similar sentiment during the inaugural address for the first theology professor of a new seminary: "O, my fathers and brethren, let it never be said of us ... that we take more pains to make polite scholars, eloquent orators, or men of mere learning, than to form able and faithful ministers of the New Testament."[29] The theology professor being inaugurated, Archibald Alexander, had advocated the founding of the seminary before the General Assembly of the Presbyterian Church four years earlier. Princeton Theological Seminary, the Presbyterian Church's first official center for theological training, was soon to become a bastion of American Calvinism and defender of the faith, the home of what would later be known as "the Princeton Theology."

The first year of the new seminary gave no hint of what was to come. The students— only three — met in Alexander's home. Until that time theological students customarily studied with a tutor in preparation for examination by the presbytery.

Born in a log cabin in Virginia, Alexander would forever be "confirmed in his stance as a Virginian and Southerner."[30] Although he was reading the New Testament and could recite the Westminster Shorter Catechism by the age of seven, the young Alexander had showed no particular inclination toward pursuing a clerical vocation. But he liked to read, and came across some religious literature which sparked his interest. That and some experience with revivalism set him upon a soulful self-examination. Soon his heart was set on the Christian ministry. Alexander spent several years as a rural pastor and itinerant missionary on the frontier of Virginia and Ohio before accepting the presidency of Hampden-Sydney College. There the young theologian had an opportunity to teach science. Science and mathematics remained an interest for the rest of his life.

Not only had Alexander originated the idea of a Presbyterian seminary, he chaired the planning committee, and then as the seminary's first professor designed and instituted its curriculum. He did so within the guidelines laid down in the official "Plan of the Seminary" which stated that "every student ... must have read and digested the principal arguments and writings relative to what has been called the deistical controversy — thus he will be qualified to become a defender of the Christian faith."[31]

In a series of books which began publication about a decade after the founding of the seminary, Archibald Alexander attempted to set out a theology of Scripture. For Calvinist Protestants the Bible is *the* religious authority. Since Deists and other skeptics claim that the Bible is just another piece of human literature, the Bible becomes the main bulwark of the faith, which must be defended at all cost. Its authority must be set upon a firm and certain basis.

In his doctrine of Scripture Alexander claimed that evidence for the authority of Scripture must come from the experience of reading the Bible. The Bible overpowers the reader, convincing him or her of its authority: "Nothing tends more to confirm and elucidate the truths contained in the word than an inward experience of their efficacy on the heart."[32] Alexander insists that this "genuine religious experience is nothing but the impression of divine truth on the mind by the energy of the Holy Spirit."[33] Recalling his own salvation experience in revivalism, Alexander was sure that reason alone did not suffice to arrive at true religious knowledge. The evidence of the Bible's authority, on reading Scripture, could not be "perceived by the unaided intellect of man, but as it is exhibited to the mind by the illumination of the Holy Spirit."[34]

When Alexander died in 1851 he could rest easy in the knowledge that the defense of the Bible had been left to a man passionate in holding fast to the faith. Charles Hodge, in a speech delivered many years later during the celebration of his (Hodge's) fiftieth year as professor at the seminary, said (inaccurately), "I am not afraid to say that a new idea never originated in this seminary."[35]

Hodge's father died during a yellow-fever epidemic when Charles was still an infant. The family's pastor at their home in Philadelphia had become the president of Princeton College. So Hodge's mother moved the family to the town of Princeton where she could support her sons by boarding college students. This happened to be the very year the seminary was founded.

As a lad of fourteen Hodge was present at Archibald Alexander's inaugural where he met the man who would soon be his teacher and would guide and direct his early career. When Hodge began his study of theology at the seminary under Alexander in 1815, he had come to stay. For most of his remaining long life he would remain a fixture at the seminary, living in the same house, patronizing the same tailor shop for sixty years. During his later years both of his sons would join him as professors at the seminary. First hired to teach Greek and Hebrew, he would later become chair of theology while continuing to teach New Testament exegesis until his death. His two-thousand-page *Systematic Theology* and his other copious writing, along with his teaching, would have a powerful conservative influence upon the Presbyterian Church, and indeed upon much of American Protestantism for several generations. Hodge would teach more than three thousand students at the seminary — more than any other American during his century.[36] Formerly Hodge's students, preachers and teachers and college presidents would spread his ideas throughout the nation.

Hodge's most protracted absence from the seminary came after he had been teaching for four years. He asked to be granted a two-year leave to acquire a more thorough grounding in the biblical languages. Hodge had boarded at the Alexander home for the first two years after his hiring, and the older man regarded the younger as almost a son. In Germany? Alexander would prefer his protégé not be exposed to the rationalism and skepticism so prevalent in the German universities. But the younger man persisted, so he gave his consent. Alexander need not have worried. Once in Germany, Hodge sought out only the more conservative theologians, scholars who taught him how best to argue against the prevalent rationalist thinking. Hodge was appalled to learn the extent of German biblical criticism and vowed to fight it the rest of his life. In this respect he was in the vanguard among American scholars. In 1840, the year of Parker's review, Hodge assailed Strauss in an article titled "The Latest Form of Infidelity."

Over the years Hodge kept abreast of developments in German biblical criticism. Know your enemy. He never recovered from his initial shock on learning that the Bible should be treated like any other literature, literature created out of the human mind.

Hodge believed that the best counter-offensive was to present a systematic doctrine of inspiration — that the Bible was the very word of God — which he did in 1857. Hodge's doctrine of inspiration was something new. As historian Ernest R. Sandeen notes, "Most twentieth-century fundamentalists and many twentieth-century historians have mistakenly assumed that Protestantism possesses a strong, fully integrated theology of biblical authority ... no such theology existed before 1850."[37] That many today believe that the doctrine of verbal inspiration existed since the time of the first Christians shows how thoroughly Hodge's ideas have become part of contemporary American Protestant belief.

Unlike Alexander, Hodge never mentioned the Holy Spirit as the cause of a person's belief in the inspiration of Scripture, presumably because he wanted, in the face of his skeptical German opponents, to appear strictly rational and objective. But unlike Alexander, he was deviating from tradition. The Westminster Confession of 1648 said, concerning Scripture: "...our full persuasion and assurance of the infallible truth, and divine authority thereof, is from the inward work of the Holy Spirit, bearing witness by and with the Word in our hearts."[38] Notwithstanding that he was a devout Calvinist, Hodge contradicted what Calvin had said on this subject. For Calvin the witness of the Holy Spirit was of primary importance for faith: "But those who wish to prove to unbelievers that Scripture is the Word of God are acting foolishly, for only by faith can this be known."[39] Hodge asserted that "the Scriptures were written *dictante spiritu dei* [dictation by the Spirit of God]."[40] Hodge was very clear that the biblical writers "were controlled by Him in the words which they used."[41] Every word in the Bible is the very word of God: "What David said, the Holy Ghost said. What Jeremiah said, the Holy Ghost said."[42]

This was entirely different from what Alexander had said and from Calvinist tradition. Alexander believed that the Holy Spirit provided the biblical writers with *ideas, but not the exact words*: "...the writer did not need a continual suggestion of every idea, but only to be so superintended, as to be preserved from error; ... there existed no necessity that very word should be inspired...."[43] Alexander used the analogy of a father and child: "The child walks by its own activity and takes steps according to its ability; but the father preserves it from falling and keeps it in the straight path."[44] Under this divine superintendence the biblical writers could retain their own idiosyncratic style of writing and expression "as fully as if they were writing or speaking without inspiration."[45]

The doctrine of *verbal* inspiration originated with Hodge, despite his claims to the contrary. By contrast, theologians of the early church and the Reformation had held only that Scripture *contained* communication from God, but in the fallible language and thought forms of human beings. Nevertheless, these human words of the Bible sufficed to bear divine meaning, and functioned to save souls.

The important point for Alexander was that the Holy Spirit "preserved" the biblical writers "from error." Hodge took this concept and said that the biblical writers were "infallible organs of God, so that what they taught, God taught."[46]

The Christian church had never maintained that the Bible pretended to teach matters of science. Nor had Calvin. Yet Hodge, a strict Calvinist, insisted that the Bible did communicate even "the last results of science."[47] He wrote, "All the books of Scripture ... are infallible ... inspiration ... is not confined to moral and religious truths, but extends to the statements of facts, whether scientific, historical, or geographical."[48] For Hodge the Bible was a veritable encyclopedia of all knowledge: "If the Bible be the word of God, all the great questions which for ages have agitated the minds of men are settled with infallible certainty."[49]

Hodge maintained that the truths natural scientists discover, even those discoveries that lie far in the future, are consistent with Scripture: "The Bible is found to harmonize with all its [the universe's] new discovered wonders."[50] When scientists come up with discoveries which seem to contradict the Bible, the fault lies with human interpretation of Scripture, not with Scripture inself: "Science has in many things taught the Church how to understand the Scriptures. The Bible was for ages understood and explained according to the Ptolemaic system of the universe; it is now explained without doing the least violence to its language, according to the Copernican system."[51]

What was important, Hodge insisted, was not what those who wrote the Bible *believed* to be true, but what they *wrote*: "...it is not the question, Whether they thought that the earth is the center of our system but, Did they teach that it is?"[52] Hodge writes, "An inspired man could not, indeed, err in his instruction on any subject. He could not teach by inspiration that the earth is the center of our system or that the sun, moon, and stars are mere satellites of our globe, but such may have been his own conviction. Inspiration did not elevate him in secular knowledge above the age in which he lived; it only, so far as secular and scientific truths are concerned, preserved him from teaching error."[53]

All was well until Charles Darwin's *The Origin of Species*. Although publication was in 1859, historian Ahlstrom notes, "Only after 1869 was the real impact of Darwinism felt in the American churches, partly because of the vast distractions of the Civil War and Reconstruction."[54] Ironically Darwin's ideas presented a threat because the Princeton Theology maintains that each and every word of the Bible is literally true with regard to the latest discoveries of science.

Up until this time Hodge had believed that science affirmed the glory of God's creation, the marvels of God's design. In 1874 in *What is Darwinism?*

Hodge remarked that this strange new notion of "natural selection" concocted by some man — who wasn't even German! — denied the omnipotence and omniscience of the Creator: "The conclusion of the whole matter is, that the denial of design in nature is virtually the denial of God. Mr. Darwin's theory does deny all design in nature, therefore his theory is virtually atheistical."[55]

Perhaps it was a blessing that Hodge was by this time an old man, nearing the end of his career and his life. In the year of his death there was published in Germany what has become a classic in the literature of biblical criticism. Julius Wellhausen's *Geschichte Israels* (*History of Israel*) placed the first books of the Old Testament into the context of the history of the Jewish religion. Recognized to this day as the basis of a new orthodoxy in Old Testament scholarship, Wellhausen's conclusions are the starting point for any contemporary scholarly endeavor in the areas of Old Testament literature and history.

So vehement an uproar did Wellhausen's publication provoke amongst conservative exegetes, he felt it necessary to resign his university chair. Realizing he had broken with traditional religious beliefs and the principles of the theological faculty, he tendered his resignation "freely and in the conviction that he could no longer adhere to the Evangelical Church or even to Protestantism."[56] But Wellhausen's resignation in no way slowed the spread of his ideas. The history and religion of the ancient Israelites was understood as an evolving entity, and treated no differently than the history of any other ethnic group. Any appeal to the supernatural was ruled out on principle. Everything prior to the accounts found in the two books of Samuel was considered to be a thick carapace of myth and legend, beneath which might exist a slight grain of historical truth.

With this addition to the arsenal of biblical criticism it was fortunate that a year before Charles Hodge died his son Archibald Alexander Hodge (named after the seminary's founder) had joined his father on the faculty of theology. The younger Hodge was from the beginning devoted to the ideals and principles his father held close to his heart. He had studied theology at the seminary under his father, and spent several years as a missionary, pastor, and chair of theology at another seminary. After his father's death he became Princeton's third professor of theology.

The younger Hodge had every intention of supporting his father's legacy. A. A. Hodge had published *Outlines of Theology* back in 1860, based to a large extent on notes taken from his father's lectures when he had been a student at the seminary.

In an 1869 publication he had virtually echoed his father's thinking concerning the inspiration of the Bible: "The books of Scripture ... are, one and all, in thought and verbal expression, in substance and form, wholly the Word of God.... This was accomplished by a supernatural influence of the Spirit of God acting upon the spirits of the sacred writers, called 'inspiration,' which ... directed them in all they wrote, and secured the infallible expression of it in words."[57]

The elder Hodge had conceded that the biblical writers were not always completely consistent in what they wrote. In his three-volume *Systematic Theology* (1872–1873) he remarked: "The errors in matters of fact which skeptics search out bear no proportion to the whole. No sane men would deny that the Parthenon was built of marble, even if here and there a speck of sandstone should be detected in its structure."[58] Charles Hodge brushed any discrepancy in Scripture aside as "so minute" as only to be "sought as with a microscope, and picked out with the most delicate forceps of criticism."[59]

But by the time the younger Hodge replaced his father as professor of theology those microscopes and forceps had been put to effective work by an army of diligent biblical critics, and the specks of sandstone in the edifice of Scripture were threatening to disastrously weaken its structure. If the father's doctrine of biblical inspiration and inerrancy were to hold in the face of increasingly cogent criticism, the son must take urgent action.

So in 1879 he issued a new, and much larger, revised edition of his *Outlines of Theology* in which he made a striking amendment to his father's doctrine by seizing upon an idea initiated by his father toward end of his life. Charles Hodge seems to have anticipated that some new device would be necessary to combat the escalating intensity of critical threats to the authority of the Bible. He attributed discrepancies in the text of the Bible to errors in copying over the centuries. The "original autographs" (the words penned by the biblical authors), however, were infallible: "It is of the Bible as it came from the hands of the sacred writers ... that this infallibility is asserted."[60]

A. A. Hodge recognized the true significance of his father's idea. He would elaborate upon and refine the original kernel of the concept of original autographs, honing it into an effective weapon to be used against the biblical critics. The younger Hodge had hit upon what seemed a foolproof argument. Because the original autographs no longer existed, the Princeton doctrine of biblical inerrancy and inspiration would forever remain unassailable.

Under Hodge's terms biblical critics had several impossible mountains to climb. Should the critics obtain the original autographs (and who would adjudicate that they were so, and how?), and should they find that a statement in these autographs contradicts some historical fact (and how would one know for sure that this historical fact was indeed true? and who would determine this?), then they must demonstrate that "they are in themselves essentially incapable of being reconciled."[61] All of this would have to "secure the recognition of the community of believing scholars,"[62] and be proved "beyond the possibility of doubt."[63] Clearly the younger Hodge missed his calling; he should have been a lawyer.

A. A. Hodge insisted that "the original autographs ... are absolutely infallible when interpreted in the sense intended, and hence are clothed with absolute divine authority."[64] But if Hodge was going to insist upon the original autographs in his war with the critics, did he not render Scripture as it existed in his own time fallible, error-laden, and therefore inauthorative? Had Hodge not fought off Scylla, only to be devoured by Charybdis? Aware that he had exposed his doctrine to this dilemma, Hodge said that according to the "unanimous testimony of Christian scholars"[65] the accumulated errors of transcription had not resulted in the loss of any essential Christian doctrine. (How would they know?) Moreover, Hodge was confident that the church now possessed "a more perfect text of the original Scriptures than she has enjoyed since the apostolic age."[66] (But unless the original autographs were available for comparison, how could this be known?)

Then in 1886, suddenly and without warning, Princeton Theological Seminary lost its third professor of theology. A. A. Hodge was dead. His replacement was called from Western Theological Seminary in Pennsylvania where he served as a professor of biblical languages and New Testament.

Installed as Professor of Didactic and Polemic Theology (a strange but exceedingly appropriate title, as it would turn out), Benjamin Breckinridge Warfield could be trusted to uphold the party line. He had studied for three years at the seminary under Charles Hodge, and was a close friend of the younger Hodge. His inaugural address at Western back in 1880 had been titled "Inspiration and Criticism," followed that same year by a pamphlet titled "The Divine Origin of the Bible."

No one could have guessed at Warfield's future when he was young. Even before entering college he had read *The Origin of Species* and was a confirmed Darwinian — a position he later rejected as youthful error. In college he majored in mathematics and physics, and would have pursued graduate studies in experimental science had his wealthy father not persuaded him to take some time off to travel in Europe. After less than a year abroad he wrote home to say that he had decided to enter the ministry.

Warfield never published a major work on theology, despite prompting from friends and associates. That was because he was kept fully occupied fending off attacks against the Princeton Theology. His writing in this regard amounted to ten sturdy volumes, the first being *Revelation and Inspiration*. He was well prepared to defend the Princeton Theology. As a youth he had won prizes for essay and debate.

Warfield adopted, and vigorously defended, the whole cloth of the doctrine of biblical authority previously presented by the Princeton theologians.

This included verbal inspiration and inerrancy: "...the Spirit's superintendence extends to the choice of the words by the human authors (verbal inspiration) ... thus securing, among other things, that entire truthfulness which is everywhere presupposed in and asserted for Scripture by the Biblical writers (inerrancy)."[67] Warfield insisted that it was only the original autographs which were infallible: "It is *the Bible* that we declare to be 'of infallible truth'—the Bible that God gave us, not the corruptions and slips which scribes and printers have given us, some of which are in every copy."[68] Nevertheless, Warfield declared the present form(s) of the text were not fallible, error-laden, or inauthorative, but were entirely adequate: "God has not permitted the Bible to become so hopelessly corrupt that its restoration to its original text is impossible."[69]

In 1881, while still teaching at Western, Warfield had co-authored an article on inspiration with A. A. Hodge which soon became the classic statement of the Princeton Theology concerning the authority of the Bible: "...all the affirmations of Scripture of all kinds, whether of spiritual doctrine or duty, or of physical or historical fact, or of psychological or philosophical principle, are without any error, when the *ipsissima verba* of the original autographs are ascertained and interpreted in their natural and intended sense."[70] The article appeared in the second volume of *The Presbyterian Review*, a journal supported by several Presbyterian seminaries as a locus for the expression of divergent theological viewpoints, with the hope of reconciliation.

A. A. Hodge and Charles Augustus Briggs were chosen as managing editors of the new journal, the latter a leader in its founding. As a young man Briggs had traveled to Germany to study under the proponents of biblical criticism. Almost immediately he was fired with excitement: "I cannot doubt but what I have been blessed with a new divine light. I feel a different man from what I was five months ago. The Bible is lit up with a new light."[71] By the time he returned to the United States he was convinced that critical methods should be adopted by conservative Christian scholars rather than leave them to the skeptics. In his 1876 inaugural address as Davenport Professor of Hebrew and Cognate Languages at Union Seminary in New York he advocated that critical methods be widely used and liberated from dogma: "So long as the Word of God is honored ... what matters it if a certain book be detached from the name of one holy man and ascribed to another, or classed among those with unknown authors?"[72] It was to help promote these new critical methods that Briggs wanted to found a new journal. Those who opposed German higher criticism proposed that *The Presbyterian Review* begin publication with a series of articles expressing both positive and negative views on the use of these new methods.

In an article titled "The Right, Duty, and Limits of Biblical Criticism"

Briggs responded to the article by Warfield and Hodge published in the previous issue of the *Review*. It was the first shot in a war which would continue for more than a decade.

Briggs took issue with the fact that the Princeton theologians had severely deviated from the Reformed tradition and the Westminster Confession: "It is well known that the great Reformers recognized errors in the Scriptures and did not hold to the inerrancy of the original autographs. Are these Princeton divines entitled to pronounce Luther and Calvin heterodox, and to define the faith of the universal Church?"[73] In addition, Briggs pointed out that the doctrine of verbal inspiration originated with the Princeton theologians: "No confession of faith or catechism of recognized standing in the Reformed or Lutheran Church teaches that the Scriptures are inspired in their verbal expressions."[74]

Briggs insisted that the Princeton doctrine of the authority of Scripture made the Bible more vulnerable to critical attack. The younger Hodge had written: "We determine what books have a place in this canon or divine rule by an examination of the evidences which show that each of them, severally, was written by the inspired prophet or apostle whose name it bears, or, as in the case of the gospels of Mark and Luke, written under the superintendence and published by the authority of an apostle."[75] Briggs immediately pointed out that "the inspiration, the canonicity, and the authority of the Bible depends, therefore, upon the results of the Higher Criticism."[76] Hodge and Warfield were playing right into the hands of the biblical critics. Because the authorship of many biblical books cannot be proved, it follows that they may very well not be inspired — *if* one accepts as presupposition the Princeton doctrine of inspiration. Briggs maintained that this problem is avoided in the Westminster tradition: "The authority of the Holy Scripture, for which it ought to be believed and obeyed, dependeth not upon the testimony of any man."[77]

In the 1881 article on inspiration Warfield wrote: "A proved error in Scripture contradicts not only our doctrine, but the Scripture claims and, therefore, its inspiration...."[78] Here Warfield's flawless logic led to a horrifying conclusion. If biblical critics can find *one single instance* of error in all of the Bible, then the Bible is not inspired and therefore not authoritative. As Briggs responded in his article: "...these Princeton divines risk the inspiration and authority of the Bible upon a single proved error. Such a position is a serious and hazardous departure from Protestant orthodoxy. It imperils the faith of all Christians.... They cannot escape the evidence of errors in the Scriptures."[79]

Moreover, as Briggs observes, "the theory of verbal inspiration cannot admit inspired thoughts in other than inspired words. It therefore results in the denial that there are inspired thoughts in the English Bible."[80] Any translation of the original Greek and Hebrew — the inspired words of God — would not be in God's words, and therefore not inspired.

The Presbyterian Church considered Briggs the standard bearer of biblical criticism in America. In 1891 he was formally charged with heresy. Briggs's able response led to the charges being dismissed, but the case was appealed to higher ecclesiastical courts. Two years later, after a trial which was perhaps most forcefully encapsulated in words from the opening argument of the prosecution — "It is the Bible and Christ against Dr. Briggs"[81] — Briggs was suspended from the Presbyterian ministry.

Briggs became an Episcopal priest. Although he continued to believe he had been scapegoated as a convenient target by those who opposed biblical criticism, he was a forgiving man and spent his remaining years working for Christian unity.

The results of Briggs's trial reverberated far beyond the Presbyterian Church: "The Bible as we now have it, in its various translations and versions, when freed from all errors and mistakes of translators, copyists, and printers, is the very Word of God, and consequently wholly without error."[82] It would be too easy from this time forward to leave out the details of this deliberation and assume that all present versions and translations of the Bible are "the very Word of God, and consequently wholly without error." As historians Rogers and McKim observe: "Now, at least in the popular mind, the English Bible in the layperson's hands was declared to be a technically true source of information on science as well as religion."[83]

The Princeton theologians had instituted two innovative concepts — verbal inspiration of Scripture and the inerrancy of the Bible. So much did their status as scholars give informal imprimatur to these new doctrines, the Princeton doctrine of the authority of Scripture has become part of the fabric of evangelical belief long after its origins have been forgotten.

8

The Birth of Liberalism

The Princeton Theology, with its concept of the original autographs, had provided a weapon, in the opinion of some, to counter the forces of biblical criticism. By redefining biblical inspiration and introducing the doctrine of biblical inerrancy, the Princeton theologians had stoutly defended the Bible, *the* basis for American Protestant Christianity, against an insidious threat from abroad.

But by the late nineteenth century criticism of the Bible was not the only invasive force entering the United States from Europe which threatened the nation's Calvinist religious foundation.

Calvinism placed God at the center of its theology. God was *totally* in control of everything human. The fate of every individual was predestined before birth. Human beings were powerless before this all-powerful God. The idea that human beings could bring on the millennium by their efforts was nonsense.

Beginning in the late eighteenth century several strands of thought were combining to displace God from this central position, and place humanity and its endeavors front and center.

In 1762 Jean-Jacques Rousseau's *The Social Contract* marked the beginning of an innovative, even revolutionary, way of thinking which later flowered forth as the Romantic Era. His writing breathed new life into European culture, a culture beginning to tire of the Enlightenment's staid cerebral spirit. Rousseau's writings reflected the character of their author. A man of spirit, of feeling, he had begun his literary career as a music copyist writing about music.

Rousseau advocated what came to be called "natural religion." The purpose of natural religion was not to worship God, but to guarantee the proper and orderly functioning of society — as such it would be supported by the state.

The seeds of this innovative idea had been planted during the Enlightenment when the concept of a specifically *Christian* God began to be questioned. Different cultures displayed various manifestations of the religious

96

spirit. Religion, with its moral and spiritual truths, was, it seemed, a "natural" part of human life. Reason should be able to discover the spiritual and moral principles which lay behind the world's religious traditions. The resulting "reasonable" or "natural" religion could then replace the moribund practices and traditions and dogma which cluttered the Christian faith. The Bible and Christian doctrine contained many of these natural religious and moral truths, but both needed a winnowing to remove the chaff of culture.

Published in 1781, Immanuel Kant's *Critique of Pure Reason* added further force to this trend toward a human-centered religion. Kant was a sober sedate professor, a man who never married and never fathered children, a man whose coming and going was so regular people could set their watches by it — not a personality one would expect to crack the carapace of the Enlightenment and reinforce the liberating spirit of Rousseau's thinking.

Kant used reason to critique reason, setting limits on reason's abilities, thereby sounding the death knell of the Enlightenment: the human mind cannot have knowledge of the transcendent, the supernatural, the "noumenal" realm, or even of its existence or non-existence; it can only know the natural "phenomenal" world. Reason can tell us nothing about God or the existence of God; that is the domain of faith.

At first appearing to be a considerably limiting philosophy, Kant's ideas energized human consciousness. No longer was the mind simply the Lockean blank slate which passively received data from the outside. Now it was considered to play a creative, active, constitutive role, for Kant had posited a "practical reason" to complement "pure" reason. With boundless expectation the human spirit proclaimed a new era of hope. The individual spirit took on new value. It was the age of the poet and artist, as self-expression reigned supreme. Nature and humanity interacted in a dynamic organic whole. The Enlightenment's static universe of absolutes yielded to a spiritual universe of becoming, of constant living change.

Kant's philosophy opened new vistas for the religious imagination, and Friedrich D. E. Schleiermacher, renowned today as "the father of modern theology," did not hesitate to exercise it. Raised a Moravian pietist, he had reacted as a youth to the authoritative pressure of strict doctrinal principles, yet retained a strong sense of religious feeling. In this felt dichotomy between the emotions and the spontaneous versus the reasoned and the static he was very much a man of the Romantic Era. He made a clear distinction between religious dogma and the religious spirit. In his two major publications, *Addresses on Religion to Its Cultured Despisers* (1799) and *The Christian Faith* (1821), Schleiermacher attempted to defend Christianity from rationalist attacks by restating Christian belief in a fresh and modern way, demonstrating its compelling power over the human spirit.

Schleiermacher said that beneath the accretion of theological doctrine (which is specific to each particular religious tradition, and a result of the history of that tradition) all human beings are aware of the Infinite, the Transcendent (which Christians label "God"). This awareness results from a feeling of "absolute dependence": "All attributes which we ascribe to God are to be taken as denoting, not something special in God, but only something special in ... the feeling of absolute dependence."[1] When we say that God is all-powerful, for example, we are simply expressing our own lack of power.

But what about Christianity? How is it to be distinguished from other religions, or from religion in general? Christianity traces its history back to Jesus of Nazareth. Jesus was "distinguished from all [other persons] by the constant potency of his God-consciousness, which was a veritable existence of God in him."[2] Jesus's "divinity" was simply a continual and more powerful God-consciousness than that possessed by other persons. He was more aware of his inadequacy, his imperfection.

What about the Bible? Schleiermacher said that the Bible shapes and informs the particularly Christian form of God-consciousness. Reading the Bible gives the general form of God-consciousness a more specific fuller shape.

Schleiermacher may have been trying to protect Christianity from rationalist attacks, but his concept of the Bible and of Christianity was far from orthodox. For he had placed human consciousness at the center, not God. Jesus was "divine," but only in a way that we all are (albeit less so).

Some years before, at intervals between 1774 and 1778, the German dramatist and literary figure Gotthold Ephraim Lessing had published the *Wolfenbüttel Fragments*— excerpts from the private research of Hermann Samuel Reimarus. Reimarus had died years earlier and had never intended his work for publication, only in answer to his own personal curiosity. Reimarus was a professor of oriental languages and a true child of the Enlightenment. As a Deist, he believed that God did not intervene in earthly events. Hence, Jesus was not resurrected. Instead, his disciples stole his body, as suggested in Matthew 28:13. They invented the myth that Jesus had been resurrected and was, therefore, some sort of universal savior. Reimarus insisted that Jesus was simply a man.

Publication of the *Wolfenbüttel Fragments* caused a violent reaction (it wasn't until 1813 that Reimarus's identity was disclosed), but set the stage for what was to follow. The idea that Jesus was not divine came to full flower in 1835 with David Friedrich Strauss's *Das Leben Jesu*.

The core, the substratum of fact underlying the gospels was that Jesus began as a follower of John the Baptist, then went out on his own, like the Baptist, to preach the coming of a messiah. After Jesus's death his disciples came to believe that Jesus *himself* was the messiah. They wrote the gospels from this viewpoint, finding support for their beliefs in the messianic prophecies of the Old Testament.

For Strauss, Jesus is a representative figure. When the authors of the gospels told about Jesus's death, resurrection, and ascension they were giving expression to their faith in humankind, that it could progress toward sinless perfection. What we are to take from the gospels is this faith of the writers, their faith in humankind.

The philosopher Ludwig Feuerbach went a step further. He frankly stated that there is no God. God is nothing but an idea, an ideal, a projection whereby humanity seeks to transcend its limitations. Yet Feuerbach did not wish to dismiss religion; like Rousseau he believed it had a valid social function. Like Schleiermacher and Strauss, for Feuerbach religion was about humanity, not about God.

In 1841 Feuerbach published *The Essence of Christianity*. In 1900 Adolf von Harnack published a book with the same title. Harnack said that Jesus's "divinity" was an accretion of the early church; Jesus had never proclaimed himself divine. What was important was Jesus's teaching: the gospel of love and the infinite worth of the human soul.

This idea of the "essence" of Christianity had occurred independently to the American, Theodore Parker. In 1840 he credited Strauss for daring to breach tradition "for the welfare of the race," for opening to humanity the "domain of *free religious thought*, where the only *essential* creed is the Christian motto, 'Be perfect as your Father in Heaven is perfect,' and the only *essential* form of religion is to love your neighbor as yourself, and God with the whole heart, mind, and soul."[3]

Parker wanted to preach about God's universal love for all of humanity, but the Bible presented a God who "loved only a few, and them not overmuch."[4] The Bible was getting in the way: "I found this worship of the Bible ... hindering me at each progressive step."[5] So one year after the publication of his review of Strauss Parker preached an ordination sermon titled "The Transient and Permanent in Christianity" in which he attacked the dogmatic and uncritical approach to the Bible so common in America, observing that "modern criticism is fast breaking to pieces this idol which men have made out of the scriptures."[6]

For Parker, the truths which Jesus taught were more important than the person of Jesus: "It is hard to see why the great truths of Christianity rest on the personal authority of Jesus, more than the axioms of geometry rest on the personal authority of Euclid or Archimedes.... If Jesus had taught at Athens ... [if] none but the human nature had ever been ascribed to him ... Christianity ... would have lost none of its truths."[7]

Around that time there was in the United States a blossoming enthusiasm for the European Romantic spirit. Reviews and articles concerning these new interests appeared in the journals. Great impetus came from a young man who had been born into the parsonage and had begun a clerical career as the pastor of Second Church, Boston.

Ralph Waldo Emerson had not shown particular promise as a student at Harvard; he graduated at the middle of his class. But in one of those coincidences which can alter the direction of cultural history, he attended Harvard during Edward Everett's brief five-year sojourn at the college. Emerson fell under the spell of Everett's rhetoric, and drank deeply of his teacher's culture and erudition.[8]

For several years Emerson engaged in ministerial duties at various churches. Then in 1838, in an address to the graduating class of Harvard Divinity School which would become a classic in American culture and literature, he revealed the real man hidden under clerical robes.

At first there seems nothing startling or unusual in Emerson's address: The world is the product "of one will, of one mind; and that one mind is everywhere active, in each ray of the star, in each wavelet of the pool...." But then the thinking shifts: "Christianity ... has dwelt, it dwells, with noxious exaggeration about the *person* of Jesus." Emerson insisted that emphasis should come off Jesus and onto the fact that every human being is "an infinite Soul."[9]

This address, historian Sydney Ahlstrom comments, made Emerson "America's first 'death-of-God' theologian."[10] The death of the Puritan Calvinist God, anyway. Emerson, a true child of the Romantic era, fused humanity, nature, and God into one pantheistic whole, a dynamic progressive growing whole, reflected in, and subsumed by, the individual self: "Nothing is at last sacred but the integrity of your own mind."[11]

That Emerson emerged as a cultural hero to so many Americans indicates new winds were blowing over the once-Puritan once-Calvinist nation.

Emerson was not alone. Horace Bushnell, "the American Schleiermacher," "the father of American religious liberalism," was raised in an orthodox religious background, and showed little inclination toward a clerical career until as a student at Yale he was converted during one of its revivals. His first congregation was urban, urbane, educated, socially-aspiring, affronted by Calvinism, and filled with American optimism and a passion for self-improvement. Bushnell adapted to the temper and thinking of his congregation.

Bushnell's reputation as an eloquent preacher and the excitement created by his first book in 1847 elicited invitations to deliver lectures to the three leading New England theological institutions—Harvard, Yale, and Andover. Published as *God in Christ* (1849), these lectures were prefaced with an essay titled "Preliminary Dissertation on the Nature of Language," in which Bushnell came out against the literal interpretation of the Bible: understood literally, "There is no book in the world that contains so many repugnances, or antagonistic forms of assertion, as the Bible."[12] To understand the Bible literally was to deviate from the intention of its authors, who had striven to express religious truths in a nuanced metaphorical manner using language which was primarily symbolic and evocative, even poetic.

Bushnell was accused of heresy. The years he spent defending himself provided his ideas widespread exposure.

As the decades passed the liberal ideas of Parker, Emerson, and Bushnell gained favor. In *An Outline of Christian Theology* (1894) William Newton Clarke claimed that Jesus's words were not meant to be understood literally. Jesus meant not that he would return in physical form, but that he would be present spiritually after his death, working in and through the church to bring about his millennial Kingdom.

The cultural climate in the United States was becoming more secular in outlook. Back in 1839 fifty-one of the fifty-four presidents of the largest colleges in the United States had been clergymen.[13] Consistent with this, American higher education at that time had a distinctly moral and spiritual, even evangelical, flavor. But as the nineteenth century grew long in tooth more and more young American students followed the lead of Edward Everett and George Bancroft, completing their education at German universities. (In 1920 their total number had swelled to nearly nine thousand.[14]) By the 1870s the German model of the university, with an emphasis on the secular and scientific, was common in American universities. In like fashion Christian seminaries like Harvard, Yale, Union, Colgate, Rochester, Crozer, and Lane underwent a sea-change. They became "liberal," "modernist" (a term that implied affirmation of the modern emphasis on science, philosophy, and secular humanism). Chicago Divinity School soon became the epicenter of this development.

Modern science presented no conflict with religion. Following Kant, there are two realms of existence: the material, open to objective scientific inquiry, and the spiritual, revealed in religious experience. The two could coexist in splendid isolation from each other. Even Darwinism presented no problem. A growing number of liberal Christian writers, theologians, and clergy thought Darwinism supported the traditional idea of Christian progress toward Christ's kingdom on earth. John Fiske gave expression to this spirit of optimism in his *The Destiny of Man* (1884): "It is Darwinism which has placed Humanity upon a higher pinnacle than ever.... Peace and love shall reign supreme ... the kingdoms of this world shall become the kingdom of Christ, and he shall reign for ever and ever...."[15] In *The Evolution of Christianity*

(1892) Lyman Abbott opted for evolution. The church and Christian society was progressing onward and upward under the direction of a loving Providence—Hegel's concept of a progressive history of the Spirit in new dress. The static universe of religious tradition was now understood to be a dynamic cosmos monitored by a loving Providence.

Nor were creeds and dogma static. Like the Bible, these needed to be understood within the context of human history, subject to constant reinterpretation as human needs and culture evolved. Liberals were optimistic about human nature and the future. Human nature was fundamentally good. There was no such thing as "original sin" or "human depravity"—cornerstones of traditional Calvinist theology. "Sin," a measurement of deviation from God-given potential, would decrease and virtually vanish in the face of ethical preaching, moral education, and social reform. Jesus was the model, in his acts and teaching; his Sermon on the Mount represented the very essence of Christian thinking.

The Protestant laity was unaware of this new thinking, restricted to the ivory towers of academe and clerical colloquia, a tempest in a teapot, until the Briggs heresy trials and the novel *Robert Elsmere* brought it to public attention.

Robert Elsmere originated in Britain in 1888, selling 40,000 copies in the first year.[16] In America people lined up to buy. A newsdealer located where ferries embarked quickly sold 3000 copies. By March of 1889 American sales had reached an estimated 200,000.[17] By the early years of the twentieth century total sales figures would climb to almost one million.[18] A survey of the nation's major libraries five years after the book's publication revealed that thirty percent of the time it made the lists of novels most frequently borrowed.[19]

William S. Peterson describes *Robert Elsmere* as "a deeply authentic account of that crisis of religious belief which shook the foundations of Western thought in the nineteenth century."[20] Although the author professed to be describing "the destructive effect of biblical criticism upon Christian orthodoxy," her novel also laid bare "her own private religious anxieties."[21] *Robert Elsmere* was less a popular novel "than an oracular pronouncement on God and human destiny. 'Do you agree with Robert Elsmere?' became ... in the United States a shibboleth designed to expose every shade of orthodoxy or heterodoxy."[22]

While conservative clergy were alarmed, critical response in the American secular press was wildly positive. *Robert Elsmere* was hailed as the greatest novel of the decade, even of the century. In a lengthy symposium in *North American Review*, America's most prestigious quarterly, a contributor remarked, "I know of no story since *Uncle Tom's Cabin* whose appearance has excited so much comment [and] intellectual interest of so high a character."[23]

In a form available and palatable to the average reader, *Robert Elsmere* got Americans thinking about their religious beliefs. As one contemporary remarked, "Where one person reads Hume, Renan, Strauss, Theodore Parker ... a hundred read *Robert Elsmere*."[24]

With the general public beginning to come onside, theological issues gathered force. The advances in technology and science and all facets of human knowledge helped the liberal cause. Optimism concerning human destiny supported the idea of progress toward an earthly "kingdom of God." Its pragmatic application found apt description in the writing of Walter Rauschenbusch, the iconic representative of the new Social Gospel movement, the practical pinnacle of liberal theology. His 1907 publication *Christianity and the Social Crisis* encapsulated the essence of the new liberal thinking: "The swiftness of evolution in our own country [the United States] proves the immense latent perfectibility in human nature ... nineteen centuries of Christian influence have been a long preliminary stage of growth, and now the flower and fruit are almost here ... that great day of the Lord...."[25] As historian Ahlstrom observes, "The Social Gospel was a form of millennial thought."[26] Rauschenbusch called for a "restoration of the millennial hope."[27] The millennialism endemic from the beginning of American history was flowering forth once more, albeit in new colors.

9

The True Church

It might seem that the forces of technological and scientific progress would assure the new liberal concepts of Christianity positive momentum in their struggle against the conservative Calvinism of tradition, and perhaps final victory. Yet several decades earlier, at the time German criticism of the Bible was making inroads into the United States and Ralph Waldo Emerson was preaching the Romantic spirit, there arose in Ireland a figure whose theology would invigorate the conservative Calvinist forces in American Protestantism and guarantee them a sure place in the future.

John Nelson Darby came from a well heeled well connected background. His father was a wealthy Irish landowner and merchant who had amassed a fortune providing supplies for the British navy. His uncle was a knighted admiral in that marine force; Darby's middle name came from this connection — his godfather was none other than the famous Lord Nelson, a good friend of his uncle. With a secure material start in life, Darby attended Trinity College in Dublin and graduated a Classical Gold Medallist, then progressed into the legal profession in association with a brother-in-law who later became Lord Chief Justice of Ireland. Clearly a successful and prosperous life lay before him.

Then, shortly after being called to the bar, he experienced a spiritual crisis and decided to become a clergyman. In 1826, at the age of 26, Darby was ordained priest with the Church of England and appointed curate of a large parish in Ireland. His father, annoyed that his youngest son should ungratefully abandon a promising legal career, disinherited him; but an uncle subsequently bestowed upon him a considerable fortune.

Darby threw himself into his new vocation with a passion. He worked long hours, seldom retiring before midnight. Worn out, undernourished, he looked like the stereotypical biblical prophet. It seemed he intended to convert every Roman Catholic in Ireland to Protestantism. But a decree from the local archbishop that all converts must swear allegiance to the British monarch — sure to stick in the craw of loyal inhabitants of the emerald isle and prevent their conversion — militated against his proselytizing efforts.

When an accident, in which Darby was thrown by his horse against a doorpost, left him lame and convalescent at the home of a relative, he had time to think: "...much exercise of soul had the effect of causing the Scriptures to gain complete ascendancy over me. I had always owned them to be the word of God."[1] Darby began to study the Bible with the same feverish passion he had previously harnessed to the conversion of Catholics.

In the biblical book of Acts he came upon passages which fed his disillusionment with the institutional church as nothing more than a handmaiden to the state: "The careful reading of the Acts afforded me a practical picture of the early church, which made me feel deeply the contrast with its actual present state."[2] Darby began to distinguish what he called "the true church" from the traditional institutional church of the denominations. The latter is steeped in sin and is really just another branch of secular society: "Christendom, as seen externally, was really the world, and could not be considered as 'the church.'"[3] By contrast, the true church is comprised of those scattered individuals who have been predestined from eternity to be the saved: "The true body of Christ ... is composed of those who are united to Christ by the Holy Ghost, who, when the professing church is cut off will have their place with him in heaven...."[4] In the end-time the true church will be taken up to reside in heaven with Christ: "...the Christian, having his place in Christ in heaven, has nothing to wait for save the coming of the Saviour, in order to be set, in fact, in the glory which is already his portion in Christ."[5] Everyone else will suffer a horrible fate.

In 1829 Darby published a pamphlet which summarized his developing eschatology. He rejected postmillennialism, the prevalent religious opinion in Britain. Only divine intervention (the Second Coming of Christ) could bring on the millennium, not human action (like preaching the gospel). The true church would be gathered up before any of the violence of the end-times occurred: "The operation, everywhere given, of the gospel, is the gathering out of souls before the wrath come."[6] Christ's own had nothing to fear regarding the eschaton.

Most noteworthy was Darby's concept of "dispensations." He did not invent the word; it had been used in religious contexts for centuries. But the way he used it, and the fact that he made it the basis of his theology and biblical hermeneutic, was entirely new in Christian thinking. Clarence B. Bass in his book *Backgrounds to Dispensationalism* remarks again and again on this: "Dispensationalism, as a system of theological interpretation [originating with Darby] ... was not known before in the history of Christian thought."[7] These "basic principles of interpretation ... depart radically from the historic Christian faith, and ... are often diametrically opposed to what the church always believed."[8]

Darby insisted that the Bible must be interpreted in accordance with two exclusive "dispensations," one concerning the Jews (as an extension of the ancient Israelites) and one concerning the Christian church. These were "the hinge upon which the subject [prophecy] and the understanding of scripture turns."[9] God's treatment of, and plans for, and promises to, Jews and Christians were exclusive of one another. Moreover, the prophesied glorious millennium involved not the Christian church, but rather the restoration of the Jews to Palestine as the fulfillment of God's biblical promise to his chosen people. God did not go back on his word; he would keep his promises to Israel and the Jews.

Darby was not alone in his eschatological interests. Back in 1821 the Reverend James Haldane Stewart of the Church of England, distressed by the worldly occupations and ambitions of the church, had gathered a group of clergymen from several denominations to pray for an outpouring of the Holy Spirit to overcome the disunity of the body of Christ, the Christian church.

Among those present was Edward Irving. Irving believed that the established church had reached such a lapsed state it would soon suffer divine judgment. He had been reading the recent translation into English of Manuel Lacunza's *The Coming of the Messiah in Glory and Majesty*, in which the traditional symbolic interpretation of the biblical book of Revelation was supplanted by a literal futurist rendition: In the end an Antichrist will persecute Christians during a violent era of "tribulation," followed by Christ's return to destroy the Antichrist and establish the millennium. Irving was soon preaching this end-time scenario in London, causing quite a sensation.

Then, beginning in 1826 and running to 1830, the wealthy evangelical banker Henry Drummond convened the Albury Park Conferences at his home in Surrey for the discussion of "biblical prophecy"—a term referring to anything concerning the end-time. Irving virtually dominated the discussions.

At the last of these conferences it was announced that miraculous gifts of the Spirit, such as those experienced at Pentecost, had been received in Scotland. In a rustic cottage a teen-aged girl named Margaret Macdonald had had a vision of the end-time in which she saw Christ take up his church in the "Rapture." As well, she witnessed "a fiery trial which is to try us [for] the purifying of the real members of the body of Jesus."[10] Those who pass through this oppression of the church by the Antichrist "will be counted worthy to stand before the Son of man."[11] Was Margaret Macdonald's vision, along with speaking-in-tongues in a London church, a sign that the Last Days were imminent?

All of this added to Irving's prestige. He was invited to play a key role in another series of discussions on eschatology at Powerscourt House, the home of Lady Powerscourt, located in the same Irish county as Darby's ministry. Back in 1826 Lady Powerscourt attended the Albury Park Conference and was so impressed with Irving she had been holding tea every second Tuesday for the discussion of biblical prophecy, presided over by the rector, the Reverend Robert Daly. Then in 1830 Irving stayed with Lady Powerscourt while he presented a series of lectures in Dublin on the Second Coming. At that time it was decided to hold three conferences from 1831 to 1833 at Powerscourt House, to which persons from all over Britain were invited.

Excitement concerning the Second Coming was rampant around 1830. Reverend E. Synge invited a number of clergymen to his estate to discuss biblical prophecy. The monthly *The Christian Herald*, edited by "a clergyman of the established Church," was founded in Dublin as a forum for the discussion of unfulfilled biblical prophecy. The Reverend S. Madden published *The Nature and Time of the Second Advent of Messiah* in which he stated that the Second Coming was imminent. Christ would return to destroy the apostate church, restore the Jews to Palestine, and institute his kingdom on earth.

The new directions of Darby's religious thinking caused him to search out and fellowship with others of like religious convictions. Through a friend he became acquainted with individuals centered around Trinity College in Dublin who, dissatisfied with the legalism of the Church of England, wished to recreate what they believed to be the essence of the New Testament church. They gathered together for worship and prayer to focus on Christ and the Bible. All shared an evangelical Calvinistic perspective: belief in the supreme authority of Scripture, and the expectation of an imminent and premillennial Second Coming.

At his brother-in-law's in Dublin Darby met Francis William Newman, tutor to his brother-in-law's family. The two discussed theology and Newman was overwhelmingly impressed with Darby, both the man and his thinking. Newman wrote to Benjamin Wills Newton at Oxford University concerning his enthusiasm for Darby's end-times ideas. In 1830 Newman persuaded Darby to accompany him to Oxford, where he invited Newton to join him and Darby for tea. He was delighted to find Newton just as excited about this Irish clergyman as he was.

Newton had begun a brilliant scholarly career at Oxford intending to become a priest with the Church of England. But at Oxford he turned to Calvinism, much as a result of the influence of Henry Bellenden Bulteel. Bulteel was the curate at St. Ebbe's Church in Oxford. A passionate Calvinist, he was attracting so many university youths to his ministry that the university blacklisted those who attended his sermons. Newton's name was at the top of the list.

Calvinism was gaining such disfavor at the university that Newton would later say that had he not been awarded his fellowship back in 1826 he would not have received it in the years immediately following. Then in 1831 things came to a head. It was Bulteel's turn to preach a sermon at the University Church. The procession began from Newton's rooms in Exeter College. Newton had read the sermon beforehand and knew there would be fireworks. He was not mistaken.

Bulteel's sermon might as well have been titled "The Calvinist Manifesto." He proclaimed Calvinist doctrine from that prestigious pulpit, and denounced the established church: Why was the church the servant of the state? Why were pious Calvinists being denied ordination, while youths of notorious repute were being ordained?

A few months later Bulteel was defrocked. Newton decided not to proceed to ordination with the Church of England. He left the established church, never to return.

Newton invited Darby to come with him to his home town of Plymouth. In late 1831 Darby and Newton started a fellowship much like that Darby had joined in Dublin. At Plymouth Darby became the guiding spirit and dominating personality of a movement to be known as the Plymouth Brethren.

Brethren theology came out of the crucible of heated controversy and the battle for leadership of the movement. Darby's willful confidence in the rightness of his ideas, and the magnetism of his person, allowed his ideas to supplant those of others in the fierce controversies which characterized the early years of the movement. Nothing was allowed to stand in Darby's way if he thought others were perverting what he believed to be Christian truth. Close friends of long standing soon became "enemies of Christ," "seducers of the faith." He felt duty-bound to expose and refute anything he regarded as fallacious doctrine. Darby felt chosen by God, much like the biblical prophets of old: "The Lord always gave me different work to do from what I lay out for myself ... and puts me into positions I little seek."[12]

Exact clarity concerning the details of Darby's innovative theology is not possible because he wrote more than forty volumes of six hundred pages each containing many inconsistencies. Moreover, Darby's writing has been described as "slovenly, tortuous and obscure,"[13] "almost uniformly unintelligible."[14] Even Darby's closest friend, perhaps greatest admirer, and the editor of his *Collected Works* could not deny the defects of Darby's writing style: "He delighted in a concatenated sentence, sometimes with parenthesis within parenthesis.... This made his writings, to the uninitiated, anything but pleasant reading ... almost unintelligible...."[15] Nevertheless, what was lacking in Darby's style of writing was more than compensated for in the force and passion of his words. As one of his theological opponents admitted, "J. N. D. writes with a pen in one hand and a thunderbolt in the other."[16]

Darby's system of dispensations implied a special hermeneutic, a special manner of interpretation of the Bible. To properly understand the Bible, Darby insisted, one must know how to "rightly divide the Word"—know which parts of Scripture pertain to which dispensation. Much of Scripture is addressed to the Jews; some is addressed to the true church. Even within the gospels there are passages addressed to the Jews and passages addressed to the true church.

Darby maintained that when correctly administered, his hermeneutic eliminates apparent contradictions in Scripture. When two passages appear to be inconsistent, they are not; God does not contradict himself. Instead, the reader is confusing passages belonging to different dispensations. When Scripture is "rightly divided" it can be read literally; there is no need for difficult or spiritualized interpretation.

Dispensationalism leads to a restricted Scripture for the Christian. Because—as dispensationalists insist, against Christian tradition—the church did not begin until Pentecost, some dispensationalists claim that nothing in the gospels is applicable to Christian living. Not the Sermon on the Mount. Not the Lord's Prayer. None of Jesus's ethical teaching.[17]

Darby's idea of dividing Scripture up in this manner caused a furor among some of the leading Brethren. B. W. Newton, in particular, was dead set against any discontinuity between Israel and the Christian church. He insisted upon the integrity and unity of God's dealings with humankind. Scripture, from Old Testament through New Testament, was a unit.

Newton's cousin by marriage, Samuel P. Tregelles, was also a prominent member of the Brethren. Tregelles was a leading biblical scholar and textual critic and had worked on the *Englishman's Greek and Hebrew Concordances.* He considered Darby's innovative hermeneutic as the "height of speculative nonsense."[18] Historian Clarence Bass notes, Darby "became absorbed in a system of interpretation which carried him far beyond the historic faith."[19]

By the mid-1840s Darby and Newton disagreed over several points of doctrine. Newton became alarmed over what he saw as Darby's "overbearing manner, both in speech and action in which he seeks to occupy this censorial position."[20] He feared Darby was intent on establishing "the supremacy of one mind ... that has wandered from the orthodox truth of God and has ceased to be in subjection to His Word."[21]

For Darby, the Rapture occurs before the tribulation. Newton believed the true church would have to endure the tribulation. Yet by placing the Rapture *before* the tribulation Darby's version was sure of eventually winning out. Why should the true Christians have to endure the violence and horror of the tribulation? Certainly no Christian would want to. Hence, almost a century later in America, what became known as "pre-tribulational" premillennialism would dominate the fundamentalist movement. As Charles B.

Strozier notes, this "is probably the single most significant theological inno-vation in contemporary fundamentalism,"[22] "a crucial part" of the end-time scenario. Instead of fearing the end-time, fundamentalist Christians look for-ward to the Last Days with anticipation. Without this pre-tribulational Rap-ture the eschaton would be a living nightmare. To this day the expectation of a pre-tribulational Rapture offers believers an abiding comfort and secu-rity: The End "is definitely coming ... but it doesn't scare me, because I'm a Christian. It'll be other people who will suffer."[23]

To be included in the Rapture a person must be part of the true Christian church. As doctrinal disputes increased Darby became ever stricter regarding who was included. He saw himself as "guarding the beloved sheep of Christ against the work and power of Satan."[24] The Christian must "set a barrier against ... the infection of an abominable evil."[25]

Just as the Brethren had separated from the defiled established church, one must separate from Brethren who do not follow Scripture in doctrine and practice. (This really meant separation from any who did not agree with Darby's theology.) Darby refused to "break bread" with Newton's group; he set up his own "table," gathering to him a loyal following.

Darby recommended separation from anyone who came in contact with anyone who did not believe and practice according to the Bible. If one person in a congregation was not strictly biblical in belief and practice, the whole congregation was tainted because they fellowshipped with that person. The same would apply to anyone who had any contact with any member of that congregation, and so on and on.[26] A congregation could not accept an indi-vidual excommunicated by another congregation. There seems no end to this "progressively centrifugal nature"[27] of separatism, until eventually those who remain may find themselves "eating their gingerbread all by themselves in a corner."[28]

This practice of separation plagues dispensationalists to this day. As his-torian Clarence Bass observes, "The devastating effects of this spirit upon the total body of Christ cannot be underestimated."[29]

Separatism continually reduced the number of true Darbyite acolytes. Darby must have felt a need for new blood. America beckoned.

10

Made in the USA

In his book *With God on Our Side* William Martin observes that dispensationalism was "a relatively new scheme of biblical interpretation that would have an incalculable impact on evangelical theology."[1] This has been particularly true in the United States where, from its introduction in the mid-nineteenth century, dispensationalist theology has been of profound significance.

Darby had developed a theological system which appealed to millenarians reeling from the aftermath of the Great Disappointment. While it was true that just after this disaster American premillennialists sought to distance themselves from Millerism and any hint of the fanaticism so often associated with this movement, millennialism had not lost a beat. It remained the essence of the American national ethos. Almost upon the heels of the Great Disappointment the moderator of the General Assembly of the Presbyterian Church, clergyman Samuel H. Cox, proclaimed: "I really believe that God has got America within anchorage, and that upon that arena He intends to display his prodigies for the millennium."[2]

On several levels Darby's dispensationalism fit the needs of American millenarians wishing a scriptural base for their beliefs. In 1853 an article in *The Princeton Review* noted: "Millenarianism has grown out of a new 'school of Scripture interpretation'.... The central law of interpretation by which millenarians profess always to be guided, is that of giving the literal sense."[3] A few years later another writer observed: "A literal interpretation is, indeed, the basis on which the Millennial edifice chiefly rests."[4] Here is where Darby would have special appeal. Literal reading of the Bible was a distinctive characteristic of Darbyism. As historian Ernest Sandeen notes, "One major characteristic of the dispensationalists is their particular concern for biblical literalism."[5]

A bulwark against the biblical critics, Darby's dispensationalist hermeneutic allowed for a tight literal interpretation, while at the same time providing a way around the many anomalies found in the Bible without resorting to the looser metaphorical interpretation of the liberals.

Finally, the doctrine of the imminent Second Coming and the Rapture would prove to be a major selling point for dispensationalism in America.

Americans were aware of Darby at least as early as 1853 when an article in the *Quarterly Journal of Prophecy* reviewed one of his books. Darby's opaque style of writing drew a humorous comment: "When a person undertakes to expound Scripture, it is supposed ... that he can make himself understood."[6]

In 1854 James Inglis began to publish *Waymarks in the Wilderness*—an echo of the early New England colonists' "errand into the wilderness." *Waymarks* consistently preached Darby's doctrine of the imminent Second Coming and secret Rapture; and the writing of the Brethren—Darby, Newton, Tragelles, and many others—was continually reviewed and repeatedly referred to.

By 1863 a new journal, *Prophetic Times*, edited by a widely diversified group of clergymen—Lutheran, Episcopal, Presbyterian, Baptist, Dutch Reformed, among others—had begun publication. The title page indicated its *raison d'être* and major interest: "A new serial devoted to the exposition and inculcation of the doctrine of the speedy coming and reign of the Lord Jesus Christ, and related subjects."[7] In the first issue the editors stated their creed, one heavily influenced by Darbyite dispensationalism. Not only is the term "dispensation" employed three times, the postmillennialist viewpoint is called "an unchristian delusion." A few passages from the creed deserve quoting: "That we are living in the last periods of the present dispensation.... That Christ will soon reappear upon the earth to avenge His elect.... That the saints ... received up in the glorified state ... shall escape the dreadful tribulations which are to mark the last years of this dispensation...."[8] Here clearly is reference to Darby's pre-tribulation Rapture. The diversification of the denominational backgrounds of these editors indicates how widespread these dispensationalist beliefs had become in the United States at this early date.

Darby first came to the United States in 1862, staying for four weeks. After this he became a steady sojourner. From 1862 until 1877 Darby made seven visits, residing for forty percent of that time. He spent most of his time in the big cities—Detroit, Chicago, Saint Louis, New York, and Boston—visiting New York nine times and staying five months in 1867–1868 and four months in 1874–1875, and visiting Boston eight times and staying two months in 1875 and again in 1876. During his final trip he remained in those two cities for fifteen months.

Darby professed that his mission in the United States was to spread the gospel of dispensationalism and to get converts to leave their respective backsliding churches: "Our real work ... is to get Christians clear practically of a great corrupt baptized body."[9] Although he won many converts, only a small number of these left their denominations.

While Darby may have been frustrated in his desire to woo Christians away from their traditional denominations, he did make one convert who would have a profound influence on the direction of conservative Christianity in the United States in the upcoming decades. Darby preached from the pulpit of Saint Louis's Walnut Street Presbyterian Church. Its pastor was none other than James Hall Brookes, soon to become a leading advocate for dispensationalism and a leader in the premillennialist movement.

A type of Darbyite premillennialism began to catch hold, but not as a popular movement. Instead, this brand of thought new to America fascinated a small number who preached to their congregations, wrote books, and published in millennialist journals.

Then in 1868 occurred a seminal event in the evolution of American millennialism. James Inglis, the founder of *Waymarks in the Wilderness*, along with an editor of *Prophetic Times*, a preacher from the Plymouth Brethren in Ireland, and several others, held a small private conference in New York City. They agreed to gather for conferences in future years in such places as Philadelphia and Saint Louis to emphasize "the doctrines of the verbal inspiration of the Bible ... and the personal imminent return of our Lord from heaven."[10] This was the beginning of a series of conferences which would run through the end of the century, fostering the broad dissemination of premillennialist and dispensationalist beliefs, providing an occasion for forming longtime like-minded friendships and networking, and eventuating in a protodenominational fellowship with an acquired leadership and specific doctrinal interests.

In 1875 the Reverend James Hall Brookes took over leadership of the conferences. Brookes had studied at Princeton Seminary, had spoken at earlier conferences, and was widely known through his writing in *Waymarks in the Wilderness*. He was the principal speaker in the 1875 conference known as the Believers' Meeting for Bible Study.

For the next several years this conference met annually for one or two weeks in the summer, usually at a resort setting. Because it convened at Niagara-on-the-Lake from 1883 to 1897, it became known as the Niagara Bible Conference. As historian Sandeen notes, "Virtually everyone of any significance in the history of the American millenarian movement during this period attended the Niagara conference."[11] This included more than 120 leaders and speakers. Many in attendance were not Darbyite dispensationalists, but all came from that Calvinist heritage which formed a cornerstone of American Protestantism from the time when the *Arbella* arrived at the shores of America.

Brookes attended virtually every conference until his death in 1897, and served as its president and guiding light. Brookes describes the idyllic scene which greeted attendants: "...the porches were filled with eager hearers of the Word. The place too becomes more beautiful as the years go by, and it would be difficult to find a spot better suited to the quiet and prayerful study of the Sacred Scriptures. The building in which the Conference meets, overlooking Lake Ontario and the River Niagara, and surrounded by green trees, is secluded from the noise of the world; and so excellent were the arrangements for the accommodation of the guests, both in Queen's Royal Hotel and in the boarding houses of the village, that not a word of complaint was heard from anyone."[12]

These conferences involved more than pleasant and congenial company and dozing in the warm summer sun in "the quietest and sweetest of retreats."[13] The focus was on "study concerning 'the things of the Kingdom of God.'"[14] A standard day comprised two addresses in each of the morning and afternoon, and a fifth in the evening.

To avoid theological controversy Brookes drew up a creed. Considering that Brookes recommended works by the Brethren, that he visited B. W. Newton back in 1862, and that Darby was invited to preach in his Saint Louis church, it is not surprising that Brookes's creed was replete with dispensationalist theology.[15] It included a denial of the postmillennialist position that the world will improve; it affirmed the verbal inspiration and inerrancy of Scripture; it affirmed the premillennial Second Coming of Christ. Leaders and speakers at the Bible conferences consistently adhered to the Darbyite doctrine of the any-moment Second Coming, particularly at the 1884 conference where "it came to be the 'fashion' of every speaker to 'ring the charges' on the possibility of Christ coming any moment—before the morning dawned, before the meeting closed, and even before the speaker had completed his address."[16] To those who attended the Bible conferences none of this seemed unusual or innovative.[17] Indeed, one described the Plymouth Brethren as nothing more than the "ultra-Protestant movement."[18]

On October 30, 1878, at Holy Trinity Episcopal Church in New York City American dispensationalism took a giant step forward. On that date was called to order the first session of a new type of conference — the First American Bible and Prophetic Conference. It was organized by eight premillennialists drawn from the leaders of the Niagara conferences. Its purpose was not only to focus on the premillennial Second Coming through the reading of papers exclusively on that topic, but to draw public attention to the vigor of the premillennialist movement. It was a mustering of forces, the recognition of a common front against postmillennialist clergy. The great majority of those at the conference came from New England, New York, New Jersey, and Pennsylvania, but not a single person from the Deep South. Most significant was a group of conservative Calvinists related to Princeton Theological Seminary. Historian Sandeen writes, "The 1878 Premillennial Conference marks the beginning of a long period of dispensationalist cooperation with Princeton-oriented Calvinists."[19] Beginning with the 1878 conference these two groups could be found speaking at the same occasions and publishing in the same journals in an informal alliance against "modernism."[20]

The 1878 conference provided the premillennialist movement the publicity it craved. For an entire week it received good coverage in the *New York Tribune* which published an extra edition of fifty thousand copies providing the addresses in full. The proceedings were published in book form under the title *Premillennial Essays*, and several religious journals mentioned the conference.

The Second American Bible and Prophetic Conference was held in November 1886. An article in a Baptist paper indicates a widening acceptance and growing support for premillennialism among clergy and Christian scholars: "Premillennial views, whatever may be said of them, have become so widespread in the various denominations, not excluding the Baptists, that it is folly to ignore this mode of Christian thinking."[21] Historian Ernest Sandeen observes, "Darbyite dispensationalism dominated late nineteenth-century American millenarianism."[22]

There were many conferences during the last decades of the nineteenth century and the early years of the twentieth on various subjects of interest to Princeton-style Calvinists, premillennialists, and dispensationalists. Notable among these was the Northfield Conference, not only because of its duration (1880 to 1902), but because of its connection with Dwight L. Moody. Moody's presence, and his vast influence upon the Protestantism of his day, lent credence to the dispensationalism promoted at these conferences.

In 1909 American dispensationalism marked another milestone. In that year was published the *Scofield Reference Bible*, acclaimed "the most effective tool for the dissemination of dispensationalism in America."[23]

The Scofield Bible was the brainchild of Cyrus I. Scofield. Scofield had fought for the South in the Civil War, then was admitted to the bar and served in the Kansas legislature before converting to dispensationalism and deciding upon a career in the ministry. With no formal biblical education, Scofield learned from his pastor, none other than James Brookes. Brookes took the younger man under his wing: "During the last twenty years of his life Dr. Brookes was perhaps my most intimate friend, and to him I am indebted more than to all other men in the world for the establishment of my faith."[24] Under Brookes's tutelage Scofield became a staunch supporter of the premillennialist movement, the Scofield Bible being only one of his major contributions and innovations.

Scofield conceived the idea of his Bible almost two decades before starting work on it in 1902. When he completed a first draft in 1908, he consulted other dispensationalists for their suggestions before going to press. In the preface to the published version Scofield called his work "a perfected text,"[25] claiming that until this point "the many excellent and useful editions of the Word of God left much to be desired."[26] Scofield added copious editorial notes on the same page as the biblical text, focusing the biblical text into neat dispensational divisions for the reader. The Scofield Bible so subtly mixes text and dispensationalist interpretation that many readers find it difficult to differentiate between dispensationalist doctrine and the words of Scripture. Hence for many, Scofield's notes have come to acquire almost biblical authority.

The project was backed and financed by a large group of influential men for the purpose of spreading the dispensationalist message. A parody of a popular gospel song at that time — "My hope is built on nothing less / Than Scofield's notes and Moody Press"[27] — speaks of their success. The Scofield Bible brought dispensationalist theology to the laity as nothing had before, or has since. In the words of one fundamentalist, it remains to this day "the single most influential publication in Fundamentalism's history."[28] The *Scofield Reference Bible* has remained "the Bible" for fundamentalists since the time of its initial publication.[29] Considering the fact that there are over three thousand different translations and editions of the Bible, this is a real boasting point.[30] Sales to date are estimated to be between thirty and fifty million copies.[31] It continues to be updated and revised for today's readers. As Charles B. Strozier observes, "It may well be that the Scofield Bible has touched the lives of more people than any other single book published in this [twentieth] century."[32] Scofield's Bible proved to be a brilliant instrument for the promulgation of the Darbyite doctrine of the secret Rapture of the true church.

Shortly on the tail of the *Scofield Reference Bible* came a series of publications collectively called *The Fundamentals,* published over several years from 1910 to 1915 in twelve volumes. This project was the brainchild of wealthy oil baron Lyman Stewart. A confirmed Darbyite dispensationalist, Stewart regularly traveled across the continent from his home in California to attend the Niagara and Northfield conferences. It was while attending one of the Niagara conferences that he conceived the idea of *The Fundamentals.* Although Stewart was an active lay member of the Presbyterian church he chafed at what he considered steadily increasing doctrinal laxity. The seminaries were not providing the clergy with an adequate biblical foundation. Eventually he would withdraw his support from the Presbyterian denomination and advise his friends to do likewise. But something needed to be done immediately to stem the tide of apostasy, to reassert Christian truths, and to counteract the Satanic forces of biblical criticism.

To rectify this Stewart dedicated his vast wealth to the publication and distribution of free Christian literature. But he was, by his own admission, a shy retiring man. He never mentioned the idea of *The Fundamentals* to anyone, even his wife. Then one Sunday afternoon in August of 1909 he attended an address given by the Reverend Amzi Clarence Dixon at Temple Auditorium in Los Angeles. Dixon was a regular speaker at premillennialist conferences. As Stewart heard Dixon attack the writing of a liberal professor at the University of Chicago, he knew he must speak with him. He gathered up courage and mentioned the idea of his pet project to Dixon. When Dixon said that this conception was "of the Lord" Stewart knew he had found his man. Six months later, in February of 1910, the first volume of *The Fundamentals* was published.

Stewart had already gained some experience in religious publishing. He had helped finance the *Scofield Reference Bible*. Before that he had originated and financed another publication. Decades earlier W. E. Blackstone's *Jesus Is Coming* had become one of the most popular dispensationalist books. Stewart republished it and paid for its free distribution to missionaries, seminarians, professors—he himself drew up a list of these. Hundreds of thousands of copies of the book were eventually printed.

Stewart chose Dixon to overlook the publication of his pet project, and set aside three hundred thousand dollars for its financing. Stewart left virtually all decisions about publication and the selection of material completely to Dixon. The project aimed at a balanced reaffirmation of fundamental Christian truths in, as Stewart worded it, "the chaste and moderate language which causes even the opponent to stop and read."[33] This was to be no militant manifesto, but rather an effort to build and maintain alliances within conservative American Protestantism, to establish a peaceful coalition of biblical forces in the face of a deteriorating religious environment.

Articles covered the gamut of conservative Christian thought and doctrine on subjects ranging from missions and evangelism to attacks on criticism of the Bible and the relationship between science and religion. The Bible was the most prominent topic. Twenty-nine articles were devoted to biblical apologetics. Five articles focused on the inspiration of Scripture, all written by dispensationalists. These authors went beyond the Princeton doctrine of inspiration and inerrancy, opting for the "dictated inspiration" of the entire Bible, "a Book dropped out of heaven."[34]

The first volume of *The Fundamentals* was mailed to 175,000 persons, "Compliments of Two Christian Laymen"—Lyman Stewart and his brother Milton, whose names did not appear anywhere in any of the volumes. By the third volume, later in 1910, this number had risen to three hundred thousand copies. Altogether three million volumes were distributed,[35] the goal being to reach every pastor, missionary, seminary student and professor, college professor, Sunday school superintendent, YMCA/YWCA secretary, and religious editor.

The Fundamentals would later be looked upon as a symbolic point of reference by more militant conservatives, but at the time of publication there was no intention of firing the first shot in some theological war. Rather, this project represented the final bow of a moderate irenic spirit among those in a conservative-premillennialist coalition dedicated to defending what they believed to be the doctrines fundamental to the belief of anyone calling himself "Christian."

Those in this coalition, "comprised of an alliance between two newly-formulated nineteenth-century theologies, dispensationalism and the Princeton Theology,"[36] ranged over a spectrum of personalities; two of the movement's leaders, Dwight L. Moody and Reuben A. Torrey, provide representative examples.

Moody was steadfastly opposed to religious controversy. Even his physical appearance did nothing to suggest controversy or emotion, but rather a reasoned calm, a model of middle-class respectability. A contemporary clergyman wrote, "...he looked like a business man; he dressed like a business man; he took the meeting in hand as a business man would."[37]

Unlike other evangelists, Moody did not preach hellfire and the wrath of God. Instead, like the liberals, he preached God's love. He was close to liberalism in his almost postmillennialist concept of America as a republic of virtue which could be saved by religious revival. Nothing should be allowed to get in the way of spreading the gospel. To meet this practical end he cultivated the friendship of prominent liberals. As a contemporary commented, "Not the least of the many services which Mr. Moody rendered to the age has been this practical demonstration that religion is more than theology, and that, based upon this principle, a true Christian catholicity is always possible."[38] George Marsden remarks concerning Moody, "His theology, although basically orthodox, was ambiguous to the point of seeming not be theology at all."[39]

While Moody was a confirmed premillennialist who believed in an imminent Second Coming he did not endorse the detailed doctrine and precise formulation of Darbyite dispensationalism. Because creeds are divisive, he avoided them whenever possible: "Christ's teaching was always constructive.... His method of dealing with error was largely to ignore it, letting it melt away in the warm glow of the full intensity of truth expressed in love.... Let us hold truth, but by all means let us hold it in love, and not with a theological club."[40]

Moody's words are strongly contrasted to those written in the same year by Reuben A. Torrey, a close associate of Moody, later to become a leading figure in the emerging fundamentalist movement: "Christ and His immediate disciples immediately attacked, exposed and denounced error. We are constantly told in our day [by the liberals] that we ought not to attack error but simply teach the truth. This is the method of the coward and trimmer; it was not the method of Christ."[41]

Torrey was the very picture of the staid severe Calvinist. An austere, rather pompous figure, "on the street he usually wore a high hat, and he always talked as though he had one on."[42] Torrey took pride in his "scholarly" preaching style. Even an admirer had to admit that he did "not remember his ever getting a laugh from any congregation."[43] A sympathetic biographer described Torrey as almost immune to emotion: "Rather was he swayed by the logical element of cold reason."[44]

Like the Princeton theologians, Torrey regarded ideas as things which are collected, then sorted and arranged — like the facts of science. This was painfully exemplified in his *What the Bible Teaches: A Thorough and Comprehensive Study of What the Bible Has To Say concerning the Great Doctrines of which It Treats*, a dry-as-dust five-hundred-page collection of thousands of biblical "propositions" supported by proof texts, as inspiring as a dictionary. Torrey despised any concession to aesthetics. He declared, as if they were mutually exclusive, "Beauty ... must always yield to precision and clearness."[45] He described the contents of *What the Bible Teaches* as "simply an attempt at a careful, unbiased, systematic, thorough-going, inductive study and statement of Bible truth.... The methods of modern science are applied to Bible study — thorough analysis followed by careful synthesis."[46]

Torrey's emphasis on "propositions" which formed the basis for religious creeds was strict Calvinist tradition. Adherence to the cognitive aspects of faith, to right doctrine, to correct belief had always been at the foundation of traditional Calvinism. Calvinism stressed ideas, ideology: "Calvinism in America nearly always demanded intellectual assent to precisely formulated statements of religious truth."[47] Then along came Jonathan Edwards and Finney with their concessions to the experiential aspects of faith over intellectual rigor. It is not surprising that dispensationalism, with its insistence on explicit statements of faith, received its greatest support among Presbyterians and Calvinist Baptists— both strong in the Calvinist tradition — and so little support among Methodists (who stress experiential faith).

That individuals of such opposite personalities as Moody and Torrey were found under the same religious umbrella was characteristic of that heterogeneous conservative Protestant movement of the late nineteenth and early twentieth century. What united these disparate individuals was their common cause against liberalism, and a staunch determination to defend the Bible against all critical inroads.

In the early years of the twentieth century the forces of biblical criticism were gaining ground. A whole generation of American seminary students at the more liberal institutions had been indoctrinated with this new and foreign learning. It was time for a more active defensive role than mere passive attendance at biblical and millenarian conferences. Most of the grand old leaders of the biblical premillennialist movement had passed on to their eternal reward. Younger conservatives needed to take up the torch.

The alliance between the two novel movements—the dispensationalists and the Princeton-oriented Calvinists—had been forged. Their respective doctrines had been woven into new cloth. As historian Sandeen observes, "Both dispensationalism and the Princeton Theology were marked by doctrinal innovations and emphases which must not be confused with apostolic belief, Reformation theology, or nineteenth-century evangelism."[48] As Sandeen correctly points out, "Their innovations were more significant than their preservations."[49]

Then came the First World War. Tensions induced by wartime fever, experienced by the population in general, exploded with particular vehemence between premillennialists and modernists. The division between liberals and conservatives was exacerbated. The calmer moderate spirit of pre-war times gave way to a decided militancy, as both sides participated in a verbal war. Soon each was declaring the other in league with Germany.

Early in 1918 there occurred an event which enlivened the hearts of premillennialists. British forces under General Allenby captured Jerusalem, freeing the holy city from the Ottoman Turks. Soon the Jews would once again be in possession of the promised land. All was falling into place within the dispensationalist timetable.[50] It was now only a matter of time until Christ returned. To celebrate and discuss the capture of the holy city premillennialists organized a conference to be held in late May. An enthusiastic audience of over three thousand packed the grand hall of the Philadelphia Academy of Music. The premillennialist movement had received a very definite shot in the arm.

At that conference anti-German sentiment was expressed: We must "make war against foreign innovation into our religious world." German theology "has been forcing its way into the veins and arteries of all our religious life. We ought to fight it to the finish."[51]

W. H. Griffith Thomas, a staunch premillennialist, saw a direct connection between German critical scholarship of the Bible and the collapse of German civilization and the resultant war. Thomas was not alone in his thinking. Words published in the dispensationalist periodical *Our Hope* made this premise abundantly clear: If the churches had "entered the conflict against German rationalism fifty years ago, as loyalty to Christ demanded, this most destructive and hideous of wars could never have occurred.... The new theology has led Germany into barbarism, and it will lead any nation into the same demoralization."[52] This theme was repeated in William B. Greene's opening address at Princeton Seminary in the fall of 1918. He blamed German atrocities in the war on evolutionary naturalism and the atheistic philosophy of Friedrich Nietzsche. Addressing an audience at the Bible Institute of Los Angeles, premillennialist Howard W. Kellogg said, "Loud are the cries against German Kultur.... Let this now be identified with Evolution, and the truth begins to be told." This philosophy of evolution, Kellogg maintained, would eventuate in "the wreck of civilization and the destruction of Christianity itself."[53]

The emotional climate of wartime provided premillennialsts with an unprecedented opportunity to air their views, and the apocalyptic aspect of war furnished a powerful example to support their view of history as regressive rather than progressive. It was all part of God's plan, and should be ground for hope in an imminent and glorious Rapture. Conservatives cited liberalism as evidence of the increased apostasy expected just before the end-time. Premillennialist doctrine concerning the end-time made more sense during this time of international chaos than ever before. Converts flocked to the call.

The melding of Darbyite dispensationalism with the Princeton theology concerning biblical inerrancy and verbal inspiration and with the Calvinist tradition of American Puritanism yielded a new religious force distinctively American. Made in the U. S. A.

And then the war was over. Just days later premillennialists gathered for a conference in New York City, flexing the muscle of a newly resurgent premillennialist movement. The anti-premillennialist attacks by liberals during the war years had brought together several strands of conservative thinking, uniting them in defense, forging a strong coalition ready to do battle. In contrast to the conferences of the former century, only a few of the leaders attending this conference had firm denominational ties; instead most were affiliated with Bible institutes. The modernist onslaught had stiffened opposition, made it more extreme and militant. The war in Europe might be over, but that among Christians in America was just beginning. It would be an intramural war, as proclaimed by David James Burrell, pastor of Marble Collegiate Church in New York (venue for some of the November 1918 conference sessions): "...the only atheism and infidelity in the world today which has any fight left in it is within the professing Church ... where Christ is denied and travestied and reduced to the meanest dimensions of diminutive man; and where the Bible is derided.... the Trojan horse that has been wheeled within our gates."[54]

The forces were gathered. The war for the religious soul of America was about to begin.

11

The Fundamentalists

The ink was barely dry on the armistice agreement, ending the war which was to end all wars, when President Woodrow Wilson penned his message to the American people: "Everything for which America fought has been accomplished. It will now be our fortunate duty to assist by example, by sober, friendly counsel, and by material aid in the establishment of just democracy throughout the world."[1] Later Wilson addressed the Senate, again outlining his high aspirations for the nation, reminding America of its Puritan beginnings, of its God-given destiny: "The stage is set, the destiny disclosed. It has come about by no plan of our conceiving, but by the hand of God who led us into the way. We cannot turn back. We can only go forward, with lifted eyes and freshened spirit, to follow the vision. It was of this that we dreamed at our birth. America shall in truth show the way."[2]

But Wilson was a tired sick man. His party did not nominate him for re-election. Not that it mattered. On November 2, 1920, Americans voted overwhelmingly Republican. The new president, Warren G. Harding, was the polar opposite of Wilson. All smiles and winning handshakes, Harding was a simple man, a friendly man, a small-town man, "just folks." Harding had no special vision for the American people, no high-sounding goals. He spoke not of the birth of the nation, not of its destiny. Americans were tired. Tired of war, tired of bearing the burden of some conceived noble "destiny," tired of feeling they must lead the world onward and upward, tired of some moral obligation as the hope of the world. Americans wanted to forget Europe, to forget the rest of the world. They wanted to crawl back into a safe cocoon, and avoid further involvement with the big bad evil world out there. Americans wanted to relax, to live life. And with this new president in the Whitehouse they would be allowed to relax. Months earlier they had taken solace in his words: "America's present need is not heroics but healing; not nostrums but normalcy; not revolution but restoration; ... not surgery but serenity."[3] Here was a man who understood their needs, their desires.

The emotional energies released by wartime exigency cannot be quickly turned off at war's end. The eat-drink-and-be-merry-for-tomorrow-we-die attitude which had infused the nation's youth during the war was now being translated into a craving for speed and excitement. Old moral codes had fallen to unconventional sexual liaisons and abrupt wartime marriages. These had their lingering effects on postwar society, a society tired of Wilsonian "important issues," a society ready to take a holiday. Public spirit was at low ebb, enthusiasm for private indulgence at high tide.

The revolution in societal mores began with the young generation. Their parents could read about it in F. Scott Fitzgerald's 1920 novel, *This Side of Paradise*. It could be expressed in one word — sex. It was everywhere: the new sex and confession magazines, the cinema. And in the automobile, the "house of prostitution on wheels," which allowed youth to escape parental supervision, indulge their passions in the next town where they were unknown and reputations would not be risked. Prohibition fostered a spirit of illegality. Bootleggers, speakeasies. The hip flask, the cocktail party. Times were changing. The old order was yielding to the new. A new age of harsh gaiety was dawning.

Young women no longer waited at home for that one special man to whisk them away to married life. They were out working, earning their own money. Money they spent on cosmetics, on cigarettes, and yes, on booze. Fathers and husbands no longer ruled. Women were men's equals. They had the vote.

The young woman and her man wanted nothing which hinted at the past with its "Puritan" lifestyle and "Victorian" manners. It was fashionable to be modern, to be sophisticated, to be smart, to be cynical and blasé, to flaunt a rebellious attitude, to shock. On the dance floor painted ladies in short frocks, bare arms, girated to the rhythm of a squawking sax. Guys and gals cheek-to-cheek, bodies glued together in tight embrace. Dr. Francis E. Clark, founder and president of the Christian Endeavor Society, was aghast. Such "indecent dance" was "an offense against womanly purity, the very fountainhead of our family and civil life."[4] If the women were lost, society was lost. Where would it all end?

Clark's concern was shared by other conservative Protestants. The formerly unchallenged certainties of bedrock American religious tradition were yielding to secular materialism and religious indifference. The old landmarks of church life were passing away. Why sit in a stuffy church listening to some stuffy preacher, when you could go for a nice drive in the country, or play a round of golf? The vitality of mainline denominational Protestantism was drastically declining, yielding to a more entertaining life-style. Despite a booming economy people were contributing far less than before to mission boards.[5]

The nation was going to hell on a handcart. An article in the conservative

The King's Business remarked that "there is no such thing as Christian civilization in any nation on earth today."[6] Conservative Christians were determined to stem the moral decline, to renew the religious vigor and rigor of past generations. John Roach Straton, a New York City pastor and ardent champion of moral reform, reminded Americans that their nation was "the ark of the covenant of humanity's hopes": "So surely as God led forth ancient Israel for a unique and glorious mission, so does he seem to have raised up Christian America for such an hour as this."[7] Had not America a special role in God's plan? Was not America to be a light to the nations, a city upon a hill? It was time for America to return to her Puritan roots, to *be* America.

America was undergoing a national crisis. Her very civilization was endangered. The war was over, a foreign war on foreign land, started by foreigners. But the foreign influence was threatening once again, causing paranoia concerning all things foreign. The "Red Scare": Rumors spread about a radical conspiracy against the government and institutions of the United States. Any moment bombs might begin exploding, Bolshevik hordes begin marching through the streets. There were strikes. There was a Socialist party — Russian immigrants, no doubt, who took their orders for revolution directly from Moscow. During the ensuing panic and hysteria it was wise for anyone with unorthodox political or economic ideas to keep quiet. To differ from the canons of the Legion, the precepts of the Rotary Club, was to be branded a communist. College professors could not afford to be seen reading liberal periodicals; they cancelled their subscriptions.

Conservative Protestants saw this as an opportunity. They would capitalize on the populace's paranoia concerning all things foreign, transform it into a desire to turn back to traditional "Americanism."

It was time to act, to cast off the Satanic foreign influence. It was time for America to turn inward. America had just fought a war to uphold civilization against barbarism. Now a war must be fought *within* America to preserve her nationhood. The only sure solution was a determined return to the essence of her nationhood — her biblical foundation. The words of David S. Kennedy published in *The Presbyterian* captured this sentiment: America's "foundation is the Bible, the infallible Word of God ... her perfect guide in her religious and social life.... There is but one remedy.... She must restore the Bible to its historic place in the family, the day school, the college and university, the church ... or else she might collapse and fail the world in this crucial age."[8]

With this in mind the new conservative coalition held a conference in Philadelphia in late May of 1919 which witnessed the founding of the World's Christian Fundamentals Association (WCFA).

The response was overwhelming. More than six thousand attended, demonstrating a renewed religious spirit and energy. Resolutions were formulated which would stand for the next generation. Committees were struck which were intended to function permanently, much like denominational boards. A nine-point creed highlighted the verbal inspiration and inerrancy of the Bible and the premillennial and imminent return of Christ. The vow to annihilate modernism got a resounding affirmation.

The subject of education was preeminent. Foreign influence, most specifically in the form of German biblical criticism, was undermining the very moral and spiritual foundation of the national ethos. Most American colleges had been founded by evangelical Protestants, and fostered by the Christian church. Elementary and secondary schools had been steeped in Protestantism. But that was in the distant past. Over the last generation the entire educational system had undergone a process of secularization. Professors, many educated in Europe, had replaced clergymen as presidents and educators in most colleges. Following European universities, professors encouraged students to question everything, including religious beliefs and the authority of the church. Many public universities no longer required attendance at chapel. Institutes of higher learning were turning out three times the number of students they had a half-century earlier, many of whom would go on to be educators, spreading the "Satanic poison that threatens the very foundations of the Republic."[9] In many curricula the physical and social sciences were squeezing out the classics, theology, and moral philosophy. It was a veritable invasion of science. Physics, chemistry, biology, anthropology, sociology, psychology. Moral codes were not universally valid. Human behavior, it turned out, was dependent upon chromosomes and glands. Freud, Jung, Adler. Reflexes, complexes, psychoses. Science was invading not only the educational system, but society at large. It filled magazines, occupied special columns in newspapers. Freud was discussed at cocktail parties. At luncheon Mrs. Brown asked Mrs. Green if she had heard of the latest theory about child rearing. What would science not discover, what would its handmaiden technology not invent, to improve human life? Religion, surely, was irrelevant and unnecessary. Science would provide.

Modernism must be cut off at its roots. Conservative Christians would educate their young people themselves. Christian youth would attend Bible institutes fashioned on the model of the Moody Bible Institute. A list of standards for these new schools was drawn up, and a list of approved schools.

Growth at the Moody Bible Institute indicated that these were not idle dreams, mere plans. Between 1904 and 1931 the gross operating expenses of the Moody Institute increased from $376,000 to almost six million dollars; the number of its buildings, from eight to thirty-seven; its staff, from 42 to 280; its student body, from 1100 to 17,200.[10]

The 1919 convention and the founding of the WCFA represented a decisively innovative movement within the Protestant church in America. Shortly thereafter this spirit of uncompromising radicalism became a divisive force in major Protestant denominations. In an editorial in the July 1, 1920, issue of the *Watchman-Examiner* Curtis Lee Laws coined a name for this new movement which would stick — "fundamentalist."

Fundamentalism was "comprised of an alliance between two newly-formulated nineteenth-century theologies, dispensationalism and the Princeton Theology."[11] In historian Sandeen's words, "...the millenarian movement had changed its name. The millenarians had become Fundamentalists."[12] An article in *The Christian Century* titled "The Threat of Millennialism" pointed to the doctrinal essence of this new movement: "The cult of fundamentalism with its verbal inspiration and infallibility, is chiliasm or Adventism with a new name."[13]

Millennialism had become a threat. But this was not the millennialism which had inspired the Massachusetts Bay colonists, nor that which had informed the new nationalism of 1776. This was a vocal, powerful, cohesive premillennialism, moving in a direction militantly opposed to traditional millennialism.

By 1921 denominational Protestantism was fully aware that within its bosom lay a threat to its very existence. The major problem with fundamentalism, seen from the denominational viewpoint, was its dispensationalist doctrine. Dispensationalism brought with it "a whole new theological vocabulary ... alien to many deeply versed Christians ... the new conceptions, far from being 'fundamentals,' were fundamental heresies."[14] So divergent was this new stream of thought, by 1927 even the president of Princeton Seminary felt compelled to ask, "Shall Princeton Seminary ... be permitted to swing off to the extreme right wing so as to become ... [fundamentalist]?"[15]

In May 1922 the celebrated Baptist preacher Harry Emerson Fosdick rallied the liberal side with a sermon which attracted widespread media attention: "Shall the Fundamentalists Win?" Soon it appeared that Fosdick's fears might be coming to fruition; the tide seemed to be turning in favor of the fundamentalists. By the beginning of 1924 an editorial in *The Christian Century*, the bellwether of liberal journals, titled "Fundamentalism and Modernism: Two Religions," baldly acknowledged an emergent dichotomy in American Protestantism: "Two worlds have clashed, the world of tradition and the world of modernism. One is scholastic, static, authoritarian, individualistic; the other is vital, dynamic, free and social."[16] The divergence between these two facets of Christianity, the editorial claimed, was as great as that between Christianity and Confucianism.

In his book *The War on Modern Science* Maynard Shipley feared "a political takeover" in which "much of the best that has been gained in American culture will be suppressed or banned, and we shall be headed backward toward the pall of the Dark Age."[17] The fundamentalists had the numbers — Shipley estimated twenty-five million.[18] A journalist wrote, "Heave an egg out a Pullman window and you will hit a Fundamentalist almost anywhere in the United States today."[19] From the cornfields of Iowa there rose a figure to champion the emerging spirit of fundamentalism. He preached to the common man and woman. You loved him, or you hated him. His critics, often ministers of the church, said he was a vain bigot, spewing venom and hatred. They despised this peddler of ignorance, this uneducated showman, this religious huckster whose revivals resembled a three-ringed circus act. His critics did not mince words, calling him "a vulgar harlequin, a ranting mountebank."[20]

Billy Sunday was a premillennialist. He believed that sin and lawlessness would increase until Christ returned to bind Satan; any human efforts to ameliorate the situation were both futile and misguided. But until that Second Coming he would try to save as many souls as possible. Unlike Dwight L. Moody, a roly-poly Santa Claus of a man, always ready to make peace, Sunday was of lithe athletic physique, a fiery fighter, a soldier on the front lines of a war of epic magnitude between Good and Evil. Traditional, ordinary weapons — the preaching of contemporary clergymen — would not suffice; it was "too nice; too pretty; too dainty."[21] The time had passed for such "offhanded, flabby-cheeked, brittle-boned, weak-kneed, thin-skinned, pliable, plastic, spineless, effeminate, ossified, three-karat Christianity."[22] Billy Sunday was a warrior and his God was a warrior God: "I have no interest in a God who does not smite."[23] In his battle to save souls Sunday was unrelentingly aggressive, uncompromisingly committed. Totally convinced of the validity of his beliefs, he was untiring in his efforts.

Sunday was all energy from the moment he fairly leaped onto the stage. His performance was less church service, more entertainment — acknowledged as such by the master showman and proprietor of the Barnum and Bailey Circus, Alfred T. Ringling. Sunday was always in motion. A fireball of energy, charging about the stage, arms waving, fists punching the air, sweat coursing down his face, he vomits forth a cascading Niagara of words. Always nattily attired — pressed suit, expensive patent-leather shoes, flashy new-car-salesman necktie with diamond stickpin — he is soon ripping off his jacket, rolling up his sleeves, removing collar and tie. He plays his audience like a master violinist — now soft caressing comforting words, now a machine-gun staccato of verbiage rising in volume and pitch to hysterical climax. The crowd is spellbound, filled with suspense, hanging on each word. Moved, molded, kneaded, the audience is powerless in an onslaught of sensationalism.

Sunday's fame spreads from small rural town to the big city. By 1916 he is in Detroit. Three thousand greet him as he steps off the train, more than for President Wilson a few months earlier. A crowd of 29,000 hear him speak in a structure built to hold 16,000. On his final day Sunday draws an audience of 50,000. The following year he draws even larger crowds in New York City.

Sunday spoke the language of the common man and woman. No high-falutin theological lingo. Just plain talk. Here was a man who gave voice to one's prejudices, even one's hatred and anger. He knew what it was to toil by the sweat of one's brow; he understood everyday frustrations; he was balm for the distressed soul. Billy Sunday was a steady rock in a confusing changing world, a model of virtue and sobriety in a culture gone mad. In Billy Sunday the old-time gospel with all its miracles came to life, the faith and ethics of bygone generations were reaffirmed. Billy Sunday offered reassurance, hope in a life beyond the here and now.

Mayors, governors, civic leaders supported Billy Sunday. His message of sobriety, hard work, personal pride, and religious duty could only lead to a more responsible citizenry and a healthier urban economy. Businessmen and financiers wanted their names associated with this paragon of religious conviction — it was good for their image, and for business. S. S. Kresge, Louis F. Swift, John Studebaker, H. J. Heinz ... the list ran on.

Billy Sunday was good for business, and he was good for America. In the years leading up to World War One, and during the war, he was at the peak of his popularity. It was a time when Sunday's brand of muscular Christianity hit just the right note. In a letter to Sunday former president Theodore Roosevelt remarked: "There is not a man in this country for whom I have greater respect and admiration than I have for you, and there is no man, in recent years, who has done better work than you, in this country."[24]

During the war a southern writer proclaimed Billy Sunday "the biggest force in the United States for patriotism ... Uncle Sam's bugler."[25] "The Star Spangled Banner" played as members of the audience came forward during an altar call. "Of course I shall preach patriotism. I have no more use for a man who is not loyal to his country than I have for a man who is not loyal to his religion."[26]

Sunday's brand of patriotism went much further than flags, fireworks, and lemonade on the Fourth of July: "Christianity and Patriotism are synonymous terms, and hell and traitors are synonymous."[27] Either you were for the United States *and* Christianity, or you were against the United States *and* Christianity. There was no in-between: "In these days all are patriots or traitors to your country and the cause of Jesus Christ."[28] Sunday ended his sermons with a Bible held high in one hand, the American flag in the other. For Billy Sunday Americanism and Christianity were one.

From the beginning Sunday backed America's war effort: "I am a 24 karat, one hundred cents on the dollar, twelve inches to the foot, sixteen ounces to the pound, two thousand pounds to the ton, major league rooter and booster...."[29] Sunday saw the World War as a holy war, a cosmic war between the forces of good and evil. God had chosen America as his land and his people. America was God's divinely appointed instrument for the enforcement of good in the world. The German people were the "Devil's hordes," the supreme threat to all that America stood for, the major source of "modernist" ideology, the home base of "higher criticism" of the Bible. Billy Sunday campaigned to destroy modernism. He was on a crusade to return America to her religious roots, to the Bible.

Billy Sunday reserved his most heated attacks for liberal modernist preachers and theologians and seminary professors — "fudge-eating mollycoddles," the Trojan horse, the fifth column within the ranks of the American clergy, "those damnable, infamous, vile, rotten, black-hearted, white-livered, beetle-browed, hog-jowled, weasel-eyed, good-for-nothing, dirty imps of hell and damnation."[30] These men were responsible for introducing all the "isms and schisms and ologies" which were poisoning American Christianity: "Thousands of college graduates are going as fast as they can straight to hell. If I had a million dollars I'd give $999,999 to the church and $1 to education."[31]

Americans must return to the Bible. Scripture was sufficient. It was the inspired and inerrant Word of God, the guide and sole authority for Christian life. There was no need for the fine intellectual distinctions of theology, for the abstruse concepts of religious dogma. Religious faith was not an intellectual process, a complicated philosophy, but rather a simple affirmation of the heart. With Bible in hand, Sunday could confidently say, "I know my doctrine is all right and I know that I do not need to have some doctor to doctor my doctrine."[32]

Billy Sunday's preaching inflamed the populace. He put blood in the veins of conservative Christians. He bolstered fundamentalism and infused the movement with a determined spirit of militancy. Would it prevail? Would it destroy the traditional denominations? Would the fundamentalists take over? Would premillennialism drown out postmillennial hopes of progress toward an earthly Kingdom?

12

Showdown in Dayton

Then occurred an event which dampened, even extinguished, liberal and denominational fears of fundamentalism, almost until our own time.

The "Monkey Trial"[1] was a pivotal event in the history of American Christian fundamentalism. Billed as "the trial of the century" by an excited press, it was the anticipated culmination of a slowly developing battle between science and conservative Protestant Christianity.

The target was Darwinian evolution. Half a century earlier Darwin's theory had been castigated by conservatives like Charles Hodge, viewed as anathema to Christian belief. By the time of *The Fundamentals*, however, many conservative theologians had assimilated evolution into a creationist context. James Orr wrote, "Assume God — as many devout evolutionists do— to be immanent in the evolutionary process, and His intelligence and purpose to be expressed in it; then evolution, so far from conflicting with theism, may become a new and heightened form of the theistic argument."[2] Even Princeton Seminary's B. B. Warfield conceded that evolution could be God's "procedure in creating man."[3] Some leading fundamentalists were taking a conciliatory position. A. C. Dixon was willing to accept evolution if it could be proved, and Reuben A. Torrey maintained that a Christian could "believe thoroughly in the absolute infallibility of the Bible and still be an evolutionist of a certain type."[4]

But by 1925, the year of the famous trial, much water had passed over the falls. During the intervening years paleontologists had made a series of startling discoveries which provided persuasive support for Darwin's theory of human origins. Such discoveries were bruited in the public press as "the missing link" and "the direct ancestor of modern man." For fundamentalists evolution was fast becoming *the* representative symbol of modernism, of all that was wrong with the spirit of the nation.

The South and rural areas everywhere had until this time been little touched by the secularization and liberalized Christianity most prevalent in the cities of the northeast. But when the fundamentalism of the northeast became the focus of national media attention, particularly in its emphasis on

130

Darwinism, it began to gain attention in the South. Soon a distinct anti-evolution movement swept into the South. By 1922 the annual convention of Southern Baptists ruled that evolution provided an irreconcilable contradiction to Scripture. In some cases the perceived conflict between science and Scripture took on a bizarre hue; in Kentucky, early that same year, a teacher was fired for teaching — in seeming contradiction to the Bible — that the earth is round.

One Sunday morning a Tennessee father of two lovely daughters and three stalwart sons listened to a sermon by an itinerant preacher. The sermon centered around a young woman who had left her rural community to attend a big-city university. There she learned about evolution, and as a result lost her faith; she no longer believed in God's existence. Alarmed, the man realized the same could happen to his own beloved children, for evolution was taught in the local schools.

John Washington Butler was no fire-breathing radical. A well loved and respected member of the community, he wanted only to protect the souls of his children. As a member of the Tennessee legislature, he introduced a bill making it "unlawful for any teacher in any of the universities, normals and all other public schools of the state which are supported in whole or in part by the public school funds of the state, to teach any theory that denies the story of the divine creation of man as taught in the Bible, and to teach instead that man has descended from a lower order of animals."[5] Butler justified this bill on high moral and patriotic grounds: "If we are to exist as a nation the principles upon which our government is founded must not be destroyed, which they surely would be if ... we set the Bible aside as being untrue and put evolution in its place."[6]

Educators in the public schools and at the University of Tennessee might privately have disapproved of Butler's bill, but they feared losing appropriations awaiting legislative approval if they spoke up against it. As for the legislators voting on the bill, who amongst them wanted to appear to be coming out against the Bible? Tennessee was in the heart of the Bible belt. Out of an adult population of 1.2 million, more than one million were registered church members.[7] The next election always looms large. Anyway, the governor would surely veto such a bill.

The bill passed in both houses with a huge majority. Governor Austin Peay had not only the next election on his mind, but pet reforms he wanted to push through; these required the cooperation of legislators like John Washington Butler. A delegation of Baptists—the largest denomination in the state—paid a visit to the governor's office; suddenly his mind was made up. On March 21, 1925, he signed the bill into law, but considered it primarily a symbolic act, a declaration of sentiment, "a distinct protest against an irreligious tendency to exalt so-called science, and deny the Bible in some schools and quarters—a tendency fundamentally wrong and fatally mischievous in its effects on our children, our institutions and our country."[8] Peay clearly did not believe, nor intend, that the Butler Act would carry any real legal force: "After careful examination I can find nothing of consequence in the books now being taught in our schools with which this bill will interfere in the slightest manner.... Probably the law will never be applied. It may not be sufficiently definite to admit of any specific application or enforcement. Nobody believes that it is going to be an active statute."[9]

And so things might have transpired had not Lucille Milner, secretary with the American Civil Liberties Union, noticed a small article in a Tennessee newspaper titled "Tennessee Bars the Teaching of Evolution." Thinking it might be important, she clipped it and passed it on to the director.

The ACLU had its roots in the First World War when Quakers sought a vehicle to protect religiously motivated pacifists from compulsory military service. It had since broadened its mandate to include the protection of the civil rights of individuals and minorities in any cause. Conflict between majority rule and individual liberty would be resolved by reference to the First Amendment; "freedom of speech," the rallying cry.

Notice of Tennessee's Butler Act ran through the ACLU like wildfire, for here might be an opportunity for the organization's first victory in court. On the ACLU's executive committee was Henry R. Linville. With a doctorate in zoology from Harvard, as president of the Teachers Union of New York City and chair of the biology department at New York City's DeWitt Clinton High School, Linville brought to the ACLU a special interest in a teacher's right to freedom of speech. (As it would turn out, the textbook used in Tennessee schools was George William Hunter's *A Civic Biology*. Hunter was a colleague of Linville at Clinton and succeeded him as chair of its biology department.)

A year previous to the passage of the Butler Act Linville had co-authored the ACLU's first public statement regarding academic freedom, in which anti-evolution laws were mentioned as a "chief issue" of ACLU concern. In response, the ACLU formed the Committee on Academic Freedom which promised to "deal with laws ... attempting to prohibit the teaching of evolution."[10] The ACLU would nationally spotlight any instance of abuse, and offered free legal assistance to anyone whose civil rights were violated.

On May 4 the *Chattanooga Times*, a newspaper opposed to the Butler Act, published an ACLU press release: "We are looking for a Tennessee teacher who is willing to accept our services in testing this law in the courts."[11]

That same day a young mining engineer read about the ACLU's request in his office at the Cumberland Coal Company in Dayton, Tennessee. George

W. Rappleyea was from New York City, a foreigner to southern ways. In college he came to believe in evolution and his faith had suffered. But after moving to Dayton he had again begun to attend church. Its liberal pastor convinced Rappleyea that Christianity and evolution were not contradictory. When he read the ACLU's notice in the *Chattanooga Times* he saw an opportunity to challenge the Butler Act, a statute which rankled the young engineer's sense of intellectual integrity. He needed to get some influential locals involved, and he knew just the carrot to draw them in — this issue could provide Dayton with state-wide, perhaps even national publicity, and that would be good for business.

Dayton was struggling economically. Its population had dropped to 1,800, from a peak of 3,000 in the 1890s. Back in those more prosperous and optimistic times the city fathers had envisioned Dayton as a hub for commerce and trade, a future gem in the so-called "New South." Northern money flowed into this tiny burg located close to the picturesque Tennessee River midst rising foothills. Railways were constructed, linking Dayton to wider markets. Coal and iron mines and a blast furnace attracted immigrants from faraway Scotland. In those sunny times Daytonians could imagine their city surpassing the competition in Knoxville and Chattanooga. But all too soon things went awry. The blast furnace ceased production, and even a newly-opened hosiery mill could not stem the downward tide. Growth stopped. The town was bleeding.

Rappleyea showed the ACLU notice to Fred E. Robinson, chairman of the county school board. Robinson's drugstore sold Hunter's *A Civic Biology*. Rappleyea convinced Robinson about the viability of staging a test case for the teaching of evolution in Dayton, and phoned ACLU headquarters in New York. The ACLU would pay expenses, even those of the prosecutor. Now to find a compliant teacher.

John T. Scopes was suggested. Scopes's father was an immigrant, a labor organizer, an avowed socialist, and an agnostic. The younger Scopes inclined toward his father's religious views; when he had been a student at the University of Kentucky he had admired the stand of its president against that state's anti-evolution legislation. But he was no hot-headed soapbox radical. Although he disapproved of the Butler Act, and accepted the evolutionary theory of human origins, he taught physics and mathematics, not biology — except while temporarily substituting for the regular teacher who was ill. Nor was Scopes anti-religious; he occasionally attended the local Methodist church, mainly to make friends.

A personable young man, Scopes seemed perfect for the part. He was shy and well-liked, a first-year teacher who coached football. His blond hair, innocent blue eyes, and boyish demeanor gave him a non-threatening and guileless air, while his horn-rimmed glasses suggested a certain earnest and youthful idealism. Moreover, Scopes was single and had no intention of remaining in Dayton for any extensive period of time, unlike the regular biology teacher who was a settled family man. He would have left Dayton by now for the summer break, but for two things—concern over two students recently involved in an automobile accident, and a certain blonde young lady.

Scopes was summoned to the drugstore. Rappleyea laid out the proposal. Scopes was not sure. Couldn't evolution be squared with the biblical account of creation? Besides, while he had made use of Hunter's textbook, he wasn't sure he had expressly taught evolution[12]—a technicality which mattered not to men hell bent to go to court.

After some discussion Rappleyea and associates were able to convince the young teacher to allow his name to stand. Business completed, Scopes drank a soda, then returned to the tennis match he had been playing.

Rappleyea lost no time contacting local newspapers and the ACLU. The latter agreed to provide financial assistance, legal advice, and publicity. It had really been all about publicity right from the beginning, both for the town and for the ACLU.

Scopes was instantly a national figure. A *New York Times* headline claimed that a motion-picture company had offered him $50,000 to appear in a production, and that an additional $100,000 was offered by syndicates. Scopes denied these claims.

To generate publicity big names were needed. The Dayton promoters invited H. G. Wells to present the case for evolution. Wells refused. Then in mid-May William Jennings Bryan agreed to offer his services for the prosecution. Three times on the Democratic ticket for president of the United States, Secretary of State under Woodrow Wilson, Bryan was a sure drawing card. Renowned and sought after for his speaking ability, Bryan had been campaigning against evolution in his own denomination (Presbyterian) and before several southern state legislatures. "I am now engaged in the biggest reform of my life. I am trying to save the Christian Church from those who are trying to destroy her faith!"[13] Never one to back away from the spotlight, Bryan eagerly anticipated the Dayton test case.

With a heavyweight like Bryan for the prosecution, the defense needed an equally prestigious figure. There was no need to go calling; days after Bryan entered the fray Clarence Darrow offered his services for free—the only time in his lengthy career.

Darrow was the most celebrated defense attorney of his time. His name constantly made national headlines. Both his legal expertise and his personal philosophy made Darrow the perfect opponent for Bryan. A proclaimed agnostic, Darrow delighted in challenging traditional morals and religious belief: "My object was to focus the attention of the country on the program of Mr. Bryan and the other fundamentalists in America."[14] The prosecution wanted to build up its ranks. But fundamentalist luminaries William Bell Riley, John Roach Straton, J. Frank Norris, and T. T. Shields had turned down pleas for assistance. What about Billy Sunday? At a Memphis crusade a few months earlier he had praised the Tennessee legislature for its leadership, focusing his rage against "the old bastard theory of evolution," holding high the flag of biblical literalism. Spotting among his audience a theologian who supported Darwinism, Sunday shook his fist in the man's direction and screamed, "Stand up, you bastard evolutionist; stand up with the infidels and atheists, the whoremongers and adulterers."[15] Billy Sunday mocked the idea that one thing could evolve into something else: "Old Burbank has developed the potato, but he hasn't made an orange out of it!"[16] He praised the mysteries of God's magnificent creation: "Why is it that what a cow eats turns to hair, what a chicken eats turns to feathers, and what a sheep eats turns to wool?"[17]

But Sunday sent his regrets. Even a personal request from none other than William Jennings Bryan could not convince Sunday to attend the trial. Sunday sent his best wishes: "All the believing world is back of you in your defense of God and the Bible."[18] His God-given talents did not include theological hair-splitting, nor the type of intellectual thrust and parry required for courtroom debate. Thanks, but no thanks.

With the cast in place for the trial the town made preparations for the big show. Newspapers had estimated crowds of up to 30,000. Six blocks of the main street were roped off as a pedestrian mall. Town officials had the Southern Railway schedule extra trains from Chattanooga, and asked the Pullman Company to park sleeping and dining cars on sidings. The county's first airstrip was laid out on a nearby pasture. Chattanooga supplied extra police and firefighters. To make sure Dayton would have enough safe drinking water and proper sanitation the state furnished a mobile chlorination unit and tended waste facilities. The Ladies' Aid Society supplied lunches for a dollar.

The Progressive Dayton Club formed the Scopes Trial Entertainment Committee to arrange visitor accommodations. They prepared a card index of rooms available in private homes. Vacant land owned by the coal company was turned into a temporary camp. Army tents and cots were requisitioned through Congress. The hotels did their part; the Aqua filled its halls with cots. A nearby mountain resort, Morgan Springs Hotel, engaged a jazz orchestra for nightly performances. Rappleyea fixed up an abandoned eighteen-room mansion outside town limits for the visiting defense team.

The scene of the trial got extensive refurbishing. The courtroom was painted, five hundred seats were added, and a movie camera platform was constructed. For visiting reporters a bank of phone booths was added in an adjoining room, and a makeshift press room was made ready in a storage loft over a downtown hardware store. Microphones would feed loudspeakers on the courthouse lawn and at four auditoriums around town. A speaker's platform was built on the courthouse lawn which was crisscrossed by newly installed water pipes and dotted with privies. Media outlets proliferated. Western Union strung telegraph wires from the courtroom to nearby cities and supplied twenty-two operators. Radio station WGN in Chicago would broadcast the trial live—a first in the history of radio—by connecting the courtroom microphones to special telephone lines. All of this would be put to good use. During the trial the print media put out 165,000 words a day; a total of two million words went out by telegraph.[19]

The citizens of Dayton embraced the upcoming event in festive fashion. The monkey theme was ubiquitous: pictures of monkeys in shop windows, a police motorcycle with the sign "Monkeyville Police," a delivery van with the words "Monkeyville Express." Robinson's drugstore, bearing the banner "Where It Started," offered "simian" sodas and stocked relevant reading material. The Progressive Dayton Club condemned what it viewed as a frivolous attitude to a serious courtroom issue. Some merchants complied and toned down their displays; others did not — why should they when the Progressive Dayton Club itself issued a souvenir coin with a monkey wearing a straw hat?

Then the big stars began to show. Greeted by a large crowd, Bryan arrived in Dayton three days before the beginning of the trial, along with a heat wave which pushed the temperature into the nineties. There the mercury would remain throughout, twenty degrees above normal.

The day before the trial the New York defense lawyers arrived. A young fellow grabbing their luggage caused alarm. Rappleyea intervened: it was okay, the young fellow was Scopes. The trial bore his name, but otherwise he was virtually forgotten in the glaring lights of the circus atmosphere, and would be throughout the proceedings.

Clarence Darrow arrived on the last train into Dayton the night before the trial was to begin. Movie cameras captured Darrow and Scopes embracing. Darrow announced his position: "Scopes is not on trial. Civilization is on trial.... Nothing will satisfy us but ... to prove that America is founded on liberty and not on narrow, mean, intolerant and brainless prejudice of soulless religio-maniacs."[20]

July 10. A Friday. Opening day of the trial. By seven o'clock in the morning, two hours before proceedings were scheduled to begin, spectators started to file into the courthouse. By 8:45 all seats were occupied. People stood in the aisles and around the walls, filling every possible space. The crowd spilled out into the hallways. Two hundred reporters were in attendance, including some of the nation's most renowned journalists. Their reports would dominate front pages around the country for the next few weeks. But most of the crowd consisted of locals—citizens of Dayton and farmers in overalls.

Then came the shining stars of the event. Cameras were rolling as Bryan and Darrow shook hands. The room thundered with applause. While the two men differed sharply over religion, they had worked together for political causes in years past and remained on cordial terms. Jackets were removed—daytime temperature was forecast to hit 100 degrees, and air circulation was inadequate for a room jammed with perspiring bodies. There was no air-conditioning. Several spectators and a member of the prosecuting team would drop from heat exhaustion before the day was over.

Born in the mountain hamlet of Gizzards Cove and a local resident all his life, the presiding judge, John T. Raulston, billed himself as "jist a reg'lar mount'neer jedge." Raulston was all smiles. This was his show. He had originally hoped to cover a vacant lot with a roof and seat twenty thousand people in tiers. As it was, he had set no time limit on the trial, expecting, and willing to allow, both Bryan and Darrow to give extensive speeches. He would keep daily sessions brief to draw out the total number of days; the town's businessmen would be glad of the extra business. All of this would help foster his career on the bench. This was his big chance. Up to this point his biggest cases had involved bootlegging and murder, none of which attracted widespread attention.

Outside the courthouse a carnival atmosphere was underway. Hot-dog stands. Sandwich stands. Watermelon stands. Youngsters peddling lemonade. Four steers roasting over an open pit. Vendors of this, that, and everything else. Step right up and for pennies get your picture taken with a live chimpanzee. View the fossilized remains of the missing link. Books on biology and religion. Signs everywhere—"Read Your Bible," "Come to Jesus," "Prepare to Meet Thy Maker," "Be Sure Your Sins Will Find You Out." A rationalist from Brooklyn railed against the stupidity of Christianity next to the Anti-Evolution League's display. Evangelists spouted the Word. A blind mountaineer bore a sign claiming he was the world's authority on the Bible, next to a representative of the flat-earth school of geology. "Every Bible-shouting, psalm-singing pulpit hero in the state poured out of the hills and brought his soapbox with him."[21] The action started early every morning and went late into the night. Dances and parties nightly. As Scopes would later write in his memoir: "From the beginning to the end of the test case Ringling Brothers or Barnum and Bailey would have been pressed hard to produce more acts and sideshows and freaks than Dayton had."[22]

The town took a beating in the national press. Many big-city journalists came to Dayton no doubt expecting, like arch-cynic H. L. Mencken, "to find a squalid Southern village, with darkies snoozing..., pigs rooting under the houses...."[23] What many were determined beforehand to find, they did find, even if that meant journeying into the neighboring hills. Nocturnal Holy Roller revivals furnished sensationalist print, typifying backwards southern culture. In his daily dispatches to Baltimore Mencken referred to the locals as "morons," "hillbillies," and "peasants." He told of the "degraded nonsense which country preachers are ramming and hammering into yokel skulls."[24] A group of mountain men determined to ride Mencken out of Dayton were persuaded by the chief commissioner to disperse. Mencken got the message; he slipped quietly out of town.

A few mountaineers showed up in town with their rifles in plain view, causing fear amongst out-of-towners, but they meant no harm; this was a common sight in Dayton. One Holy Roller left town for her mountain retreat, fearing "the mark of the beast" was on the inhabitants of Dayton: "They'll go down to the lake of fire.... I'm going to stay away, for something might happen to the courthouse."[25] These relatively rare examples provided good press, but they were mountain folk, not Daytonians. Most of those making a spectacle of themselves were from out of town, even out of state.

Many who crowded the downtown were curious Daytonians, civilized townfolk who came to see the show. Other Daytonians fled the city to avoid the chaos, or lease their homes to visitors. A spirit of hospitality prevailed. . A Bostonian was offered the key to a local house: "The house is yours." Even Mencken, in a quieter more reflective moment, had to admit, "The town, I confess, greatly surprised me.... What I found was a country town full of charm and even beauty."[26] Yet the caricature of Dayton as a southern hick town, created by journalists wanting a good story-line, never died.

The first days of the trial passed in jury selection and various motions and legal procedures. A powerful thunderstorm — which was jokingly attributed to divine displeasure at the anti-religious tone of one of Darrow's speeches— knocked out the town's power and water. The court was then without fountains and electric fans. Darrow's shirt was soaked in sweat. His wife fussed: shouldn't he put on another shirt? Still able to smile in the unbearable heat, Darrow replied, "Surely, my dear, do you not think it too hot for two shirts?"

On the second Monday, during the afternoon session, Judge Raulston moved the proceedings from the courtroom outside onto the platform which had been constructed on the courthouse lawn. Cracks had appeared on the ceiling below the courtroom due to the large crowd, and there was some fear of collapse.

Outside the crowd numbered close to 3,000, rather than the five hundred the courtroom could hold. The ambiance changed; it was a relaxed atmosphere. Spectators sat on the grass and makeshift wooden benches, in the sunlight and in the shade beneath the maple trees, and perched upon the branches of those trees. Boys moved among the crowd selling bottled pop.

A week had passed. The real action was to begin. Darrow called Bryan to the witness stand as the defense's expert on the Bible. An audible gasp passed through the crowd. The leader of the prosecution knew this was a mistake, but could not restrain the old man. William Jennings Bryan looked out over the people, sure this was to be his moment. He would stand up for his God. This was why he had come to Dayton.

But the William Jennings Bryan of 1925 was not that of 1896 — the young political wonder who had wowed the nation with his Cross of Gold speech. The passing years had laid a heavy hand upon this champion of morality and Christian faith. The young man had become an old man. Where once had flourished a flowing black mane, now a fringe of scraggly gray circled a shining bald pate. The former athletic frame had given way to an older man's paunch; the former bull neck was now shrunken and wattled. In his prime Bryan had a voracious appetite. Breakfast consisted of a whole cantaloupe, six eggs, ham, quail, fried potatoes, and two heaping stacks of pancakes swimming in butter, all washed down with several cups of coffee generously fortified with sugar. Now a victim of diabetes, he had to curb his appetite. Yet despite his physician's warnings he continued to enjoy the delights of the table. The handwriting was on the wall. He was jousting with death. Little did he know he was on his last days, that this was to be his last stand.

But within the old man's body throbbed the heart of the younger Bryan. His spirit showed no sign of waning. He was ready, and eager, to enter the fray. Pointing scornfully toward the defense team, Bryan issued a challenge: "They did not come here to try this case.... They came here to try revealed religion. I am here to defend it, and they can ask me any questions they please."[27]

Despite the gravity of the occasion, Darrow and Bryan often engaged in witty repartee.

> DARROW: What do you think?
> BRYAN: I do not think about things I don't think about.
> DARROW: Do you think about things you do think about?
> BRYAN: Well, sometimes.[28]

The spectators broke out in laughter. Judge Raulston was enjoying himself, laughing along with everyone else. He made no effort to restrain either gentleman, going with the flow, keen to see where things were heading. Journalists picked up on the humor. One remarked that Bryan was right to deny Darrow's definition of "mammal"; for clearly Bryan's shining pate had no hair, and clearly he did not suckle his young. Bryan, the experienced orator, could string words together effectively: "It is better to trust the Rock of Ages, than to know the age of the rocks." "*Some* believers in Darwinism retained their belief in Christianity ... some survive smallpox."[29]

Darrow's strategy was to demonstrate that the Bible cannot always be taken literally. Therefore, it is possible to interpret the biblical account of creation so that it does not contradict evolution. Hence, anyone teaching evolution would not be contravening the Butler Act, would not be teaching a "theory that denies the story of the divine creation of man as taught in the Bible." Darrow began to honed in on the attack. Bryan agreed that the Bible said God created the sun on the fourth day. But how could you count the previous days without a sun? Darrow asked. Bryan was forced to admit that these were "periods" of time, not necessarily days marked by the coming and going of the sun. Then Darrow asked the crucial question: Was the earth created in six days? "Not six days of twenty-four hours," Bryan conceded.[30] The fundamentalists were aghast. With those six words Bryan had slain biblical literalism. If "six days" did not *literally* mean six days, if it required interpretation, where would interpretation of God's Holy Word stop?

The leader of the prosecution tried to end Bryan's testimony. What was the purpose of this line of questioning? Bryan was incensed; he didn't wait for the judge's reply: "No other purpose than ridiculing every Christian who believes in the Bible."[31] A member of the defense team claimed Bryan was trying to get evidence into the trial record for use in a possible later appeal. "I am simply trying to protect the word of God against the greatest atheist or agnostic in the United States!" Bryan shouted, pounding his fist in rage.[32] The crowd thundered its approval. "I want the Christian world to know that any atheist, agnostic, unbeliever, can question me any time as to my belief in God, and I will answer him."[33] Soon Darrow and Bryan were standing, shaking their fists at one another, casting slurs and insults. Judge Raulston knew it was time to adjourn for the day.

The following day Darrow asked the jury to find the defendant guilty, which it did. This prevented Bryan from launching into a closing speech, and averted a hung jury, which would prevent a later challenge of the constitutionality of the Butler Act in a higher court.

The famous, or infamous, Scopes trial was over. That evening the reporters showed their appreciation for the hospitality of Dayton's citizens. They hired a hall, imported a band from Chattanooga, and invited the whole town. The townspeople joyfully danced the night away. It was a great finish to two wild weeks.

A few days later the *Nashville Banner* noted that "Dayton is back where it was before the trial began, a sleepy little town among the hills."[34] The 2,310 daily newspapers across the nation[35] which every day for two weeks smeared their front pages with every twitch of the trial quickly turned to other topics. As for Scopes, he had been virtually forgotten in all the hoopla. Despite the guilty verdict, the school board offered to renew his teaching contract provided he comply with the Butler Act. He declined. Expert science witnesses from the trial had gathered scholarship money for any field of graduate study Scopes might choose. He decided on geology at the University of Chicago. Passing up huge amounts of money for movies and lecture circuits — he wanted his privacy back — Scopes eventually settled down to life as a petroleum engineer.

Bryan remained in Dayton for a few days revising and expanding the closing address he had intended to deliver in court. Despite his far from positive showing during the trial, he was not discouraged. This address would be the clarion call to a new crusade against the teaching of evolution. The fight had just begun.

On Friday, July 24, arrangement was made for the *Chattanooga News* to publish this address. The next day Bryan addressed an audience of 2,000 to an overwhelmingly positive response. Things were looking up. "If I should die tomorrow," Bryan told a reporter, "I believe that on the basis of the accomplishments of the last few weeks I could truthfully say, well done."[36] That evening he continued to polish his address.

The next morning it was back to Dayton where Bryan led a Sunday congregation in prayer. After enjoying a hearty mid-day dinner at the home of friends, Bryan went upstairs for a nap. He never woke up. Fittingly, the final words of his last address were from a popular hymn — "We will be true to thee till death." His soul could rest easy. He had remained true to the faith, true to his Lord. Governor Peay announced a state holiday to mark Bryan's passing, proclaiming the man a "martyr to the faith of our fathers."[37]

It is ironic that Bryan was front and center in a trial that popular opinion came to see as the decisive battle between fundamentalism and the modern scientific worldview. While Bryan was quick to take issue with anyone who denied the divine authorship of the Bible, he did not consider himself a fundamentalist. Indeed, his emphasis on practical Christianity, on the moral life, on the need for social reform, placed him close to the thinking of such liberal advocates of the Social Gospel as Washington Gladden and Walter Rauschenbusch.

Bryan never became a dispensational premillennialist. The debate between premillennialists and postmillennialists seemed unimportant: "There are so many people who do not believe in the first coming of Christ, that we ought not to worry them about the second coming until we can get them to accept the first."[38] Bryan was not even against evolution per se, provided people understood that it was merely an unproven theory, not fact. Never a vindictive man, he did not gloat over the legal victory achieved during the famous trial, and offered to pay Scopes's fine of $100.

Unfortunately the trial cast a long and distorting shadow upon the image of this man of noble and upright character. Bryan was a fine example of a Christian gentleman who might have done much to bridge the gap between fundamentalist and modernist. Scopes found Bryan "a very warm person, who seemed to truly love people."[39] Concluding his biography of Bryan, Michael Kazin writes: "Bryan's sincerity, warmth, and passion for a better world won the hearts of people who cared for no other public figure in his day."[40] Bryan's love for his fellows and desire to better their lives rested upon "the doctrine that man, being a child of God and a brother of all the other children of God, must devote himself to the service of his fellows."[41] The idea that we are all children of God, all brothers and sisters, was no mere slogan, no idle dictum. Bryan and his wife counted Catholics and Jews among their personal friends in a day when this was risky for a politician.

Bryan, it seemed, was unable to see why his fellow humans could not better get along with one another. He insisted that "most of the conflicts between individuals and between nations grow out of misunderstandings."[42] While Bryan didn't back down when cherished principles or beliefs were at stake, "he showed a praiseworthy tolerance towards those who disagreed with him."[43] He was always a man of the middle road, a man willing to compromise, a man of peace. Bryan was always ready to fight the good fight, but he bore no ill will.

The subtle doctrinal differences which separate Baptist from Methodist, Methodist from Presbyterian, Christian from Christian, were not of importance to Bryan, but what they held in common. Bryan admitted there are many passages in the Bible which are difficult to interpret and could lead to theological differences. But why focus on these when so much of the Bible can be clearly understood? "If we will try to live up to that which we can understand, we will be kept so busy doing good that we will not have time to worry about the things that we do not understand."[44]

The "truth" of the Bible was not Bryan's ultimate concern. Rather, he emphasized its power to guide human life; he emphasized the Christ in the Bible who "went about doing good." As biographer Robert W. Cherny notes, Bryan "found Christian love more compelling than logic."[45] Sounding much like a postmillennialist, Bryan remarked, "Christian civilization ... rests on a conception of life that makes life one unending progress toward higher things, with no limit to human advancement or development."[46] Bryan represented the evangelicalism of former generations in which spiritual piety went hand in hand with an almost postmillennialist ideal of progress toward the Kingdom, an evangelicalism that fused national and religious interests. Ever the optimist, Bryan never lost faith in the destiny of the United States to lead the world in matters of morality and religion, or in "the essential goodness of Man who would respond immediately and wholeheartedly to the truth once he was made to see it and understand it."[47]

If fundamentalism wanted a poster-boy, a representative figure, Billy Sunday better fit the bill. A year after the Dayton trial Sunday had a chance to go up against a Unitarian minister from New York City who had studied at Leipzig. Each expressed his view in *Collier's* magazine. Sunday's opponent, the Reverend A. Wakefield Slaten, tolled the death knell of Christianity. Christ had never been more than a mere man, and Christianity no more than exaggerated myth, superstitious nonsense which the light of science and reason was rapidly showing to be misguided, an anachronism in these enlightened times. The next generation would revere the mighty processes of nature, and God as the "controlling force in the vast process of cosmic evolution."[48] Sunday launched his standard attack against intellectuals, foreigners, and modernists, while staunchly defending the foundations of his fundamentalist old-time-religion Americanism: premillennialist theology and the inerrancy of Scripture.

Sunday had done much to bring on prohibition and the Eighteenth Amendment — something he considered one of his greatest achievements. But the decade of the 1920s ate away at this accomplishment with its speakeasies, its bathtub gin, its hip flasks. Many men at Sunday's mature age would quit the good fight. Not Billy Sunday. Desperately treading water against the rising tide of secularism, pressing heroically into the hurricane winds of cultural change, Sunday stubbornly continued to pack his bags for the next town on the preaching circuit. He continued to fight uncompromisingly for the cause, despite the fact that his big-time crusades were now just memories preserved in scrapbook clippings. Now he could garner crowds of just one thousand for just one night. His wild antics in the pulpit were beginning to take on a spirit of frantic desperation.

His star was in decline. America was growing tired of his message. Just when Billy Sunday was most needed as a crusader against the forces of modernism his candle began to flicker. He was becoming old news in an era when novelty was everything. In an age noted for ballyhoo the great ballyhooer was losing his audience. The press was no longer eager to capture his latest bombast. Those who only a few years before might have entered tents and tabernacles to be entertained by this fiery pugilist of a man, now found a plethora of new competing forms of entertainment.

The stars of screen and stage had eclipsed those of the pulpit. As Sunday was leaving the tabernacle after one of his performances he asked a newsboy the direction to the local post office. The newsboy knew he was talking to the great Billy Sunday, but was clearly unimpressed. When Sunday invited the boy to "come to tonight's revival, I'll show you the way to heaven," the boy replied matter-of-factly, "How can you show me the way to heaven when you don't even know the way to the post office?"[49] In a culture of increasing secularism, the post office was infinitely more important than some faraway heaven.

But Billy Sunday left a legacy. He had shown fundamentalists how to organize for success, how to build a campaign machine. When he first came to New York City he was supported by nearly 50,000 persons, local volunteers who formed committees and helped map strategy. Women's groups, labor, clubs, organizations, businesses, church leaders— all were solicited for support. The press was informed and kept updated. Telephones were manned, flyers mailed. An army of supporters knocked on doors in every neighborhood.

Billy Sunday bequeathed a significant twist to fundamentalism, which would not become manifest until much later in the twentieth century. He had forged an ironclad link between fundamentalism and Americanism. He had melded premillennialism with an ardent patriotic Americanism formerly mostly found among postmillennialists.

During the trial William Jennings Bryan had made special appeal to southern hearts, to the culture of the South, to sectional pride. He praised southerners for their piety, for holding to the faith of their fathers while the rest of the nation was going astray. The biblical faith of the South would result in a new awakening, he assured his audiences, a religious revival which would start in the South and spread from there throughout America, perhaps throughout the world.

Southerners listened. Southern pride was stirred. Passing anti-evolution laws took on an almost patriotic flavor in the South, a symbol of southern pride and regional identity, although it must be pointed out that many anti-evolution bills were not passed into law. In Kentucky, for example, an anti-evolution bill was joined with another requiring that water in the state should run uphill! Oklahoma, in 1923 the first state to ban evolutionism, repealed its law. In nine states anti-evolution bills were defeated. Nevertheless, here and there throughout the South school boards restricted the teaching of evolution. Textbooks were sanitized. The Scopes trial hardly rang the death knell of the anti-evolution movement. Today 44 percent of Americans believe that "God created man pretty much in his present form at one time during the last 10,000 years."[50]

In the final analysis the famous Scopes trial was trial by public opinion and the press. In the popular press of the big cities modernism had won a clear victory. The South and rural America, but moreso fundamentalism and conservative religion in general, had lost. The journalist H. L. Mencken, writing after the Scopes trial, did much to fix upon the public mind a derogatory image of the fundamentalist Christian: Fundamentalists "are everywhere where learning is too heavy a burden for mortal minds to carry.... They march with the Klan, with the Christian Endeavor Society.... Poor and unhappy folk...."[51] Mencken was not alone in pouring scorn on the heads of fundamentalists. One writer remarked, "for the first time in our history organized knowledge has come into open conflict with organized ignorance."[52] The popular novelist Sinclair Lewis claimed that the Hebrew Bible was "interpreted by men superbly trained to ignore contradictions."[53]

During the years immediately following the trial northern journalists wrote about "the inquisition in Tennessee" and the South as "a cultural wilderness." In his highly regarded 1928 publication *The Rise of American Civilization* Charles A. Beard understood the Scopes trial as a "spectacular battle" in an ongoing "war" between rural fundamentalists and urban modernists. This dichotomy has remained imprinted upon the thinking of many in our own time. While the Scopes trial did nothing to slow fundamentalism in the South, it did brand the South and fundamentalism with a distinct "hillbilly" hue. Fundamentalism became associated with the poor, the uneducated, the country, the South. Fundamentalists suffered the disparagement and disdain of their fellow Christians in the mainline denominations as "'hicks' and 'rubes' and 'drivers of second-hand Fords.'"[54]

As historian Ernest Sandeen points out, "No stereotype of the Fundamentalist dies harder than the picture provided by the Scopes trial."[55] Although the campaign against evolution during the twenties may have been strongest in rural and southern areas, it is a mistake to identify fundamentalism with anti-evolutionism. Fundamentalism originated in the big cities of the northeast and was principally concerned with the verbal inspiration and inerrancy of the Bible, and with the premillennial and imminent Second Coming of Christ.

Fundamentalism was much larger than the anti-evolution movement. Dispensationalist premillennialism remained the "central"[56] doctrine of fundamentalism. As historian Sandeen, observes, "It is millenarianism which gave life and shape to the Fundamentalist movement."[57] Sandeen goes further: "Fundamentalism ought to be understood ... as one aspect of the history of millenarianism."[58] The millennialism which came across the Atlantic with the *Mayflower* and the *Arbella* was still very much alive and well. In fundamentalism it had merely found a new ship upon which to steal passage.

After the public spectacle of the Scopes trial conservative Christians and liberal Christians went their own ways, both religiously and culturally. For a few years following the disaster at Dayton fundamentalist leaders fought a desperate and strident battle to regain for fundamentalism the status it had attained just previous to the Scopes trial. But to no avail. It was over, it appeared; the movement in shambles. Overwhelming public ridicule so embarrassed large numbers of moderate Protestant conservatives that they fled the movement more quietly and quickly than those who had fled Millerism. Those who remained tended to be uncompromising radicals, isolated individuals who retreated into separatist minorities hoping some day in the future to regroup. While the Scopes trial changed the public's *image* of fundamentalism, it certainly did not write the last chapter in its history. Dayton, Tennessee, was not the last stand of Christian fundamentalism in the United States.

13

Conservatives Resurgent

Viewing the 1920s from the vantage point of a chastened 1931, historian Frederick Lewis Allen in his book *Only Yesterday* waxed nostalgic: "Soon the mists of distance would soften the outlines of the nineteen-twenties, and men and women ... would smile at the memory of those charming, crazy days when the radio was a thrilling novelty, and girls wore bobbed hair and knee-length skirts.... They would talk about the good old days."[1]

As a result of the Scopes trial it appeared that the good old days for the fundamentalists had passed into history as well. In June 1926 an editorial in *The Christian Century* titled "Vanishing Fundamentalism" proclaimed the demise of that militant brand of conservative Christianity. The Scopes trial had rendered it a "decisive rout." Fundamentalism was "hollow and artificial ... [an] accidental phenomenon making its sudden appearance" and its just as sudden disappearance. Like some biological "sport" it had managed to flourish during a specific and abnormal set of social circumstances, but that auspicious environment had now passed. "Wholly lacking the qualities of constructive achievement or survival ... it [fundamentalism] is henceforth to be a disappearing quantity in American religious life, while our churches go on to larger issues."[2]

It was true after the Scopes trial that many conservatives within the mainline churches began to distance themselves from the movement and adopt a more liberal modernist viewpoint, thereby nullifying any threat fundamentalism might have had *within* those churches. But it was also true that many conservatives held fast to fundamentalist ideas and "came out" from the mainline churches to found their own denominations.

Hardcore fundamentalists did not abandon their faith. Instead, they withdrew from a culture which was growing increasingly secular, and set about founding their own subculture with separate religious, educational, and social institutions. Historian Edward J. Larson writes, "Although the Scopes trial helped push fundamentalists out of mainstream American culture, they seemed almost eager to go. A separatist streak marked elements of conservative American Protestantism ever since the Pilgrims set foot on Ply-

147

mouth Rock in 1620."[3] By the 1930s so thoroughly independent had this new subculture become from mainstream American life, it was virtually hidden, to the degree that "outside observers thought the movement had died."[4]

As conservative Christians retreated into their own subculture their concept of the imminent millennium faded from public cognizance. But that changed with the instant annihilation of two Japanese cities during the last days of the Second World War. One of the physicists who worked on the atomic bomb remarked that the Day of Judgment seemed suddenly to be the next day.

The imminent millennium gained new life in the broader culture as the words "apocalyptic" and "Armageddon" brought the idea of religious finality to even the most secular of periodicals. The *Philadelphia Inquirer* heralded the atomic bomb as "the new beast of the apocalypse."[5] William L. Laurence chose the word "Armageddon" as the title for the last section of his history of the bomb project.

Preachers of doom and doomsday prophecies abounded. Scripture was searched for the slightest allusion to anything which might be interpreted as atomic destruction. Did Zechariah's "small things" (4:10) refer to the atom? Second Peter 3:10 lent scriptural significance to prevalent concerns: "The heavens shall pass away with a great noise, and the elements shall melt with fervent heat, the earth also and the works that are therein shall be burned up." New ears were listening to ancient words.

President John Kennedy's assassination on November 22, 1963, added to general uncertainty about the future. Soon it seemed that all was chaos: more assassinations, Vietnam, burning cities, race riots, runaway inflation. *Life* magazine had long been America's picture-book, capturing the kaleidoscope of the times. Now its covers screamed disaster: battered soldiers, the inferno in the cities.

The 1960s proved to be a decade of social revolution. It began in the nation's universities, where angry student voices shouted through megaphones that society needed to be reconstructed from the ground up. It was time to make changes, to overthrow "the establishment."

By the 1970s a more strident voice was heard. Women. As the women's movement advanced the place of women, it had a profound effect on the future of men and children. Just as it appeared that the building blocks of traditional society were tumbling down, there came news that American Protestantism, too, was undergoing cataclysmic change.

In 1972 Dean M. Kelley, a minister of the United Methodist Church and an executive with the National Council of Churches, published a book filled with statistics and observations which gained the attention of major newsmagazines and religious periodicals. His findings were surprising: Church attendance at most mainline Protestant denominations had peaked during the mid-1960s, then began to fall off. For example, in just the few years between 1965 and 1972 the Episcopal Church lost 12 percent of its members, the Presbyterian Church (USA) lost 9 percent, and the United Church of Christ lost 9 percent.

In the time since Kelley's report things have gotten considerably worse. By 1975 the mainline church's share of American Protestantism had dropped to forty percent, down from sixty percent at the beginning of the century.[6] A 1976 Gallup survey found twice as many Americans involved in Transcendental Meditation as there were Presbyterians.[7] At the end of the 1980s Isabel Rogers, former moderator of the Presbyterian Church (USA), conceded that the mainline churches were "no longer the primary shapers of values in American society."[8] Over a period when the national population had increased by 47 million, five mainline denominations lost a total of more than five million members.[9] Muslims outnumbered Episcopalians, and Methodists were losing adherents at the rate of more than 1000 a week.[10] By 1990, Presbyterians accounted for only three percent of the population of the United States; Episcopalians, only two percent.[11] By 1993, using 1965 as a base, losses in membership amounted to 33 percent for the Episcopal Church, 33 percent for the Presbyterian Church (USA), 20 percent for the United Church of Christ, and 21 percent for the United Methodist Church.[12] Three years later mainline churches were closing their doors at the rate of fifty a week.[13]

The beat goes on. Between 1980 and 2008 the United Methodist Church lost 18 percent, the Episcopal Church lost 23 percent, the United Church of Christ lost 31 percent, and the Christian Church (Disciples of Christ) lost 43 percent. In all these examples the losses have been consistent and steady over that time span.[14] During the last ten years the major mainline Protestant denominations have lost one million adherents, so that they now comprise only sixteen percent of the national population.[15] Considering that these denominations have long defined the spiritual and moral ethos of the nation, all of this is alarming.

Yet these numbers do not tell the whole story. Not only are mainline pews half empty on a Sunday morning, a disproportionate number of those present are seniors, indeed *senior* seniors. Forty-nine percent of active Presbyterians are near retirement, and Sunday school enrolment is down 55 percent over two decades.[16] Failure to attract a representational proportion of younger people means that these traditional bastions of religious belief have to a great degree moved from mainline to sideline. The increasing age of mainline church memberships is a major concern of these denominations regarding the future.

But the decline of the mainline Protestant church was not the whole picture. Kelley found that at the same time mainline churches had declining numbers, conservative churches were gaining adherents at an explosive rate. From 1958 until 1975 membership of the Church of the Nazarene increased 52 percent, Seventh-Day Adventists 66 percent, the Church of Jesus Christ of Latter-Day Saints 68 percent, the Jehovah's Witnesses 155 percent, Assemblies of God 157 percent.[17] By 1984, a Gallup survey revealed that 22 percent of Americans counted themselves "evangelical," compared to 18 percent in 1976[18]— an increase by almost one quarter in just eight years. In 1989 *Time* magazine noted that among the 500 fastest growing Protestant congregations, only five were mainline.[19] By 1990, Baptists, at twenty percent of the national population, were flourishing,[20] and historian Garry Wills stated that "evangelicals make up the largest number of Christians in America."[21] In 1993 *Newsweek* revealed that a new conservative congregation is founded almost daily.[22] In his study of fundamentalists, the most conservative of conservatives, Charles B. Strozier wrote, "Christian fundamentalism in America at the end of the millennium is a mass movement that broadly describes the religious orientation of roughly a quarter of the population."[23] The strictest fundamentalists were estimated to comprise one third of all conservative Protestants in the United States.[24] So rapidly was conservatism growing, Protestantism as a whole was on the rise, despite a dwindling mainline church population.

One reason why mainline churches "as American as apple pie and the Fourth of July" had so suddenly fallen on hard times was found in an article in the newsmagazine *Maclean's*: By 1993 38 percent of all conservative church members were converts from mainline churches.[25] The mainline church was losing members to the conservative competition down the street. In their study of the changing shape and the future of American mainline religion, Wade Clark Roof and William McKinney explained that the cultural and religious center of the United States had shifted, resulting in a polarized and fragmented religious culture. Mainline churches had become "the major suppliers of recruits to other faiths."[26]

In addition to those who left mainline churches for conservative churches, sixty percent of born-agains were found *within* mainline churches.[27] The composition of the mainline denominations was changing. They were neither the monolithic nor the homogeneous institutions they once were thought to be. A 1984 survey disclosed that in the United Methodist Church (a fairly liberal denomination) 9 percent of denominational officials considered themselves evangelical, as did 21 percent of the clergy and 30 percent of the laity.[28] A Gallup survey that year showed that the forty percent of Americans who said they were "born again,"[29] included 57 percent of Baptists, 32 percent of Methodists, 29 percent of Lutherans, 27 percent of Presbyterians, and 14 percent of Episcopalians.[30] Adding to the mix, some mainline denominations were fracturing into liberal and conservative branches.

The trend to conservatism has continued to this day. Overall, conservative Christians form a large and continually increasing sector of the American population. According to a recent Gallup poll, forty-six percent of Americans call themselves "born-again" Christians.[31] Figures published in 2005 indicate 26 percent of the population of the United States consisted of white evangelicals; another ten percent, black evangelicals.[32] During the years between 1980 and 2008 growth has been consistent and constant. Using the Southern Baptist Convention and Assemblies of God as examples, the numbers are 23 percent and 119 percent, respectively.[33] Figures from the *Statistical Abstract of the United States, 2008* indicate that fundamentalists increased 126 percent and evangelicals 326 percent over a ten-year period when the American population increased 13 percent.[34] A group of sociologists studying the demographics have recently concluded that "the Protestant population will continue to shift in the conservative direction for many years to come."[35] Why?

Writing in the early 1960s, a decade before Kelley's study, sociologist Peter L. Berger rued the dull complacency of liberal mainline denominations. These institutions had become the handmaiden of an increasingly secular society; too often they "sanctified" societal norms and values. Virtually identifying with a respectable middle-class way of life, the mainline Protestant churches failed to present any real "encounter with the Christian message."[36]

Mainline churches had long represented the status quo. At one time the various denominations could be ranked in a graded pecking order of social prestige: A Methodist was a Baptist who wore shoes; a Presbyterian was a Methodist who attended college; an Episcopalian was a Presbyterian who lived off his investments. As you moved up the economic ladder you not only purchased the appropriate automobile, you drove it to the right church. Attendance at church was part of correct social life. No one expected to be preached the prophetic gospel; church was a place to meet new friends and business acquaintances on your way up. The title of a contemporary book, *The Comfortable Pew*, summarized the Sunday morning mood in a great many Protestant mainline churches.

When the secular culture began to change in the 1960s, the mainline church followed. Mainline pastors went out of their way to be "with it." They too could be "cool." They grew their hair longer. They experimented with a little street argot. Mainline churches, it seemed, were willing to bend and grant concessions of any nature if this would hold their membership.

These changes in the mainline church only made matters worse. People were fleeing "tolerant," "reasonable," and "relevant"[37] religion for the "wrong" churches at an accelerated rate. The attempt to "meet the needs" of the religious shopper suggested a loss of theological integrity and identity. To the man and woman in the pew, liberal clergy appeared willing to sell the soul of the church. One third of those who regularly attended one mainline denomination said that their church was too liberal.[38] They objected to recent innovations.

While some mainline clergy tried to be "with it," others of a liberal bent decided it was time for the church to take a leadership role. The social unrest of the 1960s and early 1970s had brought a series of new moral issues to the forefront — war, justice, equality. A Methodist minister phrased the challenge: "We must recognize that a desperate struggle is on for the soul of the world. That requires ... a great godly company of men and women ... desiring only to save, serve, help and heal."[39] Ninety percent of the clergy in some mainline denominations believed that ministers should try to influence the power structures of society for the good.[40]

As the liberal mainline church championed what it considered progressive causes (women's rights, gay rights, etc.) the laity felt alienated. A survey in 1967 found that 72 percent of the laity said they would be very upset if their own minister or priest became involved in such campaigns.[41] Yet as late as 1998 eighty percent of Episcopal clergy were still beating the social justice drum — agitating for more government action to alleviate poverty, expand social welfare, protect the environment — often in opposition to the private wishes of their membership.[42] Clearly, the clergy and the officials of the national denominational bodies were losing touch with the grass roots. They just didn't get it.

They were not alone. Back at the end of the 1960s, noting a declining church and the changes in society, many were beginning to think religion had lost its significance, that it would pass quietly into history. Sociologists, in particular, predicted that traditional Protestantism would disappear amidst the attractions and abundant prosperity promised by secular materialism. Surely once people were educated and adopted an urban lifestyle, their religious beliefs would wither on the vine.

But the sociologists were engaging in idle speculation, rather than observing what was happening. First, there was the unease of the time, summarized in Alvin Toffler's 1970 book *Future Shock*, characterized by *Newsweek* a "disquieting study." While some found the societal changes of the late 1960s and early 1970s exciting and liberating, just as many others found them disorienting and profoundly disturbing. Where once there had seemed to be answers, now just questions. In a world of shock upon shock upon shock, many were left searching for a still and stable point of reference.

"Stop the world, I want to get off," said a hit musical of the late 1960s. But if one could not get off the world, one could find solace in the belief that there exists *another* world, a supernatural realm over and above this earthly realm. And so it was that many turned to religion, as had generations before in times of change and uncertainty.

Second, sociologists failed to observe the actions of the nation's youth, or misinterpreted their actions. When America's young people revolted against "the establishment" the mainline church was on their hit list. But it wasn't because they were against religion. *True* religion was one of the things they most craved. Young people saw in the mainline church a skeleton without a soul. Their spiritual quest was leading them from the church to Zen Buddhism, witchcraft, astrology, yoga, Vedanta, and all manner of innovative cults. Religion wasn't dying, it was flourishing under new banners.

In an era of future shock people were turning to the past, to that "old-time religion." One Anglican priest defied mainline trends and made the Bible central in his ministry. His congregation went from sixty to a capacity of five hundred, most aged 18 to 40.[43] Contrary to the expectation of liberal pundits, people seemed suddenly to be craving the stricter religious practices and even the belief systems of more conservative brands of Christianity. In an era of future shock, liberalization of church liturgy and belief only added to a growing sense of chaos. Dean Kelley related how one woman was "won away" right from under his nose. Jehovah's Witnesses had come to her home to provide Bible study, so she joined them. Why did she leave the Methodist church Kelley pastored? "I wish *your* church was one-tenth as serious about *its* message as *they* are about theirs!"[44]

People were choosing the religious option which offered a clear identity, strong and consistent leadership, and a definite and unchanging set of beliefs. Any increase in church discipline was gladly accepted in return for a solid rock on which to base one's life, a stable center in a world apparently spinning out of control. The more conservative churches promised balm to the soul in need of comfort, and a rich religious experience for the individual in search of meaning and self-fulfillment, at a time when seven out of ten Americans were spending a great deal of time thinking about their inner lives.[45] People turned to church for comfort and reassurance, solace in troubled times. The fulfillment and salvation of one's own spirit and soul took priority over helping others.

When a born-again president was elected in the person of Jimmy Carter, and the Moral Majority brought the New Christian Right into sharp focus,[46] the stage was set for a public resurgence of conservative Christianity. The word "fundamentalist" once again gained the attention of the American public. Since the Scopes trial fundamentalists had lived apart from the wider culture, defining themselves as the true Christians, awaiting the day when Christ would return. But now many willingly came into public view, proud to wear the badge "fundamentalist." The most conservative form of American Protestantism was clearly on the rise and in the open after decades of hiding.

The vast majority of conservative Christians, whether they consider themselves "evangelical" or "fundamentalist," are premillennialists—they believe Christ will *soon* return and then usher in the millennium. This is what the "Second Coming" is all about. A Gallup survey indicated that 93 percent of those who call themselves evangelical "have no doubts" about the Second Coming of Christ.

Thoughts of the end-time are never far from the surface. At the beginning of the atomic age prominent fundamentalists flooded the airwaves proclaiming the approach of the Last Days. Soon fundamentalist televangelists were reaching half of the nation's population every week—more than attended church. One fifth of all Americans subscribed to one religious network alone, a network which brought in four million dollars a week. Today there are over two hundred Christian television stations in the United States, the vast majority evangelical or fundamentalist.[47] The number of Christian radio stations almost doubled between 1998 and 2004, from 1089 to 2014.[48]

The fundamentalist message over radio and television is predominantly apocalyptic. Just before the final battle of Armageddon and Christ's return there will be chaos and confusion, and declining moral values. And that, the fundamentalists point out, is exactly what is unfolding on the evening news.

By the mid-1970s public moral issues were of great concern to conservative Christians. Watergate and the Supreme Court's 1973 decision on abortion meant that morality could no longer remain a strictly private concern. Conservatives reminded their fellow Americans that they were God's chosen nation, a light unto the world. The nation, conservatives insisted, must return to her roots and restore her Christian principles. Pro-choice, gay rights—such issues were the sure way to national perdition. Remember Sodom and Gomorrah, the fall of Rome? God would surely punish America if she persisted in this downward moral spiral. America must once more be governed by biblical precepts.

The moral issues which most concerned conservatives—abortion, relations between church and state, homosexuality, pornography—were not of primary interest for liberals. These differing moral concerns emphasized the fact that the religious great divide which had attracted so much attention in the early 1920s was once again alive and well.

Little Christian love is afforded those on the other side of this great divide. Stereotyping is the order of the day. Liberals find their conservative brethren to be intolerant, rigid, unsophisticated, close-minded, simplistic, and fanatical. Conservatives say liberals are immoral, overly concerned with social issues, and don't know the Bible. An article in *The Christian Century* observes: "Liberals abhor the smugness, the self-righteousness, the absolute certainty, the judgmentalism, the lovelessness of a narrow, dogmatic faith. [Conservatives] scorn the fuzziness, the marshmallow convictions, the inclusiveness that makes membership meaningless—the 'anything goes' attitude that views even Scripture as relative."[49] This cultural divide includes the clergy. Protestant mainline and conservative clergies "live in distinct intellectual and cultural worlds."[50]

At the foundation of differing moral, social, and political positions lie opposing views of the Bible held by liberals and conservatives. One hundred million conservative Christian Americans believe that the Bible is the "actual word of God and is to be taken literally, word for word."[51] The opposing views of Scripture held by liberals and conservatives are particularly noticeable with respect to the interpretation of apocalyptic passages. Conservatives interpret the book of Revelation literally. As the twentieth century approached its end and the ominous year 2000 was just over the horizon, "53 percent of adult Americans expected the imminent return of Jesus Christ and the fulfillment of biblical prophecies about a cataclysmic destruction of evil."[52] As well, 60 to 70 million Americans ("conservatively estimated") believe in the Rapture.[53] Liberals see in Revelation a millennium achieved through the work of the church, and look not to some fiery end of this world but give the issues of this present world priority.

If men and women are from different planets, liberals and conservatives are from different galaxies. Liberals and conservatives speak different languages, they do not communicate. They live their lives in separate worlds, in separate cultures.

14

A Hidden Culture

Compromise, accommodation — these are anathema to conservatives. They leave friends and family, if need be, to devote their lives to the study of the Bible, to their life within a churchly community — their Christian friends: "I live in this little world — my little Christian world ... everything else seems sorta pointless."[1] This Christian world is a protective cocoon, separate from the chaotic changes of the broader secular world.

Separate, yet not separate. A hidden culture within the wider suburban American culture. Conservatives drive every Sunday to the evangelical Gospel Tabernacle across the city. They ask if you are "saved." They knock on doors during a religious revival. They talk openly about being "born again." For a large part of their lives conservatives blend seamlessly into the broader culture. They earn money in the same corporations, live on the same streets. They ride the commuter train beside other Americans; they work next to other Americans in office and factory. They are sisters and cousins and sons and nieces and uncles and mothers of other Americans. Unless their neighbors or fellow workers know them well they would never know they're conservatives, that in addition to the wider culture in which they earn an income they also participate in a hidden biblical churchly culture. On the outside, on the surface, at least, there is nothing to distinguish conservatives from other Americans.

In the mid-1970s, while conservative Protestantism was growing on the backs of disillusionment with the traditional mainline denominations, a new phenomenon, the megachurch — defined as any church with attendance in excess of two thousand — was spawned to answer new-found spiritual needs. There were ten such churches in 1970,[2] fifty by 1980.[3] Today there are thirteen hundred, fifty of which have attendance over 10,000.[4] It is estimated that a new megachurch opens every two days.[5]

The prefix "mega" is well earned. Everything about these churches is big. Lakewood Church, located in Houston, Texas, provides some numbers. Its weekend attendance — spread over several services — is the largest in the United States at 47,000.[6] Services are held in the recently transformed — at a cost of $75 million[7]—Compaq Center, former home of the NBA's Houston Rockets, which can seat 16,000. Saddleback Church in Lake Forest, California, with a normal weekly attendance of 24,000, brings in 45,000 at Easter, and lists 82,000 as "occasional attendees."[8]

Megachurches are businesses. If they didn't conduct themselves as such, financial chaos would result. Saddleback Church in Lake Forest, California has a staff of over one hundred and fifty, and raised $52 million for an expansion of its facilities.[9] Lakewood Church takes in $55 million a year in contributions.[10] The average megachurch takes in $4.8 million a year, compared with $100,000 for the average traditional church.[11]

While not the largest megachurch—it places second with only half the attendance of Lakewood[12]—Willow Creek Community Church of South Barrington, Illinois, is the prototypical megachurch when it comes to management. It was named "the most influential church in America" for several years running, according to a poll of American pastors.[13] Nestled in the suburbs of Chicago, its duck pond provides the image of an up-to-date suburban corporate park. Even the terminology employed at Willow Creek is all business. The church's pastoral staff—overlooking one hundred ministries[14]—is known as the "administrative team"; the total of what the church community has to offer, as "product." And Willow Creek can furnish the numbers: a 7200-seat, $72-million sanctuary;[15] a $48-million budget; $143 million in net assets; $26 million in annual contributions; 427 employees; 10,000 volunteers.[16]

Willow Creek began in business-like fashion. Founded in 1975, it had its basis in a door-to-door survey which asked why suburbanites were no longer attending church on Sunday mornings. By the turn of the century Willow Creek was drawing seventeen thousand locals through its doors every week.[17]

Ambitious pastors around the nation were quick to realize that Willow Creek was onto something, and wanted to know its formula for success. Enter the Willow Creek Association, a consulting firm run under the auspices of the church and the direction of an MBA, which serves 10,500 churches from ninety denominations, and brings in $17 million annually to Willow Creek's coffers.[18] The Association is not itself a denomination; churches join, but remain in their respective denominations, or remain independent. Pastors are neither trained nor ordained by the Association; they attend conferences and workshops—but these have proven amazingly fruitful (witness the burgeoning megachurch phenomenon). Indeed, so successful has the church and the Association proven to be, Willow Church is recognized among the top five percent of 250 major commercial brands, "right up there with Nike and John Deere."[19]

Megachurches are usually founded and run as a one-man-show by a pastor with a powerful charismatic personality. Dispensationalist minister W. A.

Criswell[20], founder and former pastor of First Baptist Church of Dallas, was so dynamic and celebrated a figure in that giant metropolis that he was known simply as "the pastor." Continuing to preach at an age when most are content to reminisce, he had increased the membership to 28,000 (which included even Billy Graham) by the time he stepped down as pastor.[21]

Such dynamism is typical of conservative megachurch preachers. They preach, they write, they broadcast, they grow the Kingdom. Rick Warren of Saddleback Church (Lake Forest, California) has written the fastest-selling nonfiction book ever. Used in twenty thousand churches in 162 countries, *The Purpose-driven Life* sold over 23 million copies in its first three years of publication,[22] and is read today by 19.1 percent of Americans.[23] *Your Best Life Now*, by Pastor Joel Osteen of Lakewood Church, sold two and a half million copies in its first six months.[24] His telecast sermons are piped into two hundred million households.[25] So famous has Osteen become, he is featured in the popular commercial magazine *People*, in which is noted his luxurious 5000-square-foot home, a $13 million advance for a recent book, his success ethic — *Success for Dummies* is found on his bookshelf, and he works out and runs two miles a day.[26]

The pastors of conservative megachurches know their market; they speak fluently the language of suburbia and capture its idiom. New to the culture of California when he first arrived in that state in 1955, Robert Schuller took little time to recognize that the automobile was its epicenter. He rented the local drive-in theater, passed out handbills inviting people to "worship as you are ... in the family car,"[27] and was soon preaching to a field filled with automobiles.

The typical megachurch provides acres of parking, as far as the eye can see — the Willow Creek plant is located on 155 acres,[28] much of it for parking. As you drive onto one of the parking lots of the typical megachurch on a Sunday morning you are greeted by a parking attendant (no charge). You notice that other persons are dressed neatly, but casually. (Although at some churches you might see the more traditional Sunday morning attire.) When you enter the church you are welcomed at the door and pointed to a panoply of display tables, each advertising the various activities provided by the church community. There is, it becomes immediately obvious, a program, a club, an activity, for virtually everyone — newlyweds, young parents, seniors, divorcees, teenagers, former prisoners, alcoholics, the girth-challenged. There are dinners, parties, sports, summer camps, family counseling, self-help programs.

Called "shopping-mall churches," megachurches replicate suburbia. Some contain mall-style food courts, and other accoutrements of suburban life. Brentwood Baptist Church in Houston has its own McDonald's; Covenant Celebration Church in Tacoma has its own Starbucks.

Second Baptist Church of Houston grew to 11,000 during the 1980s, and has more than doubled that figure today.[29] The church itself seats eight thousand, but that is only a small part of this "city within a city" (as its promotional pamphlet boasts). A brochure proclaims the church's mandate: "In a fast-paced city such as Houston, a person or family needs a subculture, a group of people and a place where they can build a lifestyle."[30] And Second Baptist provides all the facilities for that lifestyle: a movie theater, an eight-lane bowling alley, a bookstore, a restaurant, pool tables, a gymnasium, a weight-training room full of the latest equipment.

Many megachurches are big on sports. First Baptist Church of Dallas provides everything for those who wish to keep fit: racquetball courts, a roller-skating rink, two gymnasiums, fitness machines, bowling alleys, a sauna. Prestonwood Baptist Church of Plano, Texas, involves 16,000 individuals in its sports program. In addition to six gymnasiums, its $100-million, 140-acre campus features eight playing fields.[31] The Fellowship of Las Colinas, in Irving, Texas, features a 38-team basketball league. It held a baseball clinic led by the New York Yankees. During football season the Fellowship shows its partisan colors; on a giant outdoor screen fans can catch the opening minutes of a Dallas Cowboys game early Sunday afternoon before leaving church grounds.

In addition to sports, megachurches often offer specific services normally found in secular business establishments. Lakewood Church provides free financial counseling and low-cost bulk food. Many churches offer extra services for a special price, the money from these services adding to the church's bottom line. Willow Creek, for example, provides auto repair ($1 million of income a year), a bookstore ($3.2 million), and a coffee shop/restaurant ($2.5 a year).[32] The restaurant associated with First Baptist of Dallas serves members and the community at large; Dallas businessmen often dine there, parking in the ample multilevel garage.

First Baptist Church of Amarillo counts as its members— over ten thousand[33]— a fair portion of the city's population (173,000).[34] By its size and its facilities it "might easily be mistaken for a small college."[35] Its Family Life Center houses bowling, skating, sauna, and crafts. The church offers "a complete, if enclosed, social life."[36] The same might be said for Chapel Hill Harvester Church in Atlanta. It has its own publishing house and television studios, and a residential housing estate. It has its own primary and secondary schools and the Institute for Advanced Education (which teaches classes in Kingdom theology). Megachurches often furnish education for the young. First Baptist of Dallas has a Christian day school for grades one through twelve. Second Baptist of Houston has a school for 900 students. Such churches are truly self-contained cities.

Megachurches offer a feeling of community in a society which has become impersonal and transient. A Gallup survey found that "'Americans are ... the loneliest people in the world' and strongly desire their churches to provide a sense of community."[37] Much of the American population is on the move, never in one location long enough to lay down roots. As one person remarked, concerning the church community, It is "family, when so many people seem not to have a family anymore."[38] Michelle Goldberg notes, "Megachurches fill the spiritual and social void, providing atomized residents [of suburbia] instant community."[39]

In order to more narrowly provide a church community conservative churches make good use of the technique of niche marketing. The Southern Baptist Convention, the nation's largest Protestant denomination at 16,300,000,[40] has plans to "plant" 1800 churches with this in mind. As Martin King, of Southern Baptist's North American Mission Board remarks, "We have cowboy churches for people working on ranches, country music churches, even several motorcycle churches aimed at bikers."[41]

In contrast to the traditional liberal mainline church, the conservative megachurch caters closely to the needs of today's suburban family. "We give them what they want," one pastor maintains.[42] Critics call this "cafeteria Christianity" or "Christianity lite," but it is difficult to argue with success. Half of the American churchgoing population attends only twelve percent of the nation's 400,000 churches; the other half are in congregations of less than seventy-five persons.[43] As Bob Buford of Leadership Network phrases it, "It's Wal-Mart versus the corner grocery. It ain't a fair fight."[44] Michael S. Hamilton observes, "Dynamic growing churches require a combination of spiritual wisdom, cultural discernment, visionary leadership, talented management, favorable demographics, and adequate financial resources."[45]

The conservative megachurch speaks to the individual alienated by today's harried lifestyle. The megachurch provides a haven from today's hurried stressful life. As one sales manager says, "When I walk out of a service, I feel completely relieved of any stress I walked in with."[46]

But it isn't just a feeling of community and a quiet time away from everyday stress that attracts so many to the conservative megachurch. It is something deeper. This becomes obvious by examining why people leave the mainline church and move to a conservative church.

One disillusioned Episcopalian remarks: "We have nothing at all to hold on to, no shared belief, no common assumptions ... no accepted definition of what an Episcopalian is or believes."[47] Persons leave because they find the mainline church too wishy-washy, too easy, too convenient and compatible. They don't want some tired version of "I'm OK, you're OK," all wrapped up in pleasant-sounding, easy-to-digest, warm-and-cosy, pithy platitudes, universal bromides. In its efforts to please, to play it safe, to provide a "consumer Christianity," the liberal church has gone too far. It is too tolerant, too accepting, too spiritually empty. Sterile. Where, people ask, is the mysterium, the magic, the miraculous? Where is the sacred? Where is Jesus Christ? Where is God?

None of this is surprising, considering what liberal mainline seminaries press upon their students. A Rockefeller Foundation report found a lack of traditional scholarly rigor in the seminaries it surveyed. The once-obligatory courses in Bible, church history, and doctrine were now optional. Greek and Hebrew? Optional. The list of elective courses had grown to the point it seemed everything was elective. Fewer and fewer attended chapel. Old-style morals were on the slide. In summarizing, the report stated that these seminaries offered a "general education for those interested in a diffuse variety of religious studies, personal quests for the meaning of life, social activism and pastorally oriented behavioral science."[48] Many students attracted to such a potpourri lack direction and focus, and after graduation abandon organized religion altogether.

Professor Christopher R. Seitz of Yale University Divinity School worries that students are trained to think critically about their faith, but lack the "substantive base" upon which such thinking can build without becoming destructive: "Most don't know the names of half of the books of the Bible, whether Calvin lived before or after Augustine, what it means to say that Christ descended to the dead or acted 'in accordance with the Scriptures' ... or how to understand a final judgment of the quick and the dead."[49] At Harvard University Divinity School sexism, homophobism, and misogyny are the new mortal sins. As one student comments, "Pluralism is the God at Harvard. The basic presumption is that Western religion is not good, and Christianity is the worst. The new slur, like being 'homophobic,' is being 'Christo-centric.'"[50]

As these liberal attitudes spread into the larger church, the laity sought a new spiritual home. There was a need for something solid, something to grab onto, something unchanging, something one could count on, something to give life meaning midst a chaotic world of constant change. And the conservative megachurch offered just that. Here was certainty, unambiguous answers to life's conundrums—backed by the authority of a solid Scriptural tradition. Here was hope, here was meaning, here was a sense of ultimate purpose to all of existence, a sense of order to human life. Here was an enlivening spiritual experience, experience of the sacred, of the transcendent, of the Holy Spirit. The experience of direct communion with Jesus Christ, of oneness with a spiritual community. So personal, so intimate.

The Bible is the center of the conservative megachurch service. Charles

Trueheart observes that although not all megachurches are strictly fundamentalist, "these churches are proudly evangelical ... [and] take the Bible very
seriously."[51] Those attending Willow Creek Community Church, for example,
believe that the Bible is both inerrant and infallible. A survey of 3,500 conservative Christians showed Willow Creek to be typical: 32 percent agreed
with the statement "The Bible is the actual word of God and is to be taken
literally, word for word"; 65 percent agreed with the statements "The Bible
is the inspired word of God. It contains no errors, but some verses are to be
taken symbolically rather than literally." A mere 3 percent agreed that the
Bible "may contain historical and scientific errors," at the same time insisting
it "is the inspired word of God."[52]

The Bible is front and center in fundamentalist and evangelical preaching; as it should be, for the Bible is at the center of all of life for the conservative. This is true to the spirit of the first Puritan colonists in America. The
evangelical's emphasis on the Bible has led some to view the resurgence of
evangelicalism as a second Protestant Reformation. The conservative preacher,
if he is faithful to his calling, is not given to rhetorical showmanship, eloquence worthy of a graying senator. While he may here and there introduce
a spot of humor, his focus is ever fixed on explicating the holy word. Any
church, even the most popular of megachurches must hew to this standard.
At Willow Creek there is recognition that it has not been teaching "a robust
enough biblical theology" and "needs to turn the ship around."[53]

The sermon is located within the context of the church service — prayer,
hymn-singing — but it is the focus, often lasting as much as one and a half
hours, and there may be more than one on a Sunday. Conservative preachers
like to work through the whole Bible systematically, covering no more than
two or three verses a session. Although one version of Scripture is regarded
as the church's "Bible," it is not unusual for a preacher to remark on the wording of another version. The Greek New Testament and the Hebrew Old Testament are consulted. Words and phrases are diligently searched in parallel
passages throughout Scripture. The verse under study is understood in the
context of surrounding verses and chapters. It is painstaking work. Those in
the pews are amazingly attentive and take detailed notes.

The biblical message is located within the context of apocalyptic belief.
In his study of the megachurch phenomenon Donald E. Miller notes the prevalence of "millenarian beliefs on the imminent end of the world and the return
of Christ."[54] In his survey of 3,500 persons the majority expected Christ to
return in the near future; the rest said it was not the place of human beings
to speculate on the time of the Second Coming. No one questioned the material and earthly return of Christ.

W. A. Criswell was a good example of a devout apocalypticist. He preached for three years from Revelation, always with a dispensationalist slant. His flock never seemed to tire of this—a collection of $1.85 million was gathered one Sunday.[55] Criswell's sermons were broadcast on radio—the church owns its own radio station—and on television. During his last forty years as pastor he published a book a year proclaiming the dispensationalist message. So that others might take up the task he founded the Criswell Center for Biblical Studies which included Criswell Bible College and the Graduate School of the Bible.

The devoted conservative is not satisfied with several hours of Bible study every Sunday. Many attend Bible study sessions at adult Sunday school, and Bible study classes offered by the church during the week, which are every bit as intense and technically demanding in their use of Greek and Hebrew as the Sunday sermons. Some megachurches offer a dozen different classes every evening of the week. At Calvary Chapel, Costa Mesa, two thousand teenagers gather once a week for Bible study. Teenagers and Bible study? No wonder the conservative church is growing. It is building for the future.

Then there are the less formal Bible study groups. These often consist of a few friends who choose a project—the gospel of John, say—which they will pursue for several months, or a theme to be studied throughout Scripture, or they may select a different passage each week. They rotate meetings at member's homes, and members take turns leading and guiding discussion. Ample use is made of recommended commentaries. Discussion may become quite heated because these sessions focus on the application of the text to situations and issues encountered in everyday life. Prayer opens and closes each session. There is, of course, the mandatory coffee and cookies and social intercourse. In addition to all of this conservatives are supposed to read the Bible every day as individuals and in the context of their families. A survey of 3,500 conservative Christians showed that, for the most part, they do devoutly read their Bibles. Two-thirds read the Bible at least once a day—one fifth more than once a day—and another quarter, two or three times a week.[56] The father usually leads and the passage selected will be discussed in relation to the life of the family, with prayerful supplication for application of the divine word in each of their individual lives.

Conservatives believe that the truths of the Bible can only be discerned after a person has been born again. Without the guidance of the Holy Spirit the Bible cannot be properly understood, which is why non-believers see apparent contradictions in the text. Conservatives speak of allowing the text to "wash over" one's spirit until one feels in direct communication with God. But this spiritual journey requires constant study of the Bible, unending effort to understand. Here the notes provided by the Scofield edition of the King James Version can be helpful.

Evangelicals by no means limit themselves to the Scofield Bible. They also read the *Good News Bible, Good News for Modern Man,* and the New International Version. They even have computerized versions in pocket size with indexed counseling guides. By contrast, liberal mainline churches are more likely to use the Revised Standard Version or the New Revised Standard Version of the Bible. This use of different Bibles helps maintain the religious cultural divide.

Churches and the communities they gather about them are just part of the massive subculture of conservative Christianity in the United States. In addition to churches, evangelicals and fundamentalists have their own publishing houses, mission societies, bookstores, and summer camps for families and children. They listen to "Christian" music, purchase "Christian" books, greeting cards, calendars, video. There are "Christian" business directories, "Christian" financial guides, "Christian" video outlets, "Christian" beauty pageants, "Christian" luxury cruises, "Christian" soap operas, "Christian" romantic novels ... the list goes on. There is even a Christian Yellow Pages. The evangelical culture is virtually identical to much of the secular culture but with that important label "Christian"—the evangelical seal of approval—affixed.

Strangely, the evangelical/fundamentalist culture is almost hidden (although not purposely) from most people who lead strictly secular lives or whose Christianity is nourished in the liberal mainline church on a Sunday morning. Until Jerry Falwell and the Moral Majority put evangelical Christianity into the public spotlight the "Christian" print media, for example, was virtually ignored by the secular press. It wasn't long thereafter before *The New York Times* was consulting religious bookstores before making up its bestseller lists and *Publishers Weekly* was listing "Christian Bestsellers"—ten hardcovers and ten paperbacks.

With Hal Lindsey's apocalyptic *The Late Great Planet Earth,* first published in 1970, selling in the millions, the big publishing houses in New York and Boston and San Francisco could no longer afford to ignore the conservative Christian market. To do so would be to lose out on a mother lode. There were over six thousand Christian bookstores doing a thriving business in the United States.[57] The Christian Booksellers Association boasted over 3500 members.[58]

The surge in evangelical print started back in 1976 when the sales of religious books, excluding Bibles and hymnals, jumped 24 percent and religious books accounted for 15 percent of all book sales.[59] By the 1980s stores affiliated with the Christian Booksellers Association were doubling their sales, then doubling them again.[60] Considering that by international standards Americans are not readers—the United States at that time placed an embarrassing twenty-fourth in per capita book sales when compared with other nations,[61] and included 72 million illiterates among its population[62]—the evangelical book business had established an amazingly successful penetration of the market. One estimate claimed that every year 50 million Americans read at least one Christian book other than the Bible.[63] By the end of the decade there were over seventy evangelical publishing houses,[64] and the number of evangelical periodicals increased by two dozen annually.[65] Religious book sales increased from $2.6 billion to $3.3 billion over the years 1998 to 2004.[66]

Large coastal publishers soon wised up to such potential windfall profits. Because evangelical publishers knew their market so well the obvious play for secular publishing houses to quickly gain a toehold in the evangelical market was to buy out an established evangelical publisher. Harper & Row purchased Zondervan, Hal Lindsey's original publisher. ABC acquired Word Books, a prosperous evangelical publisher centered in Waco with offices in Dallas, Los Angeles, Nashville, and London.

Word Books is just one division of a corporate empire which includes Word Book Club (operates much like the Book of the Month Club), a film division (very profitable), and Word Records, a music division (the largest strictly Christian music company in the world). A Word Record artist is expected to do more than sell records; he or she must also sell a way of life. But Word is not about to sign someone who has turned to "Christian" music because he or she could not cut it in the secular market. Talent is a prerequisite—Amy Grant is a shining example.

Word Records has hit a gold vein. With sales exceeding three-quarters of a billion dollars annually, the contemporary "Christian" music industry has surpassed the market for jazz, classical, New Age, and soundtracks.[67] The label "Christian" has opened up a hitherto hidden and untapped market. As a result, several labels have been taken over by secular corporations eager to profit on this captive market.

Every April musicians, publicists, journalists, and agents for recording companies and distributors flock to Nashville for the Gospel Music Association's annual convention. But Nashville is not the only center for Christian music. There is Christian contemporary country from Waco, Texas, and even Christian rap from Detroit and Christian heavy metal from Los Angeles. Indeed, virtually every type of music can be classed as "Christian"; it is the message, not the sound which counts. Christian music is just one example of how the hidden evangelical subculture mirrors and duplicates the secular culture.

The key to growing and maintaining a culture is its youth. A major reason the mainline church has lost ground over the past several decades is its failure to attract and keep young people. Its graying membership is dying off. By contrast, conservative churches are filled with young families—essential to the long-term growth of conservative Christianity.

Young people are the future, their education the principal force in acculturation. When it comes to educating the young—both in church and at school—evangelicals have excelled. Between 1971 and 1978 the number of "Christian" schools—those with born-again teachers and a "Christ-centered curriculum"[68]—increased by an astounding 47 percent and the number of teachers and students doubled.[69] By 1984 student enrollment had doubled again, with 10,000 Christian private primary and secondary schools, a doubling in five years[70]—a pace of three new schools a day.[71] Three decades earlier more than ninety percent of school-aged children attended public schools, but with the influx into private Christian schools that fraction had dropped to less than three quarters.[72] By the time the general public had heard of the Moral Majority one and a half million students were enrolled in "Christian" schools,[73] with a further half to one million educated at home,[74] the motivation for home education almost always religious.

In one church community, studied by Nancy Tatom Ammerman, nine out of ten children attend specifically "Christian" schools and academies, then go on to study at Christian colleges.[75] Emphasis is on the basic verbal and mathematical skills, and rote memorizing and recitation, as opposed to critical thinking. The Bible is front and center, the context for all other learning. History becomes "American Christian History," events understood in light of the nation's godly purpose and origin.

Fearing what their children might be exposed to in the secular educational system, conservative parents often provide their own brand of schooling at home. The *Statistical Abstract of the United States, 2008* puts the number of homeschooled children at 2.2 percent of students.[76] Children grow up in a protective cocoon, isolated from the evils of the broader society. By the time they reach adulthood many will feel uncomfortable in anything but their own conservative subculture, where they socialize and lead their lives almost exclusively in the company of their fellows.

Back in 1982 when, with his wife Vickie, Michael Farris began educating his children at home, he didn't know anyone else doing it; it was illegal in many states. The following year he founded the Home School Legal Defense Association and became a full-time homeschooling advocate. In large part because of Farris's activism homeschooling is now a legal right in every state.

Today an annual Christian Home Educators convention features three days of lectures and workshops. Parents attending the convention can choose from a wide array of educational games, videos, and Christian curricula.

Countless booths display instruction manuals, biblical coloring books, and for the very young — adventure stories with Christian heroes.

Farris is also the founder and president of Patrick Henry College in rural Virginia, catering specifically to homeschooled evangelical students. Although this college has been in service only since 2000 and accepts less than 100 students a year it furnished seven percent of the White House's interns during George W. Bush's administration and twenty-two conservative congressmen employed one or more of its graduates as interns.[77]

Education beyond the primary and secondary levels has long been on the agenda of fundamentalists. After the Scopes trial they had been subjected to ridicule. As usual, H. L. Mencken was in the lead, pouring contempt on the fundamentalist college: "You will find one in every mountain valley of the land, with its single building in its bare pasture lot, and its faculty of half-idiot pedagogues and brokendown preachers. One man, in such a college, teaches oratory, ancient history, arithmetic and Old Testament exegesis."[78] Smarting from the wounds of 1925, fundamentalists yearned to forestall the notion that they lacked a good education.

Fortunately fundamentalism had devised its own form of special education, central to the structure and coherence of the movement, decades before — the Bible institute. Historian Ernest Sandeen places great value upon this institution; he claims that after the devastation of the Scopes trial "fundamentalism owed its survival to the Bible institutes."[79]

Back in 1882, flushed with the success of the Niagara conferences, James Brookes had proposed the establishment of a summer school for the training of young men who had neither the means nor the time for formal education at a college or seminary. He insisted that there were hundreds of these young Christian men who "would receive more instruction out of the Scriptures in one month at such a school than in three years at most of the theological institutions."[80] Such a school would provide laymen with sufficient Bible knowledge and practical training to advance the cause of premillennialism and dispensationalism through the wider culture.

Although Brookes's particular concept did not materialize, leading premillennialists began teaching pilot classes in Chicago during the mid-1880s in response to Dwight L. Moody's plea for the training of "gap men — men to stand between the laity and the ministers."[81] By 1889 these efforts had culminated in a full-time school, named after his death the Moody Bible Institute. This institute was followed in short order by others, so that by the early years of the new century "most of the millenarians without pastoral charge found their base of operations in one of these schools."[82] This significant piece of the fundamentalist program was standardized with the founding of the World's Christian Fundamentals Association in 1919.

At first these institutes offered a two-year program. At the Moody institute students attended lectures on the Bible during the morning, then engaged in practical work in the city during the afternoon and evening. As Moody had recommended, "Never mind the Greek and Hebrew; give them plain English and good Scripture. It is the sword of the Lord and cuts deep."[83] A typical curriculum consisted of nine subjects: biblical and practical theology, synthetic study of the Bible, biblical exegesis, special biblical studies, Bible readings, Christian work, missions, sermons, sacred music. During the 1920s and 1930s some schools expanded their programs to three years. Later some added a fourth year and granted a degree, to become full-fledged Bible colleges.

The focus of study in the Bible institutes is apocalypticism: the Second Coming, the Rapture, Last Days, and the millennium. So successful an enterprise have these Bible institutes become, historian Sandeen can assert that "millenarianism has been taught in the twentieth century principally by Bible institute instructors and in Bible institute classrooms."[84] The Bible institute has long been in the vanguard regarding the propagation of dispensationalist fundamentalism. But it has served the fundamentalist movement in more than just education and training. While it has provided the movement with preachers, teachers, missionaries, musicians, and sundry other dedicated individuals—two hundred Bible institutes graduate 100,000 students every year[85]—it has also served as a social and administrative center, providing a spiritual home for those strong in the faith. Many attend, not as a trainee intending to serve in some formal vocation, but simply to enrich their own personal religious life and to obtain a sound grounding in proper doctrine. In many cases son will follow father, and attend the same institute. Graduates of the various Bible institutes regard instructors and fellow students met during their student days as not only lifelong friends, but "their community of primary allegiance."[86] Former students renew fellowship at the annual Founder's Day and summer conferences, receive a monthly alumni magazine, and stay in close touch with the old school in many other ways.

Bible institutes have become particularly important in recent decades as more and more conservative American youth seek higher education. College education has proved anathema for young people raised in a conservative faith. College educated young people too often abandon the church of their parents—a trend that began in earnest in the 1960s and has continued since. A survey disclosed that the majority of Americans who had only grade school education believed the Bible to be the literal word of God, but only one in five of those with a college education did.[87]

Caught in this trend, several Bible institutes have undergone a transformation. The Bible Institute of Los Angeles (acronym BIOLA), subsidized by the Lyman Stewart of *The Fundamentals* fame, was renamed Biola College in 1949, then in 1981 as Biola University. Along with such changes in name, many Bible institutes have introduced courses in the sciences and liberal arts in order to gain the accreditation enabling them to grant degrees.

Bible institutes are undeniably important for the spread of dispensationalism, but Dallas Theological Seminary is its Vatican. Many leading dispensationalist luminaries have served as faculty. With 1,937 students[88] and 12,800 alumni[89] Dallas Seminary has been the most important training center for dispensationalist teachers and pastors. Dispensationalist colleges, Bible institutes, and seminaries, as well as many conservative churches, prefer to hire Dallas graduates over those from denominational seminaries. In the words of its statement of purpose: "The Seminary is committed to the primacy of the authoritative, inerrant Scriptures ... applying the truths of the Christian faith ... given within the framework of evangelical, premillennial, dispensational theology."[90] This in the face of local opposition: Grace Presbytery of Texas declares dispensationalism a heresy "out of accord with the system of doctrine set forth in the Westminster Confession of Faith."[91]

Dallas Seminary bills itself as "the largest independent evangelical seminary in the world,"[92] and in fact it is the largest nondenominational seminary in the world. It has extension schools in Philadelphia and San Antonio, and boasts 1600 master's students and 99 students working on the Ph. D.[93]

On October 1, 1924, Lewis Sperry Chafer's decade-long dream was realized. Evangelical Theological College, as the seminary was called for its first twelve years, opened its doors to its first class—just thirteen students. This new establishment in every way bore Chafer's image. He had been the driving force behind its founding, had helped phrase its doctrinal statement, had chosen its location. Chafer wanted his seminary to be nondenominational so that students would come from various denominations to study, then return to their denominations to spread the dispensationalist message. He made sure every member of his faculty was a devoted dispensationalist.

Although Chafer had no formal theological education, he had closely associated with C. I. Scofield for several years at various Bible institutes and schools. In 1923 he succeeded Scofield as pastor of First Congregational Church in Dallas. Scofield was the father Chafer had lost as a child. No one had greater influence on his life. When Scofield died Chafer replaced him as leading luminary among dispensationalists.

Chafer felt free to tinker with dispensationalist doctrine over which he alone seemed curator. He believed that Armageddon would involve Iran, Iraq, and Israel—a notion passed along to future generations. Chafer wrote the definitive systematic theology of dispensationalism — an eight-volume work of 2700 pages. In the first volume he boldly asserted, "Apart from a sane

recognition of the great purposes and time-periods of God, no true understanding of the Bible has ever been received."[94] Chafer served his beloved
seminary as theology professor and president until his death in 1952.

In 1926, shortly after the ground had been broken for Dallas Seminary,
another fundamentalist institute of higher learning was founded — Bob Jones
University, named after Bob Jones, Senior. Although the original venue has
been changed a few times, the university continues to flourish, with an enrollment of 4,200 and a total of 35,000 graduates.[95]

Fundamentalist through and through, Bob Jones University is "a delib-
erately maintained time-warp which [has] essentially slammed the door on
the late twentieth century."[96] It harkens back, as one writer so eloquently
phrases it, to "that well-scrubbed, homogeneous America which *Reader's
Digest* or Norman Rockwell traded in."[97] Dubbed by its founder The World's
Most Unusual University, it houses in a special glass case a Bible once owned
by Billy Sunday, teaches "filmmaking in a Christian setting," and offers a
doctorate in Bible Studies.

Social activity between the sexes is restricted. Men are not allowed to
associate freely with female students outside classes. There is a chaperoned
dating parlor for weekends, and unmarried couples are forbidden to be seen
together out walking after seven in the evening. The university bookshop
carries no tempting newspapers or magazines. At ten each morning students
attend mandatory chapel service; seats are assigned and attendance is taken.
By 10:30 P.M. students are in their dorms for group prayers; lights out at
eleven.

Faculty and staff at Bob Jones University have produced a complete
Christian school curriculum for grades K-12, including textbooks and sup-
plementary materials, published by Bob Jones University Press.

A poll conducted in 1980 found that Oral Roberts was better recognized
than the president of that time (Jimmy Carter) or even John F. Kennedy.
Roberts began as an evangelist and faith healer then went on to found a religious empire which includes a $500 million complex in Tulsa, Oklahoma.
City of Faith Hospital and, across the street, Oral Roberts University are central to this complex. The hospital consists of three towers; the central one,
sixty stories high, is crowned with a flashing red light to warn low-flying air-
craft. Out front is a giant bronze casting — hands joined in prayer, sixty feet
in height.

Oral Roberts University is all gold and white, domes and cylindrical towers. Two hundred feet in the air is a gaslit flame beacon which never goes
out. If the buildings look twenty-first century, student life more resembles
that of bygone generations. Male and female are kept separate. Curfews
abound. Profane language is forbidden, as are student protests and petitions.

Dorm rooms are inspected regularly. Men must be clean-shaven, keep their hair short, and wear ties, even to the cafeteria and library. Women must wear dresses or skirts. Dancing is not allowed, and all students must participate in an exercise program and pass an annual fitness test. Oral Roberts University assures parents that their offspring will get a Christian education, insulated from much of modern secular life. Yet graduates get a fully accredited degree recognized by employers and graduate schools.

Another conservative Christian university has an endowment among the top one hundred universities in the United States. Regent University (formerly CBN University) is the brainchild of Pat Robertson. His aim in founding such an institution was to build for the future, to supply committed Bible-believing Christians who would spread their beliefs across the nation. Forty-seven hundred students[98] study law, education, business, theology, and communication (the latter embracing radio, television, drama, film, public relations, media management, journalism, and advertising). The School of Communication offers a doctoral program.

Liberal theology coming from the secular halls of higher education in recent decades justifies the fears of conservative Christians, and warrants the founding of specifically "Christian" institutes of higher learning.

In his massive three-volume work on the history of liberal theology Gary Dorrien draws a bead on the core difference between liberals and conservatives: "Fundamentally, liberal theology is the idea of a Christian perspective based on reason and experience, not external authority."[99] For conservative Christians *the* external authority is, of course, the Bible. The Bible is at the center of all conservative Christian education, from home-schooling to the Bible institutes to Bob Jones University and Dallas Seminary.

Some liberal theologians make no reference whatsoever to the Bible. They can get along—and apparently would prefer to do so—without God. Late in 1965 issues of the *New York Times, The New Yorker,* and *Time* magazine shouted the proclamation of several theologians: God was dead. This death-of-God theology maintained that modern humanity had come of age. It was time to realize that "God" was just an idol, and needed to be relinquished.

Many liberal theologians saw value in the *concept* of God, even if they did not believe in the *existence* of a god. Theologian Gordon Kaufman said that God is "the mind's most profound and highest creation ... it brings unity and significance into all dimensions of its life."[100] Other liberal theologians criticized their colleagues for such meaningless word games, for engaging in practical atheism. Frederick Herzog lambasted theological schools as "enclaves of self-perpetuating intellectual elites reversing the order of God's priorities."[101] One theologian candidly admitted that while she had a very successful academic career, something was missing in her spiritual life.

The sociologist Peter Berger claims that liberal theology once functioned to keep Christianity alive in the modern world. But in this postmodern time it has become "a recipe for the self-liquidation of the Christian community."[102] Liberal theologian John Shelby Spong's books are controversial. Their provocative titles—*Born of a Woman, Resurrection: Myth or Reality?, Why Christianity Must Change or Die*—reflect the revolutionary thinking between their covers: that the apostle Paul was a homosexual; that virgin birth narratives were commonplace mythology in Jesus's time.

But, as Dorrien notes, by the late 1970s liberal theologians had lost most of their audience. The public could not understand their esoteric academic vocabulary, virtually incomprehensible to all but their colleagues. Liberal theologians had shifted so far toward secular modernism as to be out of touch with the beliefs of church-going Christians. Dorrien writes, "Postmodernized Americans, faced with a wider array of religious options than their parents, increasingly opted for dogmatic certainty or secular disbelief."[103] There was a shift from the 1970s onward away from the mainline center of the traditional denominations toward fundamentalism at one pole and secularism at the other pole, a widening rift between conservatives and liberals.

15

The Seventh Angel

The fundamentalist's life is lived separate from the larger secular culture, a life of discipline and structure, an orderly existence with no gray areas. Absolutes and predictability, rather than uncertainty. Answers, instead of questions. Submission to authority — pastoral, biblical, divine. "[God] has all the answers. I don't have responsibility.... He makes the decisions for me, and that is great!"[1] The pathway is clear, everything set in stone. The members of one church found 7,834 promises made by God in the Bible — a veritable legal contract, because God does not break a promise.[2] Every facet of human life is laid out, a roadmap for Christian living.

That roadmap ends in the last book of the Bible, where fundamentalists and other conservatives find what they consider God's most reassuring promise — the Second Coming of Jesus Christ and the millennium. Even liberal Christians believe these promises, but differ in the details, in the sequence of events; they interpret this final book of the Bible less literally, and give it less importance within the context of the rest of the New Testament. Because, relative to liberals, conservatives place so much emphasis on the last book of the New Testament (Revelation, also known as the Apocalypse), they are considered "apocalypticists" or "millennialists."

Conservatives are reading authors like Jerry Jenkins and Tim LaHaye (a graduate of Bob Jones University). These two have collaborated on fifty-one apocalyptic novels[3] in which the Rapture takes central place. Their *Left Behind* series has spawned movies, CDs, children's books, and board games. Total sales for this fictional depiction of premillennial dispensationalism exceed sixty million,[4] garnering the authors fifty million dollars apiece.[5] A recent survey indicated that 17.7 percent of the population has read at least one of the books in the *Left Behind* series.[6] Jenkins notes, "We've had many unsaved [read "liberal"] people say they have accepted Christ because of reading *Left Behind* or one of the other books."[7]

Conservatives read Hal Lindsey's *The Late Great Planet Earth*, a commercial rehash of the dispensationalist end-time scenario he learned as a student at Dallas Theological Seminary.[8] Despite the fact that *The Late Great*

Planet Earth is a cultural phenomenon with sales over thirty-one million,[9] translation into thirty-one languages, and circulation in over fifty countries[10] ("the bestselling Christian book in history" other than the Bible[11]), it is unlikely to be found on the shelves of secular university libraries. A movie version of the book starring Orson Welles played in commercial theaters throughout the United States to scant critical praise and little critical attention.

Conservatives tout Lindsey as "the most widely read writer on prophetic themes in history"[12]— at one time he had three books on *The New York Times* bestseller list, and his other books have sold a further seventeen million. Lindsey had a television program syndicated throughout the United States on several Christian networks, yet he is unknown to most people in the wider culture, even professors of religious studies.

But thanks to authors like LaHaye and Lindsey, apocalypticism — particularly in its dispensationalist garb — is spreading. The chaotic and horrific events of recent times contribute. News of the terrorist destruction of the twin towers of the World Trade Center in New York City on September 11, 2001, led to a 60 percent jump in sales for *Left Behind* books.[13] Even in staunch mainline churches apocalypticism has reared its head since 9/11. The senior minister of Manhattan's Fifth Avenue Presbyterian Church remarks, "I would go for years without anyone asking about the end-times. But since Sept. 11, hardcore, crusty, cynical New York lawyers and stockbrokers who are not moved by anything are saying, 'Is the world going to end?,' 'are all the events of the Bible coming true?' They want to get right with God. I've never seen anything like it in my 30 years in ministry."[14]

The experience of the senior minister of Manhattan's Fifth Avenue Presbyterian Church is not unexpected. Such end-time anxiety is ever present, albeit at most times hidden from public view, simmering below the surface, waiting like subterranean embers to burst into flame. The Persian Gulf crisis of 1991 demonstrated the latent force of apocalypticism and how quickly, in times of crisis, it can move from the periphery to the center of public consciousness. At the height of that crisis renowned apocalypticist John Walwoord appeared on CBS and CNN to explain what was happening in light of biblical prophecy. Within days books about the end of the world were published and selling in the millions.

One half of all Americans believed that Christ might "possibly" return around the year 2000.[15] Many watched websites like "raptureready. com" which tracks precursors of the end-time — earthquakes, floods, plagues. As the year 2000 approached, the number of apocalyptic websites shot up to 239.[16] To this day apocalypticists remain on red alert; "raptureready. com" receives over eight million hits a day, as measured by the "Rapture Index," the "Dow Jones Industrial Average of End Time activity."[17]

Because of their beliefs, conservative Americans can be vulnerable to rogue apocalypticists, false prophets. There follows the stories of three minor apocalypses, three tragedies, highlighted in the media, burned into the public psyche. The first resulted from gross failure by authorities and the media to comprehend the religious significance of apocalypticism, to know about this hidden culture.

All three serve as a warning: If not understood and put into proper historical and religious context, apocalypticism can have dangerous, even violent, consequences. These stories can be seen as social experiments which ended in tragedy, but they convey a lesson.

April 19, 1993, was a nice spring day in most parts of the United States. People turned on their television to catch the evening news.

Their television screens captured a nightmarish scene. Black billowing smoke and a raging fire. As the commentator's voice explained what was playing out before their eyes, people heard and watched in shock, horror, and disbelief. It was the final episode in a drama that had lasted fifty-one days, the final episode in a drama which would sear its way into the collective consciousness.

Those who happened to be home earlier that day could have switched on their TV and seen the drama play out in real time. In less than one hour wood frame buildings burned to the ground, the flames driven by a thirty-mile-an-hour wind. It was estimated at the time that eighty-six persons had died in that fiery inferno, including seventeen children under ten years of age.[18] Later it was determined that the final death toll was seventy-four, including twenty-one children.[19]

At 6:02 that Monday morning military M-60 tanks modified for demolition duty had begun punching holes in the flimsy wooden structure. Tear gas was inserted through these holes, intended to drive the occupants from the building.

But no one was coming out, for inside the occupants had donned gas masks. Over the next six hours the onslaught escalated. Four military Bradley vehicles fired gas canisters through the windows. Still no one exited the building. Then, around noon, the first puffs of smoke, coming from second-story windows.

How the fire started was not known at the time, and may never be known. But one thing is clear. The whole operation, over the extended period of almost two months, resulted in the highest death toll of any federal law enforcement action in memory.[20] And it was one of the most massive in the history of U. S. enforcement. The cost ran into the millions of dollars. There was never less than seven hundred personnel on hand on any day of the siege:

from the Federal Bureau of Alcohol Tobacco and Firearms, the FBI, the Texas Rangers, the local police and sheriff's office, U. S. Customs, the National Guard, the Texas Department of Public Safety, and the United States Army.[21] But from any humane perspective the real cost was in human lives. Uncounted among the dead, two fetuses, one near full-term, the other seven months.[22] Lives that never got started.

It had all begun six weeks earlier, on the last day of February, an incident also seen by millions watching the evening news. "Operation Trojan Horse" was the official designation, but front-line personnel had facetiously nicknamed it "Showtime." For those watching their TV screens, no made-for-TV movie could have been more exciting. Helicopters buzzed over a ramshackle building. Law enforcement officers in combat gear were scaling the walls, smashing windows, lobbing in grenades. Gunfire. There was lots of gunfire, from the officers and from inside the building. A full-fledged gun battle.

Soon it seemed that those inside the building were winning. The so-called "dynamic entry" had been turned back. Wounded federal agents were being swiftly carried away by their comrades, bleeding profusely. When the numbers came out later four of the seventy-six who took part in the raid had died and fifteen had been wounded,[23] along with six dead who resided in the building. Never had there been such carnage among federal agents in a single day.

Now, in April, all was readied for the main event. The news media were on the spot right from the beginning. Several days earlier local television stations had been apprised of the situation by Public Information Officers of the Bureau of Alcohol, Tobacco, and Firearms. But the BATF was not about to trust filming the event to the local news media. The public relations people of the BATF filmed the raid themselves, planning to turn the footage over later to the TV stations. For this was to be its biggest operation since the Prohibition. Extensive training for the raid had taken place at the Army's Fort Hood, sixty miles southwest, and as an eighty-vehicle convoy approached on the interstate, cameras were rolling. The BATF wanted to put a positive spin on things to counter recent bad publicity. Later, when the raid turned into a disaster, it was found that, strangely, those BATF cameras had "malfunctioned."

But that didn't matter. More than a thousand reporters and cameramen had responded. Soon a veritable media Satellite City rose out of the flat Texas plains, costing two million dollars a day to maintain.[24] Tents and portable toilets were set up. Daily Fed Ex and mail deliveries arranged, exclusive telephone and electric lines in place. A mile-long collection of trailers packed with electronic gear, sixty-foot satellite dishes. CNN's Winnebago came with a roll-out artificial lawn complete with yard ornaments—apparently they planned to stay awhile. The locals got in on the circus, ready to make a quick buck, selling this and that. A Salvation Army truck dispensed sandwiches and other goodies.

There were, of course, rumors (a constant with media gatherings): those inside the raided building had been stockpiling plutonium, and had been tunneling their way to a nearby federal research station over the past year.

Rumors would have to suffice, because reporters were not allowed access to the raw facts. Telephone lines to the building were cut. Barricades thrown up. The press would have to shoot photos by telephoto lens from two miles away.[25] There would be official spokespersons; all other officials were under gag orders. Key documents would be sealed. Later, when a few residents left the building, reporters were denied opportunity to interview, and all hearings were closed to the public. With the situation so tightly managed, news journalists were no more than lackeys to government spinmeisters. Their diet was restricted to whatever officialdom felt it could safely divulge.

And what was the official line? The BATF had initiated the raid on the grounds of weapons charges, based on a tip from the local sheriff's office that powdered aluminum and gunpowder had been delivered to the building. These substances can be used to make grenades, prohibited by federal law. But they can also be used to reload spent rifle cartridges, something entirely legal. The residents had amassed a large collection of guns. They claimed that this was part of a business that helped support life in the building. They bought and sold guns at a profit. What was the problem? Texas is a "gun state"; with four registered weapons for every man, woman, and child.[26] There is no federal or Texas law forbidding stockpiling guns. You could own thousands if you wished. But there was other evidence that residents had purchased parts which allowed them to convert semi-automatic guns to fully automatic guns (machine guns). Once again, this was legal at the time; more than 234,000 Americans owned machine guns.[27] Automatic weapons could be purchased, or made—conversion kits were available. Rather than ban machine guns, the government preferred to collect hefty registration fees. Finally, it came down to one thing: no one had applied for a permit to own homemade machine guns.

But it wasn't just guns. The story coming out in the press was much more spectacular, even lurid. It wasn't just that the flimsy wooden building located outside the city of Waco, Texas, was considered "a heavily-fortified compound." The news media reported that the residents, including children, were "hostages" under the "mind control" of a "charismatic leader," one David Koresh. Koresh was reputed to be a religious fanatic, the autocratic leader of a "cult," who, among other things, molested children. And would continue to do so, if no action was taken to stop him, and soon. Moreover, hadn't the State Department received a cable from the United States Embassy in Australia in April 1992 concerning a tip which said that the small community occupying the compound — known as the Branch Davidians — were contemplating mass suicide? If the legal authorities didn't do something soon, a mass tragedy was surely in the offing.

The very mention of the word "cult" caused ears to prick up. The public knew all about cults. Cults had been a lively topic in the news media for the past few decades: Cult leaders are crazies, and their followers mindless robots, unable to free themselves from their leader's powers. Because cult leaders use psychological manipulation, government authorities deemed it legitimate and fair and even ethical to use similar weapons. Using psychological harassment, they hoped to grind down the spirit of the Branch Davidians. During the six weeks between the February raid and the April denouement, night and day, the residents of the building were subjected to inhumane treatment. High-decibel noises and glaring floodlights were employed to annoy, irritate, and disorient the residents, and deprive them of sleep. The sounds of crying babies, dying rabbits, sirens, and Tibetan chants alternated with those of bagpipes, crowing roosters, and dental drills. All this was accompanied by the ever-present helicopter flypasts. Or was that just the *sound* of helicopters coming over the high-volume sound system?

Despite media branding, the locals saw nothing unusual or demonic in David Koresh, the man. "If you're gonna write somethin' bad about David, I don't want to talk to you," a farmer told Ivan Solotaroff who was doing research for an *Esquire* article.[28] Koresh was known to pay his bills promptly. He came across as a regular guy, with a passion for high-performance cars and expensive guitars, who would "crack a cold Bud" and "bird-dog the babes." He kept his grass cut and stocked tanks with Florida bass and black crappie for local fishermen. He was a good and helpful neighbor. When a farmer's combine broke Koresh's people harvested his hay, then Koresh invited the farmer for a swim in his pool. Koresh would haul his guitar to a bar in town and play whenever the opportunity arose. Sometimes he would proselytize. Some of the locals found his music too religious and his ethics too restrictive. But as for his religious beliefs? "Saying God talks to you is not unusual. Down here, that's like saying the Avon lady called."[29]

David Koresh had begun life as Vernon Wayne Howell, the illegitimate offspring of a fourteen-year-old girl who dropped out of school when she became pregnant. His mother moved on to Dallas alone to start a new life, so for his first five years the boy lived with his maternal grandparents in Houston. At the end of that time young Vernon, nicknamed "Sputnik" on account of his hyperactivity, rejoined his mother who had found a new man — a lounge operator and carpenter.

Vernon's boyhood was relatively normal for the Texas working class. He went fishing and learned to shoot with a .22 and shotgun. The adult Howell loved his family enough to invite them for protracted visits at his new Waco residence. When he was wounded in the February 28 raid, afraid he might be dying, he phoned his mother: "I'm dying, alright? But I'll be back real soon, okay? ... I'll see ya'll in the skies."[30]

Vernon failed first grade at school twice, and failed second grade, until it was recognized that he suffered from a learning disability. He received remedial training and continued in school until the eleventh grade. By all counts he was no trouble maker, despite that fact that his home life as a teen-ager was less than exemplary. (By her own admission his mother liked to party, and his half-brother went to prison on charges of burglary and drugs.) But Vernon was an obedient son, got good deportment grades at school, and was regular in attendance — an average student.

Young Vernon liked tinkering, working with his hands. Anything mechanical fascinated him — cars, radios. He loved music. He found a guitar in an abandoned barn, got a few lessons at a local music store, and was soon playing country and western with garage bands.

But his real passion was religion. His grandmother took him to church often, his mother seldom. Most kids hate going to church and are restless in the pew. Not Vernon. He paid close attention to every word. Church wasn't enough. Vernon listened to local radio preachers and watched the big-time evangelists on TV. His mother didn't know what to make of it: "I was raised in the Adventist Church, but I didn't know what I believed."[31] Apparently religion was not in the genes. But it was Vernon's "thing." He had a love affair with the Bible. By the age of twelve he had memorized long passages. In high school he preached the Bible to his classmates.

Adolescence took its usual toll. Vernon was working as a carpenter, bringing in lots of cash, the new owner of a prized pickup, when a young girl approached him one evening for a lift home. Things happen, and soon she was pregnant. By Vernon. The young man's soul experienced a religious dilemma. He was confused. He didn't do drugs, drank little, and now this? The girl's father told Vernon to disappear.

Vernon prayed and prayed, and listened for the voice of his Lord. He moved from Dallas to Tyler and started attending a Seventh-Day Adventist church where a friend told him about a religious community related to the Seventh-Day Adventists. Mount Carmel. Apparently that group was led by a prophet who claimed to receive revelations. So one afternoon in 1981 a bearded young man, troubled in his religion, showed up at what would be the locale of his death some twelve years later.

Soon he was working at Mount Carmel as a handyman, valued for his carpentry and mechanical skills. He found living conditions Spartan. The building itself was of simple structure — wood frame, covered on the outside with wood paneling, on the inside in some places with fiberboard, in other places with sheetrock, or plywood. These thin walls provided little protection from the cold and the heat. There was no furnace, no air conditioning. Electric space heaters did little to hold off the cold Texas winters. In summer you melted.

There were no bathrooms. Running water was a luxury found only in the kitchen. The men had devised makeshift facilities, including a shower, under a tree outside. The women and children took sponge baths and used chamber pots which they emptied into plastic buckets and thence into an old septic tank.

The residents slept in tiny rooms, several to a room. Most rooms had no door, so people hung sheets or blankets across the entrance to afford some minor degree of privacy. Residents were allowed their own private possessions; this was not a commune. Some even put name tags on such simple items as washcloths, and initials on clothespins. The sleeping quarters had no closets, and few had chests of drawers. So clothing was hung on improvised hooks and rods. Other possessions were kept in boxes; where there was insufficient room these were piled in the hallway or, for those who had one, in the trunk of their car.

Vernon Howell liked things just the way he found them. Years later he remarked, "I want to keep the building kind of rough in shape and not really finished and that way people that come here, they're coming for one reason, because they're coming to know something."[32]

That something was the Bible. As one of the residents commented, "For many years Mt. Carmel was a place where people came from many parts of the world, for serious pursuit of the Scriptures. The Center had been graced by the presence of a succession of inspired teachers.... As a matter of fact, the way Mt. Carmel was organized was really no different from a monastery."[33] Later, under Howell's leadership, life would become even more monastic, as he forbade men and women to sleep together. The men slept in bunks on the first floor, the women and children in separate quarters on the floor above. Sexual intercourse would take one's focus away from the primary concern — the Bible.

The news media used the term "Branch Davidians" for the residents of Mount Carmel because property deeds stated that ownership belonged to the "Branch Davidian Seventh-Day Adventist Association." While all were welcome at Mount Carmel, the vast majority had Seventh-Day Adventist backgrounds.

The lineage of the Seventh-Day Adventist Church goes back to William Miller. Belief in an imminent apocalypse was his legacy to the church which followed his lead. It was left to Ellen G. White to set the foundation of the new church. At just nineteen years of age she began to have visions in which, she believed, God revealed to her great truths. Her first revelation was that the Sabbath should be kept on Saturday, the seventh day, rather than on Sunday, a pagan practice. This focused new interest in the Old Testament, something Christians in general tended to neglect.

Ellen White added another radical revision to standard Christian thinking. She believed that Jesus was not the final act of God's work with humankind. Jesus was but one step in a long history of the revelation of God's Truth. God's Truth is found in the Bible, but it is hidden — which is why large portions of Scripture make no sense. Our human abilities fall short of being able to understand. But every so often God chooses a special man or woman to be his voice. God reveals to this individual a portion of God's Truth in Scripture. Ellen White believed herself to be one of the chosen few.

Seventh-Day Adventistism grew in numbers and became an established church. Then along came Victor T. Houteff. Houteff saw himself as a prophet, following in the tradition of Ellen White. He believed his fellow Adventists were becoming too lax. Original precepts had been abandoned, Adventist practices compromised by worldly pursuits. It was time for reform, for getting back to the basics.

By 1935 church leaders were charging Houteff with heresy. Severed from church membership, he and a few followers established a community outside of Waco, Texas— Mount Carmel. This separatist group —called the Davidian Seventh-Day Adventists— worked at converting other Adventists to their stricter view, in light of their belief that the end of the world and the Second Advent of Christ was fast approaching.

In 1955 Houteff died, leaving his wife Florence in charge. Two years later she sold their property and established a new Mount Carmel nine miles east of Waco, near the town of Elk. Florence Houteff is best known for her prediction that the world would end on April 22, 1959. She called on Davidians worldwide to come to Mount Carmel. Prior to the big day some nine hundred gathered, many having quit their jobs and sold their homes. They camped in seventy-five tents and awaited The End in the spring rain.

The big event failed to materialize. The Davidians were in disarray. Their numbers declined and parcels of the property were sold. Eventually the Davidians split into eight smaller groups, many of these settling in various locations around the United States. One group, to be named the Branch Davidians, remained in Mount Carmel.

Ben and Lois Roden had moved into Mount Carmel shortly after Victor Houteff's death. Ben had many ideas and put them into writing to share with other Davidians. Eventually he was able to command the loyalty of those residing at Mount Carmel and became their new leader. Roden believed that The End was close at hand and that his followers, the Branch Davidians, should lead strict lives in preparation. Among other things, he introduced the observance of the biblical celebrations of Passover, Pentecost, and the Feast of the Tabernacles.

When Roden died his wife Lois took over. But her son George felt he should lead the community. A bitter struggle followed, with George engaging in legal maneuvering in an attempt to wrest control from his mother.

Enter Vernon Howell. Lois Roden had many religious conceptions of her own, which Howell readily accepted. Lois Roden was greatly impressed with Howell's knowledge of Scripture and his earnest comportment. Soon she was grooming Howell as her replacement. This did not go unnoticed, or appreciated, by her son George. The dispute over control of the community escalated. When the dust settled Vernon Howell and those who chose to side with him were in charge.

Howell made a trip to Israel in 1985. Something happened there — something simply described as a profound "experience." He believed that he had undergone a transformation; he had been remade as a new being. Before the trip he had great knowledge of Scripture; now he was inspired. He could weave together seemingly disparate passages in novel and meaningful ways. He no longer simply *studied* the Bible. Now he *knew*. Its meaning, from Genesis to Revelation, was day by day being revealed to him, as if spoken directly into his ears.

Howell took the name "David Koresh" — emblematic of the change in his being — from the Hebrew of the first verse of the forty-fifth chapter of the book of Isaiah which says that God spoke "le-meshichoh le-koresh" — "to his anointed one, to Koresh." The Hebrew for "anointed one" is "messiah," which in the Greek of the New Testament becomes "christos." Hence, "Jesus Christ" is to be understood as "Jesus, the Christ," or "Jesus, the anointed one." This was how David Koresh understood Jesus — as a messiah, one in a long line of individuals chosen, anointed, by God for a special purpose.

The news media made a big point of implying that Koresh saw himself as Jesus Christ. This simply was not true. He did not claim to be Jesus Christ. By taking the name "David Koresh," Howell saw himself, like King David of the Old Testament, to be chosen by God for a special purpose, another in a long line of God's "anointed," God's "messiahs."

Koresh believed himself to be the "seventh angel," the one anointed by God as the final messenger before the Second Advent of Jesus Christ. ("Angel" in the Greek New Testament means "messenger.") In the Adventist tradition, like William Miller, Ellen White, Victor Houteff, and Ben Roden before him, Koresh was to bring the end-time message to his fellow Adventists. He understood Miller to be the first of the seven angels mentioned in the book of Revelation. Miller had begun to open the seven seals mentioned in Revelation. Koresh would continue to open these seals. Those at Mount Carmel would be privileged to be present at the opening. For opening the seals would not only reveal the hidden meaning of the Bible, it would also, by that very act, signal the beginning of the end-time, the coming of the millennium.

David Koresh's followers called themselves "Bible students" or "students of the seven seals." They were not attracted to Koresh as a charismatic figure, but for his ability to reveal the meaning of Scripture. He focused on the book of Revelation — "All the books of the Bible begin and end in Revelation"[34] — but then moved onto passages throughout the Bible, bringing everything into perfect harmony. He could quickly go from here to there in the Bible with great facility. His elucidation of Scripture made of the Bible a consistent and internally logical whole.

The residents of Mount Carmel were there to learn all that David Koresh could teach them about what the Bible revealed, about what had been revealed and was being revealed to him. They believed Koresh was the messenger mentioned in Revelation, sent from God to open the seven seals, to reveal the hidden meaning of Scripture. The fact that he could so skillfully elucidate Scripture was proof that this was so. As one of them said, "I learned more with him in one night than I had learned in a lifetime of going to church."[35] Another, who had a master's degree in theology, said that in three hours with Koresh, "I had perceived more significant biblical truths than I had done the entire eight years I had been involved with organized religion."[36] One woman who had been a Branch Davidian for twenty-five years said that the Mount Carmel residents did not like being sent into town for errands or business for fear of missing something that Koresh might be teaching that day. She mentioned the long hours of Bible study as a joyful experience: "We might sit there for 15, 19 hours, 10 hours, 6 hours. It would depend. It was never a bore."[37]

The residents of Mount Carmel met morning and evening for Bible study, along with communion service of bread and wine. Community life totally revolved around Bible study. As one of the group commented, "We lived, ate, and breathed the Bible.... It was the whole center of our being."[38] Some who survived the holocaust of April 19 said one of the last things they saw in the compound was parents in gas masks reading the Bible to their children.

The opening of the seven seals would bring on the end-time. By 1992, when Koresh renamed Mount Carmel "Ranch Apocalypse," his people were in a sense already living in the end-time. They saw themselves as the fortunate few, God's true people. They felt their lives in common with the disciples and martyrs, who down through history had stood firm, proclaiming God's truth in the face of the sinful majority. As one of them said, "Mt. Carmel was designed for purposes of holistically transcending this present artificial and sensory based consciousness.... Mt. Carmel was designed of heaven for purposes of accomplishing the above transcendence.... while blocking out the artificial noise of humanity."[39]

When the events of February and April 1993 transpired, the residents of Ranch Apocalypse were ready to die, to partake in the end-time. They were not worried, because "we've got God on our side."[40] Why be concerned? God was scripting events, and his script was found in the book of Revelation. Even those who were sent out by Koresh for one purpose or another during the siege had not wanted to leave. As the flames consumed the building on April 19, one woman ran from the fire and then, perhaps feeling a traitor to her own belief, started back toward the blaze. At least one Branch Davidian who was away from the compound when it burned down expressed regret that she had missed the millennium.

16

False Prophets

On the hot humid nights of August 9 and 10, 1969, seven people were brutally butchered in two of Los Angeles' finer residential districts. The goriest of movie scripts could not approach the stark reality of these grisly murder scenes. A total of 169 stab wounds, many five inches deep. A male victim shot twice, bludgeoned thirteen times, stabbed fifty-one times.[1] Another male with multiple stab wounds, the word "war" carved on his belly, a knife and fork stuck in his dead body.[2] Another victim stabbed forty-one times.[3] Words smeared in the blood of the victims: "pig" on a front door, "death to pigs" and "rise" on living-room walls, "helter skelter" on a refrigerator door.

A year and a half and 8750 hours of detective work[4] later a jury found Charles Manson and three women in their early twenties, Susan Denise Atkins, Leslie Van Houten, and Patricia Krenwinkel, guilty of murder in the Tate-LaBianca killings—what *Time* magazine termed "one of the grisliest ... crimes of the century."[5] A half year later Charles Watson, also in his early twenties, would be convicted as well. When the trials were over and the sentences delivered, one question remained: What was the motive?

Neither Manson nor the members of his "Family" knew their victims personally. On several occasions members of the Family had taken part in "creepy-crawls"[6]—they went through a house while the residents were sleeping and made some minor rearrangement which would alert the residents that someone had been through their home. Rosemary LaBianca, one of the Family's seven victims, had told a close friend only weeks before her death that someone had been coming to their home while they were away. Things had been gone through and the dogs, which were normally inside the house, were outside. On the nights of the murders items worth thousands of dollars were in plain view, but there was no evidence of theft. Rosemany LaBianca's wallet was taken but was later found, money intact. What, then, was the motive?

The prosecutor in the Tate-LaBianca trials, Vincent Bugliosi, discovered that the words "helter skelter," written in blood in the LaBianca home, provided the clue to the motivation behind the killings. Bugliosi had found the same words on a door at Spahn Movie Ranch, the headquarters of a group which called themselves "the Family." This suggested a link to the Tate-LaBianca deaths.

While in prison Susan Atkins bragged about the murders to a fellow inmate. In a note she indicated that the "motive behind all this ... was to instill fear into the pigs and to bring on judgment day ... the second coming of Christ, M [Manson] is he who has come to save."[7] Questioned before the grand jury, Atkins revealed that Helter Skelter was "the last war on the face of the earth. It would be all the wars that have ever been fought built one on top of the other."[8] Bugliosi concluded that "Judgment Day, Armageddon, [and] Helter Skelter ... were one and the same."[9]

Manson was convinced that he personally could start Armageddon, the final war. One witness reported that Manson believed that "God's getting ready to pull down the curtain," to start "over again with his chosen people."[10] God's chosen people were, of course, the Family. The Family would multiply in the desert until they numbered the biblical 144,000. Manson got this "from reading things into the Bible, from Revelations."[11] Manson found mention in Revelation of a "bottomless pit." Members of the Family spent days searching for the bottomless pit which would shelter them from Helter Skelter, protect them from Armageddon.

Once while being booked, Manson was asked his occupation. A minister, he replied. He would preach and lecture the Family for hours at a time. He "avidly read the Bible."[12] His favorite book of the Bible was Revelation, as many people told Bugliosi.[13] He "read and reread the book of Revelation."[14] The lurid imagery of this book was grist for Manson's fertile and diabolical imagination. He was particularly fascinated with chapter 9. He quoted it often.

Revelation 9 talks about locusts with "hair as the hair of women" (verse 8). Verse 15 mentions "four angels," and verse 19 has the words "their power is in their mouth." Who else could this be, Manson reasoned, but the British rock group, the Beatles? Beatles, locusts, what's the difference?

In the Beatles' White Album Manson found inspiration for his own personal interpretation of Revelation. Beginning in late 1968, when he first heard the White Album, Manson seemed on a collision course with destiny. His dreams of being a rock star frustrated, Manson assumed the mantle of the Beatles' glory by fancying himself the interpreter of the musical four. In the White Album's hidden lyrics Manson detected a clarion call; the Beatles were indirectly communicating with Manson: "You say you got a real solution.... We'd all love to see the plan."[15] Clearly, the Beatles wanted Manson to show the way to Helter Skelter. One of the songs in the album was titled "Helter Skelter"—the source of Manson's term for Judgment Day, Armageddon. From this song Manson connected the words "coming down" and "helter skelter"[16] to mean all hell was about to break. That the song was about a children's playground slide didn't matter to Manson. He grasped at the words "the bottom" as reference to the bottomless pit.[17]

But perhaps Charlie's favorite piece from the White Album was "Revolution 9." The only words were "number 9, number 9," repeated over and over. It was clear to Manson that "Revolution 9{in} was a thin disguise for "Revelation 9." Did he not hear the word "rise," once as a whimper, once as a long slow scream? He played the recording over and over for the Family.

According to Manson, the Beatles were waiting for Jesus Christ and he was that Christ. After Helter Skelter was completely acted out he would rule the world. Even Manson's name was tailor-made for the role he sought. Or at least he made it that way. He altered Charles Milles Manson slightly to get Charles Willis Manson. Say it slowly: "Charles' will is Man's Son."[18] In other words, with "Manson" an anagram for "the Son of Man," Manson's will is the same as that of the Son of Man. Manson claimed to have lived two thousand years ago and to have died on the cross. All the pieces had come together. "Charlie has set up the whole thing, it's kind of like a storybook."[19] Now the Family had a script. It only waited for the drama to begin. It played on the evenings of August 9 and 10, 1969 — the Tate-LaBianca killings. Revelation 9 ends, ironically, poignantly, with the words "Neither repented they of their murders," a verse Manson never tired of quoting to the Family.[20]

On November 18, 1978, more than nine hundred people died in an isolated clearing in the South American jungle called Jonestown.

A few weeks later the story unfolded in the media: a cult of religious fanatics had joined their deranged leader Jim Jones in a final rite of mass suicide, drinking cyanide-laced fruit punch. *Time* and *Newsweek* splashed their pages with lurid photographs under the headline, "Cult of Death." The spectacle of Jonestown fascinated, repulsed, terrified. It rendered a vicarious leer at the pornography of others' lives. Sensationalistic journalists pandered to the popular imagination with accounts of sexual exploitation, beatings, mind control, brainwashing.

Church leaders seized upon the label "cult" in a frantic effort to disassociate their denominations, and Christianity in general, from the Jonestown tragedy. Those who died at Jonestown were from Peoples Temple, a registered congregation within a large Christian denomination, the Disciples of Christ, also known as the Christian Church. The Disciples issued an official press release disavowing any close relationship with Peoples Temple. The latter was "totally unrelated" to the home mission work of the Disciples, and Jonestown was "totally unrelated" to the overseas ministries of the Disciples.[21]

Those in Peoples Temple would not have considered themselves members of a cult, forced against their will. One woman who missed the communal death said that her time at Jonestown had been the happiest of her life: "If I had been there, I would have been the first one to stand in that line and take that poison and I would have been proud to take it."[22] Two other women not at Jonestown agreed with this sentiment.[23] Another woman remarked: "I believed, and still do, that the majority of the people in Jonestown ... were a principled, hard-working, sacrificing crew of people who had given up everything to build a community.... We had a sense of pride...."[24]

As time passed, there evolved a more considerate, thoughtful approach to the tragedy at Jonestown, a sincere effort at understanding the members of Peoples Temple, acknowledging their fundamental humanity. Tim Reiterman observed that "the Temple attracted a variety of basically good people."[25] John R. Hall writes, "Jim Jones was a deeply flawed yet somehow visionary man whose movement attracted to Peoples Temple many decent and deeply committed people."[26]

One of those was survivor Odell Rhodes, whose account of his experiences in the Guyana community are related in Ethan Feinsod's book *Awake in a Nightmare: Jonestown: The Only Eyewitness Account*. Rhodes finds extraordinarily prejudiced the idea that Jonestown was a jungle concentration camp. At the conclusion of the book he writes, "To me Jonestown's about the best thing I ever did in my life.... I loved it there, and up to the minute I left I never wanted anything in my life as much as I wanted Jonestown to succeed."[27]

Jonestown was an experiment in communal living, a social experiment. In Jonestown those who had been discriminated against and economically deprived, those who had led a life of misery and error back in the United States, would be provided for and forgiven. In Jonestown all would live as one, regardless of age, sex, or color, in a "common commitment to a certain set of shared ideals about what it might mean to be a human person in a human community."[28] The experiment ended in tragedy, but there was something to be learned, even in failure. As Tim Reiterman observes, "The lessons of Jonestown, while hard for some to accept, raise fundamental issues about this country [the United States] — about the failure of institutions, including the churches."[29]

One of the "lessons," one of the "fundamental issues," involved apocalypticism. Those who have studied Jones's life and personality are quick to comment on his apocalypticism. Stephen C. Rose notes the "power" of "Jones' apocalyptic vision."[30] John R. Hall remarks on the "apocalyptic struggle ... found in pronouncements by Jim Jones."[31] He elaborates: "For all his support of progressive causes, Jones shared the pessimism of Pentecostals and other

Adventists who take seriously the Book of Revelation prophecies about the apocalyptic downfall of the present evil world order as a prelude to the Second Coming."[32]

Peoples Temple was the embodiment of Jones's ideology, its spirit steeped in apocalypticism. Listening to over nine hundred tape recordings of sermons, rallies, and conversations,[33] David Chidester experienced the cadence and powerful persuasiveness of Jones's oratory, gained a feeling for the coherence of his theology, and witnessed the compelling range of his imagery. He was able to state conclusively that "Peoples Temple ... was an apocalyptic movement, having much in common with other militant millenarian movements."[34] Jones harnessed the force of the Bible's authority to accomplish his purposes. He appropriated the "biblical paradigm" of "the heavenly city of a New Jerusalem described as descending from the skies in the Book of Revelation"[35] as the role for his churchly community. In apocalyptic mode, Jones spoke of "the world of fire, the Apocalypse, the burning elements,"[36] "Judgment Day,"[37] "Armageddon."[38]

John R. Hall sees "Peoples Temple as an emerging 'apocalyptic sect'—a group preoccupied with the final struggle between good and evil and the end of the world in its present form."[39] Those who joined Peoples Temple "became people of the Apocalypse who acted as if an evil world was coursing on the brink of disaster ... they lived in opposition to what they perceived as the direction of world history."[40]

Jim Jones painted contemporary American society as an evil cesspool. The evil forces in American life would meet their end in nuclear Armageddon. David Chidester notes, "Nuclear apocalypse was a central preoccupation in the mythic worldview of the Peoples Temple."[41] The world would be cleansed of evil forces, and those who followed Jones would get to live in a better world—the millennium. Jones proclaimed, "We're close to the end. We're close to the time of the settling day, of Judgment Day."[42]

The world would soon end in Armageddon. An advertisement published by Peoples Temple proclaimed that Jim Jones "can protect you from the effects of the Dangerous Forces that are loose in these Last Days."[43] The "protection that Christ offers you through Pastor Jones"[44] was available to those who sent away for an anointed prayer cloth. In capital letters readers were warned, "Time is short!"[45] Another advertisement cautioned, "As prophesied in the book of Revelation: The horsemen of the apocalypse are now unleashed, bringing death and destruction throughout the nation."[46] The evils of today's world were listed, to demonstrate that these were, indeed, the Last Days.

Jones convinced his people that Jonestown was to be their refuge from the upcoming Armageddon. They would escape in "Operation Exodus" from Pharaoh's Egypt, from Babylon (the United States), to this "Promised Land across the sea," the new Jerusalem that appears after the holocaust (as in the book of Revelation).

The apocalypticism of Jim Jones and Peoples Temple shared much of the style and spirit of Christian fundamentalism. As Judith Weightman remarks, Peoples Temple had "quite a bit to do with fundamentalism."[47] Shiva Naipaul writes: "Peoples Temple was laid out along the latitudinal and longitudinal grids of the Fundamentalist imagination; an imagination obsessed with sin and images of apocalyptic destruction, authoritarian in its innermost impulses, instinctively thinking in terms of the saved and the damned, seeking not to enlighten but to terrorize into obedience."[48]

The community of Peoples Temple shared many characteristics with Christian fundamentalists. They were a group set apart: "In Peoples Temple the world of society at large is seen as totally evil, and in its last days; at the end of history as we know it, the current dispensation is to be replaced by a community of the elect, those who live according to the revelation of God's will."[49] In the words of Jim Jones: "You're all ordained to be here. You're a chosen people."[50]

As a chosen people, those of Peoples Temple (like Christian fundamentalists) are called to "come out"[51]—Jones used this standard fundamentalist phrase—from the larger society. They must "establish a radical separation between themselves and the established social world, which they regard as hopelessly evil."[52] So "the Temple became a world in and of itself, with little interaction with the larger reality to counteract their increasingly deviant theology."[53]

The Temple winnowed prospects for its membership, to insure total commitment. A prospective member was interviewed as to their motivations for wanting to join, then had to sign a blank form — who knew what might be filled in later?— which said that everything on it was true. The process of vetting and initial membership took about four months. The neophyte started small, then gradually was expected to undergo ever more rigorous tests of commitment. Members had to attend services which went into the early hours of the morning. They sold their homes and turned the proceeds over to the Temple; then moved into Temple housing. They worked for the Temple from dawn to dusk, or at outside employment and turned their wages over to the Temple.

Proving oneself to be among the chosen people required commitment to the cause. There were rules: "no drinking, no smoking, no sex, no pictures of departed relatives, no funerals, no diamonds, no furs, no jewelry, no nice furniture, no new clothes, ... no vacations, no potato chips, no wigs, no pork, no coffee, no tea, no new cars."[54] A detailed dossier was kept on every member: attendance record, a schedule of church commitments, daily timetable, biographical and financial information, fears, temptations, closest friends, et cetera, et cetera. Those who showed signs of sliding were disciplined. This could take the form of a physical beating, in severe cases with a two-foot length of rubber hose — "only a few swats were needed to persuade even the most recalcitrant offender to toe the line. The dull thud of the length of rubber squashing flesh was also more effective a deterrent for the witnesses."[55] The victim could end up covered in searing welts, so painful the person was kept on suicide watch.[56]

Such discipline insured that members did not slip back into the evil life of the outside world. As Shiva Naipaul says, it was "a war between the forces of Good and Evil"[57]— a standard litany among Christian fundamentalists. Sociologist Constance A. Jones has neatly tied together this "dualism" of good and evil with the need for social separation and submission to authority: Jim Jones and the Temple were defined "as exemplars of absolute good and opponents ... as exemplars of absolute evil. Polarization ... engendered a policy of social isolation which branded normal participation in the processes of the larger society as undesirable."[58]

This dualism, this polarization, led to conflict with the outside society. "Peoples Temple took the widespread religious motif of Babylon's apocalypse to an extreme, cultivating a sense of persecution and siege. It thus accentuated ... the boundary between the Temple and society at large."[59] This "siege mentality"[60] was both welcomed and fostered by Jim Jones, for it tightened his forces about him and eventually led to the jungles of Guyana. Persecution by those from the broader society was a welcome sign that the Temple's cause was just, and its enemies evil — a type of thinking the Temple shared with apocalyptic Christian fundamentalism.

The 1960s, when Jim Jones was establishing Peoples Temple, was much like the 1920s, when fundamentalism was a force against what it saw as a profligate society. During the 1960s it seemed that everything traditional was being re-evaluated. The moral and religious foundations of a nation which had from the beginning considered itself a chosen elect people, a light to other nations, were crumbling. It was, as Robert N. Bellah and Phillip E. Hammond phrased it, "the erosion of the legitimacy of the American way of life."[61] Many Americans were deeply concerned regarding fundamental changes in the national ethos. Jim Jones capitalized on this. He gave traditional fundamentalist apocalypticism a twist. "America," he boldly proclaimed, "is the Antichrist." America bore "the mark of the Beast." Over and over Jones called America "Babylon."[62]

Those in the pews recognized these references to the book of Revelation. They eagerly grabbed hold of the challenge Jones presented. "In the zeal of its proponents, Peoples Temple stood squarely in the tradition of early Protestants. With its apocalyptic sense ... the Temple simply radicalized the historic quest of Protestantism to found a 'city on the hill. ' The Temple, too, sought to migrate to a promised land."[63] As David Chidester points out, the exodus to Jonestown was no "anomalous aberration," but rather "a recent instance of a religiopolitical utopianism that was integral to the original colonization of America."[64] Peoples Temple in Jonestown was "like the Massachusetts Bay Puritans with their theocratic utopia in the New World."[65] Jones had managed to reconcile two seemingly opposing strands of American religious history: "the fundamentalist concern with individual salvation and the social gospel emphasis on saving 'this' world in God's name. Somehow he inspired others by bringing the overriding social concerns of the day into a millennialist resentment that sought redemption, one way or another ... [all the while] presuming the reality of American ideals."[66]

Jones went back to the example of the earliest church, taking the biblical text of Acts 4:34–35 as the basis for the establishment of Peoples Temple. That passage describes how those who owned land or houses sold them and turned the proceeds over to be distributed "unto every man according to his need." "I saw that where the early believers stay together they sold all their possessions and had all things in common,"[67] said Jones.

Peoples Temple catered to the same social needs as today's megachurches. Like many megachurch members, for those in Peoples Temple their church was their life and their identity.[68] They spent virtually all of their time there. It provided community, social life, friends. It was "an organizational totalism which consumed participants."[69] Participants felt welcomed into, and surrounded by, an enlarged family. "I had never before witnessed the warmth and love I was seeing in this totally integrated group."[70]

Under Jones's direction Peoples Temple engaged in a form of practical Christianity he termed "apostolic socialism." The church's letterhead bore wording from Matthew 25:35–40: "I was hungry, and you gave me meat; I was thirsty, and you gave me drink; a stranger, and you took me in; naked, and you clothed me...." And Peoples Temple did just that. Every Sunday before the church service a free meal was laid out for whoever wished to come — often more than a thousand people.[71] Canned goods and clothing were available for any in need. For those who might otherwise have gone cold, fuel was delivered to their homes. The Temple generously donated to charities and institutions and worthy causes: cancer, heart disease, and sickle-cell anemia research, the Ecumenical Peace Institute, the American Civil Liberties Union, a senior citizens' escort program, the American Indian Movement, the National Association for the Advancement of Colored People.

Praise for the work of Peoples Temple and for its leader was abundant.

Jones was declared by one person to be the most loving, Christ-like human being he had ever met; by another as "the best thing that ever happened to San Francisco."[72] A reporter wrote that Peoples Temple was "a religious organization that follows the precepts of Jesus Christ more diligently than does any other group that professes to follow the teachings of Jesus Christ."[73]

More significant, perhaps, was the praise uttered by clergy. Concerning Jim Jones, a Baptist pastor said: "The depth of his character and his dedication to humankind are measured each and every day.... In Peoples Temple the most essential teachings of the early church are revived ... translated into actions."[74] Another man of the cloth observed that Jones "was doing things that we read about in the Bible but never saw in action."[75]

Compliments from Jones's denomination overflowed. The regional minister-president of the Disciples took pride in Peoples Temple as an exemplary Christian community. After a visit a regional pastor reported that Peoples Temple was "the human race at its best."[76] A denominational official asserted, "The ministry of this man [Jones] and his congregation is surpassed by none in our denomination."[77] Another denominational official wrote that Peoples Temple is "the most committed and dedicated group of people I have known in any church anywhere."[78] The general counsel of the Disciples of Christ had generous words for Jones: "humble, unpretentious, self-sacrificing, completely dedicated and committed to the fulfillment of the Gospel...."[79]

Accolades for Jones came not only in words. He was feted with various awards and citations. *Religion in Life* magazine named him among the nation's one hundred outstanding clergymen. The *Los Angeles Herald* proclaimed him Humanitarian of the Year. He was presented the *Sun Reporter*'s Special Merit Award. The year previous to the tragedy in Jonestown he was declared Martin Luther King, Jr. Humanitarian of the Year.

Civic authorities recognized Jones's contribution. He had been director of the Human Rights Commission of Indianapolis, foreman of a county grand jury, on a juvenile justice commission, and chairman of San Francisco 's Housing Authority.

Jones mingled with the rich and famous. As one writer noted, "Jones had friends or admirers in the state legislature and the U. S. Congress, the offices of the governor, the mayor, the police chief, the sheriff, and district attorney...."[80] He got invited for a private visit aboard vice presidential candidate Walter Mondale's jet, and received a personal handwritten thank-you note from Rosalynn Carter.

In the public eye Jim Jones was a rising star and Peoples Temple was a good corporate citizen. But as the years passed the public image and the inside reality began to diverge. By 1971 the Temple's doors were closed to drop-in visitors. Only card-carrying members gained entrance. Outsiders who wanted to attend a service had to provide a list of personal information to a member who would submit it to a committee for vetting. If it was cleared, a date would be set and the congregation alerted to a special performance.

Closed doors, of course, arouse suspicions. So does an eight-foot chain fence topped with barbed wire surrounding the property. Neighbors and passers-by began noticing what appeared to be armed guards, some on the roof with binoculars. A guard tower was equipped with bright spotlights that glared through the night. Late at night and into the morning hours the pastor's voice was heard booming over a loudspeaker. By 1977 investigators from the San Francisco District Attorney's Office were looking into charges of homicide, battery, child abduction, property extortion ... the list went on. No indictments were forthcoming, however.

Jones's church services were unusual, to say the least. Those entering Peoples Temple were pat-searched, in extraordinary cases strip-searched, all after presenting their membership cards. Wearing dark shades, Jones enters the sanctuary to thunderous applause, surrounded by guards in army surplus jackets—two in front, two to the rear, one on each side. After a lecture on the evils of smoking and drinking, Jones asks everyone who has smoked a cigarette or indulged in a beer or a glass of wine over the past week to stand up. Jones beckons them to the front. Minor offences are punishable by stripping down to one's underwear, occasionally to the skin, and running down the aisle through the whole church. But drinking and smoking are not minor offences. Punishment is five strokes of a two-inch-wide leather belt. There are shouts from the congregation. "Harder. Harder." No one wants to be caught silent, for fear of the same punishment.[81]

Jones's language in the pulpit was bold, daring, irreverent, graphic. He used street lingo, and talked openly about sex. People were hooked. They found themselves laughing at Jones's earthy sense of humor, and nodding a hesitant agreement. "I'm sick of your hypocrisy! I want you to come down off your pedestals and learn about the gut level of life! Get down where it's really at. Come on now — everybody say 'Shit'!"[82] They did. It was cathartic, and great entertainment.

Jones had always been irreverent, his language florid, meant to shock. As a child he greeted neighbors with "Good morning, you son of a bitch."[83] Jones hated the America he grew up in, and its religion: "I filled the holy water with real water and they didn't know they were anointing themselves with my pee."[84] He put cow manure in a minister's Bible. Jones couldn't understand that someone might really believe or have genuine heartfelt sentiments about their religion; to him they were all hypocrites.

Jones, right from the beginning, wanted revenge on the church, on Christianity. He wanted to expose all Christians as closet atheists. Sharon Amos, one of Jones's staunchest supporters confessed, "I came [to the Temple] with a Bible in my hand.... I was very religious, but it is from that type of background that Jim has educated us to what we are today, and I'm a positive atheist."[85]

To turn Christians into atheists Jones needed a church. He chose one which allowed wide latitude in doctrine and practice — the Disciples of Christ, also known as the Christian Church. As a regional president of that denomination phrased it, "Every church is an entity unto itself. It calls its own pastor. It fires its own pastor. It is a completely autonomous group of people."[86] The denomination had no set procedure for disinheriting a member congregation. Jim Jones would have open season.

The Disciples of Christ gave Jones, as an ordained minister with that denomination since 1964, and Peoples Temple a mantle of respectability. Certainly in no way sectarian, the Disciples is a mainline Protestant denomination. With over four thousand independent congregations, the Disciples was the eighth-largest Protestant denomination in the nation.[87] Temple publicity made use of such facts, citing their pastor as "an officially ordained minister of the 1.4 million member Christian Church (Disciples of Christ) denomination,"[88] and President Lyndon Johnson and FBI Director Clarence Kelly as members of their denomination. Peoples Temple grew to be one of the largest Disciples congregations in northern California. Its attractive ivy-covered building at the corner of Alvarado and Hoover in Los Angeles spoke tradition and solidity.

Jones *used* religion to accomplish his goals. James Reston, Jr. writes: "Jones carefully studied the speech rhythms of Pentecostal and Free Will Baptist ministers, as well as their lines of reasoning and the quotations in the Bible important to them, so that he could reproduce the sounds and cadences and biblical references that made the newcomers from that background feel more comfortable in his presence."[89]

The style, the atmosphere, the feel, of a Peoples Temple service was Pentecostal/fundamentalist. "Temple life essentially replicated the conventional popular culture of Pentecostal evangelical Christianity."[90] There was an overflowing of spirit — enthusiastic, dynamic, emotional, expressive: an "amen," a "you got that right, Father," applause, speaking in tongues. There was a band, a full choir. Services began with joyful hand-clapping singing. "We Shall Overcome," sung over and over again. But all of this was parody, caricature, for Jones was really mocking the religion of those in the pews. Much of the music was written by Temple members specifically for Temple services. It soon became obvious to the neophyte that "traditional Christian hymns were conspicuous by their absence."[91]

Jones learned how to please his audience early in life. A female Pentecostal preacher had placed the eight-year-old boy in the pulpit. Jones's biographer Tim Reiterman writes: "Already he was an actor and even a con man. He had cultivated the knack not only for perceiving what people wanted to hear but also for saying it in an appealing way with a performer's timing."[92] Over the years Jones honed and developed these skills. Jonestown survivor Odell Rhodes remarked, "He was the best con man I ever saw — and I've seen quite a few."[93]

For Jones religion was merely a vehicle, an instrument, in his master plan. Religious people were his pawns. Religious people were conditioned to self-sacrifice and discipline, and were devoted followers. They often possessed high ideals. Ex-member Sherwin Harris said that Jones "used the religious message to his own ends. He played upon the very sensitivities instilled in those people by their churches; and by the time people realized where they had gone astray, it was too late."[94] Annie Moore had grown up in a Christian home; her father was a minister. Yet she remarked, concerning Peoples Temple: "It's the only place I have seen real true Christianity being practiced."[95] Shortly after joining the Temple she wrote her concerned parents: "You obviously think that the Peoples Temple is just another cult or religious fanatic place or something like that.... I can tell what's real and what's not. People have a hard time fooling me."[96] Later a nurse and one of Jones's most dedicated followers, she would commit suicide at Jonestown.

Jones's wife Marceline wasn't fooled; she knew that her husband "used religion to try to get some people out of the opiate of religion."[97] Jones had been frank with Huey Newton: "He told me in Cuba that he didn't believe in any religion, that he only used that as a tactic to organize the religious community."[98] Jones made his position clear from the pulpit: "That's my purpose in being here. When the transition comes.... Religion, the opiate of the people, shall be removed from the consciousness of mankind. There shall no longer be any need for anything religious when freedom comes."[99]

Jones despised religion and religious people. From the pulpit of Peoples Temple he ridiculed those who had come from fundamentalist backgrounds. In biblical idiom he twitted those who were preoccupied with whether the Rapture was coming before or after the tribulation: "You strain at gnats and you swallow camels."[100]

Because the Bible stood as an authority over against Jim Jones, he waged war against it. Potential members of Peoples Temple had to wade through a series of ten tapes, the first of which delineated the "errors" in the Bible. Jones issued a pamphlet titled *The Letter Killeth* to further elaborate on what he saw as errors and lies in the Bible.

From the pulpit Jones railed against the Bible. It was "a paper idol. It's just another goddamned book."[101] Jones said the Bible instructed women to submit to their husbands, and the poor to accept their poverty. "The Bible has taught you to be content."[102] The Bible was not some sacred text written in ancient times; it was written in 1611 by King James, "as mean a rascal that ever walked on earth."[103] He "was a drunk, he was an oppressive king, he was a practicing deviant of the worst nature, he ... wrote your Bible, along with eighty other drunks just like him."[104] "Are you gonna sit there and read this garbage?"[105]

Often in the midst of long angry tirades Jones threw the Bible onto the floor. "No fears of doing that.... No, it's not sacred. You won't die if ... you drop it. You won't die if you stand on it." Jones demonstrated. "You won't die if you jump up and down on it," which Jones proceeded to do with obvious relish.[106] Sometimes he tore pages from the Bible, once even set fire to it. Jones hated the Bible so much he had a shipment of free Gideon Bibles sent to Jonestown to be used as toilet paper.

As one adherent said, Jones "was dealing with a strictly religious crowd, so he had to talk Bible...."[107] Whenever it served his purpose Jones would quote the Bible, or use biblical language and concepts and stories. The exodus from America to Guyana would be like "under Moses from Egypt."[108] Jones twisted Scripture to support his ideas. James Reston, Jr. remarks, "As always, he was a distorter and defiler of the Word."[109] Even while people were taking the final poison at Jonestown Jones was quoting Scripture.[110] He never dropped the religious facade.

Jeannie Mills relates an episode from a Peoples Temple service. Jones had been reviling Scripture, noting errors in its text, using florid language. Mills was shocked and offended. How could he say things like that about God's Holy Word and get away with it? Just then, as if he had read her thoughts, Jones said, "If there were a God in heaven, do you think he would let me say these things about His Holy Word?" At this, Jones lifted his eyes upward, shook his fist in rage, and challenged, "If there is a God in heaven, let Him strike me dead!" Mills, raised a fundamentalist, waited in horror. Then, his face beaming a broad smile, Jones mocked, "Someone in this room is waiting." The congregation broke out in laughter. As for Mills, "my faith took a sharp nose dive."[111]

Jones liked these performances. On another occasion he again shouted his challenge at the heavens: "If you're all-powerful, send one of your magic wands. Send your electric lightning. Send your thunder. Let it rain!"[112] Nothing. People laughed.

As Jones relates it, looking back, he had never believed in God even during his first days as pastor: "Here I am, raving against the church, knocking the church, ridiculing God.... I said, you giving me a church? I don't believe in anything.... [I] believed in nothing — that is how religious I was and still am."[113] Jones was amazed at some of his successes as a pastor but, "hell, it didn't make me believe any more in the living deity than I did before."[114]

Jones berated his congregation, "All you sanctimonious hypocrites, all you religious idiots who have gone your whole life believing in the Bible and Jesus Christ and God."[115] Jones worked himself into a rage. "What's your sky God ever done?... You prayed to your sky God and he never heard your prayers. You asked and begged and pleaded in your suffering...."[116] "I've long since put out a warrant for his arrest, charging him with murder, ... torture, cruelty, inhuman treatment beyond description."[117] "You're free! You're free of God!"[118] Many in Peoples Temple followed Jones's lead. One of his chief supporters emphatically declared, "We don't believe in God."[119]

"I am God!" Jones had shouted in earlier times.[120] But during Jones's final days at Jonestown he was a broken, pitiable figure. Things were not working out as he had envisioned. In the end, deeply troubled, with everything crashing down upon him, he retreated into a fog of drugs.[121] As his San Francisco physician said, Jones was "frying his brain" with drugs.[122] U. S. Embassy Consul in Guyana Richard McCoy remarked, "I knew he was irrational the day I met him. By May 1978, it was clear he was on drugs."[123] Jones's voice, once riveting, had lost all strength. His words were slurred. He read from notes, often not ending sentences. When he was unable to read, his closest aides read him a sentence and urged him to repeat it over the loudspeaker. Sometimes they had to take over and read his message to the people themselves.

Two weeks after the tragedy Dr. Carlton Goodlett said that based upon his recent examination of Jones he believed the man would have been dead in another ten days anyway, from natural causes.[124]

17

True Believers

Death in Los Angeles, Texas, Guyana. Three minor apocalypses, high-lighted in the media, burned into the public psyche. Three willful leaders. Three groups of vulnerable persons. The book of Revelation. The Apocalypse.

James Tabor and Eugene V. Gallagher write: "An accurate, truthful portrayal of David Koresh and his followers ... is essential for understanding contemporary religious life in our country [the United States]."[1] The same could be said regarding Manson's Family, and those in Peoples Temple. All three groups had much in common. They came from conservative Christian backgrounds where the Bible had preeminent status. The desire for commitment, for dedication of self, characterized the members of all three groups. They sought religious "meaning" in their lives and found it in apocalypse.

That all three groups were considered "cults" obscures what they had in common. The designation "cult" demonizes, making understanding impossible. As Tabor and Gallagher remark, "When the term 'cult' is used to describe any religious group, it becomes easier to view that group as religiously illegitimate, psychologically and physically harmful to its members, and dangerous to society."[2]

Right from the beginning those at Ranch Apocalypse were designated a "cult" by law enforcement agencies and the news media. Cult "experts" were called in for consultation. An FBI report admitted that one of its anticult consultants "has a personal hatred for all religious cults" and would happily aid law enforcement to "destroy a cult."[3] Another anticult consultant insisted he saw no evidence of any "certain hope for an early end to the standoff."[4] This opinion hastened the timetable and precipitated the tragedy.

David Koresh was rumored to have molested children. But child welfare investigators from the Texas Children's Protective Services visited the Waco residence several times and found no evidence of child abuse.[5] The United States Department of Justice said there was no evidence of child abuse during the fifty-one day siege.

Nor were Koresh's people "hostages." Fourteen adults and twenty-one children exited the Waco residence during the siege. With all those guns, had he so desired, surely Koresh could have held these persons captive. But he did not. One of those who left said that people were always coming and going. People would come, stay a while, and leave.

On viewing videos of the Branch Davidians after the tragedy, the Department of Justice reported that they appeared calm and articulate: "The abiding impression is not of a bunch of 'lunatics,' but rather of a group of people who, for whatever reason, believed so strongly in Koresh that the notion of leaving the squalid compound was unthinkable."[6]

Many of those who resided with Koresh were highly educated. One had a Master of Religious Studies, another a degree in comparative religion, a third had a graduate degree in theology. There was a secondary school teacher, a lawyer who had graduated from Harvard Law School and lectured at university, a high school physics teacher who had been educated as an electrical engineer, a design engineer, a nurse ... the list goes on. These were people who could think for themselves.

Because the residents of Mount Carmel were considered a cult, little effort was made to enter their world of belief. Instead, confrontation and brute force prevailed.

The tragedy at Waco resulted from lack of understanding, from gross failure to comprehend the religious significance of apocalypticism: "In order ... to have any chance for a peaceful resolution of the Waco situation ... one would need to enter into the apocalyptic world of David Koresh and his dedicated followers."[7] A scholar who specialized in biblical apocalyptic, James Tabor contended that had those in authority fully understood "the religious dynamics" and the "apocalyptic significance" of the situation, it "could very likely have led to a peaceful resolution of the standoff."[8]

The Branch Davidians were not a cult. If anything they were more loyal to Seventh-Day Adventist precepts than the broader denomination.[9] As Tabor and Gallagher note, the Branch Davidians "stand firmly within the Millerite-Adventist tradition and it is impossible to properly understand them outside this broader context."[10] As one Branch Davidian remarked, "If we're a cult, then all these churches are cults."[11]

Nancy Ammerman says she was surprised when she began to study Koresh's teachings: "They are but a variant on what could be found in many fundamentalist and millennialist churches."[12] Malise Ruthven agrees: "There may be more similarity between modern 'fundamentalisms' and New Age cults or new religious movements than many observers suppose."[13]

Ammerman remarks, "The methods of study and exegesis he [David Koresh] used would be familiar to many conservative students of the Bible...."[14] As Tabor and Gallagher observe: "[David Koresh] insisted that 'scripture must be its own expositor' and one must not rely upon human creeds and the 'traditions of men' in arriving at the truth. This 'democratization' of biblical studies has proven to be of incalculable influence in the development of American religion...."[15]

There are estimated to be between one thousand and fifteen hundred independent Bible-based groups— in many ways resembling that led by David Koresh — in the United States.[16] Right from the beginning, from the time of the Puritan colonists, American Protestantism has been a Bible-based religion. Today the Bible maintains its central place for American Christians. Four of five Americans believe the Bible is the literal and inspired word of God.[17] Bible reading has been increasing over the last few decades. In the year 2000, forty percent of American adults were reading the Bible at least once a week outside of church; today this has increased to 47 percent. This increase is most noticeable among conservatives— an increase of seventeen percent from 2001. Ninety-six percent of evangelicals engage in frequent reading of the Bible.[18]

The residents of Ranch Apocalypse were true believers: "The difference is that we live the Bible. Other people go to church on Saturday or Sunday and the rest of the week do their own thing. We lived it."[19] As another resident commented, "Religion is a bad thing when you can do what you want to do, and just go to a religious social club once a week.... Christianity two thousand years ago wasn't that way."[20]

The Branch Davidians saw themselves as Christians more dedicated and committed to their faith than the majority. Even a Branch Davidian apostate admits that the "Branch Davidians lived their faith to a degree most Christians would never dream of doing.... They put to shame many who profess religion, but only do so verbally."[21]

Commitment. That was a key characteristic of the Branch Davidians, but also of many Americans who have in recent years moved from liberal to more conservative, even fundamentalist, forms of Christianity. Dean M. Kelley, ordained Methodist minister and formerly on the executive board of the National Council of Churches, the author of *Why Conservative Churches Are Growing*, says that "the dedication of the whole self" can be "very attractive to people with intense needs for ultimate meaning in their lives."[22]

Like many in the conservative Christian church, those in the Family, in Peoples Temple, and at Ranch Apocalypse were, for the most part, idealists; they were true believers, ready to follow, ready to commit, ready to dedicate themselves.

Family member Charles Watson showed no signs of turning into a cold-blooded killer before he met Charles Manson. Indeed, he must have been the pride and joy of the small town in which he grew up. He was all-district in football and basketball, a track star in virtually every event, setting many records. He belonged to 4-H, was a Boy Scout, a sports editor, helped with the school play, a member of the school band and the Spanish Club, an American history enthusiast, and on top of all this he worked afternoons and summers in a factory, saving to go to college. Three times he was chosen "Campus Kid."

More than the average youth he was religiously motivated. He was very involved in church activities. As a child he attended vacation Bible School every summer. He led devotions for the youth group and gave talks for evangelistic services. After he had been convicted and was serving his term in prison, Watson helped with chapel services. Eventually he became senior deacon, counseling inmates. He began to prepare for ordination, studying six hours a day, serving as student chaplain.

While he was a member of Manson's Family the Bible provided a religious rationalization for Watson's life, but it was a steady diet from the book of Revelation as interpreted by Charles Manson. Watson admits that before he met Manson the Bible had simply been there. Manson made the imagery of Revelation come alive.

Before her days with the Family Susan Atkins attended church, frequently standing to ask forgiveness for her sins. She claims to have had a vision of the cross. She participated in Girl Scouts, and was a good student in school. After conviction Susan Atkins returned to her religious roots as a born-again Christian.

Patricia Krenwinkel was a serious student whom teachers enjoyed having in their classes. She was baptized in the Presbyterian Church, assisted with children's summer church programs, and read her Bible. Leslie Van Houten was a well-behaved girl who became Homecoming Princess and Homecoming Queen. Raised in the Presbyterian faith, she attended church regularly, was a Bluebird and a Campfire Girl, and held offices in Job's Daughters, a religious group.

A strong religious upbringing, with special emphasis on the Bible, characterized many of the leading figures in Peoples Temple. Carolyn Moore, the person closest to Jim Jones, grew up in a Christian home; her father was a Methodist minister. As her sister observed, "Ironically, it was our own religious training that made Carolyn an activist and prepared her for Peoples Temple. The message of the Bible was clear: serve the poor. But the churches she'd known didn't seem to care about the poor, at least, not enough. The pietism of traditional white Protestantism bored and frustrated her."[23]

Rebecca Moore, commenting on another sister, Annie, a nurse at Jonestown and another of Jones's most dedicated followers, writes, "Like Carolyn ... her religious upbringing had prepared her for a life of commitment."[24]

Maria Katsaris was one of Jones's closest aides. She, too, had grown up in a Christian home; her father was a Greek Orthodox priest. "Maria's religion was an integral part of her humanitarianism. She had always gone to Mass regularly."[25]

Like those in Manson's Family and those at Ranch Apocalypse, a Bible-centered Christian upbringing left many in Peoples Temple vulnerable. Jeannie Mills deserted Peoples Temple before the Jonestown disaster, but she admits that she was "extremely naive."[26] "I think my religious upbringing had made me gullible."[27] Mills attended a Seventh-Day Adventist school, went to church, was a Campfire leader. She believed the straight-A student, the best child in the family, the cheerleader, is most likely to join a group like Peoples Temple. They are "so pure and noble"[28] they expect their religious leaders to be likewise, and commit themselves to them in implicit trust.

Tabor and Gallagher warn of the dangers of "total commitment to the leader's interpretation of the Bible" and "strong belief that we are in the times prior to the end of the world."[29] Manson's aura of religious charisma hooked many an unwary youth. His self-assured interpretation of Revelation exposed the vulnerability of those who had been raised in a religious home which revered the authority of the Bible. This potentially dangerous combination of religious charisma and cunning use of the Bible was something he shared with Jim Jones.

Charles Manson, Jim Jones, and David Koresh all played upon the religious vulnerability of their followers, especially with regard to their biblical upbringing. Those in the Family, in Peoples Temple, and at Ranch Apocalypse fell under the spell of seriously egotistic leaders, each with his own plan, his own script, for an apocalypse. As Robert Endleman notes in his comparative study of Jones and Manson, "Each was impassioned with apocalyptic visions,"[30] and their "philosophies ... were very much alike ... laced with apocalyptic vision."[31] Manson, Jones, Koresh — each used the biblical text of Revelation, the Apocalypse — something those under their sway knew and respected — to persuade and convince.

18

Book of Sevens

The book of Revelation gave Charles Manson a skeleton on which to build his vengeful script. Jim Jones spoke the apocalyptic language of Revelation. David Koresh centered his biblical teaching on Revelation. Falsely interpreted, the book of Revelation is an explosive fuse, potentially dangerous.

Revelation, also known as the Apocalypse, has fascinated generations of believers, and non-believers, yet remains an enigma. Thomas Paine said it "is a book of riddles that requires a revelation to explain it."[1] As Saint Jerome remarked fourteen centuries earlier, "Revelation has as many mysteries as it does words."

The lurid, even nightmarish, imagery of the Apocalypse has been a magnet to many non-Christians. The Four Horsemen of the Apocalypse, the Seven Seals, the Millennium, the Antichrist, Armageddon — these images are all part of popular American culture, and exert a "mythical power capable of profoundly effecting the imagination."[2] The novelist D. H. Lawrence writes, "The Revelation of John is ... a book to conjure with. It ... has been used, throughout the ages, for occult purposes, for the purpose of divination and prophecy especially."[3] Lawrence focuses on the number seven, which he insists is a "magical number," "the number now of divination and conjuring," tainted with "magic, prognostication, and occult practice."[4]

The Apocalypse is constructed around the number seven; it consists of seven series of seven.[5] There are the seven messages to seven churches, seven seals, seven trumpets, seven bowls, seven signs, seven kings, a seven-headed beast, two groups of seven visions.

Seven is the most prevalent number, but many others are mentioned in Revelation. Indeed, the Apocalypse is a treasure trove for numerologists. The mystical meaning of numbers has a long history that includes the ancient Greek Pythagoreans, Philo of Alexandria, the Gnostics, Hebrew cabalists, and even Christians.

Saint Augustine was smitten by the numerological bug. In his *Tractates on the Gospel of Saint John* he provided an elaborate numerological analysis of the number 153 — the number of fish Simon Peter drew up from the Sea of Tiberias in John 21:11. He added the number of Commandments (10) to the number of the gifts of the spirit (7) to get 17. He then summed the numbers from 1 to 17. The result, 153, signified for Augustine the union of God's work in both Old and New Testament times.

The number 153 has special numerical properties on its own. If each of the numbers 1, 5, and 3 is raised to its third power, the sum of the resulting powers is 153 (1 plus 125 plus 27). Only three other numbers are equal to the sum of the cubes of their digits— 370, 371, 407.[6]

The number 666 is closely associated with the book of Revelation. This sign of the Beast (the devil) has been applied to figures like Napoleon and Hitler, and by Seventh-Day Adventist Carlyle B. Haynes to the Roman Catholic Church. But this can be turned against Seventh-Day Adventism and applied to its founder, Ellen Gould White.[7] The Old Testament leader Joshua is mentioned in the sixth verse of the sixth chapter of the sixth book of the Bible.

Martin Gardner remarks on one particularly disturbing finding. Medieval numerologists, he notes, made much of the number 1480, obtained by summing the values assigned to the Greek letters of "Christos." Construct a square with sides of length 1480 units. Its diagonal measures 2093. If a circle of circumference equal to 2093 is constructed, its diameter measures 666.[8] But surely Christ cannot be the Beast! The trouble is, as Gardner notes, "it's easy for a skilled numerologist to find 666 in any name."[9] Numbers may appear to have magical significance, but one who has made numbers his special study remarks, "You can no more find a patternless arrangement of digits or letters than you can find a cloud without a shape."[10]

Revelation has fascinated numerologists, both pagan and Christian. It is also the favored domain of dispensationalists. Dispensationalist writers like Hal Lindsey base their popular accounts of the end-time scenario primarily on their interpretation of the biblical Apocalypse.[11]

Because dispensationalists relate the symbolism of the Apocalypse to current events, they tend to see the end-time as just around the corner. As historian Paul Boyer notes, "upwards of 40 percent" of Americans "believe that Bible prophecies detail a specific sequence of end-times events," and "read the headlines and watch the news through a filter of prophetic belief."[12]

These Americans see the world's events in a different light, and vote accordingly.[13] Here is what political commentator and former White House strategist Kevin Phillips said in 2008, near the end of the Bush administration. "The principal ethers at work [while George W. Bush was president] were evangelical, fundamentalist, and Pentecostal Christianity, infused with a millennial preoccupation...."[14] Phillips says that "at least 30 percent" of those who voted for Bush in the 2000 and 2004 elections—by some polls perhaps even a majority—"were end-time believers."[15] Phillips is concerned about "the preoccupation of Americans awaiting the Rapture or the tremors of Armageddon."[16] He observes that "three-quarters of U. S. evangelicals" believe that the world will "end in Armageddon" and that the Antichrist is already here.[17]

But, as Phillips notes, "most theologians point out" that "the Bible includes no specific sequence of end-times events ... so belief that it does is largely a product of a century of amplified Darbyism."[18] Professor of New Testament, Barbara Rossing, pulls no punches: "The Rapture and the dispensationalist chronology is a fabrication.... The system is not true to a literal reading of the Bible, as they claim."[19] One dispensationalist, a professor at the Moody Bible Institute in Chicago, goes against his fellows. He calls the practice of "anachronistically correlating current events" with Bible prophecies "an obsession" which has "undoubtedly caused more harm than good."[20]

The biblical Apocalypse has too often appealed to the dark side of the human soul. It has led to fatalism, causing people to retreat from this world and abandon the fight for human progress and betterment. It is used to sanctify our natural human tendencies of revenge and aggression, to bless our demonization of enemies. This has led to excesses, atrocities, and all forms of human violence, from the individual to the international scale. As Jonathan Kirsch observes, far too often has Revelation functioned as a "petri dish for the breeding of dangerous religious eccentricity."[21]

Many consider Revelation the creation of a vivid, even fevered or insane, imagination. Robert P. Carroll in his book *When Prophecy Failed* writes, "Apocalyptic may be considered the triumph of the imagination over reality. A triumph brought about by the felt need to overcome the restrictions of grim reality."[22] The Apocalypse has been considered the result of "the creative imagination of a schizophrenic."[23] It has been called "an insane rhapsody" (Northrop Frye),[24] "the ravings of a maniac" (Thomas Jefferson).[25] Clergy in Jefferson's time said the book of Revelation "either finds a man mad, or makes him so."[26] In our time Harold Bloom has only damning words: "The influence of Revelation always has been out of all proportion to its ... spiritual value." It "has enthralled the quacks and cranks of all ages ... a lurid and inhumane work ... without wisdom, goodness, kindness, or affection of any kind."[27]

Novelist D. H. Lawrence finds the "chief spirit" of Revelation "repellent."[28] The violent angry tone of Revelation leads Lawrence to assert a strong contrast between the "Christianity of the Apocalypse" and the "Christianity of Jesus."[29] Many would agree. Richard K. Emmerson and Bernard McGinn remark that the Apocalypse of John is unusual among ancient apocalyptic literature in that it is full of "a spirit of vengeance, both divine and human, that seems at war with much of the rest of the New Testament."[30]

There are glaring differences, noticeable at a glance, between the gospels' depiction of Jesus and God and that found in Revelation. The God of Revelation is not the loving "Father" of the gospel of John, who "so loves the world" (3:16). The "Lord God Almighty" of Revelation, one who appears "like jasper and carnelian" (noted for their hardness), is powerful and wrathful, austere and distant, aloof and judgmental.

John's gospel announces that "whoever believes in him [Jesus] should not perish, but have everlasting life" (3:16). Nothing more than belief is needed; no special works required. But in Revelation belief is no longer sufficient: "I will give unto every one of you what your works deserve" (2:23). "I am coming soon ... to repay everyone for his actions" (22:12). "And the dead were judged ... according to their works" (20:12).

Where in the Apocalypse is the loving Jesus who fed the hungry and healed the sick? The gentle Jesus of the gospels has been replaced in the Apocalypse by a raging warrior. In his hand is neither loaf nor wine, but sword and sickle. He has come not to give life, but to take it away. Rather than bring the good news of mercy and life, the Apocalypse is filled with judgment and punishment and death. Instead of the Jesus of the gospels, there is the "Son of God whose eyes burn with a flame of fire" (2:18); there is the mysterious and terrifying figure on the white horse who "judges and makes war" (19:11); there is "one like a son of man" with "a sharp sickle in his hand" (14:14).

Because Revelation is so different from the other books of the Bible in style and content and spirit, its authenticity was suspect from early times. Around 200 A.D., Gaius of Rome, a respected theologian, rejected Revelation as part of Christian Scripture. He maintained that the heretic Cerinthus had written it from his imagination,[31] and craftily attributed it to John (meaning the apostle of that name), knowing that this would inspire confidence in its authenticity. Gaius noted that in the letters of Paul, long accepted and respected by the church, Christ was to return without warning "like a thief in the night." By contrast, Revelation indicated specific events which would occur just prior to Christ's return. Moreover, Revelation contained false prophecy: the letter to the church of Thyatira contained promises which could not be fulfilled because by Gaius's time this church had ceased to exist.

The position of Revelation was even weaker in the eastern church, the cradle of Christianity. Cyril of Jerusalem listed the books of the New Testament in his lectures to those preparing for church membership. His list included all our present books except Revelation. In many regions the Apocalypse was banned. In the third century Bishop Dionysius of Alexandria rejected Revelation because it was not by the apostle John and its text was obscure and full of contradictions.[32] Dionysius presented strong arguments—many of which are considered valid to this day[33]—to prove that Revelation's "John" was not the apostle by that name.[34]

It wasn't until 367 that the Apocalypse was officially included in the sacred canon. But its status continued to be disputed. During the Reformation Martin Luther declared Revelation to be "neither apostolic nor prophetic,"[35] which was equivalent to saying that Revelation had no proper place in the Bible.

Revelation was considered for inclusion in the Christian canon only because several important figures in the early Christian church believed it was written by John the apostle. At that time there existed many pieces of religious literature which displayed the same type of wild imagery and visions found in the Apocalypse, but none became part of the Christian canon. Without the attribution of the apostle John as its author, Revelation might, like so much similar literature, have disappeared.

There is good reason to believe that the apostle John was not the author of the Apocalypse. He was martyred before 70 A.D., and ancient witnesses are almost unanimous that the Apocalypse was written late in the reign of Domitian (around 95 A.D.). The gospel of John, the three epistles of John, and Revelation were all originally composed in Greek, but the quality of Greek in Revelation is grossly inferior to that in the other four books. Not only does the John of Revelation use a style and theology which contrasts that of the other four books, he never claims to be an apostle (he calls himself a prophet, and makes a clear distinction between "apostles and prophets" [18:20]), or to have known Jesus personally.

That John called himself a prophet is strange, considering that the Jews believed prophecy had ceased well before John's time. The biblical book of 1 Maccabees, written about 140 BC, has the words "since the time that prophets ceased to appear among them" (9:27). The Jewish historian Josephus, writing about a generation before John's time, noted that from about 450 B.C. whatever was written gained little credence, because there was "no longer a reliable succession of prophets."[36] Early rabbinic literature remarked that "after the last prophets, Haggai, Zechariah, and Malachi died [about 500 B.C.], the Holy Spirit departed from Israel."[37]

Not only was prophecy extinct long before John's time, John was not consistent with the tradition of the classical Old Testament prophets. The visions and words of the Old Testament prophets were transcribed later by persons other than the prophets themselves. By contrast, John recorded his own prophecy in written words. Unlike the prophets of old, John makes ample use of material from other written sources, particularly Hebrew Scripture. In the Apocalypse there are extensive allusions to various books of the Old Testament — 518, by one count.[38]

The great prophets of the Old Testament warned the people to turn from their wicked ways. This implied a malleable future. By contrast, John tells of "things which must be" (4:1). The beast of the Apocalypse is given power over "every one whose name has not been written before the foundation of the world in the book of life" (13:8). It does not matter what anyone does in this life. Either one's name has been in the book of life since before the earth was created, or not. No longer can human beings influence their destiny. Nothing can alter the course of God's eternal plan. History is in a sense already complete, its end and goal set in stone.

This fatalism and determinism was found in other Jewish apocalypses. The first Jewish apocalypses appeared in the third century BC, and purported to reveal ancient, but previously secret, knowledge about the cosmos and human destiny. They were filled with strange symbols and esoteric ideas not found in Jewish tradition.

The source of this foreign content is not difficult to trace. Beginning with the Babylonian captivity Jews lived among the Persians for more than two hundred years. Consequently, Jewish culture was influenced by Persian culture, including its religion — Zoroastrianism. Zoroastrianism saw everything as part of a divine plan. There is a time of tribulation for all people, even the righteous, just before a glorified virgin-born savior defeats the demonic forces, resurrects the dead for judgment (granting all righteous persons everlasting life), and ushers in a new and eternal world governed by God.

John, then, was clearly not a prophet in the Old Testament tradition, but an apocalyptic seer. He wrote in the tradition of Jewish apocalypticism, and used much of Zoroastrian theology concerning the end-time, with one major exception — his pessimism. Zoroastrianism had a positive and optimistic outlook concerning this earthly life. The earth was not hopelessly drowning in evil. Human beings could overcome evil.[39] Jewish apocalyptic, however, was steeped in pessimism because of the environment which gave it birth. The Jewish people were so oppressed that some believed there was no longer reason to hope for this world. Instead they focused their hopes on an end to this world and the coming of a new world.

Early Christianity was no more monolithic than Christianity today. Apocalyptic eschatology, as witnessed in John's apocalypse, may have been a facet of developing Christianity, but it "by no means exhausted the total meaning of the Christian religion."[40] How much of early Christianity was apocalyptic remains an unanswered question.[41]

Revelation is an extended letter from John to the seven churches of Asia Minor (now Turkey). It was not intended for all of Christendom or for all time. John wrote the Apocalypse for the benefit of a certain group of people at a specific time of stress.

John's purpose in writing was to encourage Christians to maintain the faith in the face of harassment by the surrounding community. The emperor cult — in which the emperor was worshiped as "Lord and God" — benefited these seven cities economically and politically. But John urged Christians in these cities to turn away from pagan practices and worship the true lord, Jesus Christ. John wanted Christians in the seven cities to withdraw from the surrounding pagan community — "Come out of her, my people" (18:4) — and form a separate community with strict social and religious rules, in the expectation of an imminent end to the world.

Not to participate in the emperor cult was to cut oneself off from the social, economic, and commercial life of the city. There would be "tribulation" — public harassment and persecution, even more than presently experienced — but this is all part of God's plan, which would end in the punishment of the persecutors and new life for the persecuted. The cosmic picture revealed in the Apocalypse gives meaning to present suffering. John proclaims the ultimate triumph of good over evil; God's kingdom on earth is coming. John expected The End to be imminent.

Beginning shortly after John's time Christians examining Scripture found many differing theological threads woven into the tapestry of the New Testament writings: "There appears to have been, among the early Christians, no single understanding of the meaning of Jesus and his resurrection, even from the apocalyptic perspective."[42] Observing that the language of the Apocalypse was symbolic and open to interpretation, Origen of Alexandria suggested it was not meant to be understood literally, in the "Judaistic" sense, but required a spiritual rendering. Soon the majority in the East were following Origen's lead.

In the West this change in the interpretation of the Apocalypse came later, when the expectations of the early Christians in an imminent Second Coming began to wane. It took the influence of Augustine to dehistoricize the message of the Apocalypse. Christians should not look forward to some future thousand years of glory. The parousia had not been delayed. The kingdom of God was already here; it had arrived with Jesus. The war between good and evil was already unfolding in the actions of human beings, in the presence of the church. The Holy Spirit is with us, its power available to effect the kingdom of God within individual souls, empowering us to do good in this world and improve the status of human existence. The church was the instrument of salvation. Revelation's "millennium" was an allegory for the age of the church, that period between Jesus's sojourn on earth and his Second Coming. A sacramental view of existence — below/above — was to replace the apocalyptic now/future. Christian hope was to reside in the salvation of the individual soul after death, not in some corporate end of the world. The kingdom of God was now to be viewed no longer as imminent, but immanent.

The language and imagery of the Apocalypse would serve a churchly purpose — the horror of its depiction of hell would spur parishioners toward a better life. Augustine had led the way to the official interpretation of the Apocalypse. A year after his death the Council of Ephesus (431) decreed literal interpretation of the Apocalypse erroneous. Since that time the official view of the Christian church has been that Revelation must be understood spiritually, not literally.

The church had spoken. But that has not prevented individual Christians from interpreting the Apocalypse as they please. A fascination with the literal interpretation of the Apocalypse has never died. As Bernard McGinn notes, all through Christian history "the apocalyptic mentality has continued to produce new religious challenges, no matter how often it has been domesticated."[43]

Centuries after Augustine, Martin Luther, the father of the Protestant Reformation, found the Apocalypse an "obscure book"[44] which does not teach Christ's message.[45] He noted the "great affection" and the "excessive zeal" the "unlearned mob" had for the Revelation of John. Because of its lurid imagery and its use of allegory, Luther labeled Revelation a dangerous book. It attracted "fanatics"[46] who read into the allegories whatever they wished, then claimed biblical authority for their crank schemes: "Everyone claims to be a master interpreter."[47] "There one is free to fabricate anything whatever."[48] Luther issued a warning: "He who either fabricates allegories without discrimination or follows such as are fabricated by others is not only deceived but also most seriously harmed...."[49] The Reformation era was not sympathetic to a literal interpretation of the Apocalypse. Both the Augsburg Confession and the Helvetic Confession went against it.

In the eighteenth century Thomas Paine scoffed at those who saw in Scripture long-range "predictions"; the biblical prophets were clearly referring to events of their own times: "Scarcely anything can be more absurd than to suppose that men situated as Ezekiel and Daniel were, whose country was overrun and in the possession of the enemy, all their friends and relations in captivity abroad, or in slavery at home, or massacred, or in continual danger of it ... should find nothing to do but that of employing their time and their thoughts about what was to happen to other nations a thousand or two thousand years after they were dead."[50]

The Old Testament book of Deuteronomy decrees the punishment for false prophets: "And thou shalt stone him with stones, that he die." The false prophet is one whose predictions prove incorrect. Since the false prophet must be stoned within his own lifetime, it follows that a prophet's predictions relate only to his own lifetime. The prophets of the Bible never made predictions concerning the distant future. Their words referred to the immediate future. John claimed to be a prophet. Like other biblical prophets his visions told of a time which was near, of "that which must shortly happen" (22:6). An angel told him to "seal not the prophecies of this book: for the time is at hand" (22:10). John was not writing to us about our time. He was writing to the churches of his own time concerning what was about to happen.

Too often is Revelation seen as a book of gloom and doom, a sword of Damocles hanging menacingly over our heads. Some see every evil, man-made or natural, as a sign that we are in the end-time. They feel powerless. They believe we cannot get ourselves out of this mess, that we must await the Second Coming before the golden millennium occurs. We will not have long to wait. The signs, they believe, are everywhere.

Others find this interpretation misguided. Christians should feel empowered by the Apocalypse, for it speaks of the eventual triumph of good over evil. God will help the courageous overcome the evils of this world and bring about a better world, an earthly "millennium": "God is with humankind" (21:3). "To the thirsty I will give water.... He who conquers ... I will be his God...." (21:6–8).

They read Revelation in the context of the Bible as a whole — as promise rather than threat. In the story of Noah, related in the biblical book of Genesis, God's promise prevailed over the curse of the flood: "The Lord said in his heart, I will never again curse the ground because of man's evil" (8:21). So he set upon the clouds a rainbow, as the sign and reminder of his "covenant which is between me and you and every living creature of all flesh" (9:15). Revelation is a continuation of God's promise. Good *will* triumph over evil. The millennium will come.

19

The Millennium:
Hope for the Future?

The core beliefs of conservative American Christians have left them vulnerable to rogue preachers, false prophets. The same core beliefs of conservatives have left the nation vulnerable, polarized into "Reds" and "Blues."

Many of these core beliefs—those introduced by John Nelson Darby and the Princeton theology—are innovations upon Christian tradition, which is why fundamentalism has been so divisive. Fundamentalists place undue emphasis upon one book of the Bible, the Apocalypse, which they interpret literally. Ironically, the Apocalypse is the one book of Scripture which has had doubtful authority through much of Christian history. The mainline church, throughout that history, has either rejected it entirely, or insisted that it be interpreted symbolically. To get around this, Darby and the dispensationalists simply write off the mainline church as not "the true church," a trick the rogue preachers, false prophets, have brought to perfection.

More than half of Americans, conservative Americans, believe that the prophecies in the book of Revelation will literally come true. Paul Boyer notes, "prophecy belief is far more central in American thought than intellectual and cultural historians have recognized."[1] He goes on to state that "one cannot fully understand the American public's response to a wide range of international and domestic issues without bearing in mind that millions of men and women view world events and trends, at least in part, through the refracting lens of prophetic belief."[2] As historian Leonard Sweet quips, "Watching, waiting, and working for the millennium ... has become, even more than baseball, America's favorite pastime."[3]

The millennium. Beginning with the Massachusetts Bay colony, the religious ethos of the nation which followed has been nourished and underpinned by the hope for an American millennium. The Puritans who first colonized America believed that by living according to strict biblical precepts they could precipitate the coming of Christ's Kingdom in this world, the millennium promised in the Bible. Jonathan Edwards carried this millennial hope into the Age of Science. He was convinced that the Great Awakening heralded the "advancement" of Christ's Kingdom on earth, and that America would be the site of the coming millennium. The Great Awakening raised millennial expectations amongst the populace, providing a unifying self-consciousness throughout the thirteen colonies which did much to facilitate the movement toward independence as a new nation. The millennialist tradition provided the ideological leverage which inspired American colonists to break from Britain.

With victory over the British, the millennium seemed imminent. Millennialism provided a common ground between liberals and conservatives and defined the national purpose, providing an intellectual framework for much of the thinking regarding the new nation. The new nation would, indeed, be a city upon a hill, a religious example to other peoples, a nation with cosmic significance, a special people, a divinely chosen instrument in the realization of the Kingdom. Millennialism underpinned the nature, purpose, and destiny of the nation. The very *idea of the nation*—held by both liberals and conservatives—involved the concept of the United States as God's chosen nation, God's chosen people, chosen to have a special role in his plan for humanity. From the time of its first colonists, America, as a people, *as a nation*, has considered itself a religious entity. This is how it differs from other nations. This religious idealism of Americans, both liberal and conservative, is evident to this day in the words "in God we trust," "one nation under God."

The traditional belief at the time of independence from Britain was that the millennium would arrive gradually, brought about by the continual progress in human behavior, after which Christ would return to reign over his Kingdom. William Miller changed that. He believed that human action was futile. Only Christ could inaugurate the millennium. These divergent concepts of the millennium provided the seedbed for the growth of two religious cultures. As the most significant millenarian expression in American history, Millerism forced the religious center to polarize into a dichotomy. Darby's influence and the Princeton theology hardened this dichotomy, eventuating in a battle between fundamentalists and modernists. After the famous "Monkey Trial," fundamentalists separated from secular society until the 1980s, when once again they blossomed forth, responding to new-found spiritual needs. Today conservative Christians have created a separate subculture.

A nation with two divergent cultures. The polarization of America's populace into the "Reds" and the "Blues," into religious conservatives and liberals, has profound implications for the future of the nation, the direction the nation will take in the decades to come. Robert Wuthnow speaks of "two distinct civil religions"—one liberal and one conservative: "While each of these expresses certain truths about the character of the American republic, the tensions between the two have rendered each less than satisfactory as unifying, legitimating belief systems."[4] In place of a former "single voice" and set of "common ideals," Wuthnow sees "different visions of what America can and should be. Religious conservatives and liberals offer competing versions...."[5] And it has much to do with differing concepts of the millennium.

The millennium, for both liberals and conservatives, is a time when humanity will live under God's reign — the Kingdom of God. The details of when and how it will happen differ for conservatives and liberals. Unfortunately, liberals and conservatives insist on emphasizing these differing details, rather than what they have in common. William Jennings Bryan said that it is not what separates Christian from Christian, but what they have in common that matters. For Bryan, Christianity was a practical faith. It taught people how to love and live in harmony with others, even if their concepts of Christianity might differ somewhat. Bryan never took sides in the millennialist debate between premillennialists and postmillennialists; it seemed unimportant in the broader picture.

Dwight L. Moody was a confirmed evangelical who believed in an imminent Second Coming, but he, like Bryan, was ready to overlook theological nuances in favor of the common ground in Christ. John Robinson, pastor to the Pilgrims back in the early seventeenth century, wrote: "We ought to be firmly persuaded in our hearts of the truth and goodness of the religion which we embrace in all things; yet as knowing ourselves to be men whose property it is to err and to be deceived in many things. And accordingly, both to converse with men in that modesty of mind as always to desire to learn something better or further by them, if it may be."[6]

Conversing. Learning. Understanding. The alternative is really no alternative. Kevin Phillips writes, "Our collective failure to challenge presuppositions, think anew, and openly debate central religious concerns affecting society is a recipe for disaster."[7]

If the concept of the American millennium could forge a new independent nation two centuries ago, if Americans of both liberal and conservative religious persuasions could work together to one purpose *then*, they should be able to do so *now*. Robert Wuthnow maintains that "America's legitimating myths," "deeply intertwined" with its "religious traditions," have in the past allowed the nation to see "its star rise in the galaxy of economic and political power."[8] In the past this focus on the millennium, this sense of divine origin and direction, provided strength of purpose. It can do so today if Americans take seriously the proclamation "one nation under God"; if American Christians of liberal and conservative persuasions consider what they have in common as Christians, to come together in understanding and common purpose; if American Christians row vigorously on both sides of the boat, so that its course be straight, and not allow ambitious politicians to draw them into warfare over partisan issues.

Bill Bright, founder of Campus Crusade for Christ, writes: "God has given this country unlimited resources and manpower and finances ... [and] has called America to help bring the blessing of His love and forgiveness to the rest of the world."[9] It is the old mantra: A city upon a hill. It remains to be seen whether Americans will rise to the challenge. Only the future will tell.

Notes

Preface

1. James Davison Hunter, *Culture Wars: The Struggle to Define America* (New York: Basic-Books, 1991) 64.
2. *Ibid.*, 42.
3. *Ibid.*, 43.
4. E. Brooks Holifield, *God's Ambassadors: A History of the Christian Clergy in America* (Grand Rapids: William B. Eerdmans, 2007) 320.
5. Robert Wuthnow, *The Reconstruction of American Religion: Society and Faith Since World War II* (Princeton: Princeton University Press, 1988) 133.
6. Kevin Phillips, *American Theocracy: The Peril and Politics of Radical Religion, Oil, and Borrowed Money in the 21st Century* (New York: Viking, 2006) 104.
7. *Ibid.*, 100.
8. Peter L. Berger, "Democracy and the Religious Right," *Commentary* (January 1997) 55.
9. Paul Boyer, *When Time Shall Be No More: Prophecy Belief in Modern American Culture* (Cambridge: Harvard University Press, 1992) 3–4.
10. Harold Bloom, *The American Religion: The Emergence of the Post-Christian Nation* (New York: Simon & Schuster, 1991) 257.
11. Robert C. Fuller, *Spiritual, but Not Religious: Understanding Unchurched America* (Oxford: Oxford University Press, 2001) 1.
12. *Ibid.*
13. Vincent Crapanzano, *Serving the Word: Literalism in America from the Pulpit to the Bench* (New York: The New Press, 2000) 30.
14. Fuller, 1.
15. Phillips, 119.
16. William G. McLoughlin, *Modern Revivalism: Charles Grandison Finney to Billy Graham* (New York: Ronald Press, 1959) 529.
17. Fuller, 3.
18. Quoted in Phillips, 108.
19. *Ibid.*, xiii.
20. *Ibid.*, 101.
21. Quoted in *ibid.*, 124.
22. Quoted in *ibid.*, 171.

23. For the Christian Right, particularly with respect to the Middle East, see David S. New, *Holy War: The Rise of Militant Christian, Jewish and Islamic Fundamentalism* (Jefferson, NC: McFarland, 2002).
24. Quoted in Douglas Kennedy, *In God's Country: Travels in the Bible Belt, USA* (London: Unwin Hyman, 1990) 165.
25. Quoted in Jonathan Kirsch, *A History of the End of the World: How the Most Controversial Book in the Bible Changed the Course of Western Civilization* (San Francisco: HarperSanFrancisco, 2006) 245.
26. Michael D'Antonio, *Fall from Grace: The Failed Crusade of the Christian Right* (New York: Farrar Straus Giroux, 1989) 242.
27. Phillips, viii.
28. *Ibid.*, 194.
29. *Ibid.*, vii.
30. *Ibid.*, ix.
31. Quoted in *ibid.*, xv.
32. Hunter, 67.
33. David W. Wills, *Christianity in the United States: A Historical Survey and Interpretation* (Notre Dame: University of Notre Dame Press, 2005) 13.
34. *Ibid.*, 13.
35. Any attempt to define "fundamentalism" is pointless. It is simply a more extreme form of conservative Christianity, and shares its beliefs. It is these beliefs, as they developed against liberal beliefs, which provide the focus of this study.
36. Nancy Gibbs, "Apocalypse Now," *Time* (July 1, 2002) 32–33.

Chapter 1

1. Quoted in Os Guinness, *The Gravedigger File* (London: Hodder and Stoughton, 1983) 175.
2. Three out of four Americans attend church, compared to only one in ten Britishers (*ibid.*, 50).
3. Quoted in John C. Miller, *The First Fron-*

tier: *Life in Colonial America* (New York: Dell, 1966) 31. Hereafter, material quoted from early works will be altered in spelling to modern English usage.

4. Quoted in *ibid.*, 30.

5. Quoted in James Truslow Adams, *The Founding of New England* (Boston: Atlantic Monthly Press, 1921) 99.

6. T. H. Breen and Timothy Hall, *Colonial America in an Atlantic World: A Story of Creative Interaction* (New York: Pearson Longman, 2004) 112.

7. Miller, 32.

8. Breen and Hall, 114. These words do not reflect their opinion, but that commonly held by others.

9. Allen Carden, *Puritan Christianity in America: Religion and Life in Seventeenth-Century Massachusetts* (Grand Rapids: Baker Book House, 1990) 11.

10. Perry Miller, *Nature's Nation* (Cambridge: Harvard University Press, 1967), 234.

11. Sydney E. Ahlstrom, *A Religious History of the American People*, 2d ed. (New Haven: Yale University Press, 2004) 128.

12. The Puritans themselves knew that their attempt to establish a "society of saints" and lead a godly life brought contempt: We are "despised, pointed at, hated of the world, made a byword, reviled, slandered, rebuked, made a gazing stock, called Puritan, nice fools, hypocrites, hair-brained fellows, rash, indiscrete, vainglorious... ." (Written in 1616, quoted in Avihu Zakai, *Exile and Kingdom: History and Apocalypse in the Puritan Migration to America* [Cambridge: Cambridge University Press, 1992] 131.)

13. Both quotes from Ahlstrom, 79.

14. Ahlstrom's wording, 80–81.

15. Ahlstrom's wording, 80.

16. Ahlstrom's wording, 92.

17. Quoted in Carden, 44.

18. Quoted in *ibid.*

19. John Danforth, quoted in *ibid.*, 38.

20. *Ibid.*, 122.

21. Thomas Shepard, quoted in *ibid.*, 36.

22. Figures cited in *ibid.*, 39.

23. Urian Oakes, quoted in *ibid.*, 40.

24. Quoted in *ibid.*, 42.

25. Quoted in *ibid.*, 131.

26. Quoted in Ahlstrom, 147.

27. Quoted in Sacvan Bercovitch, *The Puritan Origins of the American Self* (New Haven: Yale University Press, 1975) 191.

28. From Mather, *Theopolis Americana: An Essay on the Golden Street of the Holy City* (1710), quoted in Stephen J. Stein, "Transatlantic Extensions: Apocalyptic in Early New England," in C. A. Patrides and Joseph Wittreich (eds.),

The Apocalypse in English Renaissance Thought and Literature: Patterns, Antecedents and Repercussions (Ithaca: Cornell University Press, 1984) 277.

29. Carden, 94.

30. J. F. Maclear, "New England and the Fifth Monarchy: The Quest for the Millennium in Early American Puritanism," *William and Mary Quarterly* 32 (April 1975) 223.

31. *Ibid.*, 224.

32. Paul Boyer, *When Time Shall Be No More: Prophecy Belief in Modern American Culture* (Cambridge: Harvard University Press, 1992), 68.

33. Reiner Smolinski, "Apocalypticism in Colonial North America," in Stephen J. Stein (ed.), *The Encyclopedia of Apocalypticism, vol. 3: Apocalyticism in the Modern Period and the Contemporary Age* (New York: Continuum, 1999) 48.

34. Stein, "Transatlantic Extensions," 273.

35. See, for example, Austin C. Dobbins, *Milton and the Book of Revelation: The Heavenly Cycle* (Tuscaloosa: University of Alabama Press, 1975).

36. Quoted in Zakai, 124. These words echo Revelation 12:6,14, where the woman who flies into the wilderness is interpreted to be the true church. In a section of the *Winthrop Papers* titled "Reasons to be Considered, and Objections with Answers" is the wording "seeing the Church has no place left to fly into but the wilderness... ." (Quoted in Zakai, 143).

37. Quoted in *ibid.*, 132.

38. *Ibid.*, 134.

39. *Ibid.*, 125.

40. Ahlstrom, 124.

41. *Ibid.*, 135.

42. Maclear, 225.

Chapter 2

1. Sacvan Bercovitch, *The Puritan Origins of the American Self* (New Haven: Yale University Press, 1975) ix.

2. *Ibid.*, 108.

3. Philip F. Gura, *A Glimpse of Sion's Glory: Puritan Radicalism in New England, 1620–1660* (Middletown, CT: Wesleyan University Press, 1984) viii.

4. Quoted in Stephen J. Stein, "Transatlantic Extensions: Apocalyptic in Early New England," in C. A. Patrides and Joseph Wittreich (eds.), *The Apocalypse in English Renaissance Thought and Literture: Patterns, Antecedents and Repercussions* (Ithaca: Cornell University Press, 1984) 275.

5. Perry Miller, *Errand into the Wilderness* (Cambridge: Harvard University Press, 1956) 218.

6. Quoted in Bercovitch, 91.

7. Quoted in *ibid.*, 96.

8. Quoted in Stein, 280.

9. J. M. Bumsted and John E. Van de Wetering, *What Must I Do to Be Saved? The Great Awakening in Colonial America* (Hinsdale, IL: Dryden, 1976) 3.

10. Quoted in Frank Lambert, *Inventing the "Great Awakening"* (Princeton: Princeton University Press, 1999) 41.

11. Quoted in Perry Miller, *Jonathan Edwards* ([New York]: William Sloane, 1949) 22.

12. Quoted in *ibid.*

13. Quoted in *ibid.*, 31.

14. Quoted in Sydney E. Ahlstrom, *A Religious History of the American People,* 2d ed. (New Haven: Yale University Press, 2004) 299.

15. *Ibid.*

16. Edwards, quoted in *ibid.*, 351.

17. Quoted in Miller, *Jonathan Edwards,* 58.

18. Quoted in *ibid.*, 50.

19. *Ibid.*, 72.

20. Edwards, quoted in Iain H. Murray, *Jonathan Edwards: A New Biography* (Edinburgh: Banner of Truth, 1987) 117.

21. Edwards, quoted in Lambert, 67.

22. Quoted in Murray, 117.

23. Kenneth P. Minkema, "Jonathan Edwards: A Theological Life," in Sang Hyun Lee (ed.), *The Princeton Companion to Jonathan Edwards* (Princeton: Princeton University Press, 2005) 1–2.

24. Edwards, quoted in Murray, 115–116.

25. Edwards, quoted in *ibid.*,116.

26. Quoted in John E. Smith, *Jonathan Edwards: Puritan, Preacher, Philosopher* (Notre Dame: University of Notre Dame Press, 1992) 29–30.

27. Ahlstrom, 351.

28. Edwards, quoted in Miller, *Jonathan Edwards,* 158.

29. Edwards, quoted in *ibid.*

30. Quoted in Lambert, 67.

31. Quoted in Miller, *Jonathan Edwards*, 140.

32. Quoted in Murray, 118.

33. The full title was *A Faithful Narrative of the Surprising Work of God in the Conversion of Many Hundred Souls in Northampton, and the Neighbouring Towns and Villages of New Hampshire, in New England.*

34. Quoted in James West Davidson, *The Logic of Millennial Thought: Eighteenth-Century New England* (New Haven: Yale University Press, 1977) 123.

35. Quoted in Frank Lambert, *Pedlar in Divinity: George Whitefield and the Transatlantic Revivals* (Princeton: Princeton University Press, 1994) 16.

36. Whitefield, quoted in *ibid.*,17.

37. Quoted in *ibid.*, 15, 18.

38. *Ibid.*, 62.

39. *Ibid.*, 8.

40. Quoted in Lambert, *Inventing,* 97.

41. Quoted in Robert W. Brockway, *A Wonderful World of God: Puritanism and the Great Awakening* (Bethlehem: Lehigh University Press, 2003) 105.

42. Quoted in Bumsted and Van de Wetering, 75.

43. Quoted in Lambert, *Inventing,* 96.

44. Quoted in Brockway, 109–110.

45. Quoted in Lambert, *Inventing,* 97.

46. The designation "the Great Awakening" was probably first used a century later in 1841, at a time of great revival, in a book by Joseph Tracy titled *The Great Awakening: A History of the Revival of Religion in the Time of Edwards and Whitefield.*

47. Miller, *Jonathan Edwards,* 134.

48. Ahlstrom, 263.

49. Stein, 283.

50. Alan Heimert, *Religion and the American Mind, from the Great Awakening to the Revolution* (Cambridge: Harvard University Press, 1966) 59.

Chapter 3

1. Habakkuk 2:3.

2. Psalm 102:13.

3. Quoted in Robert W. Brockway, *A Wonderful Work of God: Puritanism and the Great Awakening* (Bethlehem, PA: Lehigh University Press, 2003) 120.

4. Quoted in J. M. Bumsted and John E. Van de Wetering, *What Must I Do to Be Saved? The Great Awakening in Colonial America* (Hinsdale, IL: Dryden, 1976) 89.

5. Quoted in Brockway, 126.

6. Quoted in *ibid.*,138–139.

7. Quoted in *ibid.*,141.

8. Quoted in Bumsted and Van de Wetering, 83.

9. Quoted in *ibid.*

10. Quoted in *ibid.*

11. Quoted in Sydney E. Ahlstrom, *A Religious History of the American People*, 2d ed. (New Haven: Yale University Press, 2004) 285.

12. Quoted in Brockway, 111.

13. Quoted in *ibid.*

14. Quoted in *ibid.*

15. Quoted in Perry Miller, *Jonathan Edwards* ([New York]: William Sloane, 1949) 145.

16. Quoted in *ibid.*, 27.

17. Quoted in Bumsted and Van de Wetering, 90.

18. Miller, 183.

19. Quoted in *ibid.*,143.

20. Contemporary commentator, quoted in Brockway, 147.

21. Quoted in *ibid.*,149.

22. Quoted in *ibid.*

23. Quoted in *ibid.*,151.

24. Quoted in Miller, 173.

25. Ahlstrom, 301.

26. Quoted in Miller, 27.

27. Quoted in James West Davidson, *The Logic of Millennial Thought: Eighteenth-Century New England* (New Haven: Yale University Press, 1977) 174.

28. Quoted in *ibid.*,173.

29. Quoted in *ibid.*

30. Quoted in Bumsted and Van de Wetering, 11–12.

31. Brockway, 142.

32. Quoted in Miller, *Jonathan Edwards,* 173.

33. Alan Heimert, *Religion and the American Mind, from the Great Awakening to the Revolution* (Cambridge: Harvard University Press, 1966) 51.

34. Ruth H. Bloch, *Visionary Republic: Millennial Themes in American Thought, 1756–1800* (Cambridge: Cambridge University Press, 1985) 15.

Chapter 4

1. Robert W. Brockway, *A Wonderful World of God: Puritanism and the Great Awakening* (Bethlehem, PA: Lehigh University Press, 2003) 35.

2. Ruth H. Bloch, *Visionary Republic: Millennial Themes in American Thought, 1756–1800* (Cambridge: Cambridge University Press, 1985) 16.

3. Alan Heimert, *Religion and the American Mind, from the Great Awakening to the Revolution* (Cambridge: Harvard University Press, 1966) 66–67.

4. *Ibid.,* 66.

5. Perry Miller's words in Perry Miller, *Jonathan Edwards* ([New York]: William Sloane, 1949) 320.

6. Quoted in Brockway, 129–130.

7. Quoted in Stephen J. Stein, "Transatlantic Extensions: Apocalyptic in Early New England," in C. A. Patrides and Joseph Wittreich (eds.), *The Apocalypse in English Renaissance Thought and Literature: Patterns, Antecedents and Repercussions* (Ithaca: Cornell University Press, 1984) 284.

8. Stein's expression, *ibid.*

9. Quoted in Nathan O. Hatch, *The Sacred Cause of Liberty: Republican Thought and the Millennium in Revolutionary New England* (New Haven: Yale University Press, 1977) 29.

10. Quoted in Stein, 284.

11. All passages from this document quoted in Stein, 284–285.

12. Perry Miller, *Errand into the Wilderness* (Cambridge: Harvard University Press, 1956) 233.

13. Quoted in Iain H. Murray, *Jonathan Edwards: A New Biography* (Edinburgh: Banner of Truth, 1987) 48.

14. Quoted in *ibid.*

15. These numbers from Miller, *Jonathan Edwards,* 127.

16. Quoted in Murray, *Jonathan Edwards,* 48.

17. Miller's words, *Jonathan Edwards,* 319.

18. Quoted in *ibid.,* 70.

19. Stephen J. Stein, "Eschatology," in Sang Hyun Lee (ed.), *The Princeton Companion to Jonathan Edwards* (Princeton: Princeton University Press, 2005) 233.

20. Paul Boyer, *When Time Shall Be No More: Prophecy Belief in Modern American Culture* (Cambridge: Harvard University Press, 1992) 71.

21. Stein, "Eschatology," 229.

22. Quoted in *ibid.,* 233.

23. Heimert, 64.

24. The full title was *An Humble Attempt to Promote Explicit Agreement and Visible Union of God's People in Extraordinary Prayer, for the Revival of Religion and the Advancement of Christ's Kingdom on Earth, Pursuant to Scripture — Promises and Prophecies Concerning the Last Time.*

25. Quoted in James West Davidson, *The Logic of Millennial Thought: Eighteenth-Century New England* (New Haven: Yale University Press, 1977) 150.

26. Quoted in *ibid.*,154.

27. Sydney E. Ahlstrom, *A Religious History of the American People,* 2d ed. (New Haven: Yale University Press, 2004) 287.

28. Quoted in Heimert, 8.

29. Miller, *Jonathan Edwards,*178. This comment on a split in culture, much more in the open today, is perceptive for the 1940s.

30. Quoted in *ibid.,* 179.

31. Frank Lambert, *Inventing the "Great Awakening"* (Princeton: Princeton University Press, 1999) 10.

32. Heimert, 2.

33. Ahlstrom, 294.

34. Heimert, 9, 11.

35. J. M. Bumsted and John E. Van de Wetering, *What Must I Do to Be Saved? The Great Awakening in Colonial America* (Hinsdale, IL: Dryden, 1976) 160. See also Ahlstrom, 349, and Brockway, 175, and Jerald C. Brauer, "Puritanism, Revivalism, and the Revolution," in Jerald C. Brauer (ed.), *Religion and the American Revolution* (Philadelphia: Fortress, 1976) 2, 17.

36. Heimert, 14.

37. Bloch, 16.
38. *Ibid.*, 37.
39. Ahlstrom, 350.
40. Harry S. Stout, "The Puritans and Edwards," in Sang Hyun Lee (ed.), *The Princeton Companion to Jonathan Edwards* (Princeton: Princeton University Press, 2005) 288.
41. Ahlstrom, 287–288.
42. Hatch, 40.
43. Words of John Burt, 1759, quoted in *ibid.*, 39.
44. Differences remained, however. In general, liberals believed that the millennium would come gradually, not almost immediately after the French Antichrist was defeated (as many evangelicals believed).
45. Bloch, 22.
46. Quoted in *ibid.*, 59.
47. Quoted in Stein, "Transatlantic Extensions," 290.
48. Quoted in Davidson, 222.
49. Quoted in *ibid.*, 223.
50. Quoted in *ibid.*, 220.
51. Quoted in *ibid.*, 221.
52. Quoted in Bloch, 19.
53. Brauer, 2.
54. *Ibid.*, 27.
55. Bloch, 93.
56. *Ibid.*, xiii-xiv.
57. Quoted in *ibid.*,19–20.
58. Quoted in *ibid.*,20.
59. Hatch, 74.
60. Quoted in Davidson, 248–249.
61. Quoted in Hatch, 91.
62. Bloch, 53.
63. Quoted in *ibid.*, 85.
64. Quoted in *ibid.*, 94–95.
65. Quoted in *ibid.*, 94.
66. Quoted in Edwin S. Gaustad, *Faith of Our Fathers: Religion and the New Nation* (San Francisco: Harper & Row, 1987) 125.
67. Quoted in Hatch, 150.
68. Ahlstrom, 311.

Chapter 5

1. See Nathan O. Hatch, *The Sacred Cause of Liberty: Republican Thought and the Millennium in Revolutionary New England* (New Haven: Yale University Press, 1977) n. 97, p. 131.
2. Quoted in James West Davidson, *The Logic of Millennial Thought: Eighteenth-Century New England* (New Haven: Yale University Press, 1977) 289.
3. Quoted in Ruth H. Bloch, *Visionary Republic: Millennial Themes in American Thought, 1756–1800* (Cambridge: Cambridge University Press, 1985) 211.
4. Quoted in Hatch, 132.
5. Quoted in *ibid.*, 134.
6. To this day millennialists like Pat Robertson eschew anything not strictly American as part of the evil world beyond America's borders. Robertson sees all international associations— among these, the United Nations and, yes, he believes the Illuminati are still hard at work— as the work of Satan, out to destroy God's people. See David S. New, *Holy War: The Rise of Militant Christian, Jewish and Islamic Fundamentalism* (Jefferson, NC: McFarland, 2002) 90.
7. Boch, 231.
8. *Ibid.*,229.
9. *Ibid.*,121.
10. *Ibid.*,104.
11. Quoted in *ibid.*
12. Quoted in *ibid.*
13. Quoted in Keith J. Hardman, *Charles Grandison Finney, 1792–1875: Revivalist and Reformer* (Syracuse: Syracuse University Press, 1987) 5.
14. Quoted in *ibid.*,12.
15. Historians give various dates for the beginning and ending of this rather vaguely defined era.
16. Quoted in Bloch, 226.
17. Ruth Alden Doan, *The Miller Heresy, Millennialism, and American Culture* (Philadelphia: Temple University Press, 1987) 11.
18. *Ibid.*,12.
19. *Ibid.*,18.
20. Whitney R. Cross, *The Burned-Over District: The Social and Intellectual History of Enthusiastic Religion in Western New York, 1800–1850* (Ithaca: Cornell University Press, 1965) 79.
21. Michael Barkun, *Crucible of the Millennium: The Burned-over District of New York in the 1840s* (Syracuse: Syracuse University Press, 1986) 114.
22. Cross, 56.
23. *Ibid.*,23.
24. *Ibid.*,25.
25. Barkun, 104.
26. Quoted in Hardman, x.
27. *Ibid.*
28. Sydney E. Ahlstrom, *A Religious History of the American People* 2d ed. (New Haven: Yale University Press, 2004) 461.
29. Quoted in Hardman, 57.
30. Quoted in *ibid.*, 61.
31. Quoted in *ibid.*, 32.
32. Quoted in Cross, 174.
33. Quoted in *ibid.*,173.
34. Hardman, 87.
35. *Ibid.*,75–76.
36. *Ibid.*,80.
37. For details see Cross, 89–101.
38. *Ibid.*,93.
39. *Ibid.*,98.
40. Quoted in Hardman, 201–202.

41. Quoted in *ibid.*, 47–48.
42. Quoted in Frank Grenville Beardsley, *A Mighty Winner of Souls: Charles G. Finney, A Study in Evangelism* (New York: American Tract Society, 1937) 185.
43. Quoted in Hardman, 279.
44. Quoted in *ibid.*, 21.
45. Cross, 155.
46. Quote and figures from Hardman, 195.
47. *Ibid.*,196.
48. *Ibid.*,210.
49. Barkun, 23.
50. Quoted in Hardman, 281–282.
51. Quoted in Cross, 202.
52. Quoted in *ibid.*
53. Quoted in Hardman, 282.
54. Doan, 13.
55. *Ibid.*,14.
56. Hardman, 152.
57. Cross, 200.
58. Quoted in Hardman, 152.
59. Cross, 201.

Chapter 6

1. Quoted in Michael Barkun, *Crucible of the Millennium: The Burned-over District of New York in the 1840s* (Syracuse: Syracuse University Press, 1986) 25.
2. James D. Tabor and Eugene V. Gallagher, *Why Waco? Cults and the Battle for Religious Freedom in America* (Berkeley: University of California Press, 1995) 44.
3. *Ibid.*, n. 47, 224.
4. Quoted in Wayne R. Judd, "William Miller: Disappointed Prophet," in Ronald L. Numbers and Jonathan M. Butler (eds.), *The Disappointed: Millerism and Millenarianism in the Nineteenth Century* (Bloomington: Indiana University Press, 1987) 18.
5. Quoted in *ibid.*
6. Quoted in David L. Rowe, *Thunder and Trumpets: Millerites and Dissenting Religion in Upstate New York, 1800–1850* (Chico, CA: Scholars Press, 1985) 6.
7. Quoted in Judd, 18.
8. Quoted in Rowe, 6.
9. Quotes from *ibid.*,5,6.
10. Quoted in Judd, 18.
11. Quoted in Rowe, 7.
12. Quoted in Judd, 19.
13. Quoted in *ibid.*
14. Quoted in Rowe, 10.
15. Quoted in *ibid.*
16. Quoted in Judd, 20.
17. Quoted in Rowe, 11.
18. Quoted in Judd, 21.
19. Quoted in *ibid.*,20.
20. Quoted in Ruth Alden Doan, *The Miller Heresy, Millennialism, and American Culture* (Philadelphia: Temple University Press, 1987) 90–91.
21. Quoted in Judd, 19.
22. Quoted in *ibid.*,21.
23. Miller, quoted in Rowe, 1.
24. Miller, quoted in *ibid.*,2.
25. Quoted in *ibid.*,13.
26. *Ibid.*,12.
27. Quoted in *ibid.*,14.
28. Quoted in Judd, 22.
29. Rowe,15.
30. Quoted in *ibid.*,79.
31. Quoted in Barkun, 108.
32. Charles W. Meister, *Year of the Lord: A. D. Eighteen Forty-Four* (Jefferson, NC: McFarland, 1983) 25.
33. Judd, 30.
34. Quoted in *ibid.*
35. Quoted in David T. Arthur, "Joshua V. Himes and the Cause of Adventism," in Ronald L. Numbers and Jonathan M. Butler (eds.), *The Disappointed: Millerism and Millenarianism in the Nineteenth Century* (Bloomington: Indiana University Press, 1987) 38.
36. Quoted in *ibid.*,39.
37. Barkun, 132.
38. Meister, 30.
39. Arthur, 46.
40. Barkun, 33.
41. *Ibid.*,34.
42. David L. Rowe, "Millerites: A Shadow Portrait," in Ronald L. Numbers and Jonathan M. Butler (eds.), The *Disappointed: Millerism and Millenarianism in the Nineteenth Century* (Bloomington: Indiana University Press, 1987) 15.
43. Meister, 25.
44. Quoted in Doan, 33.
45. Quoted in Rowe, *Thunder,*121.
46. Quoted in Barkun, 55.
47. Quoted in *ibid.*,57.
48. Quoted in Whitney R. Cross, *The Burned-Over District: The Social and Intellectual History of Enthusiastic Religion in Western New York, 1800–1850* (Ithaca: Cornell University Press, 1965) 297.
49. Quoted in Arthur, 50.
50. Quoted in *ibid.*
51. Quoted in *ibid.*
52. Quoted in *ibid.*
53. Quoted in *ibid.*
54. Quoted in Rowe, *Thunder,*134.
55. Quoted in *ibid.*
56. Quoted in *ibid.*,132.
57. Quoted in *ibid.*,136.
58. Cross believes that much of what has been taken as historical fact concerning the Millerites during and leading up to October 22 is legend (305).

59. Jonathan M. Butler, "The Making of a New Order: Millerism and the Origins of Seventh-day Adventism," in Ronald L. Numbers and Jonathan M. Butler (eds.), *The Disappointed: Millerism and Millenarianism in the Nineteenth Century* (Bloomington: Indiana University Press, 1987) 197.

60. Quoted in *ibid.*

61. Quoted in Rowe, *Thunder*,137.

62. Quoted in *ibid.*

63. Quoted in *ibid.*

64. *Ibid.*,102, and Cross, 306, doubt the authenticity of these reports.

65. Quoted in Rowe, *Thunder*,139.

66. Quoted in *ibid.*

67. Quoted in Ronald L. Numbers and Jonathan M. Butler, *The Disappointed: Millerism and Millenarianism in the Nineteenth Century* (Bloomington: Indiana University Press, 1987) 215.

68. Quoted in Rowe, *Thunder*,141.

69. Quoted in Cross, 308.

70. Quoted in Rowe, *Thunder*,142.

71. Quoted in *ibid.*,141.

72. Quoted in *ibid.*,143.

73. Quoted in *ibid.*

74. Quoted in *ibid.*

75. Quoted in Arthur, 55.

76. Quoted in Cross, 313.

77. *Ibid.*,314.

78. Quoted in *ibid.*

79. Quoted in *ibid.*

80. Quoted in Rowe, *Thunder*,147.

81. Quoted in *ibid.*

82. Quoted in *ibid.*,154.

83. Quoted in *ibid.*

84. Quoted in Cross, 309.

85. Quoted in Arthur, 56.

86. Paul K. Conkin, *American Originals: Homemade Varieties of Christianity* (Chapel Hill: University of North Carolina Press, 1997) 123.

87. Quoted in Barkun, 40.

88. Quoted in Rowe, *Thunder*, 115.

89. Quoted in *ibid.*,90.

90. Quoted in *ibid.*

91. Quoted in *ibid.*,88.

92. Doan, 201.

93. Quoted in Barkun, 98.

94. Cross, 318.

95. *Ibid.*,317.

96. Stephen J. Stein, "Eschatology," in Sang Hyun Lee (ed.), *The Princeton Companion to Jonathan Edwards* (Princeton: Princeton University Press, 2005) 226.

97. Ruth Alden Doan suggests that because of Millerism a "stereotype of the premillennialist" was formed ("Millerism and Evangelical Culture" in Ronald L. Numbers and Jonathan M. Butler [eds.], *The Disappointed: Millerism and Millenarianism in the Nineteenth Century*

[Bloomington: Indiana University Press, 1987] 132, and *Miller*, 221).

98. Ernest R. Sandeen, *The Roots of Fundamentalism: British and American Millenarianism, 1800–1930* (Chicago: University of Chicago Press, 1970) 54.

Chapter 7

1. Ernest R. Sandeen, *The Roots of Fundamentalism: British and American Millenarianism, 1800–1930* (Chicago: University of Chicago Press, 1970) 42.

2. *Ibid.*,55.

3. *Ibid.*,58.

4. *Ibid.*,42.

5. *Ibid.*, xvi.

6. Quoted in *ibid.*,91.

7. Alexander Pope, *Essay on Man* (1733).

8. Quoted in Stephen Neill and Tom Wright, *The Interpretation of the New Testament, 1861–1986* (Oxford: Oxford University Press, 1988) 7.

9. *Ibid.*,21.

10. *Ibid.*,18.

11. Quoted in Jerry Wayne Brown, *The Rise of Biblical Criticism in America, 1800–1870: The New England Scholars* (Middletown, CT: Wesleyan University Press, 1969) 43.

12. *Ibid.*

13. Henry A. Pochman, *German Culture in America* (Madison: University of Wisconsin Press, 1961) 73–74.

14. Quoted in Brown, 155.

15. Quoted in *ibid.*,162.

16. Quoted in *ibid.*

17. Quoted in *ibid.*,169.

18. Quoted in *ibid.*,150.

19. Quoted in *ibid.*,164.

20. Quoted in *ibid.*,166.

21. Quoted in *ibid.*,167.

22. Quoted in *ibid.*,168.

23. Bulfinch, quoted in *ibid.*,141.

24. Quoted in *ibid.*,142.

25. Quoted in *ibid.*,143.

26. Sydney E. Ahlstrom, *A Religious History of the American People*, 2d ed. (New Haven: Yale University Press, 2004) 775.

27. *Ibid.*

28. Quoted in Brown, 181.

29. Quoted in David O. Beale, *In Pursuit of Purity: American Fundamentalism Since 1850* (Greenville, SC: Unusual, 1986) 135.

30. Jack B. Rogers and Donald K. McKim, *The Authority and Interpretation of the Bible: An Historical Approach* (San Francisco: Harper & Row, 1979) 267.

31. Quoted in *ibid.*,269.

32. Quoted in *ibid.*,270.

33. Quoted in *ibid.*

34. Quoted in *ibid.*,271.

35. Quoted in *ibid.*,276.

36. *Ibid.*,277.

37. Sandeen, 106.

38. Quoted in *ibid.*,118–119.

39. Quoted in Rogers and McKim, 331.

40. Quoted in *ibid.*,283.

41. Quoted in Sandeen, 125.

42. Quoted in Rogers and McKim, 282.

43. Quoted in Sandeen, n. 36, 123–124.

44. Quoted in Rogers and McKim, 272.

45. Quoted in *ibid.*

46. Quoted in *ibid.*,282.

47. Quoted in *ibid.*,287.

48. Quoted in *ibid.*,288.

49. Quoted in *ibid.*,287.

50. Quoted in *ibid.*

51. Hodge, quoted in *ibid.*,286.

52. Hodge, quoted in *ibid.*,287.

53. Hodge, quoted in *ibid.*

54. Ahlstrom, 768.

55. Quoted in Rogers and McKim, 288.

56. Quoted in J. Coppens, *The Old Testament and the Critics* (Paterson, NJ: St. Anthony, 1942) 18–19.

57. Quoted in Rogers and McKim, 300.

58. Quoted in *ibid.*,286.

59. Quoted in *ibid.*

60. Quoted in *ibid.*,288.

61. Quoted in *ibid.*,306–307.

62. Quoted in *ibid.*,307.

63. Quoted in *ibid.*,306.

64. Quoted in *ibid.*,303.

65. Quoted in *ibid.*,306.

66. Quoted in *ibid.*

67. Quoted in *ibid.*,337.

68. Quoted in *ibid.*,345–346.

69. Quoted in *ibid.*,346.

70. Quoted in *ibid.*,350.

71. Quoted in *ibid.*,349.

72. Quoted in *ibid.*

73. Quoted in *ibid.*,354.

74. Quoted in *ibid.*

75. Quoted in *ibid.*,355.

76. Quoted in *ibid.*

77. Quoted in *ibid.*,356.

78. Quoted in Sandeen, 126.

79. Quoted in Rogers and McKim, 355.

80. Quoted in *ibid.*,354.

81. Quoted in *ibid.*,361.

82. Deliberation of the General Assembly of the Presbyterian Church after Brigg's trial, quoted in *ibid.*,361.

83. *Ibid.*

Chapter 8

1. Schleiermacher, quoted in Alasdair I. C. Heron, *A Century of Protestant Theology* (London: Lutterworth, 1980) 28.

2. Schleiermacher, quoted in *ibid.*,30.

3. Quoted in Jerry Wayne Brown, *The Rise of Biblical Criticism in America, 1800–1870: The New England Scholars* (Middletown, CT: Wesleyan University Press, 1969) 151.

4. Quoted in *ibid.*,157.

5. Quoted in *ibid.*

6. Quoted in *ibid.*,158.

7. Quoted in *ibid.*,159–160.

8. Historian Sydney E. Ahlstrom goes so far as to say of Emerson that Everett was "his idol" (*A Religious History of the American People*, 2d ed. [New Haven: Yale University Press, 2004] 601).

9. Quotes from Emerson's address found in *ibid.*,601–602.

10. *Ibid.*,603.

11. Quoted in *ibid.*,604.

12. Quoted in Brown, 178.

13. Vincent Crapanzano, *Serving the Word: Literalism in America from the Pulpit to the Bench* (New York: The New Press, 2000) 37.

14. Brown, 38.

15. Quoted in Ahlstrom, 771.

16. William S. Peterson, *Victorian Heretic: Mrs. Humphrey Ward's Robert Elsmere* (Leicester: Leicester University Press, 1976) 159.

17. *Ibid.*,221. Number includes at least eight pirated editions.

18. *Ibid.*,222.

19. *Ibid.*,178.

20. *Ibid.*,16.

21. *Ibid.*,15.

22. *Ibid.*,181.

23. Quoted in *ibid.*,179.

24. Quoted in *ibid.*,180.

25. Quoted in Ahlstrom, 786.

26. *Ibid.*, 786.

27. Quoted in *ibid.*, 802.

Chapter 9

1. Quoted in F. Roy Coad, *A History of the Brethren Movement: Its Origins, Its Worldwide Development and Its Significance for the Present Day* (Grand Rapids: Eerdmans, 1968) 27.

2. Quoted in *ibid.*,28.

3. Quoted in *ibid.*

4. Quoted in Clarence B. Bass, *Backgrounds to Dispensationalism: Its Historical Genesis and Ecclesiastical Implications* (Grand Rapids: Baker, 1977) 111.

5. Quoted in Coad, 28.

6. Quoted in Harold H. Rowdon, *The Origins of the Brethren, 1825–1850* (London: Pickering & Inglis, 1967) 51.

7. Bass, 7.

8. *Ibid.*,17.

9. Quoted in Rowdon, 51.

10. Quoted in Larry V. Crutchfield, *The Origins of Dispensationalism: The Darby Factor* (Lanham, MD: University Press of America, 1992) 191.

11. Quoted in *ibid.*

12. Quoted in Coad, 110.

13. *Ibid.*,106.

14. Ernest R. Sandeen, *The Roots of Fundamentalism: British and American Millenarianism, 1800–1930* (Chicago: University of Chicago Press, 1970) 31.

15. Crutchfield, 8.

16. Quoted in Bass, 62.

17. For more on this, see *ibid.*,38, 148–149.

18. Quoted in *ibid.*,21.

19. *Ibid.*,98.

20. Quoted in *ibid.*,236.

21. Quoted in *ibid.*

22. Charles B. Strozier, *Apocalypse: On the Psychology of Fundamentalism in America* (Boston: Beacon Press, 1994) 120.

23. Words of a student in the early 1990s (Paul Boyer, *When Time Shall Be No More: Prophecy Belief in Modern American Culture* [Cambridge: Harvard University Press, 1992] 329).

24. Quoted in Bass, 89.

25. Quoted in *ibid.*

26. See *ibid.*, 91, for the extent of this.

27. David O. Beale, *In Pursuit of Purity: American Fundamentalism Since 1850* (Greenville, SC: Unusual, 1986) 5.

28. Dwight L. Moody, quoted in J. C. Pollock, *Moody* (Grand Rapids: Baker, 1997) 76. Moody refused to buy into separatism.

29. Bass, 99.

Chapter 10

1. William Martin, *With God on Our Side: The Rise of the Religious Right in America* (New York: Broadway Books, 1996) 7.

2. Quoted in Ernest R. Sandeen, *The Roots of Fundamentalism: British and American Millenarianism, 1800–1930* (Chicago: University of Chicago Press, 1970) 44.

3. Quoted in *ibid.*,107.

4. Quoted in *ibid.*

5. Ernest R. Sandeen, *The Origins of Fundamentalism* (Philadelphia: Fortress, 1968) 7.

6. Quoted in Sandeen, *Roots*, 85.

7. Quoted in *ibid.*, 94.

8. Quoted in *ibid.*,95–96.

9. Quoted in Sandeen, *Origins*, 9.

10. Quoted in Sandeen, *Roots,*133.

11. *Ibid.*,134.

12. Quoted in David O. Beale, *In Pursuit of Purity: American Fundamentalism Since 1850* (Greenville, SC: Unusual, 1986) 26.

13. Quoted in Sandeen, *Roots*, 132–133.

14. Quoted in *ibid.*,133.

15. Brookes never acknowledged an intellectual debt to the Brethren; he would only say that he became a premillennialist through reading the prophetic passages of the Bible.

16. Quoted in Sandeen, *Roots*, 140.

17. Although today many fundamentalists prefer to think that their beliefs are identical with original Christian doctrine, and deny the novelty of dispensationalism, some dispensationalists are willing to admit the truth. Craig A. Blaising and Darrell L. Bock, professors at a bastion of dispensationalism, Dallas Theological Seminary, "concede that dispensationalism is both recent and different from most of what went before it" (Walter A. Elwell, "Dispensationalisms of the Third Kind," *Christianity Today* [Sept. 12, 1994] 28).

18. Quoted in Sandeen, *Roots,*143.

19. Sandeen, *Origins,*11.

20. "Modernism" is a term used by conservatives, particularly in the late nineteenth and early twentieth centuries, in reference to Christian liberals—those who adopted "modern" theological ideas such as biblical criticism, and agreed with thinkers like Bushnell, Emerson, Parker, and Briggs.

21. Quoted in Sandeen, *Roots*, 154.

22. *Ibid.*, 61.

23. Larry V. Crutchfield, *The Origins of Dispensationalism: The Darby Factor* (Lanham, MD: University Press of America, 1992) preface.

24. Sandeen, *Roots*, 223.

25. C. I. Scofield (ed.), *Oxford NIV Scofield Study Bible* (New York: Oxford University Press, 1984) x.

26. *Ibid.*

27. Quoted in Timothy P. Weber, *Living in the Shadow of the Second Coming: American Premillennialism, 1875–1982* (Grand Rapids: Zondervan, 1983) 174.

28. Beale, 37. See also Sandeen, *Roots*, 222: The Scofield Bible is "perhaps the most influential single publication in millenarian and Fundamentalist historiography."

29. Some would say that the Ryrie Study Bible, the work of a former faculty member of Dallas Theological Seminary, has superceded the Scofield Bible in some ways.

30. This figure is a distributor's estimate of stock holdings. Randall Balmer, *Mine Eyes Have Seen the Glory: A Journey into the Evangelical Subculture in America* (New York: Oxford University Press, 2006) 197.

31. *Ibid.*, n. 5, 46.

32. Charles B. Strozier, *Apocalypse: On the*

Psychology of Fundamentalism in America (Boston: Beacon Press, 1994) 189.

33. Quoted in Sandeen, *Origins*, 20.

34. Quoted in George M. Marsden, *Fundamentalism and American Culture: The Shaping of Twentieth-Century Evangelicalism, 1870–1925* (New York: Oxford University Press, 1980) 122.

35. Sandeen, *Roots*, 198.

36. Sandeen, *Origins*, 3.

37. Quoted in Marsden, 32.

38. Quoted in *ibid.*,33.

39. *Ibid.*,32

40. Quoted in *ibid.*, 44.

41. Quoted in *ibid.*, 43.

42. William Gerald McLoughlin, *Modern Revivalism: Charles Grandison Finney to Billy Graham* (New York: Ronald Press, 1959) 371.

43. Quoted in Marsden, 47.

44. Quoted in *ibid.*

45. Quoted in *ibid.*, 60.

46. Quoted in *ibid.*

47. *Ibid.*,225.

48. Sandeen, *Origins*, 25.

49. *Ibid.*,22.

50. For a detailed discussion of how dispensationalism relates to everything Middle Eastern see David S. New, *Holy War: The Rise of Militant Christian, Jewish and Islamic Fundamentalism* (Jefferson, NC: McFarland, 2002).

51. Quoted in Weber, 161.

52. Quoted in Marsden, 148.

53. Quoted in *ibid.*,148–149.

54. Quoted in Sandeen, *Roots*, 237–238.

Chapter 11

1. Quoted in Frederick Lewis Allen, *Only Yesterday* (New York: Bantam, 1959) 15.

2. Quoted in *ibid.*,31.

3. Quoted in *ibid.*,41–42.

4. Quoted in *ibid.*,92.

5. Only 252 students offered themselves for foreign service to the Foreign Missionary Conference of North America in 1928, compared to 2,700 in 1920. (Sydney E. Ahlstrom, *A Religious History of the American People*, 2d ed. [New Haven: Yale University Press, 2004] 899.)

6. Quoted in George M. Marsden, *Fundamentalism and American Culture: The Shaping of Twentieth-Century Evangelicalism, 1870–1925* (New York: Oxford University Press, 1980) 160.

7. Quoted in *ibid.*,163.

8. Quoted in *ibid.*,159.

9. Quoted in *ibid.*,160.

10. Timothy P. Weber, *Living in the Shadow of the Second Coming: American Premillennialism, 1875–1982* (Grand Rapids: Zondervan, 1983) 45.

11. Ernest R. Sandeen, *The Origins of Fundamentalism* (Philadelphia: Fortress, 1968) 3.

12. Ernest R. Sandeen, *The Roots of Fundamentalism: British and American Millenarianism, 1800–1930* (Chicago: University of Chicago Press, 1970) 246.

13. Quoted in Marsden, 168.

14. Ahlstrom, 811–812.

15. Quoted in *ibid.*,812.

16. Quoted in Marsden, 175.

17. Quoted in *ibid.*,189.

18. *Ibid.*, n. 8, 281.

19. Quoted in *ibid.*,188.

20. Eugene Debs, quoted in Roger A. Bruns, *Preacher: Billy Sunday and Big-Time American Evangelism* (New York: W. W. Norton, 1992) 195.

21. Sunday, quoted in *ibid.*,138.

22. Sunday, quoted in *ibid.*

23. Quoted in *ibid.*,165.

24. Quoted in *ibid.*,204.

25. Quoted in *ibid.*,249.

26. Quoted in *ibid.*,207.

27. Quoted in *ibid.*,250.

28. Quoted in *ibid.*,210.

29. Quoted in *ibid.*,215.

30. Quoted in *ibid.*,186.

31. Quoted in *ibid.*,193.

32. Quoted in *ibid.*,127–128.

Chapter 12

1. A name resulting from a fictionalized version produced as a Broadway play a generation after the event, later adapted by Hollywood.

2. Quoted in Edward J. Larson, *Summer for the Gods: The Scopes Trial and America's Continuing Debate over Science and Religion* (New York: Basic, 1997) 20.

3. Quoted in *ibid.*

4. Quoted in *ibid.*,32.

5. Quoted in Ray Ginger, *Six Days or Forever? Tennessee v. John Thomas Scopes* (Chicago: Quadrangle, 1958) 3.

6. Quoted in Larson, 49–50.

7. *Ibid.*, 48.

8. Quoted in Ginger, 7.

9. Quoted in *ibid.*

10. Quoted in Larson, 82.

11. Quoted in *ibid.*,83.

12. John T. Scopes and James Presley, *Center of the Storm: Memoirs of John T. Scopes* (New York: Holt, Rinehart and Winston, 1967) 60.

13. Quoted in Ginger, 33.

14. Quoted in Larson, 73.

15. Quoted in Roger A. Bruns, *Preacher: Billy Sunday and Big-Time American Evangelism* (New York: W. W. Norton, 1992) 128.

16. Quoted in *ibid.*,125.

17. Quoted in *ibid.*,126.

18. Quoted in *ibid.*,280.

19. Ginger, 191.

20. Quoted in Larson, 146.

21. Scopes and Presley, 99.

22. *Ibid.*, 77.

23. Quoted in Larson, 93.

24. Quoted in Ginger, 129.

25. Quoted in *ibid.*,86.

26. Quoted in Larson, 93.

27. Quoted in *ibid.*,187.

28. Quoted in George M. Marsden, *Fundamentalism and American Culture: The Shaping of Twentieth-Century Evangelicalism, 1870–1925* (New York: Oxford University Press, 1980) 187.

29. All quoted in *ibid.*,169.

30. Quoted in Ginger, 171.

31. Quoted in *ibid.*,172.

32. Quoted in Larson, 190.

33. Quoted in Ginger, 172.

34. Quoted in Larson, 200.

35. *Ibid.*,203.

36. Quoted in *ibid.*,199.

37. Quoted in *ibid.*,203.

38. Quoted in Michael Kazin, *A Godly Hero: The Life of William Jennings Bryan* (New York: Knopf, 2006) 125.

39. Scopes and Presley, 212.

40. Kazin, 306.

41. Bryan, quoted in *ibid.*,127.

42. Quoted in *ibid.*,130.

43. L. Sprague De Camp, *The Great Monkey Trial* (Garden City: Doubleday, 1968) 36.

44. Quoted in Marsden, 134.

45. Robert W. Cherny, *A Righteous Cause: The Life of William Jennings Bryan* (Boston: Little, Brown, 1985) 204.

46. Quoted in Marsden, 134.

47. Quoted in *ibid.*,132.

48. Quoted in Bruns, 283.

49. Quoted in *ibid.*,263.

50. Vincent Crapanzano, *Serving the Word: Literalism in America from the Pulpit to the Bench* (New York: The New Press, 2000) 30.

51. Quoted in Marsden, 188.

52. Quoted in *ibid.*,189.

53. Quoted in *ibid.*

54. Hiram Wesley Evans, quoted in Sydney E. Ahlstrom, *A Religious History of the American People*, 2d ed. (New Haven: Yale University Press, 2004) 917.

55. Ernest R. Sandeen, *The Roots of Fundamentalism: British and American Millenarianism, 1800–1930* (Chicago: University of Chicago Press, 1970) xi.

56. Marsden, 31.

57. Sandeen, xv.

58. *Ibid.*, xix.

Chapter 13

1. Frederick Lewis Allen, *Only Yesterday* (New York: Bantam, 1959) 356–357.

2. All quotes from George M. Marsden, *Fundamentalism and American Culture: The Shaping of Twentieth-Century Evangelicalism, 1870–1925* (New York: Oxford University Press, 1980) 191–192.

3. Edward J. Larson, *Summer for the Gods: The Scopes Trial and America's Continuing Debate over Science and Religion* (New York: Basic, 1997) 234.

4. *Ibid.*,229.

5. Paul Boyer, *When Time Shall Be No More: Prophecy Belief in Modern American Culture* (Cambridge: Harvard University Press, 1992) 116.

6. Michael Hout, Andrew Greeley and Melissa Wilde, "Birth Dearth: Demographics of Mainline Decline," *The Christian Century* (October 4, 2005) 24.

7. George Gallup, Jr., and Jim Castelli, *The People's Religion: American Faith in the 90{ft}s* (New York: Macmillan, 1989) 13, 17.

8. Richard N. Ostling, "Those Mainline Blues," *Time* (May 22, 1989) 54–56.

9. Kenneth L. Woodward, "From 'Mainline' to Sideline," *Newsweek* (Dec. 22, 1986) 54–56.

10. *Ibid.*,54–56.

11. Garry Wills, *Under God: Religion and American Politics* (New York: Simon & Schuster, 1990) 21.

12. Kenneth L. Woodward, "Dead End for the Mainline?" *Newsweek* (Aug. 9, 1993) 46–48.

13. Charles Trueheart, "Welcome to the Next Church," *The Atlantic Monthly* (August 1996) 38.

14. All of these figures are based on calculations derived from numbers found in sequential issues of Eileen W. Lindner (ed.), *Yearbook of American and Canadian Churches* (Nashville: Abingdon, 1999–2008).

15. William C. Symonds, "Earthly Empires: How Evangelical Churches Are Borrowing from the Business Playbook," *Business Week* (May 23, 2005) 84.

16. Ostling, 54–56.

17. Dean M. Kelley, *Why Conservative Churches Are Growing: A Study in Sociology of Religion* (New York: Harper & Row, 1977) 21, 25.

18. Gallup and Castelli, 93.

19. Ostling, 54–56.

20. Wills, 21.

21. *Ibid.*,19.

22. Woodward, "Dead End," 46–48.

23. Charles B. Strozier, *Apocalypse: On the Psychology of Fundamentalism in America* (Boston: Beacon Press, 1994) 4.

24. Thomas C. Reeves, *The Empty Church: The Suicide of Liberal Christianity* (New York: The Free Press, 1996) 32. Much confusion has arisen over nomenclature. After the founding of Fuller Theological Seminary in 1947, an innovative effort to reform fundamentalism by making it more scholarly and involved in social issues, the term "New Evangelicalism" was coined. Near the end of the 1950s many fundamentalists who had separated themselves from "modernist" secular society wanted to accommodate much of the modern materialistic life without compromising basic conservative values and beliefs. These called themselves "evangelicals" to indicate their less militant and separatist attitude toward the dominant secular culture. Those who retained the proud name "fundamentalist" continued to oppose modernism in all its forms, living separate, strictly disciplined lives. "Evangelicals" are less conservative than "fundamentalists," but the terms are often used interchangeably. "Conservative" is an all-encompassing expression, and better serves to describe the dichotomy in American Protestantism.

25. Mary Nemeth, "God Is Alive," *Maclean's* (April 12, 1993) 32–37.

26. Wade Clark Roof and William McKinney, *American Mainline Religion: Its Changing Shape and Future* (New Brunswick, NJ: Rutgers University Press, 1987) 20.

27. George Barna and William Paul McKay, *Vital Signs: Emerging Social Trends and the Future of American Christianity* (Westchester, IL: Crossway Books, 1984) 120–21.

28. Leslie R. Keylock, "Evangelical Protestants Take Over Center Field," *Publishers Weekly* (March 9, 1984) 32–33.

29. Gallup and Castelli, 93.

30. *Ibid.*

31. Jonathan Kirsch, *A History of the End of the World: How the Most Controversial Book in the Bible Changed the Course of Western Civilization* (San Francisco: HarperSanFrancisco, 2006) 231. Michelle Goldberg, *Kingdom Coming: The Rise of Christian Nationalism* (New York: W. W. Norton, 2006) 8, states that one quarter of American citizens are white evangelicals, but then goes on to nuance this figure.

32. Symonds, 84.

33. These figures are based on calculations derived from numbers found in sequential issues of Lindner, *Yearbook*.

34. For the period between 1990 and 2001. These numbers seem exaggerated, and may have much to do with the definition of "fundamentalist" and "evangelical." Nevertheless, the trend is clear. (*Statistical Abstract 2008*, 7–8, 59.)

35. Hout, Greeley, and Wilde, 27.

36. Peter L. Berger, *The Noise of Solemn Assemblies: Christian Commitment and the Religious Establishment in America* (Garden City: Doubleday, 1961) 116.

37. Kelley, 25.

38. Nemeth, 32–37.

39. Quoted in Robert Wuthnow, *The Reconstruction of American Religion: Society and Faith Since World War II* (Princeton: Princeton University Press, 1988) 47.

40. E. Brooks Holifield, *God's Ambassadors: A History of the Christian Clergy in America* (Grand Rapids: William B. Eerdmans, 2007) 264.

41. *Ibid.*

42. *Ibid.,* 319.

43. Nemeth, 32–37.

44. Kelley, 76.

45. Daniel Yankelovich, *New Rules: Searching for Self-Fulfillment in a World Turned Upside Down* (New York: Random House, 1981) 5.

46. For details on this see David S. New, *Holy War: The Rise of Militant Christian, Jewish and Islamic Fundamentalism* (Jefferson, NC: McFarland, 2002).

47. William Martin, "The Christian Right and American Foreign Policy," *Foreign Policy* (Spring 1999) 71.

48. Symonds, 84.

49. Quoted in Wuthnow, 133.

50. Jackson W. Carroll, "Pastors' Picks: What Preachers Are Reading," *The Christian Century* (August 23, 2003) 32.

51. Strozier, 5.

52. Eugen Weber, *Apocalypses: Prophecies, Cults and Millennial Beliefs through the Ages* (Toronto: Random House of Canada, 1999) 208–209.

53. Strozier, 5.

Chapter 14

1. Quoted in Nancy Tatom Ammerman, *Bible Believers: Fundamentalists in the Modern World* (New Brunswick, NJ: Rutgers University Press, 1987) 102.

2. Michelle Goldberg, *Kingdom Coming: The Rise of Christian Nationalism* (New York: W. W. Norton, 2006) 58.

3. William C. Symonds, "Earthly Empires: How Evangelical Churches Are Borrowing from the Business Playbook," *Business Week* (May 23, 2005) 86.

4. Figures from the Hartford Institute, quoted in www. en. wikipedia. org/wiki/mega church (November 2008).

5. Goldberg, 58.

6. "100 Largest U. S. Churches," www. outreachmagazine. com/docs/top100_2007_largest. pdf (November 2008).

7. www. en. wikipedia. org/wiki/Lakewood _Church (November 2008).

8. Randall Balmer, *Mine Eyes Have Seen the Glory: A Journey into the Evangelical Subculture in America* (New York: Oxford University Press, 2006) 327–328.

9. *Ibid.*

10. Symonds, 80.

11. *Ibid.*,88.

12. "100 Largest U. S. Churches," www. outreachmagazine. com/docs/top100_2007_largest. pdf (November 2008).

13. www. en. wikipedia. org/wiki/Willow_ Creek_Community_Church (November 2008).

14. *Ibid.*

15. Symonds, 87.

16. All figures from *ibid.*,84.

17. Balmer, 323.

18. Symonds, 84.

19. Eric Arnson, quoted in Symonds, 88.

20. For more on this intriguing individual see David S. New, *Holy War: The Rise of Militant Christian, Jewish and Islamic Fundamentalism* (Jefferson, NC: McFarland, 2002) 20–21.

21. Jeffery L. Sheler, "Stains on Stained Glass: Tales of Treachery and Deceit inside America's Biggest Megachurch," *U.S. News & World Report* (Oct. 10, 1994) 97.

22. Symonds, 88, 84.

23. Byron R. Johnson, "The Case for Empirical Assessment of Biblical Literacy in America," in David Lyle Jeffrey and C. Stephen Evans, *The Bible and the University* (Grand Rapids: Zondervan, 2007) 251.

24. Symonds, 80.

25. www. en. wikipedia. org/wiki/Lakewood_Church (November 2008).

26. For more detail see Patrick Rogers and Vickie Bane, "Joel Osteen Counts His Blessings," *People* (December 17, 2007) 94–100.

27. Quoted in Balmer, 324.

28. www. en. wikipedia. org/wiki/Willow_ Creek_Community_Church (November 2008).

29. "100 Largest U. S. Churches," www. outreachmagazine. com/docs/top100_2007_largest. pdf (November 2008).

30. Michael D'Antonio, *Fall from Grace: The Failed Crusade of the Christian Right* (New York: Farrar Straus Giroux, 1989) 24.

31. Figures from Symonds, 88.

32. Figures from *ibid.*,84.

33. A. G. Mojtabai, *Blessèd Assurance: At Home with the Bomb in Amarillo, Texas* (Boston: Houghton Mifflin, 1986) 89, 194.

34. This figure is from the 2000 census. An estimate from July 2007, puts the population at 187,000. Figures from www. en. wikipedia. org/wiki/Amarillo,_Texas (November 2008).

35. Mojtabai, 89.

36. *Ibid.*,90.

37. Thomas C. Reeves, *The Empty Church: The Suicide of Liberal Christianity* (New York: The Free Press, 1996) 188

38. Quoted in Charles Trueheart, "Welcome to the Next Church," *The Atlantic Monthly* (August 1996) 54.

39. Goldberg, 58.

40. Eileen W. Lindner (ed.), *Yearbook of American and Canadian Churches* (Nashville: Abingdon, 2008).

41. Quoted in Symonds, 84.

42. Quoted in Trueheart, 40.

43. *Ibid.*,38.

44. Quoted in *ibid.*,47.

45. Michael S. Hamilton, "Willow Creek's Place in History," *Christianity Today* (November 13, 2000) 68.

46. Quoted in Symonds, 88.

47. Quoted in Reeves, 10.

48. Quoted in *ibid.*,153.

49. Quoted in *ibid.*,18–19.

50. Quoted in *ibid.*,17.

51. Trueheart, 46.

52. Donald E. Miller, *Reinventing American Protestantism: Christianity in the New Millennium* (Berkeley: University of California Press, 1997) 201.

53. Greg Pritchard, quoted in Matt Branaugh, "Willow Creek's 'Huge Shift,'" *Christianity Today* (June 2008) 13.

54. Miller, 108.

55. Grace Halsell, *Prophecy and Politics: Militant Evangelists on the Road to Nuclear War* (Westport, CT: Lawrence Hill, 1986) 14.

56. Miller, 130.

57. George Barna and William Paul McKay, *Vital Signs: Emerging Social Trends and the Future of American Christianity* (Westchester, IL: Crossway Books, 1984) 76; Paul Boyer, *When Time Shall Be No More: Prophecy Belief in Modern American Culture* (Cambridge: Harvard University Press, 1992) 7.

58. Ronald Nash, *Evangelicals in America: Who They Are, What They Believe* (Nashville: Abingdon, 1987) 35.

59. Gary C. Wharton, "The Continuing Phenomenon of the Religious Best Seller," *Publishers Weekly* (Mar. 14, 1977) 82–83.

60. Erling Jorstad, *Holding Fast / Pressing On: Religion in America in the 1980s* (Westport, CT: Greenwood, 1990) 103–4.

61. Barna, 75.

62. *Ibid.*

63. *Ibid.*,76.

64. Jorstad, 95.

65. *Ibid.*,95.

66. Symonds, 84.

67. Balmer, 300.

68. Barna, 150.

69. Jorstad, 9.

70. Barna, 34.
71. *Ibid.*,34.
72. *Ibid.*
73. *Ibid.*
74. *Ibid.*,37.
75. Ammerman, 106.
76. *Statistical Abstract of the United States, 2008*, 151. This amounts to over one million children.
77. Goldberg, 3.
78. Quoted in Sydney E. Ahlstrom, *A Religious History of the American People*, 2d ed. (New Haven: Yale University Press, 2004) 915–916.
79. Ernest R. Sandeen, *The Roots of Fundamentalism: British and American Millenarianism, 1800–1930* (Chicago: University of Chicago Press, 1970) 183.
80. Quoted in *ibid.*,182.
81. Quoted in David O. Beale, *In Pursuit of Purity: American Fundamentalism Since 1850* (Greenville, SC: Unusual, 1986) 89.
82. Sandeen, 183.
83. Quoted in Beale, 90.
84. Sandeen, 181.
85. Grace Halsell, *Prophecy and Politics: Militant Evangelists on the Road to Nuclear War* (Westport, CT: Lawrence Hill, 1986) 15.
86. Sandeen, 243.
87. Robert Wuthnow, *The Reconstruction of American Religion: Society and Faith Since World War II* (Princeton: Princeton University Press, 1988) 168.
88. *American Universities and Colleges*, 18th ed., 2008, 1321.
89. www. dts. edu/about/stats (December 2008).
90. Quoted in Balmer, n. 1, 45.
91. Quoted in *ibid.*,35.
92. Quoted in *ibid.*,36.
93. www. dts. edu/about/stats (December 2008).
94. Jeffrey J. Richards, *The Promise of Dawn: The Eschatology of Lewis Sperry Chafer* (Lanham, MD: University Press of America, 1991) 40, 44.
95. www. en. wikipedia. org/wiki/Bob_Jones_University (December 2008).
96. Douglas Kennedy, *In God's Country: Travels in the Bible Belt, USA* (London: Unwin Hyman, 1990) 175.
97. *Ibid.*,176–177.
98. *American Universities and Colleges*, 18th ed., 2008, 1421.
99. Gary Dorrien, *The Making of American Liberal Theology: Crisis, Irony, and Postmodernity, 1950–2005* (Louisville: Westminster John Knox Press, 2006) 2.
100. Quoted in *ibid.*,314.
101. Quoted in *ibid.*,330.
102. Quoted in *ibid.*,517.
103. *Ibid.*,537.

Chapter 15

1. Quoted in Nancy Tatom Ammerman, *Bible Believers: Fundamentalists in the Modern World* (New Brunswick, NJ: Rutgers University Press, 1987) 42.
2. *Ibid.*
3. John Cloud, "Meet the Prophet," *Time* (July 1, 2002) 40.
4. E. Brooks Holifield, *God's Ambassadors: A History of the Christian Clergy in America* (Grand Rapids: William B. Eerdmans, 2007) 318.
5. Cloud, 41.
6. Byron R. Johnson, "The Case for Empirical Assessment of Biblical Literacy in America," in David Lyle Jeffrey and C. Stephen Evans, *The Bible and the University* (Grand Rapids: Zondervan, 2007) 251.
7. Walter Kirn, "The End Is Here, Pt. 6," *Time* (Sept. 13, 1999) 39.
8. Peter Gardella, "Ego and Apocalypse in America," *Religious Studies Review*, vol. 21 (1995), 197, mentions Lindsey's professor, J. Dwight Pentecost, author of *Things To Come*.
9. Maxine Negri, "Why Biblical Criticism by Scholars Is Imperative," *The Humanist*, vol. 44, no. 3 (1984), 27.
10. Hal Lindsey, *The 1980{ft}s: Countdown to Armageddon* (New York: Bantam, 1980) 4.
11. Hal Lindsey, *The Road to Holocaust* (New York: Bantam, 1989), dust jacket.
12. Timothy P. Weber, *Living in the Shadow of the Second Coming: American Premillennialism, 1875–1982* (Grand Rapids: Zondervan, 1983) 211.
13. Nancy Gibbs, "Apocalypse Now," *Time* (July 1, 2002) 33.
14. Quoted in *ibid.*,35.
15. Daniel Wojcik, *The End of the World As We Know It: Faith, Fatalism, and Apocalypse in America* (New York: New York University Press, 1997) 212.
16. John Leland, "Millennium Madness," *Newsweek* (Nov. 1, 1999) 70.
17. Gibbs, 31.
18. Andrew Phillips, "One Lived, One Died," *Maclean's* (May 3, 1993) 16–23.
19. Listed by name in James D. Tabor and Eugene V. Gallagher, *Why Waco? Cults and the Battle for Religious Freedom in America* (Berkeley: University of California Press, 1995) 254–255.
20. Harrison Rainie, "Armageddon in Waco: The Final Days of David Koresh," *U. S. News & World Report* (May 3, 1993) 24–34.

21. Tabor and Gallagher, n. 7, 214.

22. Dick J. Reavis, *The Ashes of Waco: An Investigation* (New York: Simon & Schuster, 1995) 277.

23. Melinda Beck, "Thy Kingdom Come," *Newsweek* (Mar. 15, 1993) 52–55.

24. Ivan Solotaroff, "The Last Revelation from Waco," *Esquire* (July 1993) 54.

25. Reavis, 11.

26. Tabor and Gallagher, 65.

27. Reavis, 34.

28. Quoted in Solotaroff, 54.

29. The words of a fellow Texan, quoted in *ibid.*

30. Quoted in Reavis, 24.

31. Quoted in *ibid.,*26.

32. Quoted in *ibid.,*49.

33. Quoted in Tabor and Gallagher, 32.

34. Koresh's words, quoted in Reavis, 103.

35. Quoted in Tabor and Gallagher, 29.

36. Quoted in *ibid.,*30.

37. Quoted in *ibid.,*31.

38. Quoted in David G. Bromley and Edward D. Silver, "The Davidian Tradition: From Patronal Clan to Prophetic Movement," in Stuart A. Wright (ed.), *Armageddon in Waco: Critical Perspectives on the Branch Davidian Conflict* (Chicago: University of Chicago Press, 1995) 61.

39. Quoted in Tabor and Gallagher, 33.

40. Barbara Kantrowitz, "Was It Friendly Fire?" *Newsweek* (April 5, 1993) 50–51.

Chapter 16

1. Vincent Bugliosi and Curt Gentry, *Helter Skelter: The True Story of the Manson Murders* (New York: W. W. Norton, 1974) 32.

2. *Ibid.,*39.

3. *Ibid.,*44.

4. "Case of the Hypnotic Hippie," *Newsweek* (Dec. 15, 1969) 30–37.

5. "The Demon of Death Valley," *Time* (Dec. 12, 1969) 26–29.

6. Tex [Charles] Watson with Ray Hoekstra, *Will You Die for Me?* (Old Tappan, NJ: Fleming H. Revell, 1978) 121, 124.

7. Quoted in Bugliosi, 195. Spellings corrected from the original.

8. *Ibid.,*218.

9. *Ibid.*

10. Brooks Poston, quoted in *ibid.,*232.

11. Brooks Poston, quoted in *ibid.,*233.

12. Robert Endleman, *Jonestown and the Manson Family: Race, Sexuality, and Collective Madness* (New York: Psyche, 1993) 99.

13. Bugliosi, 224.

14. R. C. Zaehner, *Our Savage God* (London: Collins, 1974) 71.

15. Quoted in Bugliosi, 243.

16. *Ibid.,*244.

17. *Ibid.,*242.

18. Charles Manson, quoted in *ibid.,*235.

19. Paul Crockett, quoted in *ibid.,*232.

20. Zaehner, 218.

21. Quoted in David Chidester, *Salvation and Suicide: An Interpretation of Jim Jones, the Peoples Temple, and Jonestown* (Bloomington: Indiana University Press, 1988) 39.

22. Quoted in *ibid.,*162.

23. Lidia Wasowicz, "Some Jones Followers Still Believe in Him," in J. Gordon Melton (ed.), *The Peoples Temple and Jim Jones: Broadening Our Perspective* (New York: Garland, 1990) 375 (reprinted from *Chicago Sun-Times*, Nov. 18, 1979).

24. Terri Buford, quoted in Mark Lane, *The Strongest Poison* (New York: Elsevier-Dutton, 1980) 101–102.

25. Tim Reiterman, *Raven: The Untold Story of the Rev. Jim Jones and His People* (New York: E. P. Dutton, 1982) 4.

26. John R. Hall, *Gone from the Promised Land: Jonestown in American Cultural History* (New Brunswick, NJ: Transaction, 2004) ix.

27. Quoted in Ethan Feinsod, *Awake in a Nightmare: Jonestown, the Only Eyewitness Account* (New York: Norton, 1981) 221.

28. Chidester, 164.

29. Reiterman, 4–5.

30. Stephen C. Rose, "Jim Jones and Crisis Thought: A Critique of Established Religion" in Rebecca Moore and Fielding McGehee III (eds.), *New Religious Movements, Mass Suicide, and Peoples Temple: Scholarly Perspectives on a Tragedy* (Lewiston, NY: Edwin Mellen, 1989) 45.

31. John R. Hall, "Jonestown and Bishop Hill: Continuities and Disjunctures in Religious Conflict," in Rebecca Moore and Fielding McGehee III (eds.), *New Religious Movements, Mass Suicide, and Peoples Temple: Scholarly Perspectives on a Tragedy* (Lewiston, NY: Edwin Mellen, 1989) 88.

32. Hall, *Gone,*175.

33. Chidester, xii. Tapes from the archives of the FBI.

34. *Ibid.,*105.

35. *Ibid.,*109.

36. Quoted in *ibid.,*94.

37. Quoted in *ibid.,*110.

38. Quoted in *ibid.,*114.

39. Hall, *Gone,* 40.

40. Hall, *Gone,* 62.

41. Chidester, 107.

42. Quoted in *ibid.,*110.

43. Quoted in J. Gordon Melton, *The Peoples Temple and Jim Jones: Broadening Our Perspective* (New York: Garland, 1990) 92.

44. Quoted in *ibid.*

45. Quoted in *ibid.*
46. Quoted in *ibid.*,91.
47. Judith Mary Weightman, *Making Sense of the Jonestown Suicides: A Sociological History of Peoples Temple* (Lewiston, NY: Edwin Mellen, 1983) 188.
48. Shiva Naipaul, *Black and White* (London: Hamish Hamilton, 1980) 202.
49. Hall, *Gone*, 138.
50. Quoted in Chidester, 117.
51. Quoted in *ibid.*
52. Hall, "Jonestown," 78.
53. Weightman, 207.
54. George Klineman, Sherman Butler and David Conn, *The Cult That Died: The Tragedy of Jim Jones and the Peoples Temple* (New York: Putnam, 1980) 34.
55. *Ibid.*,199.
56. *Ibid.*,200.
57. Naipaul, 101.
58. Constance A. Jones, "Exemplary Dualism and Authoritarianism at Jonestown," in Rebecca Moore and Fielding McGehee III (eds.), *New Religious Movements, Mass Suicide, and Peoples Temple: Scholarly Perspectives on a Tragedy* (Lewiston, NY: Edwin Mellen, 1989) 209.
59. Hall, *Gone*, 108.
60. Hall, "Jonestown," 88.
61. Quoted in Jones, 210.
62. These quotes found in Chidester, 90.
63. Hall, *Gone*, 41.
64. Chidester, 165.
65. *Ibid.*,97.
66. Hall, *Gone*,38.
67. Quoted in Chidester, 2.
68. See, for example, the remark of Achie Ijames in Reiterman, 246.
69. Thomas Robbins, "The Second Wave of Jonestown Literature: A Review Essay," in Rebecca Moore and Fielding McGehee III (eds.), *New Religious Movements, Mass Suicide, and Peoples Temple: Scholarly Perspectives on a Tragedy* (Lewiston, NY: Edwin Mellen, 1989) 115.
70. Jeannie Mills, quoted in Weightman, 78.
71. Klineman, Butler, and Conn, 140.
72. Quoted in Reiterman, 309.
73. Quoted in Chidester, 42.
74. Quoted in Naipaul, 26.
75. Quoted in Klineman, Butler, and Conn, 88.
76. Quoted in Melton, 141.
77. Quoted in *ibid.*,143.
78. Quoted in *ibid.*
79. Quoted in Hall, *Gone*, 155.
80. Reiterman, 272.
81. Details on the physical beatings in the Temple from Klineman, Butler, and Conn, 35–36, 197–200.

82. Quoted in Weightman, 39.
83. Quoted in *ibid.*,16.
84. Quoted in Chidester, 2.
85. Quoted in James Reston, Jr., *Our Father Who Art in Hell* (New York: Times, 1981) 174.
86. Rev. Dr. Karl Irvin. Jr., quoted in Klineman, Butler, and Conn, 250. Before the Jonestown tragedy, when the Disciples tried to distance itself from Peoples Temple, Irvin had complimentary remarks concerning that congregation. (See Chidester, 39.)
87. Klineman, Butler, and Conn, 241.
88. Quoted in Hall, *Gone*, 154.
89. Reston, 48.
90. Hall, *Gone*, 109.
91. Weightman, 32.
92. Reiterman, 30.
93. Quoted in Feinsod, 94.
94. Quoted in Weightman, 185.
95. Quoted in Rebecca Moore, *A Sympathetic History of Jonestown: The Moore Family Involvement in the Peoples Temple* (Lewiston, NY: Edwin Mellen, 1985) 93.
96. Quoted in *ibid.*,93.
97. Quoted in Chidester, 37.
98. Quoted in Naipaul, 194.
99. Quoted in Reiterman, 147.
100. Quoted in Hall, *Gone*, 70.
101. Quoted in Klineman, Butler, and Conn, 78.
102. Quoted in Chidester, 64.
103. Quoted in *ibid.*,65.
104. Quoted in *ibid.*
105. Quoted in Weightman, 80 -81.
106. Quotes from Reiterman, 149.
107. Quoted in Hall, *Gone*, 44.
108. Quoted in Chidester, 94.
109. Reston, 255.
110. See *ibid.*,255, 325.
111. Related, with quotes, in Weightman, 109–110.
112. Quoted in Reiterman, 149.
113. Quoted in Naipaul, 160.
114. Quoted in Weightman, 21.
115. Quoted in *ibid.*,38.
116. Quoted in Reiterman, 148–149.
117. Quoted in Chidester, 54.
118. Quoted in Reiterman, 149.
119. Quoted in *ibid.*,387.
120. Quoted in *ibid.*,149.
121. See the list in *ibid.*,446.
122. Quoted in Moore, 221.
123. Quoted in *ibid.*,307.
124. Reston, 286.

Chapter 17

1. James D. Tabor and Eugene V. Gallagher, *Why Waco? Cults and the Battle for*

Religious Freedom in America (Berkeley: University of California Press, 1995) xi.

2. *Ibid.*,131.

3. Quoted in Nancy T. Ammerman, "Waco, Federal Law Enforcement, and Scholars of Religion," in Stuart A. Wright (ed.), *Armageddon in Waco: Critical Perspectives on the Branch Davidian Conflict* (Chicago: University of Chicago Press, 1995) 289.

4. Tabor and Gallagher, 17.

5. *Ibid.*,19.

6. Quoted in *ibid.*,23.

7. James Tabor, quoted in Dick J. Reavis, *The Ashes of Waco: An Investigation* (New York: Simon & Schuster, 1995) 253.

8. James D. Tabor, "Religious Discourse and Failed Negociations: The Dynamics of Biblical Apocalypticism in Waco," in Stuart A. Wright (ed.), *Armageddon in Waco: Critical Perspectives on the Branch Davidian Conflict* (Chicago: University of Chicago Press, 1995) 263–264.

9. See Tabor and Gallagher, 26–27, 44, 47–49.

10. *Ibid.*,47.

11. Barbara Kantrowitz, "Was It Friendly Fire?" *Newsweek* (April 5, 1993) 50–51.

12. Nancy Ammerman, n. 2, 295.

13. Malise Ruthven, *Fundamentalism: The Search for Meaning* (Oxford: Oxford University Press, 2005) 86.

14. Ammerman, n. 2, 295.

15. Tabor and Gallagher, 45.

16. Charles B. Strozier, *Apocalypse: On the Psychology of Fundamentalism in America* (Boston: Beacon Press, 1994) 163. This number excludes other religious groups which have less traditional beliefs. If these are included the estimate rises to seven thousand religious groups (*ibid.*, n. 24, 270).

17. George Gallup, Jr. and Jim Castelli, *The People's Religion: American Faith in the 90{ft}s* (New York: Macmillan, 1989) 60.

18. All statistics from Byron R. Johnson, "The Case for Empirical Assessment of Biblical Literacy in America," in David Lyle Jeffrey and C. Stephen Evans, *The Bible and the University* (Grand Rapids: Zondervan, 2007) 248.

19. Kantrowitz, 51.

20. Quoted in Reavis, 211.

21. Quoted in Tabor and Gallagher, 92.

22. Dean M. Kelley, "The Implosion of Mt. Carmel and Its Aftermath: Is It All Over Yet?" in Stuart A. Wright (ed.), *Armageddon in Waco: Critical Perspectives on the Branch Davidian Conflict* (Chicago: University of Chicago Press, 1995) 362–363. Kelley maintains that as time passes such "high-energy" religious movements gradually morph into "respectable" religious denominations, in which religion has become a peripheral aspect, rather than the central preoccupation, of the lives of the members.

23. Rebecca Moore, *A Sympathetic History of Jonestown: The Moore Family Involvement in the Peoples Temple* (Lewiston, NY: Edwin Mellen, 1985) 85.

24. *Ibid.*,94.

25. John Peer Nugent, *White Night* (New York: Rawson, Wade, 1979) 84.

26. Jeannie Mills, "Jonestown Masada," in Ken Levi (ed.), *Violence and Religious Commitment: Implications of Jim Jones's People's Temple Movement* (University Park: Pennsylvania State University Press, 1982) 166.

27. *Ibid.*

28. *Ibid.*

29. Quoted in Tabor and Gallagher, 153.

30. Robert Endleman, *Jonestown and the Manson Family: Race, Sexuality, and Collective Madness* (New York: Psyche, 1993) 167.

31. *Ibid.*,166.

Chapter 18

1. Quoted in James West Davidson, *The Logic of Millennial Thought: Eighteenth-Century New England* (New Haven: Yale University Press, 1977) 265.

2. Bernard McGinn, "Introduction: John's Apocalypse and the Apocalyptic Mentality," in Richard K. Emmerson and Bernard McGinn (eds.), *The Apocalypse in the Middle Ages* (Ithaca: Cornell University Press, 1992) 17.

3. D. H. Lawrence, *Apocalypse* (1931; rpt. New York: Viking, 1966) 174.

4. *Ibid.*,175.

5. For great detail on this, see J. Massyngberde Ford, *Revelation: Introduction, Translation and Commentary* (New York: Doubleday, 1975) 46–48.

6. Martin Gardner, *The Magic Numbers of Dr. Matrix* (Buffalo: Prometheus, 1985) 36, 179, 249. Gardner cites some other properties of 153 in a footnote, page 36.

7. *Ibid.*,14.

8. *Ibid.*,180.

9. *Ibid.*,14.

10. *Ibid.*,26. Here Gardner is quoting Dr. Matrix.

11. Revelation is not the sole source of apocalyptic beliefs found in the Bible, but it is the only book completely dedicated to apocalyptic, and the one most cited.

12. Quoted in Kevin Phillips, *American Theocracy: The Peril and Politics of Radical Religion, Oil, and Borrowed Money in the 21st Century* (New York: Viking, 2006) 253.

13. For the geopolitical results of these beliefs, see David S. New, *Holy War: The Rise of Militant Christian, Jewish and Islamic Fundamentalism* (Jefferson, NC: McFarland, 2002).

14. Kevin Phillips, *Bad Money: Reckless Finance, Failed Politics, and the Global Crisis of American Capitalism* (New York: Viking, 2008) 89.

15. *Ibid.*

16. *Ibid.*,91.

17. *Ibid.*,90.

18. Phillips, *American Theocracy,* 253.

19. Quoted in *ibid.,* 253–254.

20. C. Marvin Pate, quoted in Jeffery L. Sheler, "Dark Prophecies," *U. S. News & World Report* (Dec. 15, 1997) 69.

21. Jonathan Kirsch, *A History of the End of the World: How the Most Controversial Book in the Bible Changed the Course of Western Civilization* (San Francisco: HarperSanFrancisco, 2006) 3.

22. Robert P. Carroll, *When Prophecy Failed: Cognitive Dissonance in the Prophetic Traditions of the Old Testament* (New York: Seabury, 1979) 213.

23. Adela Yarbro Collins, quoted in Kirsch, 5. Not her personal opinion.

24. Quoted in *ibid.,*5.

25. Quoted in *ibid.*

26. Quoted in Davidson, 266.

27. Harold Bloom, *The American Religion: The Emergence of the Post-Christian Nation* (New York: Simon & Schuster, 1991) 162–163.

28. Lawrence, 34.

29. *Ibid.*,22.

30. *Ibid.*, xi.

31. Hans Von Campenhausen, *The Formation of the Christian Bible* (Philadelphia: Fortress, 1972) 237.

32. *Ibid.*,236.

33. Ford, 4, 12; R. H. Charles, *A Critical and Exegetical Commentary on the Revelation of St. John*, 2 vols. (Edinburgh: T. & T. Clark, 1920) vol. 1, xxix.

34. Charles, vol. 1, ci.

35. E. Theodore Bachmann (ed.), *Luther's Works (vol. 35): Word and Sacrament*, I (Philadelphia: Fortress, 1960) 398.

36. A. R. C. Leaney, *The Jewish and Christian World, 200 BC to AD 200* (Cambridge: Cambridge University Press, 1984) 150–52.

37. Quotes found in Harry M. Orlinsky, *Essays in Biblical Culture and Bible Translation* (New York: KTAV, 1974) 278.

38. Quoted in Ford, 37.

39. See Walter Schmithals, *The Apocalyptic Movement: Introduction & Interpretation* (Nashville: Abingdon, 1975) 120–121.

40. Bernard McGinn, "Early Apocalypticism: The Ongoing Debate," in C. A. Patrides and Joseph Wittreich (eds.), *The Apocalypse in English Renaissance Thought and Literature: Patterns, Antecedents and Repercussions* (Ithaca: Cornell University Press, 1984) 19.

41. H. -D. Betz, quoted in *ibid.*,19: "In reality, the problem as to what kinds of apocalypticism have influenced early Christianity, and what the results were, is presently much discussed and far from being settled."

42. McGinn, "John's Apocalypse," 10.

43. *Ibid.*,5.

44. Jaroslav Pelikan (ed.), *Luther's Works (vol. 1): Lectures on Genesis* (St. Louis: Concordia, 1958) 150–51.

45. Bachmann, 398.

46. Quoted in Schmithals, 170.

47. Hilton C. Oswald (ed.), *Luther's Works (vol. 20): Lectures on the Minor Prophets, III, Zechariah* (St. Louis: Concordia, 1973) 155–56.

48. Pelikan, 150–51.

49. *Ibid.*,150–51.

50. Quoted in Davidson, 265–266.

Chapter 19

1. Paul Boyer, *When Time Shall Be No More: Prophecy Belief in Modern American Culture* (Cambridge: Harvard University Press, 1992) ix.

2. *Ibid.*, xii. That issue is addressed in David S. New, *Holy War: The Rise of Militant Christian, Jewish and Islamic Fundamentalism* (Jefferson, NC: McFarland, 2002).

3. Quoted in Boyer, 12.

4. Quoted in Robert Wuthnow, *The Reconstruction of American Religion: Society and Faith Since World War II* (Princeton: Princeton University Press, 1988) 13.

5. *Ibid.*,244.

6. Quoted in James Truslow Adams, *The Founding of New England* (Boston: Atlantic Monthly Press, 1921) 95.

7. Kevin Phillips, *American Theocracy: The Peril and Politics of Radical Religion, Oil, and Borrowed Money in the 21st Century* (New York: Viking, 2006) 100.

8. Wuthnow, 243.

9. Quoted in *ibid.*,248.

Bibliography

Abrams, M. H. "Apocalypse: Theme and Variations," in *The Apocalypse in English Renaissance Thought and Literature: Patterns, Antecedents and Repercussions,* edited by C. A. Patrides and Joseph Wittreich. Ithaca: Cornell University Press, 1984. pp. 342–368.

The Academy of Humanism. *Neo-Fundamentalism: The Humanist Response.* Buffalo: Prometheus, 1988.

Adams, James Truslow. *The Founding of New England.* Boston: Atlantic Monthly Press, 1921.

Ahlstrom, Sydney E. *A Religious History of the American People,* 2d ed. New Haven: Yale University Press, 2004.

Aho, James. *The Politics of Righteousness: Idaho Christian Patriotism.* Seattle: University of Washington Press, 1990.

Allen, Frederick Lewis. *Only Yesterday.* New York: Bantam, 1959.

Altheide, David L. *Creating Reality: How TV News Distorts Events.* Beverly Hills: Sage, 1976.

Altizer, Thomas J. J. "Modern Thought and Apocalypticism," in *The Encyclopedia of Apocalypticism, vol. 3: Apocalyticism in the Modern Period and the Contemporary Age,* edited by Stephen J. Stein. New York: Continuum, 1999. pp. 325–359.

Aman, Kenneth (ed.). *Border Regions of Faith: An Anthology of Religion and Social Change.* Maryknoll: Orbis, NY, 1987.

Amanat, Abbas, and Magnus Bernhardsson (eds.). *Imagining the End: Visions of Apocalypse from the Ancient Middle East to Modern America.* London: I. B. Tauris, 2002.

American Universities and Colleges, 18th edition, 2008. Westport, CT: Praeger, 2008.

Ammerman, Nancy T. "Waco, Federal Law Enforcement, and Scholars of Religion," in *Armageddon in Waco: Critical Perspectives on the Branch Davidian Conflict,* edited by Stuart A. Wright. Chicago: University of Chicago Press, 1995. pp. 282–296.

Ammerman, Nancy Tatom. *Bible Believers: Fundamentalists in the Modern World.* New Brunswick, NJ: Rutgers University Press, 1987.

Anderson, Douglas. *William Bradford's Books: Of Plimmouth Plantation and the Printed Word.* Baltimore: Johns Hopkins University Press, 2003.

Anderson, Eric. "The Millerite Use of Prophecy: A Case Study of a 'Striking Fulfilment,'" in *The Disappointed: Millerism and Millenarianism in the Nineteenth Century,* edited by Ronald L. Numbers and Jonathan M. Butler. Bloomington: Indiana University Press, 1987. pp. 78–91.

Arendt, Hannah. *The Origins of Totalitarianism.* [1951] New York: Harcourt, 1994.

Armstrong, Karen. *Holy War.* London: Macmillan, 1988.

Arnold, J. Phillip. "The Davidian Dilemma: To Obey God or Man?" in *From the Ashes: Making Sense of Waco,* edited by James R. Lewis. Lanham, MD: Rowman and Littlefield, 1994. pp. 23–32.

Arthur, David T. "Joshua V. Himes and the Cause of Adventism," in *The Disappointed: Millerism and Millenarianism in the Nineteenth Century,* edited by Ronald L. Numbers and Jonathan M. Butler. Bloomington: Indiana University Press, 1987. pp. 36–58.

_____. "Millerism," in *The Rise of Adventism: Religion and Society in Mid-Nineteenth-Century America,* edited by Edwin S. Gaustad. New York: Harper & Row, 1974. pp. 154–172.

Averill, Lloyd J. *Religious Right, Religious Wrong: A Critique of the Fundamentalist Phenomenon.* New York: Pilgrim, 1989.

Avis, Paul (ed.). *The Study and Use of the Bible.* Grand Rapids: William B. Eerdmans, 1988.

Axthelm, Pete. "The Emperor Jones." *Newsweek,* Dec. 4, 1978, 54–60.

Bachmann, E. Theodore (ed.). *Luther's Works (vol. 35): Word and Sacrament,* I. Philadelphia: Fortress, 1960.

Bailey, Brad, and Bob Darden. *Mad Man in Waco: The Complete Story of the Davidian Cult, David Koresh, and the Waco Massacre.* Waco: WRS Publishing, 1993.

Balmer, Randall. *Grant Us Courage: Travels along the Mainline of American Protestantism*. New York: Oxford University Press, 1996.

_____. *Mine Eyes Have Seen the Glory: A Journey into the Evangelical Subculture in America*. New York: Oxford University Press, 1989.

Ban, Joseph D., and Paul R. Dekar (eds.). *In the Great Tradition: In Honor of Winthrop S. Hudson: Essays on Pluralism, Voluntarism and Revivalism*. Valley Forge, PA: Judson, 1982.

Barclay, William. *Letters to the Seven Churches*. Nashville: Abingdon, 1957.

_____. *The Making of the Bible*. Nashville: Abingdon, 1961.

Barkun, Michael. *A Culture of Conspiracy: Apocalyptic Visions in Contemporary America*. Berkeley: University of California Press, 2003.

_____. *Crucible of the Millennium: The Burned-over District of New York in the 1840s*. Syracuse: Syracuse University Press, 1986.

_____. *Disaster and the Millennium*. New Haven: Yale University Press, 1974.

_____. "Reflections after Waco: Millennialists and the State." *The Christian Century*, June 2–9, 1993, 596–600.

_____. "Reflections after Waco; Millennialists and the State," in *From the Ashes: Making Sense of Waco*, edited by James R. Lewis. Lanham, MD: Rowman and Littlefield, 1994. pp. 41–50.

Barna, George. *The State of the Church, 2006: A Report from George Barna*. Ventura, CA: The Barna Group, 2006.

Barna, George, and William Paul McKay. *Vital Signs: Emerging Social Trends and the Future of American Christianity*. Westchester, IL: Crossway Books, 1984.

Barnwell, F. Aster. *Meditations on the Apocalypse: A Psychospiritual Perspective on the Book of Revelation*. Rockport: Element, 1992.

Barr, James. *Fundamentalism*. Philadelphia: Westminster, 1978.

Bass, Clarence B. *Backgrounds to Dispensationalism: Its Historical Genesis and Ecclesiastical Implications*. Grand Rapids: Baker, 1977.

Baumgarten, Albert I. "Four Stages in the Life of a Millennial Movement," in *War in Heaven / Heaven on Earth: Theories of the Apocalyptic*, edited by Stephen D. O'Leary and Glen S. McGhee. London: Equinox, 2005. pp. 61–75.

Beale, David O. *In Pursuit of Purity: American Fundamentalism Since 1850*. Greenville, SC: Unusual, 1986.

Beardsley, Frank Grenville. *A Mighty Winner of Souls: Charles G. Finney, A Study in Evangelism*. New York: American Tract Society, 1937.

Beck, Melinda. "Thy Kingdom Come." *Newsweek*, Mar. 15, 1993, 52–55.

Bedell, Kenneth B. (ed.). *Yearbook of American & Canadian Churches, 1995*. Nashville: Abingdon, 1995.

Bellah, Robert N. "The Revolution and the Civil Religion," in *Religion and the American Revolution*, edited by Jerald C. Brauer. Philadelphia: Fortress, 1976. pp. 55–73.

Bercovitch, Sacvan. *The Puritan Origins of the American Self*. New Haven: Yale University Press, 1975.

Berger, Peter L. *The Noise of Solemn Assemblies: Christian Commitment and the Religious Establishment in America*. Garden City: Doubleday, 1961.

_____. *A Rumor of Angels: Modern Society and the Rediscovery of the Supernatural*. Garden City: Doubleday, 1969.

_____. *The Sacred Canopy: Elements of a Sociological Theory of Religion*. Garden City: Doubleday, 1967.

Berger, Peter L., and Thomas Luckmann. *The Social Construction of Reality: A Treatise in the Sociology of Knowledge*. Garden City: Doubleday, 1966.

Berrigan, Daniel. *The Nightmare of God*. Portland, OR: Sunburst Press, 1983.

Bierman, John. "Inviting Skepticism." *Maclean's*, Nov. 5, 1990, 34.

Bishop, George. *Witness to Evil*. Los Angeles: Nash, 1971.

"The Bizarre Tragedy in Guyana." *U. S. News & World Report*, Dec. 4, 1978, 25–28.

Bloch, Ruth H. *Visionary Republic: Millennial Themes in American Thought, 1756–1800*. Cambridge: Cambridge University Press, 1985.

Bloom, Harold. *The American Religion: The Emergence of the Post-Christian Nation*. New York: Simon & Schuster, 1991.

Bock, Darrell L. "Charting Dispensationalism." *Christianity Today*, Sept. 12, 1994, 26–29.

_____. "Why I Am a Dispensationalist with a Small 'd. '" *Journal of the Evangelical Theological Society* 41 (1998) 383–396.

Boettner, Loraine. *The Millennium*. Grand Rapids: Baker, 1957.

Bouchier, David. "No More Mr. Good Guy." *The Humanist*, July/Aug. 1990, 21–22.

Boyer, Pascal. *Religion Explained: The Human Instincts that Fashion Gods, Spirits and Ancestors*. London: Vintage, 2002.

Boyer, Paul. "A Brief History of the End of Time." *The New Republic*, May 17, 1993, 30–33.

_____. *By the Bomb's Early Light: American Thought and Culture at the Dawn of the Atomic Age*. New York: Pantheon, 1985.

_____. "The Growth of Fundamentalist Apocalyptic in the United States," in *The Encyclopedia of Apocalypticism, vol. 3: Apocalyticism in the Modern Period and the Contemporary*

Age, edited by Stephen J. Stein. New York: Continuum, 1999. pp. 140–178.

_____. *When Time Shall Be No More: Prophecy Belief in Modern American Culture.* Cambridge: Harvard University Press, 1992.

Bozeman, Thedore Dwight. "The Puritans' 'Errand into the Wilderness' Reconsidered." *New England Quarterly* (June 1986) 231–251.

Branaugh, Matt. "Willow Creek's 'Huge Shift.'" *Christianity Today,* June 2008, 13.

Brauer, Jerald C. "Puritanism, Revivalism, and the Revolution," in *Religion and the American Revolution,* edited by Jerald C. Brauer. Philadelphia: Fortress, 1976. pp. 1–27.

_____. "Revivalism and Millenarianism in America," in *In the Great Tradition: In Honor of Winthrop S. Hudson: Essays on Pluralism, Voluntarism and Revivalism,* edited by Joseph D. Ban and Paul R. Dekar. Valley Forge, PA: Judson, 1982. pp. 147–159.

Brauer, Jerald C. (ed.). *Religion and the American Revolution.* Philadelphia: Fortress, 1976.

Breault, Marc, and Martin King. *Inside the Cult: A Member's Chilling, Exclusive Account of Madness and Depravity in David Koresh's Compound.* New York: Signet, 1993.

Breen, T. H. *Puritans and Adventurers: Change and Persistence in Early America.* New York: Oxford University Press, 1980.

Breen, T. H., and Timothy Hall. *Colonial America in an Atlantic World: A Story of Creative Interaction.* New York: Pearson Longman, 2004.

Breen, Timothy H., and Stephen Foster. "Moving to the New World: The Character of Early Massachusetts Immigration." *William and Mary Quarterly* 30 (April 1973) 189–222.

Bremer, Francis J. *John Winthrop: America's Forgotten Founding Father.* New York: Oxford University Press, 2003.

Bremer, Francis J., and Tom Webster (eds.). *Puritans and Puritanism in Europe and America: A Comprehensive Encyclopedia.* Santa Barbara: ABC-CLIO, 2006.

Brereton, Virginia Lieson. *Training God's Army: The American Bible School, 1880–1940.* Bloomington: Indiana University Press, 1990.

Brockway, Robert W. *A Wonderful Work of God: Puritanism and the Great Awakening.* Bethlehem, PA: Lehigh University Press, 2003.

Broder, David S. *Behind the Front Page: A Candid Look at How the News Is Made.* New York: Simon & Schuster, 1987.

Bromley, David G., and Edward D. Silver. "The Davidian Tradition: From Patronal Clan to Prophetic Movement," in *Armageddon in Waco: Critical Perspectives on the Branch Davidian Conflict,* edited by Stuart A. Wright.

Chicago: University of Chicago Press, 1995. pp. 43–72.

Brower, Steve, Paul Gifford, and Susan D. Rose. *Exporting the American Gospel.* New York: Routledge, 1998.

Brown, Jerry Wayne. *The Rise of Biblical Criticism in America, 1800–1870: The New England Scholars.* Middletown, CT: Wesleyan University Press, 1969.

Brown, L. (ed.). *Advances in the Psychology of Religion.* New York: Pergamon, 1985.

Brown, Robert E. "The Bible," in *The Princeton Companion to Jonathan Edwards,* edited by Sang Hyun Lee. Princeton: Princeton University Press, 2005. pp. 87–102.

_____. "Edwards, Locke, and the Bible." *Journal of Religion* 79 (1999) 361–384.

_____. *Jonathan Edwards and the Bible.* Bloomington: Indiana University Press, 2002.

Bruce, Steve. *Choice and Religion: A Critique of Rational Choice Theory.* New York: Oxford University Press, 1999.

_____. *Fundamentalism.* Cambridge: Polity Press, 2000.

Brummet, Barry. *Contemporary Apocalyptic Rhetoric.* New York: Praeger, 1991.

Bruns, Roger A. *Preacher: Billy Sunday and Big-Time American Evangelism.* New York: W. W. Norton, 1992.

Buchanan, George Wesley. *New Testament Eschatology: Historical and Cultural Background.* Lewiston, NY: Edwin Mellen, 1993.

Bugliosi, Vincent, and Curt Gentry. *Helter Skelter: The True Story of the Manson Murders.* New York: W. W. Norton, 1974.

Bull, Malcolm, and Keith Lockhard. *Seeking a Sanctuary: Seventh-Day Adventism and the American Dream.* New York: Harper & Row, 1989.

Bumsted, J. M., and John E. Van de Wetering. *What Must I Do to Be Saved? The Great Awakening in Colonial America.* Hinsdale, IL: Dryden, 1976.

Bussell, Harold. *Unholy Devotion: Why Cults Lure Christians.* Grand Rapids: Zondervan, 1983.

Butler, Jonathan M. "Adventism and the American Experience," in *The Rise of Adventism: Religion and Society in Mid-Nineteenth-Century America,* edited by Edwin S. Gaustad. New York: Harper & Row, 1974. pp. 173–206.

_____. "From Millerism to Seventh-day Adventism: Boundlessness to Consolidation." *Church History* 3 (1986) 50–64.

_____. "The Making of a New Order: Millerism and the Origins of Seventh-day Adventism," in *The Disappointed: Millerism and Millenarianism in the Nineteenth Century,* edited by Ronald L. Numbers and Jonathan M. Butler.

Bloomington: Indiana University Press, 1987. pp. 189–208.

Campbell, Stan, and James S. Bell Jr. *The Complete Idiot's Guide to the Book of Revelation.* Indianapolis: Alpha, 2002.

Canup, John. *Out of the Wilderness: The Emergence of an American Identity in Colonial New England.* Middletown, CT: Wesleyan University Press, 1990.

Caplan, Lionel (ed.). *Studies in Religious Fundamentalism.* Albany: State University of New York Press, 1987.

Carden, Allen. *Puritan Christianity in America: Religion and Life in Seventeenth-Century Massachusetts.* Grand Rapids: Baker Book House, 1990.

Carey, James (ed.). *Media, Myths, and Narratives: Television and the Press.* Newbury Park, CA: Sage, 1988.

Carpenter, Joel. "Fundamentalist Institutions and the Rise of Conservative Protestantism, 1929–42." *Church History* 49 (1980) 62–75.

Carroll, Jackson W. "Pastors' Picks: What Preachers Are Reading." *The Christian Century*, August 23, 2003, 31–33.

Carroll, Robert P. *When Prophecy Failed: Cognitive Dissonance in the Prophetic Traditions of the Old Testament.* New York: Seabury, 1979.

Carter, Stephen L. *The Culture of Disbelief: How American Law and Politics Trivialize Religious Devotion.* New York: Basic, 1993.

"Case of the Hypnotic Hippie." *Newsweek*, Dec. 15, 1969, 30–37.

Case, Shirley Jackson. *The Millennial Hope: A Phase of War-time Thinking.* Chicago: University of Chicago Press, 1918.

Chai, Leon. *Jonathan Edwards and the Limits of Enlightenment Philosophy.* New York: Oxford University Press, 1998.

Charles, R. H. *A Critical and Exegetical Commentary on the Revelation of St. John*, 2 vols. Edinburgh: T. & T. Clark, 1920.

Chattaway, Peter T. "Christian Filmmakers Jump on End-times Bandwagon." *Christianity Today*, Oct. 25, 1999, 26–27.

Chernus, Ira. *Nuclear Madness: Religion and the Psychology of the Nuclear Age.* Albany: State University of New York Press, 1991.

Cherny, Robert W. *A Righteous Cause: The Life of William Jennings Bryan.* Boston: Little, Brown, 1985.

Cherry, Conrad. "Symbols of Spiritual Truth: Jonathan Edwards as Biblical Interpreter." *Interpretation* 39 (1985) 263–271.

Chidester, David. *Salvation and Suicide: An Interpretation of Jim Jones, the Peoples Temple, and Jonestown.* Bloomington: Indiana University Press, 1988.

Clark-Soles, Jaime. *Scripture Cannot Be Broken:*

The Social Function of the Use of Scripture in the Fourth Gospel. Boston: Brill Academic, 2003.

Claybaugh, Gary K. *Thunder on the Right: The Protestant Fundamentalists.* Chicago: Nelson-Hall, 1974.

Cloud, John. "Meet the Prophet." *Time*, July 1, 2002, 40–43.

Coad, F. Roy. *A History of the Brethren Movement: Its Origins, Its Worldwide Development and Its Significance for the Present Day.* Grand Rapids: Eerdmans, 1968.

Cockburn, Alexander. "Waco Revisited." *The Nation*, October 18, 1993, 414–415.

Cohen, Edmund D. *The Mind of the Bible-Believer.* Buffalo: Prometheus, 1986.

Cohn, Norman. *Cosmos, Chaos, and the World to Come: The Ancient Roots of Apocalyptic Faith.* New Haven: Yale University Press, 1993.

_____. *The Pursuit of the Millennium: Revolutionary Millenarians and Mystical Anarchists of the Middle Ages*, rev. ed. New York: Oxford University Press, 1970.

Cohen, Norman J. (ed.). *The Fundamentalist Phenomenon: A View from Within; A Response from Without.* Grand Rapids: Eerdmans, 1990.

Cole, Stewart G. *The History of Fundamentalism.* New York: R. R. Smith, 1931.

Coletta, Paolo Enrico. *William Jennings Bryan, vol 3. : Political Puritan, 1915–1925.* Lincoln: University of Nebraska Press, 1969.

The College Blue Book: Narrative Descriptions, 27th ed. New York: Macmillan, 1999.

Collins, Adela Yarbro. *Crisis and Catharsis: The Power of the Apocalypse.* Philadelphia: Westminster, 1984.

Collins, John J. *The Apocalyptic Imagination: An Introduction to the Jewish Matrix of Christianity.* New York: Crossroad, 1989.

Colson, Charles, with Ellen Santilli Vaughn. *Kingdoms in Conflict.* New York: William Morrow and Zondervan, 1987.

Conkin, Paul K. *American Originals: Homemade Varieties of Christianity.* Chapel Hill: University of North Carolina Press, 1997.

Conway, Flo, and Jim Siegelman. *Holy Terror: The Fundmentalist War on America's Freedoms in Religion, Politics and Our Private Lives.* New York: Dell, 1984.

Cooke, G. A. *A Critical and Exegetical Commentary on the Book of Ezekiel.* Edinburgh: T. & T. Clark, 1936.

Cooper, David E. (ed.). *The Manson Murders: A Philosophical Inquiry.* Cambridge, MA: Schenkman, 1974.

Coppens, J. *The Old Testament and the Critics.* Paterson, NJ: St. Anthony, 1942.

Coulter, Ann. *Godless: The Church of Liberalism.* New York: Crown Forum, 2006.

Cox, Harvey G. *On Not Leaving It to the Snake.* New York: Macmillan, 1964.

_____. *Religion in the Secular City: Toward a Postmodern Theology.* New York: Simon & Schuster, 1984.

_____. "The Warring Visions of the Religious Right." *The Atlantic Monthly*, Nov. 1995, 59–69.

Crapanzano, Vincent. *Serving the Word: Literalism in America from the Pulpit to the Bench.* New York: The New Press, 2000.

Crawford, Michael J. *Seasons of Grace: Colonial New England's Revival Tradition in Its British Context.* New York: Oxford University Press, 1991.

Cross, Whitney R. *The Burned-Over District: The Social and Intellectual History of Enthusiastic Religion in Western New York, 1800–1850.* Ithaca: Cornell University Press, 1950.

Crutchfield, Larry V. "C. I. Scofield," in *Twentieth-Century Shapers of American Popular Religion*, edited by Charles H. Lippy. Westport, CT: Greenwood Press, 1989. pp. 371–381.

_____. *The Origins of Dispensationalism: The Darby Factor.* Lanham, MD: University Press of America, 1992.

Curtis, Susan. *A Consuming Faith: The Social Gospel and Modern American Culture.* Columbia: University of Missouri Press, 2001.

Damsteegt, P. Gerard. *Foundations of the Seventh-day Adventist Message and Mission.* Grand Rapids: Eerdmans, 1977.

Daniels, Ted. "Charters of Righteousness: Politics, Prophets and the Drama of Conversion," in *War in Heaven / Heaven on Earth: Theories of the Apocalyptic*, edited by Stephen D. O'Leary and Glen S. McGhee. London: Equinox, 2005. pp. 3–17.

D'Antonio, Michael. *Fall from Grace: The Failed Crusade of the Christian Right.* New York: Farrar Straus Giroux, 1989.

Davidson, James West. *The Logic of Millennial Thought: Eighteenth-Century New England.* New Haven: Yale University Press, 1977.

de Camp, L. Sprague. *The Great Monkey Trial.* Garden City: Doubleday, 1968.

Delbanco, Andrew. *The Puritan Ordeal.* Cambridge: Harvard University Press, 1989.

"The Demon of Death Valley." *Time*, Dec. 12, 1969, 26–29.

Desrosiers, Gilbert. *An Introduction to Revelation.* New York: Continuum, 2000.

Doan, Ruth Alden. *The Miller Heresy, Millennialism, and American Culture.* Philadelphia: Temple University Press, 1987.

_____. "Millerism and Evangelical Culture," in *The Disappointed: Millerism and Millenarianism in the Nineteenth Century*, edited by Ronald L. Numbers and Jonathan M. Butler.

Bloomington: Indiana University Press, 1987. pp. 118–138.

Dollar, George W. *A History of Fundamentalism in America.* Greenville, SC: Bob Jones University Press, 1973.

Dorrien, Gary. *The Making of American Liberal Theology: Crisis, Irony, and Postmodernity, 1950–2005.* Louisville, KY: Westminster John Knox Press, 2006.

_____. *The Making of American Liberal Theology: Idealism, Realism, and Modernity, 1900–1950.* Louisville, KY: Westminster John Knox Press, 2003.

_____. *The Making of American Liberal Theology: Imagining Progressive Religion, 1805–1900.* Louisville, KY: Westminster John Knox Press, 2001.

Drane, John (ed.) *Revelation: The Apocalypse of St. John.* New York: St. Martin's Griffin, 1977.

Duckett, Eleanor. *Death and Life in the Tenth Century.* Ann Arbor: University of Michigan Press, 1967.

Dulles, Avery. *Revelation Theology: A History.* New York: Herder and Herder, 1972.

Efird, James M. *End-Times: Rapture, Antichrist, Millennium.* Nashville: Abingdon, 1986.

Ehrman, Bart D. *Jesus: Apocalyptic Prophet of the New Millennium.* New York: Oxford University Press, 1999.

Elliott, John Huxtable. *Empires of the Atlantic World: Britain and Spain in America, 1492–1830.* New Haven: Yale University Press, 2006.

Elwell, Walter A. "Dispensationalisms of the Third Kind." *Christianity Today*, Sept. 12, 1994, 28.

Emmerson, Richard K., and Bernard McGinn (eds.). *The Apocalypse in the Middle Ages.* Ithaca: Cornell University Press, 1992.

Endleman, Robert. *Jonestown and the Manson Family: Race, Sexuality, and Collective Madness.* New York: Psyche, 1993.

English, E. Schuyler. *A Companion to the New Scofield Reference Bible.* New York: Oxford University Press, 1972.

Erikson, Kai. *Wayward Puritans.* New York: Wiley & Sons, 1966.

Evensen, Bruce J. *God's Man for the Guilded Age: D. L. Moody and the Rise of Modern Mass Evangelism.* New York: Oxford University Press, 2003.

Farrer, Austin. *A Rebirth of Images: The Making of St. John's Apocalypse.* Westminster: Dacre, 1949.

Feinsod, Ethan. *Awake in a Nightmare: Jonestown, the Only Eyewitness Account.* New York: Norton, 1981.

Festinger, Leon, Henry W. Riecken and Stanley Schachter. "When Prophecy Fails," in *Extending Psychological Frontiers: Selected Works of*

Leon Festinger. New York: Russell Sage Foundation, 1989. pp. 258–269.

Festinger, Leon, Henry W. Riecken and Stanley Schachter. *When Prophecy Fails: A Social and Psychological Study of a Modern Group That Predicted the Destruction of the World.* New York: Harper & Row, 1956.

Fields-Meyer, Thomas, and Grant Pick. "In Heaven's Name." *People Weekly,* Dec. 14, 1998, 139–140.

Finch, Phillip. *God, Guts, and Guns.* New York: Seaview/Putnam, 1983.

Findlay, James F., Jr. *Dwight L. Moody, American Evangelist, 1837–1899.* Chicago: University of Chicago Press, 1969.

Fineman, Howard. "God and the Grass Roots." *Newsweek,* Nov. 8, 1993, 42–45.

Fiorenza, Elizabeth Schüssler. *The Apocalypse.* Chicago: Francisco Herald Press, 1976.

_____. *The Book of Revelation: Justice and Judgment.* Philadelphia: Fortress, 1985.

Focillon, Henri. *The Year 1000.* New York: Frederick Ungar, 1969.

Fogarty, Robert S. "An Age of Wisdom, an Age of Foolishness: The Davidians, Some Forerunners, and Our Age," in *Armageddon in Waco: Critical Perspectives on the Branch Davidian Conflict,* edited by Stuart A. Wright. Chicago: University of Chicago Press, 1995. pp. 3–19.

Ford, J. Massyngberde. *Revelation: Introduction, Translation and Commentary.* New York: Doubleday, 1975.

Fox, Richard Wrightman. *Jesus in America: Personal Savior, Cultural Hero, National Obsession.* San Francisco: HarperSanFrancisco, 2004.

France, John. *Rodulfus Glaber: The Five Books of the Histories,* edited and translated by John France. Oxford: Oxford University Press, 1989.

Fredriksen, Paula. "Tyconius and Augustine on the Apocalypse," in *The Apocalypse in the Middle Ages,* edited by Richard K. Emmerson and Bernard McGinn. Ithaca: Cornell University Press, 1992. pp. 20–37.

The Fundamentals: A Testimony to the Truth. Chicago: Testimony, 1910–1915.

Fuller, Daniel P. *Gospel and Law: Contrast or Continuum? The Hermeneutics of Dispensationalism and Covenant Theology.* Grand Rapids: Eerdmans, 1980.

Fuller, Robert C. *Spiritual, but Not Religious: Understanding Unchurched America.* Oxford: Oxford University Press, 2001.

Furniss, Norman F. *The Fundamentalist Controversy, 1918–1931.* New Haven: Yale University Press, 1954.

Gallup, George, Jr., and Jim Castelli. *The People's Religion: American Faith in the 90{ft}s.* New York: Macmillan, 1989.

Gamson, William A., David Croteau, William Hoyes, and Theodore Sasson. "Media Images and the Social Construction of Reality." *Annual Review of Sociology* 18 (1992) 373–393.

Gans, Herbert J. *Deciding What's News: A Study of CBS Evening News, NBC Nightly News, Newsweek, and Time.* New York: Vintage, 1980.

Gardella, Peter. "Ego and Apocalypse in America." *Religious Studies Review,* vol. 21 (1995), 196–201.

Gardner, Martin. *The Magic Numbers of Dr. Matrix.* Buffalo: Prometheus, 1985.

Garrison, David. "Tim and Beverly LaHaye," in *Twentieth-Century Shapers of American Popular Religion,* edited by Charles H. Lippy. Westport, CT: Greenwood Press, 1989. pp. 233–240.

Gatewood, Willard B. (ed.). *Controversy in the Twenties: Fundamentalism, Modernism, and Evolution.* Nashville: Vanderbilt University Press, 1969.

Gatewood, Willard B., Jr. *Preachers, Pedagogues & Politicians: The Evolution Controversy in North Carolina, 1920–1927.* Chapel Hill: University of North Carolina Press, 1966.

Gaustad, Edwin S. *Faith of Our Fathers: Religion and the New Nation.* San Francisco: Harper & Row, 1987.

Gaustad, Edwin S. (ed.). *The Rise of Adventism: Religion and Society in Mid-Nineteenth-Century America.* New York: Harper & Row, 1974.

Gellner, Ernest. *Postmodernism, Reason and Religion.* London: Routledge, 1992.

Gibbs, Nancy. "Apocalypse Now." *Time,* July 1, 2002, 30–38.

Ginger, Ray. *Six Days or Forever? Tennessee v. John Thomas Scopes.* Chicago: Quadrangle, 1958.

Goen, C. C. "Jonathan Edwards: A New Departure in Eschatology." *Church History* 28 (1959) 25–40.

Goldberg, Michelle. *Kingdom Coming: The Rise of Christian Nationalism.* New York: W. W. Norton, 2006.

Gordis, Lisa M. *Opening Scripture: Bible Reading and Interpretative Authority in Puritan New England.* Chicago: University of Chicago Press, 2003.

Gould, Ezra P. *A Critical and Exegetical Commentary on the Gospel According to St. Mark.* New York: Charles Scribner's Sons, 1903.

Gould, Stephen Jay. "Dousing Diminutive Dennis's Debate." *Natural History,* April 1994, 4–12.

Govier, Gordon. "Preparing for Pilgrims: Religious Rivalry Complicates Millennial Planning." *Christianity Today,* June 14, 1999, 24.

Graduate Programs in the Humanities, Arts &

Social Sciences, Book 2, 33rd ed. Princeton: Peterson's, 1999.

Graham, Stephen R. "Hal Lindsey," in *Twentieth-Century Shapers of American Popular Religion,* edited by Charles H. Lippy. Westport, CT: Greenwood Press, 1989. pp. 247–255.

Greene, John C. "Science and Religion," in *The Rise of Adventism: Religion and Society in Mid-Nineteenth-Century America,* edited by Edwin S. Gaustad. New York: Harper & Row, 1974. pp. 50–69.

Grenz, Stanley J. "The 1000-year Question." *Christianity Today,* Mar. 8, 1993, 34–35.

Gribben, Crawford. *The Puritan Millennium: Literature and Theology, 1550–1682.* Dublin: Four Courts, 2000.

Gritsch, Eric W. *Born Againism: Perspectives on a Movement.* Philadelphia: Fortress, 1982.

Gross, M. L. *The Psychological Society.* New York: Random House, 1978.

Guinness, Os. *The Gravedigger File.* London: Hodder and Stoughton, 1983.

Gura, Philip F. *A Glimpse of Sion's Glory: Puritan Radicalism in New England, 1620–1660.* Middletown, CT: Wesleyan University Press, 1984.

Gutierrez, Cathy. "The Millennium and Narrative Closure," in *War in Heaven / Heaven on Earth: Theories of the Apocalyptic,* edited by Stephen D. O'Leary and Glen S. McGhee. London: Equinox, 2005. pp. 47–59.

Hadden, Jeffrey K., and Anson Shupe. *Televangelism: Power and Politics on God's Frontier.* New York: Henry Holt, 1988.

Hall, Chris. "What Hal Lindsey Taught Me about the Second Coming." *Christianity Today,* Oct. 25, 1999, 83–85.

Hall, David D. "Toward a History of Popular Religion in Early New England." *William and Mary Quarterly* 41 (January 1984) 49–55.

Hall, John R. "The Apocalypse at Jonestown," in *Violence and Religious Commitment: Implications of Jim Jones's Peoples Temple Movement,* edited by Ken Levi. University Park: Pennsylvania State University Press, 1982. pp. 35–54.

_____. *Gone from the Promised Land: Jonestown in American Cultural History.* New Brunswick, NJ: Transaction, 2004.

_____. "Jonestown and Bishop Hill: Continuities and Disjunctures in Religious Conflict," in *New Religious Movements, Mass Suicide, and Peoples Temple: Scholarly Perspectives on a Tragedy,* edited by Rebecca Moore and Fielding McGehee III. Lewiston, NY: Edwin Mellen, 1989. pp. 77–92.

_____. "Public Narratives and the Apocalyptic Sect: From Jonestown to Mt. Carmel," in *Armageddon in Waco: Critical Perspectives on the Branch Davidian Conflict,* edited by Stuart A. Wright. Chicago: University of Chicago Press, 1995. pp. 205–235.

Hamilton, Michael S. "Willow Creek's Place in History." *Christianity Today,* November 13, 2000, 63–68.

Handy, Robert T. *A Christian America: Protestaant Hopes and Historical Realities,* 2d ed. New York: Oxford University Press, 1984.

Hanson, Paul D. *The Dawn of Apocalyptic: The Historical and Sociological Roots of Jewish Apocalyptic Eschatology,* rev. ed. Philadelphia: Fortress, 1979.

_____. *Old Testament Apocalyptic.* Nashville: Abingdon, 1987.

Hardman, Keith J. *Charles Grandison Finney, 1792–1875: Revivalist and Reformer.* Syracuse: Syracuse University Press, 1987.

Hargrove, Barbara J. W. "Jonestown and the Scientific Study of Religion," in *New Religious Movements, Mass Suicide, and Peoples Temple: Scholarly Perspectives on a Tragedy,* edited by Rebecca Moore and Fielding McGehee III. Lewiston, NY: Edwin Mellen, 1989. pp. 23–40.

Harper, Charles, and Bryan F. LeBeau. "The Social Adaptation of Marginal Religious Movements in America." *Sociology of Religion* 54 (1993) 171–192.

Harper, Chris J. "What I Saw." *Newsweek,* Dec. 4, 1978, 42–43.

Harrary, Keith. "The Truth about Jonestown." *Psychology Today,* March 1992, 62–69.

Harrell, David Erwin, Jr. *Oral Roberts — An American Life.* Bloomington: Indiana University Press, 1985.

Harrison, J. F. C. *The Second Coming: Popular Millenarianism, 1780–1850.* New Brunswick, NJ: Rutgers University Press, 1979.

Hartman, Louis F., and Alexander A. Di Lella. *The Book of Daniel.* New York: Doubleday, 1978.

Hatch, Nathan O. *The Sacred Cause of Liberty: Republican Thought and the Millennium in Revolutionary Nw England.* New Haven: Yale University Press, 1977.

Hatch, Nathan O., and Harry S. Stout (eds.). *Jonathan Edwards and the American Experience.* New York: Oxford University Press, 1988.

Hatcher, Chris. "Cults, Society and Government," in *New Religious Movements, Mass Suicide, and Peoples Temple: Scholarly Perspectives on a Tragedy,* edited by Rebecca Moore and Fielding McGehee III. Lewiston, NY: Edwin Mellen, 1989. pp. 179–198.

Heimert, Alan. *Religion and the American Mind, from the Great Awakening to the Revolution.* Cambridge: Harvard University Press, 1966.

Helm, Paul, and Oliver D. Crisp (eds.). *Jonathan*

Edwards: Philosophical Theologian. Burlington, VT: Ashgate, 2003.

Herman, Edward S., and Noam Chomsky. *Manufacturing Consent: The Political Economy of the Mass Media.* New York: Pantheon, 1988.

Heron, Alasdair I. C. *A Century of Protestant Theology.* London: Lutterworth, 1980.

Hill, David. *New Testament Prophecy.* Atlanta: John Knox, 1979.

Hillman, James. *Insearch: Psychology and Religion,* 2d ed. Woodstock, NY: Spring, 1994.

_____. *Suicide and the Soul.* New York: Harper & Row, 1973.

Hoekema, Anthony A. *The Bible and the Future.* Grand Rapids: Eerdmans, 1979.

_____. *The Four Major Cults: Christian Science, Jehovah's Witnesses, Mormonism, Seventh-Day Adventism.* Grand Rapids: Eerdmans, 1963.

Hoffer, Eric. *The True Believer: Thoughts on the Nature of Mass Movements.* New York: Harper & Row, 1951.

Hofstadter, Richard. *Anti-intellectualism in American Life.* New York: Knopf, 1963.

Holifield, E. Brooks. *God's Ambassadors: A History of the Christian Clergy in America.* Grand Rapids: William B. Eerdmans, 2007.

Holley, Joe. "The Waco Watch." *Columbia Journalism Review,* May/June 1993, 50–53.

Hood, Ralph W., Jr., and Peter C. Hill, and W. Paul Williamson. *The Psychology of Religious Fundamentalism.* New York: Guilford, 2005.

"The Horror Lives On." *Time,* Dec. 11, 1978, 14.

Hout, Michael, Andrew Greeley, and Melissa Wilde. "Birth Dearth: Demographics of Mainline Decline." *The Christian Century,* October 4, 2005, 24–27.

Hull, Jon D. "Anatomy of a Tragedy." *Time,* Oct. 22, 1990, 22–23.

Hunter, James Davison. *American Evangelicanism: Conservative Religion and the Quandry of Modernity.* New Brunswick, NJ: Rutgers University Press, 1983.

_____. *Culture Wars: The Struggle to Define America.* New York: BasicBooks, 1991.

Jacquet, Constant H. (ed.). *Yearbook of American & Canadian Churches, 1980.* Nashville: Abingdon, 1980.

_____. *Yearbook of American & Canadian Churches, 1985.* Nashville: Abingdon, 1985.

_____. *Yearbook of American & Canadian Churches, 1990.* Nashville: Abingdon, 1990.

Jewett, Robert. *The Captain America Complex: The Dilemma of Zealous Nationalism.* Philadelphia: Westminster, 1973.

"Jim Jones: Man Who Would Be God." *Christianity Today,* Dec. 15, 1978, 38–40.

Johnson, Byron R. "The Case for Empirical Assessment of Biblical Literacy in America," in *The Bible and the University,* edited by David Lyle Jeffrey and C. Stephen Evans. Grand Rapids: Zondervan, 2007. pp. 240–252.

Jones, Constance A. "Exemplary Dualism and Authoritarianism at Jonestown," in *New Religious Movements, Mass Suicide, and Peoples Temple: Scholarly Perspectives on a Tragedy,* edited by Rebecca Moore and Fielding McGehee III. Lewiston: Edwin Mellen, 1989. pp. 209–230.

Jordan, Anne Devereaux. *The Seventh-day Adventists: A History.* New York: Hippocrene Books, 1988.

Jorstad, Erling. *Holding Fast / Pressing On: Religion in America in the 1980s.* Westport, CT: Greenwood, 1990.

_____. *The Politics of Doomsday: Fundamentalists of the Far Right.* New York: Abingdon, 1970.

_____. *Popular Religion in America: The Evangelical Voice.* Westport, CT: Greenwood, 1993.

Judd, Wayne R. "William Miller: Disappointed Prophet," in *The Disappointed: Millerism and Millenarianism in the Nineteenth Century,* edited by Ronald L. Numbers and Jonathan M. Butler. Bloomington: Indiana University Press, 1987. pp. 17–35.

Kantrowitz, Barbara. "Day of Judgment." *Newsweek,* May 3, 1993, 22–27.

_____. "The Messiah of Waco." *Newsweek,* Mar. 15, 1993, 56–58.

_____. "Was It Friendly Fire?" *Newsweek,* April 5, 1993, 50–51.

Kaplan, Lawrence (ed.). *Fundamentalism in Comparative Perspective.* Amherst: University of Massachusetts Press, 1992.

Karlsen, Carol. *The Devil in the Shape of a Woman.* New York: Norton, 1987.

Kazin, Michael. *A Godly Hero: The Life of William Jennings Bryan.* New York: Knopf, 2006.

Kelley, Dean M. "The Implosion of Mt. Carmel and Its Aftermath: Is It All Over Yet?" in *Armageddon in Waco: Critical Perspectives on the Branch Davidian Conflict,* edited by Stuart A. Wright. Chicago: University of Chicago Press, 1995. pp. 359–378.

_____. *Why Conservative Churches Are Growing: A Study in Sociology of Religion.* New York: Harper & Row, 1977.

Kennedy, Douglas. *In God's Country: Travels in the Bible Belt, USA.* London: Unwin Hyman, 1990.

Kermode, Frank. *The Sense of an Ending: Studies in the Theory of Fiction.* New York: Oxford University Press, 2000.

Kirsch, Jonathan. "Hal Lindsey." *Publishers Weekly,* vol. 211, no. 11 (1977), 30–32.

_____. *A History of the End of the World: How the Most Controversial Book in the Bible Changed the Course of Western Civilization.* San Francisco: HarperSanFrancisco, 2006.

Klebnikov, Peter. "Time of Troubles." *Newsweek*, April 7, 1997, 48–48b.

Klineman, George, Sherman Butler, and David Conn. *The Cult That Died: The Tragedy of Jim Jones and the Peoples Temple*. New York: Putnam, 1980.

Knight, George R. *Millennial Fever and the End of the World*. Boise: Pacific, 1993.

Koch, Klaus. *The Rediscovery of Apocalyptic*. London: SCM, 1972.

Korshin, Paul J. "Queuing and Waiting: The Apocalypse in England, 1660–1750," in *The Apocalypse in English Renaissance Thought and Literature: Patterns, Antecedents and Repercussions*, edited by C. A. Patrides and Joseph Wittreich. Ithaca: Cornell University Press, 1984. pp. 240–265.

Körtner, Ulrich H. J. *The End of the World: A Theological Interpretation*. Louisville, KY: Westminster John Knox Press, 1995.

Kraus, C. Norman. *Dispensationalism in America: Its Rise and Development*. Richmond: John Knox, 1958.

Kraybill, J. Nelson. "Apocalypse Now." *Christianity Today*, Oct. 25, 1999, 31–40.

Kressel, Neil J. *Bad Faith: The Danger of Religious Extremism*. Amherst, NY: Prometheus, 2007.

Kroll, Luisa. "Megachurches, Megabusiness." *Forbes*, September 17, 2003, 41–43.

Kuklick, Bruce. "An Edwards for the Millennium." *Journal of Religion and American Culture* 11 (2001) 114–117.

Küng, Hans, and Jürgen Moltmann (eds.) *Fundamentalism As an Ecumenical Challenge*. London: SCM, 1992.

Labich, Kenneth. "Ghosts of Jonestown." *Newsweek*, Dec. 11, 1978, 29–31.

Lacayo, Richard. "The End of the World As We Know It?" *Time*, Jan. 18, 1999, 34–42.

Lambert, Frank. *Inventing the "Great Awakening."* Princeton: Princeton University Press, 1999.

_____. *Pedlar in Divinity: George Whitefield and the Transatlantic Revivals*. Princeton: Princeton University Press, 1994.

Lambrecht, J. *L'Apocalypse johannique et l'Apocalyptique dans le Nouveau Testament*. Louvain: Leuven University Press, 1980.

Land, Gary (ed.). *Adventism in America*. Grand Rapids: Eerdmans, 1986.

Landes, Richard. "Roosters Crow, Owls Hoot: On the Dynamics of Apocalyptic Millennialism," in *War in Heaven / Heaven on Earth: Theories of the Apocalyptic*, edited by Stephen D. O'Leary and Glen S. McGhee. London: Equinox, 2005. pp. 19–46.

Lane, Mark. *The Strongest Poison*. New York: Elsevier-Dutton, 1980.

Langdon, George D., Jr. *Pilgrim Colony: A History of New Plymouth, 1620–1691*. New Haven: Yale University Press, 1966.

Larson, Edward J. *Summer for the Gods: The Scopes Trial and America's Continuing Debate over Science and Religion*. New York: Basic, 1997.

Larue, Gerald A. "Surviving the Apocalypse," in *Neo-Fundamentalism: The Humanist Response*, by The Academy of Humanism. Buffalo: Prometheus, 1988. pp. 135–152.

_____. "The Threat of Neo-Fundamentalism," in *Neo-Fundamentalism: The Humanist Response*, by The Academy of Humanism. Buffalo: Prometheus, 1988. pp. 27–38.

Lawrence, Bruce B. *Defenders of God: The Fundamentalist Revolt Against the Modern Age*. San Francisco: Harper and Row, 1989.

Lawrence, D. H. *Apocalypse*. New York: Viking, 1966.

Layton, Deborah. *Seductive Poison: A Jonestown Survivor's Story of Life and Death in the Peoples Temple*. New York: Doubleday, 1998.

Leaney, A. R. C. *The Jewish and Christian World, 200 BC to AD 200*. Cambridge: Cambridge University Press, 1984.

Lee, Sang Hyun. "God's Relation to the World," in *The Princeton Companion to Jonathan Edwards*, edited by Sang Hyun Lee. Princeton: Princeton University Press, 2005. pp. 59–71.

_____. *The Philosophical Theology of Jonathan Edwards*. Princeton: Princeton University Press, 2000.

_____ (ed.). *The Princeton Companion to Jonathan Edwards*. Princeton: Princeton University Press, 2005.

Leland, John. "Millennium Madness." *Newsweek*, Nov. 1, 1999, 70–71.

Lerner, Robert E. "The Medieval Return to the Thousand-Year Sabbath," in *The Apocalypse in the Middle Ages*, edited by Richard K. Emmerson and Bernard McGinn. Ithaca: Cornell University Press, 1992. pp. 51–71.

Lesser, Allen. "Waiting for the End of the World." *The Humanist*, Sept. /Oct. 1992, 19–23, 43.

Levi, Ken (ed.). *Violence and Religious Commitment: Implications of Jim Jones's People's Temple Movement*. University Park: Pennsylvania State University Press, 1982.

Levin, David (ed.). *Jonathan Edwards: A Profile*. New York: Hill & Wang, 1969.

Levine, Lawrence W. *Defender of the Faith: William Jennings Bryan: The Last Decade, 1915–1925*. New York: Oxford University Press, 1965.

Lewis, Gordon K. "*Gather with the Saints at the River," The Jonestown Guyana Holocaust of 1978: A Descriptive and Interpretative Essay on Its Ultimate Meaning from a Caribbean View-*

point. Rio Piedras, Puerto Rico: Institute of Caribbean Studies, 1979.

Lewis, James R. "Self-fulfilling Stereotypes, the Anticult Movement, and the Waco Confrontation," in *Armageddon in Waco: Critical Perspectives on the Branch Davidian Conflict,* edited by Stuart A. Wright. Chicago: University of Chicago Press, 1995. pp. 95–110.

Lewis, James R. (ed.). *From the Ashes: Making Sense of Waco.* Lanham, MD: Rowman and Littlefield, 1994.

Lichter, S. Robert, Stanley Rothman, and Linda S. Lichter. *The Media Elite: America's New Powerbrokers.* Bethesda, MD: Adler & Adler, 1986.

Lifton, Robert Jay. *Thought Reform and the Psychology of Totalism: A Study of "Brainwashing" in China.* New York: W. W. Norton, 1961.

Lindars, Barnabas. "The New Testament," in *The Study and Use of the Bible,* edited by Paul Avis. Grand Rapids: William B. Eerdmans, 1988. pp. 229–397.

Lindner, Eileen W. (ed.). *Yearbook of American and Canadian Churches, 1999.* Nashville: Abingdon, 1999.

_____. *Yearbook of American & Canadian Churches, 2000.* Nashville: Abingdon, 2000.

_____. *Yearbook of American & Canadian Churches, 2005.* Nashville: Abingdon, 2005.

_____. *Yearbook of American & Canadian Churches, 2008.* Nashville: Abingdon, 2008.

Lindsey, Hal. *The Late Great Planet Earth.* Grand Rapids: Zondervan, 1970.

_____. *The 1980{ft}s: Countdown to Armageddon.* New York: Bantam, 1980.

_____. *The Road to Holocaust.* New York: Bantam, 1989.

Linedecker, Clifford L. *Massacre at Waco, Texas: The Shocking Story of Cult Leader David Koresh and the Branch Davidians.* New York: St. Martin's, 1993.

Lippy, Charles H. (ed.). *Twentieth-Century Shapers of American Popular Religion.* Westport, CT: Greenwood, 1989.

Livsey, Clara. *The Manson Women: A "Family" Portrait.* New York: Richard Marek, 1980.

Loetscher, Lefferts A. *The Broadening Church.* Philadelphia: University of Pennsylvania Press, 1957.

Long, Robert Emmet (ed.) *Religious Cults in America.* New York: H. W. Wilson, 1994.

Lowther, William. "The Bloody Trail behind Jonestown." *Maclean's,* Dec. 25, 1978, 27–28.

Lowther, William, William Scobie and Thomas Hopkins. "Cult of Madness." *Maclean's,* Dec. 4, 1978, 32–39.

Machen, J. Gresham. *Christianity and Liberalism.* New York: Macmillan, 1922.

Maclear, J. F. "New England and the Fifth Monarchy: The Quest for the Millennium in Early American Puritanism." *William and Mary Quarterly* 32 (April 1975) 223–260.

Madigan, Tim. *See No Evil: Blind Devotion and Bloodshed in David Koresh's Holy War.* Fort Worth: Summit, 1993.

Marcus, Joel, and Marion L. Soards (eds.). *Apocalyptic and the New Testament.* Sheffield, England: JSOT Press, 1989.

Marmon, Lucretia. [article on Hal Lindsey]. *People,* July 4, 1977, 70–72.

Marsden, George M. *Fundamentalism and American Culture: The Shaping of Twentieth-Century Evangelicalism, 1870–1925.* New York: Oxford University Press, 1980.

_____. *Jonathan Edwards: An Eighteenth-Century Life.* New Haven: Yale University Press, 2003.

_____. *Reforming Fundamentalism: Fuller Seminary and the New Evangelicalism.* Grand Rapids: Eerdmans, 1987.

_____. *Understanding Fundamentalism and Evangelicalism.* Grand Rapids: Eerdmans, 1991.

Martin, William. *The Billy Graham Story: A Prophet with Honour.* London: Hutchinson, 1992.

_____. *With God on Our Side: The Rise of the Religious Right in America.* New York: Broadway Books, 1996.

Marty, Martin E. "The Future of No Future: Frameworks of Interpretation," in *The Encyclopedia of Apocalypticism, vol. 3: Apocalyticism in the Modern Period and the Contemporary Age,* edited by Stephen J. Stein. New York: Continuum, 1999. pp. 461–484.

_____. *Modern American Religion, vol. 1: The Irony of It All, 1893–1919.* Chicago: University of Chicago Press, 1986.

_____. "Reckoning with the Millennium." *The Christian Century,* Feb. 4–11, 1998, 159.

_____. *Religion and Republic: The American Circumstance.* Boston: Beacon, 1987.

_____. "Religious Books." *The Critic,* vol. 31, no. 4 (1973), 85.

Marty, Martin E., and R. Scott Appleby (eds.). *Fundamentalisms Observed.* Chicago: University of Chicago Press, 1991.

Mathews, Shailer. *The Faith of Modernism.* New York: Macmillan, 1924.

Mathews, Tom. "The Cult of Death." *Newsweek,* Dec. 4, 1978, 38–53.

Matter, E. Ann. "The Apocalypse in Early Medieval Exegesis," in *The Apocalypse in the Middle Ages,* edited by Richard K. Emmerson and Bernard McGinn. Ithaca: Cornell University Press, 1992. pp. 38–50.

Maudlin, Michael G. "The Bible Study at the End of the World." *Christianity Today,* Sept. 1, 1997, 22–26.

McCullough, W. Stewart. *The History and Literature of the Palestinian Jews from Cyrus to Herod: 500 BC to 4 BC.* Toronto: University of Toronto Press, 1975.

McDannell, Colleen. *Material Christianity: Religion and Popular Culture in America.* New Haven: Yale University Press, 1995.

McDermott, Gerald R. *Jonathan Edwards Confronts the Gods: Christian Theology, Enlightenment Religion, and Non-Christian Faiths.* New York: Oxford University Press, 2000.

McGinn, Bernard. "Early Apocalypticism: The Ongoing Debate," in *The Apocalypse in English Renaissance Thought and Literature: Patterns, Antecedents and Repercussions,* edited by C. A. Patrides and Joseph Wittreich. Ithaca: Cornell University Press, 1984. pp. 2–39.

_____. "Introduction: John's Apocalypse and the Apocalyptic Mentality," in *The Apocalypse in the Middle Ages,* edited by Richard K. Emmerson and Bernard McGinn. Ithaca: Cornell University Press, 1992. pp. 3–19.

_____. *Visions of the End: Apocalyptic Traditions in the Middle Ages.* New York: Columbia University Press, 1979.

McLean, Herbert (ed.). "*The Untold Story of the Jonestown Massacre,*" vol. 1, issue 1, in *The Peoples Temple and Jim Jones: Broadening Our Perspective,* edited by J. Gordon Melton. New York: Garland, 1990. pp. 153–236.

McLoughlin, William G. "Revivalism," in *The Rise of Adventism: Religion and Society in Mid-Nineteenth-Century America,* edited by Edwin S. Gaustad. New York: Harper & Row, 1974. pp. 119–153.

McLoughlin, William G., Jr. *Billy Sunday Was His Real Name.* Chicago: University of Chicago Press, 1955.

McLoughlin, William Gerald. *Modern Revivalism: Charles Grandison Finney to Billy Graham.* New York: Ronald Press, 1959.

Mead, Sidney E. "Christendom, Enlightenment, and the Revolution," in *Religion and the American Revolution,* edited by Jerald C. Brauer. Philadelphia: Fortress, 1976. pp. 29–54.

_____. *The Nation with the Soul of a Church.* New York: Harper & Row, 1975.

Meiers, Michael. *Was Jonestown a CIA Medical Experiment? A Review of the Evidence.* Lewiston, NY: Edwin Mellen, 1988.

Meister, Charles W. *Year of the Lord: A. D. Eighteen Forty-Four.* Jefferson, NC: McFarland, 1983.

Melton, J. Gordon. *Religious Leaders of America.* Detroit: Gale Research, 1991.

Melton, J. Gordon (ed.). *The Peoples Temple and Jim Jones: Broadening Our Perspective.* New York: Garland, 1990.

Mendel, Arthur P. *Vision and Violence.* Ann Arbor: University of Michigan Press, 1992.

"Messiah for the Midwest." *Time,* Dec. 4, 1978, 16–18.

Middlekauff, Robert. *The Mathers: Three Generations of Puritan Intellectuals, 1596–1728.* New York: Oxford University Press, 1976.

Middleton, Richard. *Colonial America: A History, 1565–1776.* Oxford: Blackwell, 2002.

Miller, Donald E. *Reinventing American Protestantism: Christianity in the New Millennium.* Berkeley: University of California Press, 1997.

Miller, John C. *The First Frontier: Life in Colonial America.* New York: Dell, 1966.

Miller, Perry. *Errand into the Wilderness.* Cambridge: Harvard University Press, 1956.

_____. *Jonathan Edwards.* [New York]: William Sloane, 1949.

_____. *Nature's Nation.* Cambridge: Harvard University Press, 1967.

_____. *The New England Mind: From Colony to Province.* Cambridge: Harvard University Press, 1953.

_____. *The New England Mind: The Seventeenth Century.* New York: Macmillan, 1939.

Mills, Jeannie. "*Jonestown Masada,*" in *Violence and Religious Commitment: Implications of Jim Jones's People's Temple Movement,* edited by Ken Levi. University Park: Pennsylvania State University Press, 1982. pp. 165–73.

Milne, Andrew. "The Cult Awareness Network: Its Role in the Waco Tragedy," in *From the Ashes: Making Sense of Waco,* edited by James R. Lewis. Lanham, MD: Rowman and Littlefield, 1994. pp. 137–142.

Minkema, Kenneth P. "Jonathan Edwards: A Theological Life," in *The Princeton Companion to Jonathan Edwards,* edited by Sang Hyun Lee. Princeton: Princeton University Press, 2005. pp. 1–15.

Mojtabai, A. G. *Blessèd Assurance: At Home with the Bomb in Amarillo, Texas.* Boston: Houghton Mifflin, 1986.

Moody, Josh. *Jonathan Edwards and the Enlightenment: Knowing the Presence of God.* Lanham, MD: University Press of America, 2005.

Moore, George Foot. *Judaism in the First Centuries of the Christian Era,* vol. 1. Cambridge: Harvard University Press, 1962.

Moore, R. Laurence. *Religious Outsiders and the Making of Americans.* NY: Oxford University Press, 1986.

Moore, Rebecca. *A Sympathetic History of Jonestown: The Moore Family Involvement in the Peoples Temple.* Lewiston, NY: Edwin Mellen, 1985.

Moore, Rebecca, and Fielding McGehee III (eds.). *New Religious Movements, Mass Suicide, and Peoples Temple: Scholarly Perspectives on a Tragedy.* Lewiston: Edwin Mellen, 1989.

Moorhead, James H. *American Apocalypse: Yan-*

kee Protestants and the Civil War, 1860–1869. New Haven: Yale University Press, 1978.

_____. "Apocalypticism in Mainstream Protestantism, 1800 to the Present," in The Encyclopedia of Apocalypticism, vol. 3: Apocalyticism in the Modern Period and the Contemporary Age, edited by Stephen J. Stein. New York: Continuum, 1999. pp. 72–107.

Morison, Samuel Eliot. Builders of the Bay Colony. Boston: Houghton Mifflin, 1930.

Murray, Iain H. Jonathan Edwards: A New Biography. Edinburgh: Banner of Truth, 1987.

Murrin, Michael. "Revelation and Two Seventeenth-Century Commentators," in The Apocalypse in English Renaissance Thought and Literature: Patterns, Antecedents and Repercussions, edited by C. A. Patrides and Joseph Wittreich. Ithaca: Cornell University Press, 1984. pp. 125–146.

Naipaul, Shiva. Black and White. London: Hamish Hamilton, 1980.

Nash, Ronald H. Evangelicals in America: Who They Are, What They Believe. Nashville: Abingdon, 1987.

Neatby, W. Blair. The History of the Plymouth Brethren. London: Hodder & Stoughton, 1901.

Negri, Maxine. "Why Biblical Criticism by Scholars Is Imperative." The Humanist, vol. 44, no. 3 (1984), 27–28.

Neill, Stephen, and Tom Wright. The Interpretation of the New Testament, 1861–1986. Oxford: Oxford University Press, 1988.

Nemeth, Mary. "God Is Alive." Maclean's, April 12, 1993, 32–37.

Neuhaus, Richard John. Time Toward Home: The American Experiment as Revelation. New York: Seabury, 1975.

New, David S. Holy War: The Rise of Militant Christian, Jewish and Islamic Fundamentalism. Jefferson, NC: McFarland, 2002.

Nichol, Francis D. The Midnight Cry. Washington, DC: Review and Herald, 1944.

"Nightmare in Jonestown." Time, Dec. 4, 1978, 10–15.

Nock, Steven L., and Paul W. Kingston. The Sociology of Public Issues. Belmont, CA: Wadsworth, 1990.

Noel, Daniel C. "The Menace of Media-driven Public Credulity: Will a Distorted Faith Now Win Out?" in War in Heaven / Heaven on Earth: Theories of the Apocalyptic, edited by Stephen D. O'Leary and Glen S. McGhee. London: Equinox, 2005. pp. 253–261.

Noel, Napoleon. The History of the Brethren, vol. 1. Denver: W. F. Knapp, 1936.

Noll, Mark. "Edwards' Theology after Edwards," in The Princeton Companion to Jonathan Edwards, edited by Sang Hyun Lee. Princeton: Princeton University Press, 2005. pp. 292–308.

Nugent, John Peer. White Night. New York: Rawson, Wade, 1979.

Numbers, Ronald L., and Jonathan M. Butler (eds.). The Disappointed: Millerism and Millenarianism in the Nineteenth Century. Bloomington: Indiana University Press, 1987.

O'Leary, Stephen D. Arguing the Apocalypse: A Theory of Millennial Rhetoric. New York: Oxford University Press, 1994.

O'Leary, Stephen D., and Glen S. McGhee (eds.). War in Heaven / Heaven on Earth: Theories of the Apocalyptic. London: Equinox, 2005.

Orlinsky, Harry M. Essays in Biblical Culture and Bible Translation. New York: KTAV, 1974.

Ostling, Richard N. "Power, Glory — and Politics: Right-wing Preachers Dominate the Dial." Time, Feb. 17, 1986, 54–65.

_____. "Those Mainline Blues." Time, May 22, 1989, 54–56.

Oswald, Hilton C. (ed.). Luther's Works (vol. 20): Lectures on the Minor Prophets, III, Zechariah. St. Louis: Concordia, 1973.

Packer, James I. "Fundamentalism" and the Word of God. Grand Rapids: Eerdmans, 1958.

Palmer, Susan. "Evacuating Waco," in From the Ashes: Making Sense of Waco, edited by James R. Lewis. Lanham, MD: Rowman and Littlefield, 1994. pp. 99–111.

Parenti, Michael. Inventing Reality: The Politics of the Mass Media. New York: St. Martin's, 1986.

Parkes, Henry Bamford. "The Young Philosopher," in Jonathan Edwards: A Profile, edited by David Levin. New York: Hill & Wang, 1969. pp. 117–126.

Patrides, C. A., and Joseph Wittreich (eds.). The Apocalypse in English Renaissance Thought and Literature: Patterns, Antecedents and Repercussions. Ithaca: Cornell University Press, 1984.

Pelikan, Jaroslav (ed.). Luther's Works (vol. 1): Lectures on Genesis. St. Louis: Concordia, 1958.

Penton, James A. Apocalypse Delayed: The Story of Jehovah's Witnesses. Toronto: University of Toronto Press, 1985.

Peterson, William S. Victorian Heretic: Mrs. Humphrey Ward's Robert Elsmere. Leicester: Leicester University Press, 1976.

Phillips, Andrew. "One Lived, One Died." Maclean's, May 3, 1993, 16–23.

Phillips, Kevin. American Theocracy: The Peril and Politics of Radical Religion, Oil, and Borrowed Money in the 21st Century. New York: Viking, 2006.

_____. Bad Money: Reckless Finance, Failed Politics, and the Global Crisis of American Capitalism. New York: Viking, 2008.

Pitts, William L., Jr. "The Davidian Tradition," in From the Ashes: Making Sense of Waco, edited by James R. Lewis. Lanham, MD: Rowman and Littlefield, 1994. pp. 33–39.

_____. "Davidians and Branch Davidians: 1929–1987," in *Armageddon in Waco: Critical Perspectives on the Branch Davidian Conflict*, edited by Stuart A. Wright. Chicago: University of Chicago Press, 1995. pp. 20–42.

Pochman, Henry A. *German Culture in America.* Madison: University of Wisconsin Press, 1961.

Political Research Associates. "Covering the Culture War: A Resource Guide." *Columbia Journalism Review,* July/Aug. 1993, 37–40.

Pollock, J. C. *Moody.* Grand Rapids: Baker, 1997.

Pollock, John Charles. *George Whitefield and the Great Awakening.* London: Hodder and Stoughton, 1973.

Prévost, Jean-Pierre. *How to Read the Apocalypse.* London: SCM, 1993.

Quebedeaux, Richard. *By What Authority: The Rise of Personality Cults in American Christianity.* San Francisco: Harper & Row, 1982.

Rainie, Harrison. "Armageddon in Waco: The Final Days of David Koresh." *U. S. News & World Report,* May 3, 1993, 24–34.

Reavis, Dick J. *The Ashes of Waco: An Investigation.* New York: Simon & Schuster, 1995.

Redekop, John Harold. *The American Far Right: A Case Study of Billy James Hargis and Christian Crusade.* Grand Rapids: Eerdmans, 1968.

Reese, Alexander. *The Approaching Advent of Christ.* Grand Rapids: Grand Rapids International Publications, 1975.

Reeves, Thomas C. *The Empty Church: The Suicide of Liberal Christianity.* New York: The Free Press, 1996.

Reiterman, Tim. *Raven: The Untold Story of the Rev. Jim Jones and His People.* New York: E. P. Dutton, 1982.

Reston, James, Jr. *Our Father Who Art in Hell.* New York: Times, 1981.

Richards, Jeffrey J. *The Promise of Dawn: The Eschatology of Lewis Sperry Chafer.* Lanham, MD: University Press of America, 1991.

Richardson, James T. "A Comparison between Jonestown and Other Cults," in *Violence and Religious Commitment: Implications of Jim Jones's People's Temple Movement,* edited by Ken Levi. University Park: Pennsylvania State University Press, 1982. pp. 21–34, 183–84.

_____. "Definitions of Cult: From Sociological-Technical to Popular-Negative." *Review of Religious Research* 34 (1993) 348–356.

_____. "Manufacturing Consent about Koresh: A Structural Analysis of the Role of Media in the Waco Tragedy," in *Armageddon in Waco: Critical Perspectives on the Branch Davidian Conflict,* edited by Stuart A. Wright. Chicago: University of Chicago Press, 1995. pp. 153–176.

_____. "People's Temple and Jonestown: A Corrective Comparison and Critique." *Journal for the Scientific Study of Religion* 19 (1980) 239–255.

_____. "Psychological and Psychiatric Studies of New Religions," in *Advances in the Psychology of Religion,* edited by L. Brown. New York: Pergamon, 1985.

Robbins, Thomas. "The Second Wave of Jonestown Literature: A Review Essay," in *New Religious Movements, Mass Suicide, and Peoples Temple: Scholarly Perspectives on a Tragedy,* edited by Rebecca Moore and Fielding McGehee III. Lewiston, NY: Edwin Mellen, 1989. pp. 113–134.

Robbins, Thomas, and Dick Anthony. "Sects and Violence: Factors Enhancing the Volatility of Marginal Religious Movements," in *Armageddon in Waco: Critical Perspectives on the Branch Davidian Conflict,* edited by Stuart A. Wright. Chicago: University of Chicago Press, 1995. pp. 236–259.

Robbins, Thomas, and Dick Anthony (eds.). *In Gods We Trust.* New Brunswick, NJ: Transaction, 1990.

Robbins, Thomas, and Susan J. Palmer (eds.). *Millennium, Messiahs, and Mayhem: Contemporary Apocalyptic Movements.* New York: Routledge, 2004.

Robinson, Douglas. *American Apocalypses: The Image of the End of the World in American Literature.* Baltimore: Johns Hopkins University Press, 1985.

Rogers, Jack B., and Donald K. McKim. *The Authority and Interpretation of the Bible: An Historical Approach.* San Francisco: Harper & Row, 1979.

Rogers, Patrick, and Vickie Bane. "Joel Osteen Counts His Blessings." *People,* December 17, 2007, 94–100.

Rogerson, John. "The Old Testament," in *The Study and Use of the Bible,* edited by Paul Avis. Grand Rapids: William B. Eerdmans, 1988. pp. 3–150.

Roof, Wade Clark, and William McKinney. *American Mainline Religion: Its Changing Shape and Future.* New Brunswick, NJ: Rutgers University Press, 1987.

Rose, Stephen C. "Jim Jones and Crisis Thought: A Critique of Established Religion," in *New Religious Movements, Mass Suicide, and Peoples Temple: Scholarly Perspectives on a Tragedy,* edited by Rebecca Moore and Fielding McGehee III. Lewiston. NY: Edwin Mellen, 1989. pp. 41–50.

Rowdon, Harold H. *The Origins of the Brethren, 1825–1850.* London: Pickering & Inglis, 1967.

Rowe, David L. "Millerites: A Shadow Portrait," in *The Disappointed: Millerism and Millenarianism in the Nineteenth Century,* edited by

Ronald L. Numbers and Jonathan M. Butler. Bloomington: Indiana University Press, 1987. pp. 1–16.

_____. *Thunder and Trumpets: Millerites and Dissenting Religion in Upstate New York, 1800–1850*. Chico, CA: Scholars Press, 1985.

Rudolph, Frederick. *The American College and University: A History*. New York: Vintage, 1962.

Russell, C. Allyn. "W. A. Criswell: A Case Study in Fundamentalism." *Review and Expositor*, Winter 1984, 107–131.

Russell, D. S. *Apocalyptic: Ancient and Modern*. Philadelphia: Fortress, 1978.

Ruthven, Malise. *The Divine Supermarket: Shopping for God in America*. New York: Morrow, 1990.

_____. *Fundamentalism: The Search for Meaning*. Oxford: Oxford University Press, 2005.

Ryken, Leland. *Worldly Saints: The Puritans as They Really Were*. Grand Rapids: Academie, 1986.

Ryrie, Charles Caldwell. *Dispensationalism Today*. Chicago: Moody, 1965.

Sabato, Larry J. *Feeding Frenzy*, 2d ed. New York: Free Press, 1993.

St. Clair, Michael J. *Millenarian Movements in Historical Context*. New York: Garland, 1992.

Samples, Kenneth, et al. *Prophets of the Apocalypse*. Grand Rapids: Baker, 1994.

Sandeen, Ernest R. "Millennialism," in *The Rise of Adventism: Religion and Society in Mid-Nineteenth-Century America*, edited by Edwin S. Gaustad. New York: Harper & Row, 1974. pp. 104–118.

_____. *The Origins of Fundamentalism*. Philadelphia: Fortress, 1968.

_____. "The Princeton Theology: One Source of Biblical Literalism in American Protestantism." *Church History* 3 (1962) 307–321.

_____. *The Roots of Fundamentalism: British and American Millenarianism, 1800–1930*. Chicago: University of Chicago Press, 1970.

Schmithals, Walter. *The Apocalyptic Movement: Introduction & Interpretation*. Nashville: Abingdon, 1975.

Schneider, Herbert W. *The Puritan Mind*. Ann Arbor: University of Michigan Press, 1958.

Schoepflin, Rennie B. "Apocalypticism in an Age of Science," in *The Encyclopedia of Apocalypticism, vol. 3: Apocalticism in the Modern Period and the Contemporary Age*, edited by Stephen J. Stein. New York: Continuum, 1999. pp. 427–441.

Scobey, David M. "Revising the Errand: New England's Ways and the Puritan Sense of the Past." *William and Mary Quarterly* 41 (January 1984) 3–31.

Scofield, C. I. *Oxford NIV Scofield Study Bible*.

Edited by C. I. Scofield. New York: Oxford University Press, 1984.

Scopes, John T., and James Presley. *Center of the Storm: Memoirs of John T. Scopes*. New York: Holt, Rinehart and Winston, 1967.

Scott, Alice. *The Incredible Power of Cults: Hard Facts on the Soft Persuaders*. Colorado Springs: Blue River, 1994.

Sears, Clara Endicott. *Days of Delusion: A Strange Bit of History*. Boston: Houghton Mifflin, 1924.

Shachtman, Tom. *Decade of Shocks: Dallas to Watergate, 1963–1974*. New York: Poseidon, 1983.

Sheler, Jeffery L. "The Christmas Covenant." *U. S. News & World Report*, Dec. 19, 1994, 62–71.

_____. "Dark Prophecies." *U. S. News & World Report*, Dec. 15, 1997, 62–71.

_____. "Stains on Stained Glass: Tales of Treachery and Deceit inside America's Biggest Megachurch." *U. S. News & World Report*, Oct. 10, 1994, 97.

Sherrill, Rowland A. (ed.). *Religion and the Life of the Nation: American Recoveries*. Urbana: University of Illinois Press, 1990.

Shupe, Anson, David Bromley and Edward Breschel. "The Peoples Temple, the Apocalypse at Jonestown, and the Anti-Cult Movement," in *New Religious Movements, Mass Suicide, and Peoples Temple: Scholarly Perspectives on a Tragedy*, edited by Rebe-cca Moore and Fielding McGehee III. Lewiston, NY: Edwin Mellen, 1989. pp. 153–178.

Shupe, Anson, and Jeffrey K. Hadden. "Cops, News copy, and Public Opinion: Legitimacy and the Social Construction of Evil in Waco," in *Armageddon in Waco: Critical Perspectives on the Branch Davidian Conflict*, edited by Stuart A. Wright. Chicago: University of Chicago Press, 1995. pp. 177–202.

Shupe, Anson, and Jeffrey K. Hadden (eds.). *Secularization and Fundamentalism Reconsidered*. New York: Paragon, 1989.

Silverman, Kenneth. *The Life and Times of Cotton Mather*. New York: Columbia University Press, 1985.

Simon, Roger. "Miracle Worker." *The New Republic*, Oct. 7, 1996, 11.

Simpson, Alan. *Puritanism in Old and New England*. Chicago: University of Chicago Press, 1955.

"Sing Along with Manson." *Newsweek*, Mar. 16, 1970, 36–37.

Smith, John E. *Jonathan Edwards: Puritan, Preacher, Philosopher*. Notre Dame: University of Notre Dame Press, 1992.

Smolinski, Reiner. "Apocalypticism in Colonial North America," in *The Encyclopedia of Apocalypticism, vol. 3: Apocalyticism in the Modern*

Period and the Contemporary Age, edited by Stephen J. Stein. New York: Continuum, 1999. pp. 36–71.

Soggin, J. Alberto. *Introduction to the Old Testament,* rev. ed. London: SCM, 1980.

Solotaroff, Ivan. "The Last Revelation from Waco." *Esquire,* July 1993, 52–55.

Spencer, William David. "Does Anyone Really Know What Time It Is?" *Christianity Today,* July 17, 1995, 29.

Stark, Rodney, and Charles Y. Glock. *American Piety: The Nature of Religious Commitment,* vol. 1. Berkeley: University of California Press, 1970.

Starkey, Marion L. *The Devil in Massachusetts: A Modern Inquiry into Salem Witch Trials.* New York: Knopf, 1949.

Steele, Richard. "Life in Jonestown." *Newsweek,* Dec. 4, 1978, 62–66.

Stein, Stephen J. "American Millennial Visions: Towards Construction of a New Architectonic of American Apocalypticism," in *Imagining the End: Visions of Apocalypse from the Ancient Middle East to Modern America,* edited by Abbas Amanat and Magnus Bernhardsson. London: I. B. Tauris, 2002. pp. 187–211.

_____. "Apocalypticism outside the Mainstream in the United States," in *The Encyclopedia of Apocalypticism, vol. 3: Apocalyticism in the Modern Period and the Contemporary Age,* edited by Stephen J. Stein. New York: Continuum, 1999. pp. 108–139.

_____. "Eschatology," in *The Princeton Companion to Jonathan Edwards,* edited by Sang Hyun Lee. Princeton: Princeton University Press, 2005. pp. 226–242.

_____. "Providence and the Apocalypse in the Early Writings of Jonathan Edwards." *Early American Literature* 13 (1978–79) 250–267.

_____. "The Spirit and the Word: Jonathan Edwards and Scriptural Exegesis," in *Jonathan Edwards and the American Experience,* edited by Nathan O. Hatch and Harry S. Stout. New York: Oxford University Press, 1988. pp. 18–130.

_____. "Transatlantic Extensions: Apocalyptic in Early New England," in *The Apocalypse in English Renaissance Thought and Literature: Patterns, Antecedents and Repercussions,* edited by C. A. Patrides and Joseph Wittreich. Ithaca: Cornell University Press, 1984. pp. 266–298.

Stein, Stephen J. (ed.). *The Encyclopedia of Apocalypticism, vol. 3: Apocalyticism in the Modern Period and the Contemporary Age.* New York: Continuum, 1999.

Stone, Jon R. *A Guide to the End of the World: Popular Eschatology in America.* New York: Garland, 1993.

Stout, Harry S. *The Divine Dramatist: George Whitefield and the Rise of Modern Evangelism.* Grand Rapids: Eerdmans, 1991.

_____. "The Puritans and Edwards," in *The Princeton Companion to Jonathan Edwards,* edited by Sang Hyun Lee. Princeton: Princeton University Press, 2005. pp. 274–291.

Streiker, Lowell D. *The Gospel Time Bomb: Ultrafundamentalism and the Future of America.* Buffalo: Prometheus, 1984.

Strozier, Charles B. *Apocalypse: On the Psychology of Fundamentalism in America.* Boston: Beacon Press, 1994.

_____. "From Ground Zero: Thoughts on Apocalyptic Violence and the New Terrorism," in *War in Heaven / Heaven on Earth: Theories of the Apocalyptic,* edited by Stephen D. O'Leary and Glen S. McGhee. London: Equinox, 2005. pp. 263–277.

Symonds, William C. "Earthly Empires: How Evangelical Churches Are Borrowing from the Business Playbook." *Business Week,* May 23, 2005, 78–88.

Szasz, Thomas. *Ideology and Insanity.* Garden City: Doubleday, 1970.

_____. *The Manufacture of Madness.* New York: Harper & Row, 1970.

Tabor, James. "Apocalypse at Waco: Could the Tragedy Have Been Averted?" *Bible Review,* October 1993, 25–32.

Tabor, James D. "Religious Discourse and Failed Negociations: The Dynamics of Biblical Apocalypticism in Waco," in *Armageddon in Waco: Critical Perspectives on the Branch Davidian Conflict,* edited by Stuart A. Wright. Chicago: University of Chicago Press, 1995. pp. 263–281.

_____. "The Waco Tragedy: An Autobiographical Account of One Attempt To Avert Disaster," in *From the Ashes: Making Sense of Waco,* edited by James R. Lewis. Lanham, MD: Rowman and Littlefield, 1994. pp. 13–21.

Tabor, James D., and Eugene V. Gallagher. *Why Waco? Cults and the Battle for Religious Freedom in America.* Berkeley: University of California Press, 1995.

Taylor, Ann C. M. (ed.). *International Handbook of Universities,* 14th ed. New York: Stockton, 1996.

Teegarden, Kenneth L. *We Call Ourselves Disciples,* 2d ed. St. Louis: Bethany, 1983.

Teresi, Dick. "Zero." *The Atlantic Monthly,* July 1997, 88–94.

Thiering, Barbara. *Jesus of the Apocalypse: The Life of Jesus after the Crucifixion.* New York: Doubleday, 1995.

Thompson, Damian. *The End of Time: Faith & Fear in the Shadow of the Millennium.* Hanover, NH: University Press of New England, 1996.

_____. "The Retreat of the Millennium," in *War in Heaven / Heaven on Earth: Theories of the Apocalyptic*, edited by Stephen D. O'Leary and Glen S. McGhee. London: Equinox, 2005. pp. 237–251.

Thuesen, Peter J. "Edwards' Intellectual Background," in *The Princeton Companion to Jonathan Edwards*, edited by Sang Hyun Lee. Princeton: Princeton University Press, 2005. pp. 16–33.

Toffler, Alvin. *Future Shock*. New York: Bantam, 1971.

Tough, Paul. "That's the News and I Am Outta Here." *Mother Jones*, Sept. /Oct. 1998, 79–80.

Toulouse, Mark G. "W. A. Criswell," in *Twentieth-Century Shapers of American Popular Religion*, edited by Charles H. Lippy. Westport, CT: Greenwood Press, 1989. pp. 96–104.

Trimm, James. "David Koresh's Seven Seals Teaching." *Watchman Expositor* 11 (1994) 7–8.

Trueheart, Charles. "Welcome to the Next Church." *The Atlantic Monthly*, August 1996, 37–58.

Turnbull, Charles G. *The Life of C. I. Scofield*. New York: Oxford University Press, 1920.

Turner, W. G. *John Nelson Darby*. London: C. A. Hammond, 1944.

Tuveson, Ernest Lee. *Redeemer Nation: The Idea of America's Millennial Role*. Chicago: University of Chicago Press, 1968.

Tyler, B. B. *A History of the Disciples of Christ*. New York: Christian Literature, 1894.

United States Census Bureau. *Statistical Abstract of the United States, 2008*. Washington, 2007.

Vaughn, Eric. "Where's the Rapture?" *Skeptical Inquirer*, vol. 17, no. 4 (summer 1993), 367.

Von Campenhausen, Hans. *The Formation of the Christian Bible*. Philadelphia: Fortress, 1972.

Wagner, Donald E. *Anxious for Armageddon: A Call to Partnership for Middle Eastern and Western Christians*. Waterloo: Herald, 1995.

Walker, Brooks R. *The Christian Fright Peddlers*. Garden City: Doubleday, 1964.

Walker, Williston. "Jonathan Edwards," in *Jonathan Edwards: A Profile*, edited by David Levin. New York: Hill & Wang, 1969. pp. 87–116.

Wall, James M. "Eager for the End." *Christian Century*, May 5, 1993, 475–476.

_____. "Missing Connections." *The Christian Century*, July 14–21, 1999, 699.

Wallis, Jim. "Recovering the Evangel," in *Border Regions of Faith: An Anthology of Religion and Social Change*, edited by Kenneth Aman. Maryknoll, NY: Orbis, 1987. pp. 285–89.

Walters, Ray. [Hal Lindsey's books] "Paperback Talk." *The New York Times Book Review*, March 12, 1978, 45–46.

Walters, Stanley D. "Hal Lindsey: Recalculating the Second Coming." *The Christian Century*, vol. 96 (1979), 839–40.

Warfield, Benjamin B. *The Inspiration and Authority of the Bible*. Philadelphia: Presbyterian & Reformed, 1948.

Wasowicz, Lidia. "Some Jones Followers Still Believe in Him," in *The Peoples Temple and Jim Jones: Broadening Our Perspective*, edited by J. Gordon Melton. New York: Garland, 1990. p. 375. (reprinted from *Chicago Sun-Times*, Nov. 18, 1979).

Watson, Tex [Charles], with Ray Hoekstra. *Will You Die for Me*? Old Tappan, NJ: Fleming H. Revell, 1978.

Watt, David Harrington. "The *Private* Hopes of American Fundamentalists and Evangelicals, 1925–1975." *Religion and American Culture* 1 (1991) 155–165.

_____. *A Transforming Faith: Explorations of Twentieth-Century American Evangelicalism*. New Brunswick, NJ: Rutgers University Press, 1991.

Weber, Eugen. *Apocalypses: Prophecies, Cults and Millennial Beliefs through the Ages*. Toronto: Random House of Canada, 1999.

Weber, Timothy P. *Living in the Shadow of the Second Coming: American Premillennialism, 1875–1982*. Grand Rapids: Zondervan, 1983.

Weigert, Andrew J. "Christian Eschatological Identities and the Nuclear Context." *Journal for the Scientific Study of Religion* 27 (1988) 175–191.

Weightman, Judith Mary. *Making Sense of the Jonestown Suicides: A Sociological History of Peoples Temple*. Lewiston, NY: Edwin Mellen, 1983.

Wells, G. A. "Why Fundamentalism Flourishes," in *Neo-Fundamentalism: The Humanist Response*, by The Academy of Humanism. Buffalo: Prometheus, 1988. pp. 119–129.

Wendell, Barrett. *Cotton Mather: The Puritan Priest*. New York: Harcourt, Brace & World, 1963.

Wharton, Gary C. "The Continuing Phenomenon of the Religious Best Seller." *Publishers Weekly*, Mar. 14, 1977, 82–83.

Wieseltier, Leon. "Gog, Magog, Agog." *The New Republic*, May 15, 1995, 46.

Wilhelm, David. "Getting Ready." *The Christian Century*, Feb. 17, 1999, 174–175.

Wills, David W. *Christianity in the United States: A Historical Survey and Interpretation*. Notre Dame: University of Notre Dame Press, 2005.

Wills, Garry. *Reagan's America: Innocents at Home*. Garden City: Doubleday, 1987.

Wilson, Dwight. *Armageddon Now! The Premil-*

lenarian Response to Russia and Israel Since 1917. Grand Rapids: Baker, 1977.

Wilson, John F. "Comment on 'Two Roads to the Puritan Millennium.'" *Church History* 32 (1963) 339–343.

_____. "History, Redemption, and the Millennium," in *Jonathan Edwards and the American Experience*, edited by Nathan O. Hatch and Harry S. Stout. New York: Oxford University Press, 1988. pp. 133–141.

Wilson, John. "Not Just Another Megachurch." *Christianity Today*, December 4, 2000, 62–65.

Winslow, Ola Elizabeth. "A Frontier Childhood," in *Jonathan Edwards: A Profile*, edited by David Levin. New York: Hill & Wang, 1969. pp. 137–160.

Witmer, John A. "'What God Hath Wrought'— Fifty Years of Dallas Theological Seminary, Part I: God's Man and His Dream." *Bibliotheca Sacra* 130 (October 1973) 291–304.

_____. "'What God Hath Wrought'— Fifty Years of Dallas Theological Seminary, Part II: Building upon the Foundation." *Bibliotheca Sacra* 131 (January 1974) 3–13.

Witmer, Safara Austin. *The Bible College Story: Education with Dimension*. Manhasset, NY: Channel, 1962.

Wojcik, Daniel. *The End of the World As We Know It: Faith, Fatalism, and Apocalypse in America*. New York: New York University Press, 1997.

Wood, James E., Jr. "The Branch Davidian Standoff: An American Tragedy." *Journal of Church and State*, Spring 1993, 1–9.

Woodward, Kenneth L. "Arguing Armageddon," *Newsweek*, Nov. 5, 1984, 91.

_____. "The Boom in Doom." *Newsweek*, Jan. 10, 1977, 49, 51.

_____. "Dead End for the Mainline?" *Newsweek*, Aug. 9, 1993, 46–48.

_____. "From 'Mainline' to Sideline." *Newsweek*, Dec. 22, 1986, 54–56.

_____. "Playing Politics at Church." *Newsweek*, July 9, 1984, 52.

_____. "This Way to Armageddon." *Newsweek*, July 5, 1982, 79.

_____. "Uh-oh, Maybe We Missed the Big Day." *Newsweek*, Aug. 11, 1997, 15.

_____. "The Way the World Ends." *Newsweek*, Nov. 1, 1999, 66–74.

Wright, Stuart A. "Construction and Escalation of a Cult Threat: Dissecting Moral Panic and Official Reaction to the Branch Davidians," in *Armageddon in Waco: Critical Perspectives on the Branch Davidian Conflict*, edited by Stuart A. Wright. Chicago: University of Chicago Press, 1995. pp. 75–94.

Wright, Stuart A. (ed.) *Armageddon in Waco: Critical Perspectives on the Branch Davidian Conflict*. Chicago: University of Chicago Press, 1995.

Wuthnow, Robert. *Christianity in the Twenty-first Century: Reflections on the Challenges Ahead*. New York: Oxford University Press, 1993.

_____. *The Reconstruction of American Religion: Society and Faith Since World War II*. Princeton: Princeton University Press, 1988.

_____. *The Struggle for America's Soul: Evangelicals, Liberals, and Secularism*. Grand Rapids: Eerdmans, 1989.

_____. "The World of Fundamentalism." *The Christian Century*, April 22, 1992, 426–29.

Yankelovich, Daniel. *New Rules: Searching for Self-Fulfillment in a World Turned Upside Down*. New York: Random, 1981.

Yee, Min S., and Thomas N. Layton. *In My Father's House: The Story of the Layton Family and the Reverend Jim Jones*. New York: Holt, Rinehart and Winston, 1981.

Zaehner, R. C. *Our Savage God*. London: Collins, 1974.

Zakai, Avihu. *Exile and Kingdom: History and Apocalypse in the Puritan Migration to America*. Cambridge: Cambridge University Press, 1992.

_____. *Jonathan Edwards: The Reenchantment of the World in the Age of the Enlightenment*. Princeton: Princeton University Press, 2003.

Zamora, Lois Parkinson (ed.). *The Apocalyptic Vision in America: Interdisciplinary Essays on Myth and Culture*. Bowling Green: Bowling Green University Popular Press, 1982.

Index